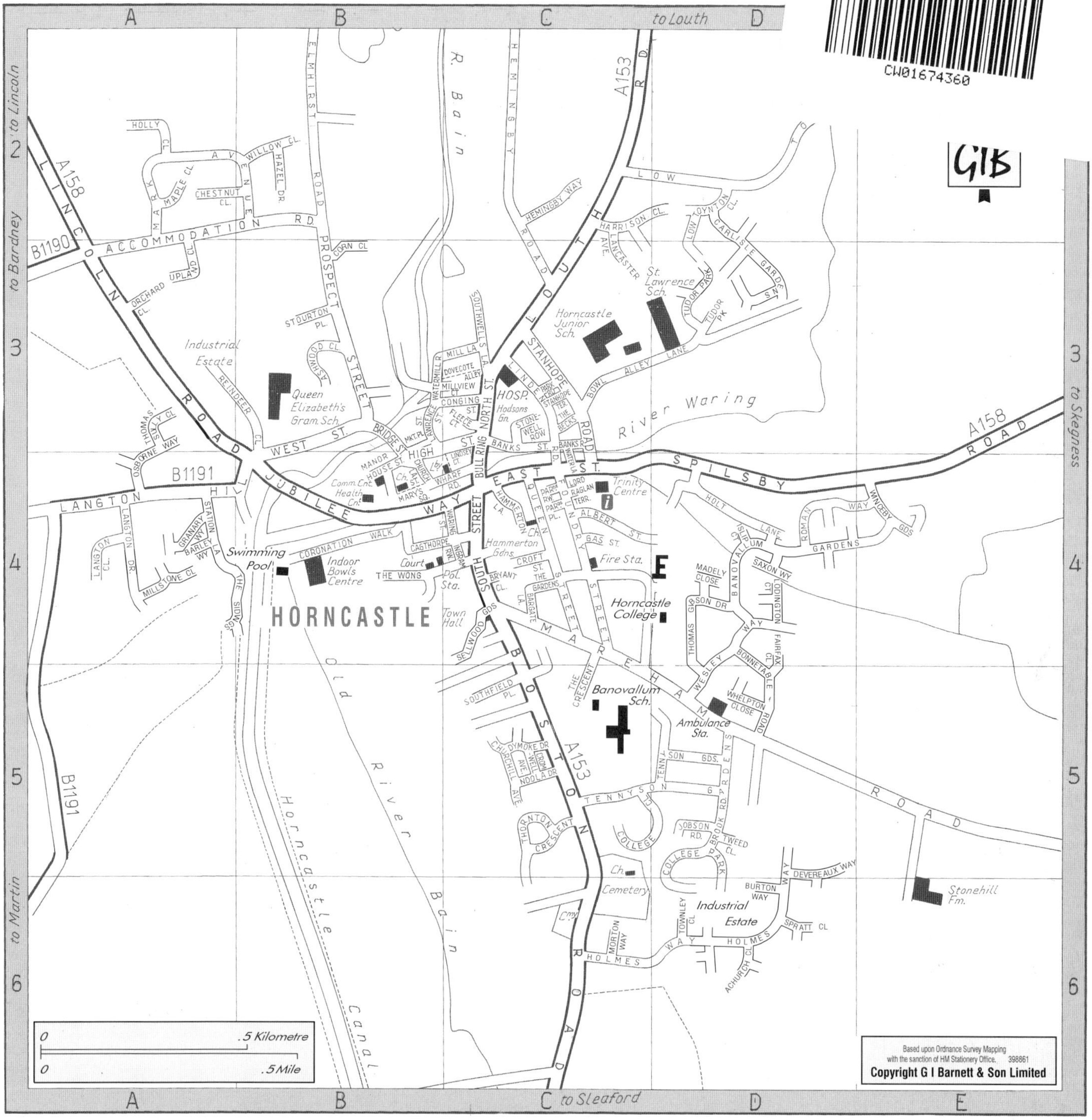

HORNCASTLE INDEX TO STREETS

Accommodation Road A.3
Achurch Close D.6
Albert Street C.4
Ashwood Close B.3

Banks Road C.3
Banks Street C.3
Banovallum Gardens D.4
Bargate Lane C.4
Barley Way A.4
Bonnetable Road D.4
Boston Road C.5
Bowl Alley Lane C.3
Bridge Street B.3
Brook Road D.5
Bryant Close C.4
Bull Ring C.4
Burton Way D.6

Cagthorpe B.4
Carlisle Gardens D.2
Chestnut Close A.2
Church Lane B.4
Churchill Avenue C.5
College Close C.5
College Park D.5
Conging Street C.4
Corn Close B.3
Coronation Walk B.4

Croft Street C.4
Cromwell Avenue C.5

Devereaux Way D.5
Dovecote Way C.3
Dymoke Drive C.5

East Street C.4
Elmhirst Road B.2

Fleece Court C.3
Foundry Street C.4

Gas Street C.4
Granary Way A.4

Hammerton Gardens C.4
Hammerton Lane C.4
Harrison Close C.2
Hazel Drive B.2
Hemingby Road C.2
Hemingby Way C.2
High Street B.4
Holy Close A.2
Holmes Way C.6
Holt Lane D.4

Ingram Row C.4
Islip Court D.4

Jobson Road D.5
Jubilee Way B.4

Lancaster Avenue C.3
Langton Close A.4
Langton Drive A.4
Langton Hill A.4
Lincoln Road A.2
Lindens Road C.3
Lindsey Court C.4
Lodington Court D.4
Lord Raglan Terrace C.4
Louth Road C.3
Low Toynton Close D.2
Low Toynton Road D.2

Madely Close D.4
Manor House Street B.4
Maple Close A.2
Marsham Road C.4
Mark Avenue A.2
Market Place B.3
Mill Lane C.3
Millstone Close A.4
Millview Court C.3
Morton Way C.6

Ndola Drive C.5
North Street C.3

Orchard Close A.3
Osborne Way A.4

Paradise Place C.4
Paradise Row C.4
Park Road C.3
Prospect Street B.3

Queen Street C.4

Reindeer Close A.3
Roman Way D.4

St. Mary's Square B.4
St. Lawrence Street B.3
Saxon Way D.4
Sellwood Gardens C.4
South Street C.4
Southfield Place C.5
Southwells Lane C.3
Spilsby Road D.4
Spratt Close D.6
Stanhope Road C.3
Stanhope Terrace C.3
Station Lane A.4
Stonewell Row C.3
Stourton Place B.3

Tennyson Gardens C.5

The Becks C.3
The Crescent C.5
The Gardens C.4
The Sidings B.4
The Wong B.4
Thomas Gibson Drive D.4
Thomas Sull Close A.3
Thornton Crescent C.5
Townley Close D.6
Tudor Park D.3
Tweed Close D.5

Upland Close A.3

Waring Street C.4
Water Lane C.4
Watermill Road B.3
Wesley Way D.5
West Street B.3
Wharf Road C.4
Whelpton Close D.5
Willow Close B.2
Winceby Gardens E.4

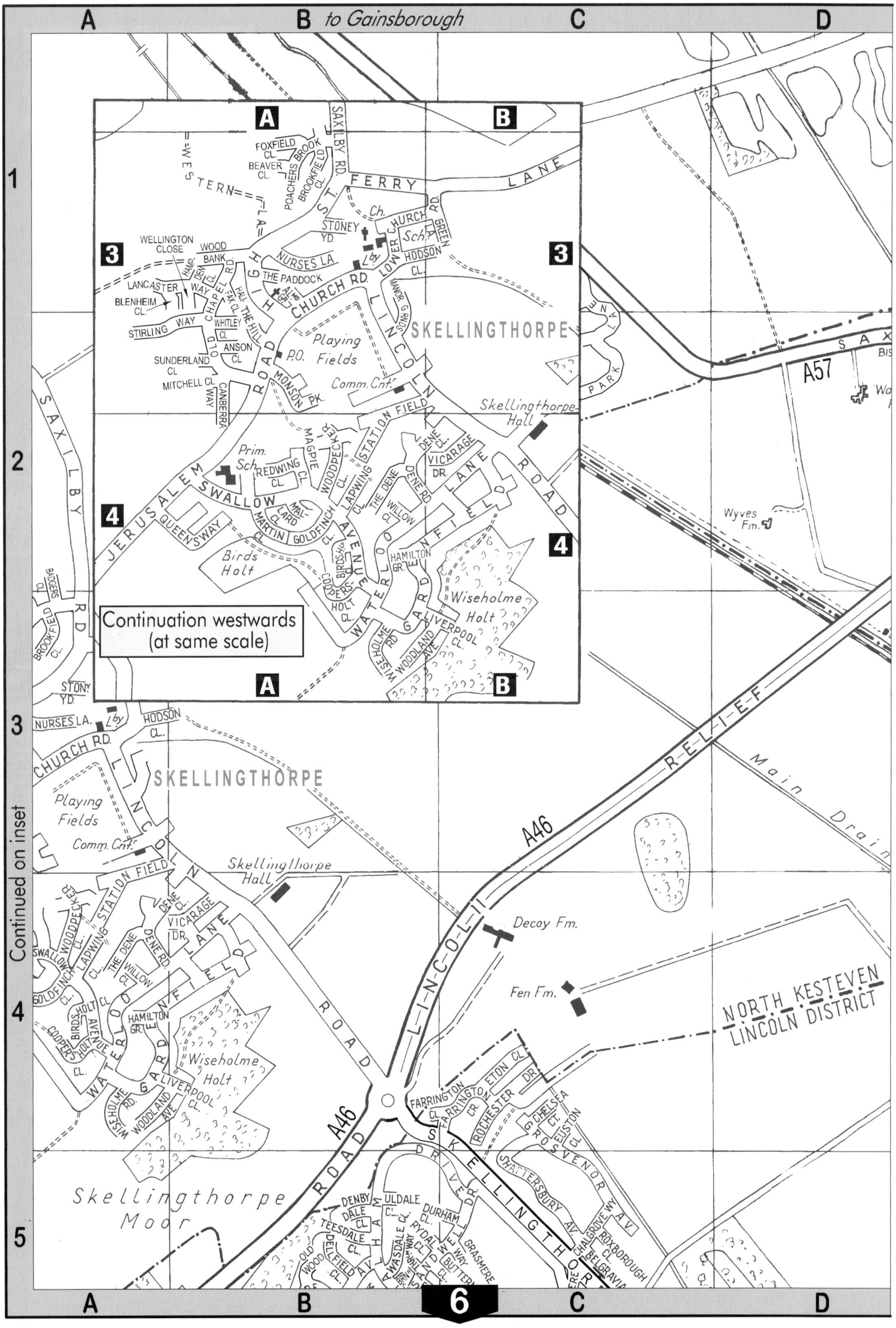
to Gainsborough
A
B
C
D
1
2
3
4
5
6
Continued on inset
Continuation westwards
(at same scale)
SKELLINGTHORPE
Playing
Fields
Comm. Cntr.
Skellingthorpe
Hall
Prim.
Sch.
Birds
Holt
Wiseholme
Holt
P.O.
FERRY
LANE
CHURCH RD.
HIGH
ROAD
LINCOLN
ROAD
JERUSALEM
SWALLOW
QUEENSWAY
STATION FIELD
WATERLOO
GARDEN FIELD
LANE
A46
A57
RELIEF
LINCOLN
ROAD
Main Drain
Decoy Fm.
Fen Fm.
Wyves
Fm.
NORTH KESTEVEN
LINCOLN DISTRICT
Skellingthorpe
Moor
SKELLINGTHORPE
DRIVE
GROSVENOR AV.
SHAFTESBURY AV.
ROCHESTER DR.
FARRINGTON CR.
FARRINGTON CL.
ETON CL.
CHELSEA CT.
EUSTON CL.
ROXBOROUGH CL.
BELGRAVIA
DENBY DALE
ULDALE CL.
DURHAM CL.
TEESDALE CL.
RYDAL WAY
GRASMERE
SANDWELL DR.
WASDALE CL.
DELFIELD CL.
OLD WOOD
SAXILBY RD
BROOKFIELD CL.
BADGERS
STONY YD.
NURSES LA.
HODSON CL.
WOODPECKER CL.
LAPWING CL.
THE DENE
DENE RD.
DENE CL.
VICARAGE DR.
WILLOW CL.
GOLDFINCH CL.
HAMILTON GR.
AVENUE
BIRDS HOLT
COOPERS HOLT CL.
WISEHOLME RD.
WOODLAND AVE.
LIVERPOOL CL.
FOXFIELD CL.
BEAVER CL.
POACHERS BROOK
BROOKFIELD CL.
SAXILBY RD.
WESTERN LA.
ST.
STONEY YD.
LOWER CHURCH RD.
CHURCH LA.
GREEN
Sch.
Ch.
HODSON CL.
MANOR GRNDS
WELLINGTON CLOSE
WOOD BANK
HAMPDEN CL.
LANCASTER WAY
BLENHEIM CL.
CHAPEL RD.
HALIFAX CL.
THE HILL
THE PADDOCK
STIRLING WAY
WHITLEY CL.
OLD CL.
ANSON CL.
SUNDERLAND CL.
MITCHELL CL.
CANBERRA WAY
MONSON PK.
REDWING CL.
MAGPIE CL.
MARTIN CL.
GOLDFINCH
MALLARD CL.
PARK
SAX
BIS

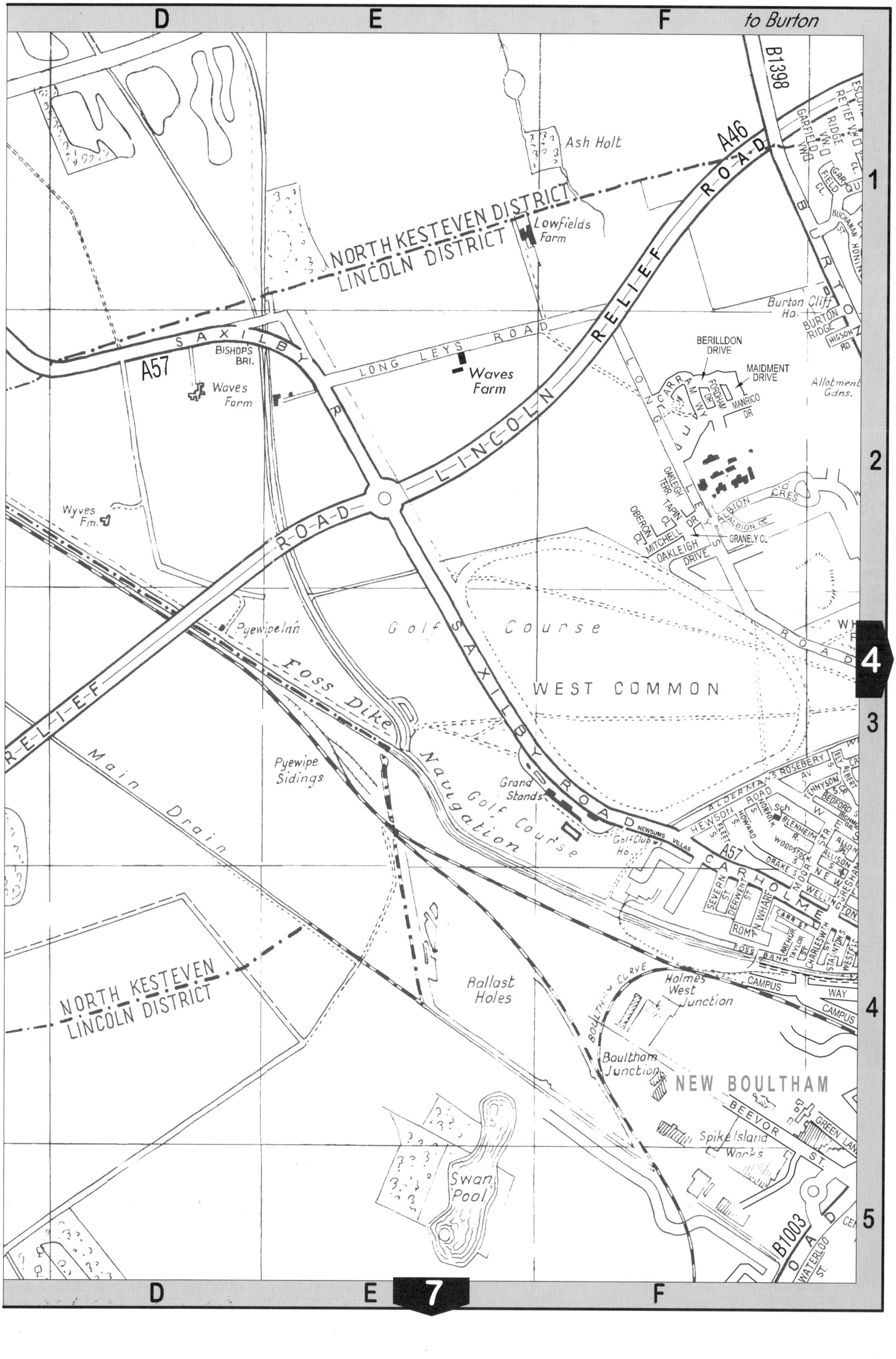
D
E
F
to Burton
B1398
A46
ROAD
RELIEF
LINCOLN
1
2
3
4
5
Ash Holt
NORTH KESTEVEN DISTRICT
LINCOLN DISTRICT
Lowfields Farm
Burton Cliff Ho.
BURTON RIDGE
HIGSON RD
BERILLDON DRIVE
MAIDMENT DRIVE
MANRICO DR
FORDHAM DR
CARRAM WY
Allotment Gdns.
SAXILBY
BISHOPS BRI.
A57
LONG LEYS ROAD
Waves Farm
Waves Farm
OAKLEIGH TERR
TAPIN CL
OBERON CL
MITCHELL DR
OAKLEIGH DRIVE
ALBION CRES
ALBION CL
GRANELY CL
Wyves Fm.
PyewipeInn
Foss Dike
Navigation
Golf Course
WEST COMMON
Main Drain
Pyewipe Sidings
Grand Stands
Golf Course
Golf Club Ho.
NEWSUMS VILLAS
ALDERMAN'S
ROSEBERY AV
HEWSON ROAD
FLEET S.
NORFOLK S.
HOWARD S.
Sch.
BLENHEIM R.
WOODSTOCK S.
TENNYSON S.
BEDFORD S.
RICHMOND
DRAKE S.
CARHOLME
NEWLAND
WELLINGTON
SEVERN ST.
DERWENT ST.
ROMAN WHARF
CARR ST.
ARTHUR ST.
TAYLOR ST.
CHARLESWORTH ST.
STAINTON S.
FOSS BANK
CAMPUS WAY
CAMPUS WAY
Holmes West Junction
BOULTHAM CURVE
Ballast Holes
Boultham Junction
NEW BOULTHAM
BEEVOR ST.
GREEN LANE
Spike Island Works
Swan Pool
B1003
ROAD
WATERLOO ST.

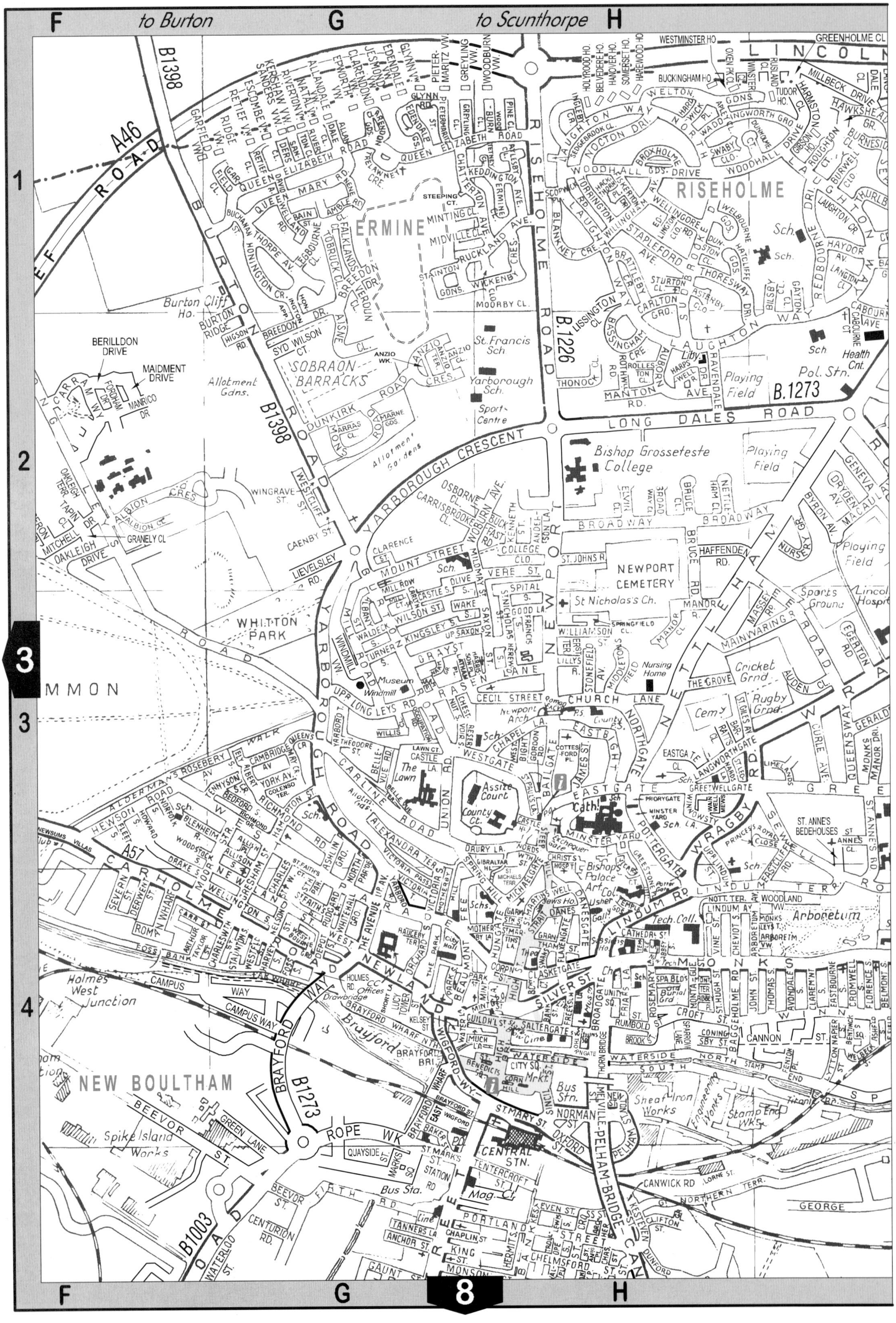
F
to Burton
G
to Scunthorpe
H
1
2
3
4
8
B1398
A46
ROAD
RISEHOLME ROAD
ERMINE
RISEHOLME
SOBRAON BARRACKS
Allotment Gdns.
Burton Cliff Ho.
St.Francis Sch
Yarborough Sch.
Sport Centre
B.1226
B.1273
LONG DALES ROAD
Bishop Grosseteste College
Playing Field
YARBOROUGH CRESCENT
BROADWAY
NEWPORT CEMETERY
St Nicholas's Ch.
WHITTON PARK
MMON
Museum
Windmill
UPR LONG LEYS RD
CHURCH LANE
NORTHGATE
NETTLEHAM ROAD
Cricket Grnd
Rugby Grnd.
Sports Ground
Nursing Home
Newport Arch
WESTGATE
CASTLE
The Lawn
Assize Court
County Ct.
BAILGATE
EASTGATE
Cath!
MINSTER YARD
POTTERGATE
WRAGBY RD
GREETWELLGATE
ST. ANNE'S BEDEHOUSES
Bishop's Palace
Arboretum
LINDUM RD
MONKS RD
CARHOLME RD
A57
WEST PARADE
NEWLAND
Holmes West Junction
CAMPUS WAY
BRAYFORD WAY
Brayford
NEW BOULTHAM
B1273
ROPE WK
Spike Island Works
BEEVOR ST.
GREEN LANE
B1003
WATERLOO ST.
CENTURION RD.
HIGH ST.
SILVER ST.
SALTERGATE
WATERSIDE NORTH
WATERSIDE SOUTH
CITY SQ.
Mrkt.
Bus Stn.
NORMAN ST.
ST MARY ST.
CENTRAL STN.
OXFORD ST.
MELVILLE ST.
PELHAM BRIDGE
Sheaf Iron Works
Stamp End Wks
Engineering Works
CANWICK RD
NORTHERN TERR.
GEORGE
TENTERCROFT ST.
PORTLAND ST.
KING ST.
MONSON ST.
CHELMSFORD ST.
Tech. Coll.
Usher Gall.
Jews Ho.
CANNON ST.

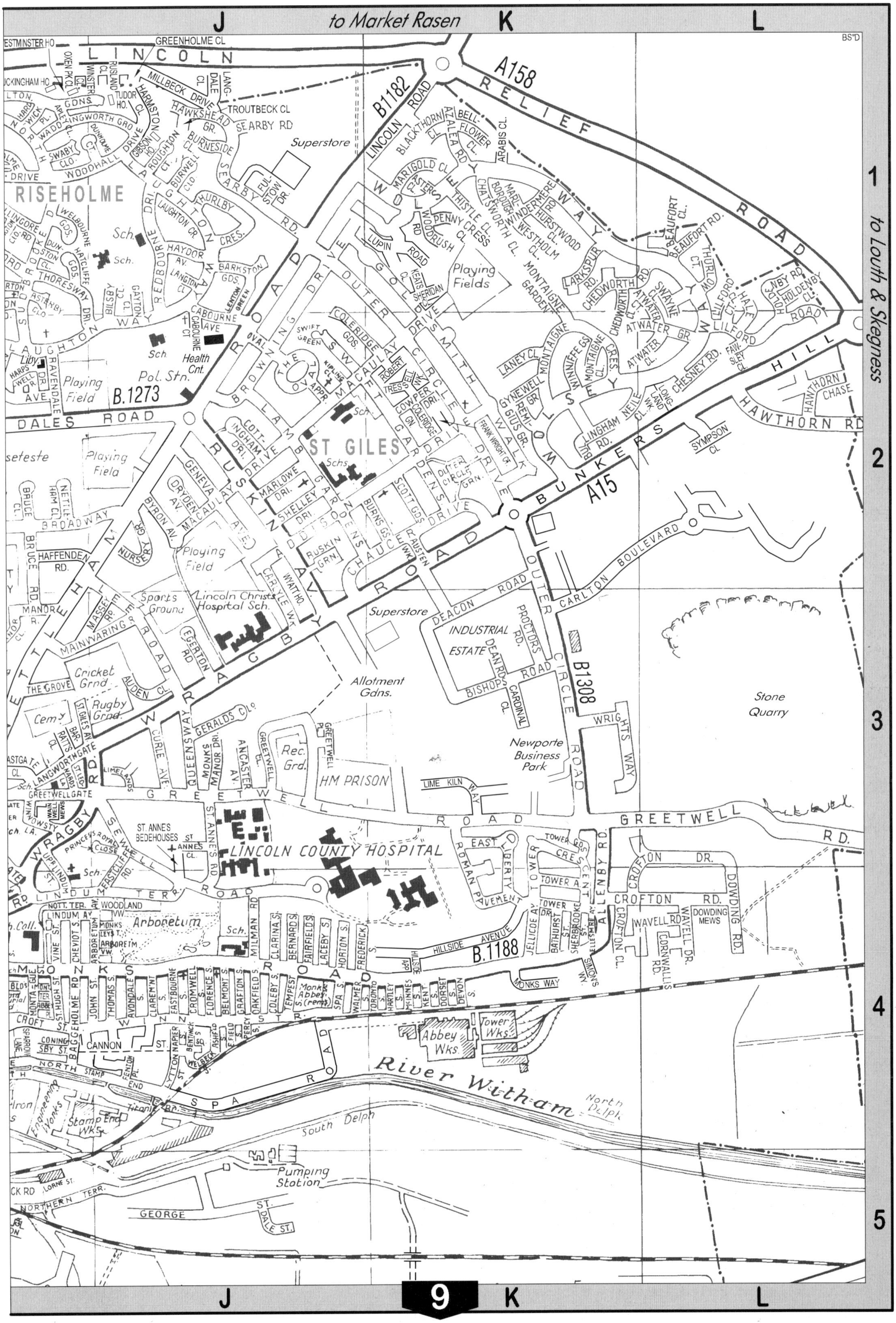
J
to Market Rasen
K
L
to Louth & Skegness
1
2
3
4
5
9
RISEHOLME
ST GILES
A158
RELIEF ROAD
B1182
LINCOLN ROAD
WOLSEY WAY
OUTER CIRCLE DRIVE
Superstore
Playing Fields
BUNKERS HILL
A15
WRAGBY ROAD
RUSKIN AV.
B.1273
DALES ROAD
LAUGHTON WAY
Pol. Stn.
Health Cnt.
Lincoln Christ's Hospital Sch.
Sports Ground
Cricket Grnd
Rugby Grnd
Allotment Gdns.
INDUSTRIAL ESTATE
DEACON ROAD
CARLTON BOULEVARD
B1308
Stone Quarry
Newporte Business Park
HM PRISON
Rec. Grd.
GREETWELL ROAD
LINCOLN COUNTY HOSPITAL
ST. ANNE'S BEDEHOUSES
Arboretum
B.1188
HILLSIDE AVENUE
MONKS ROAD
Monks Abbey
Abbey Wks.
Tower Wks.
River Witham
North Delph
South Delph
Pumping Station
Engineering Works
Stamp End Wks.
SPA ROAD
HAWTHORN RD
CROFTON DR.
DOWDING RD.
WAVELL DR.
ALLENBY RD.

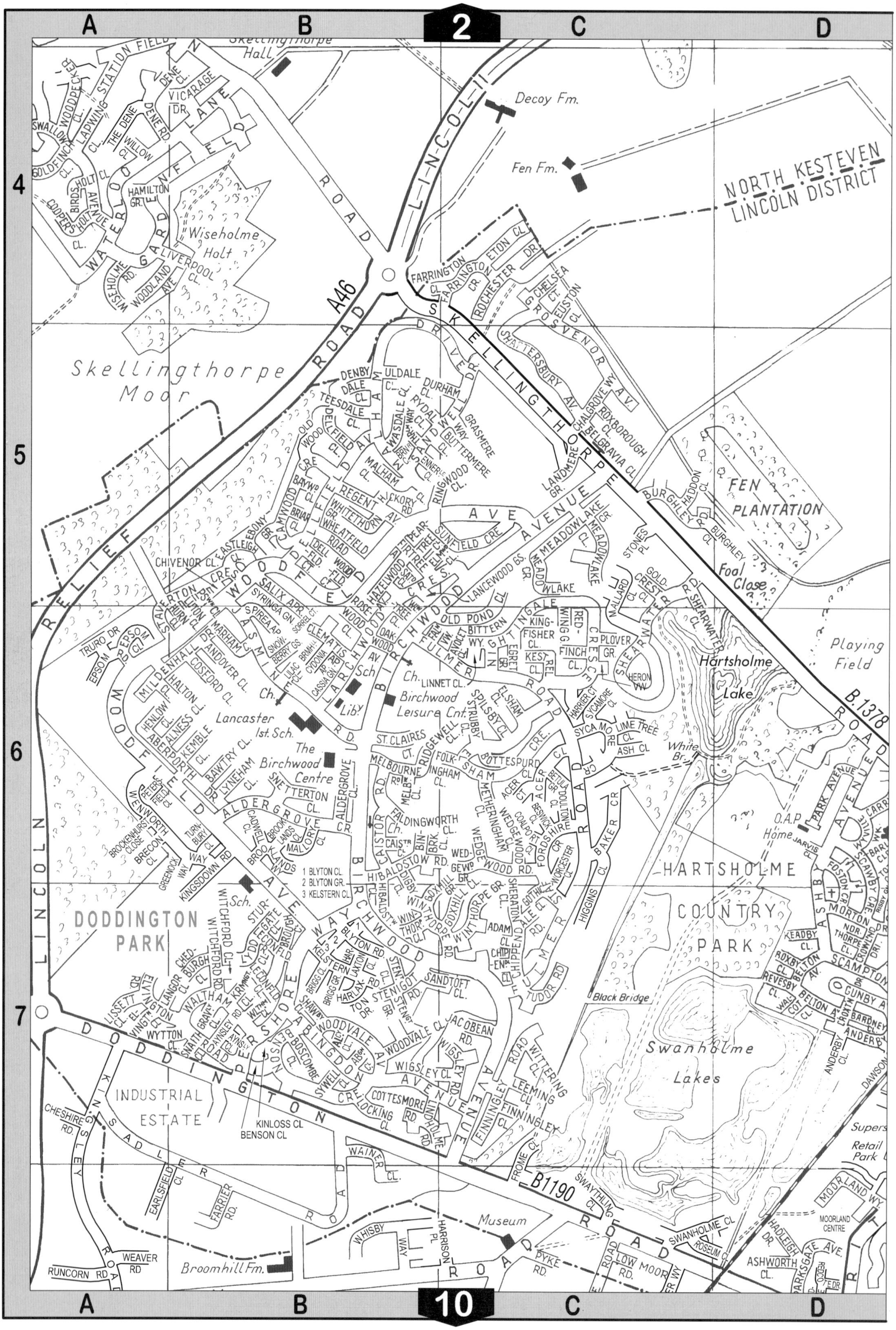
A
B
2
C
D
4
5
6
7
10
Skellingthorpe Hall
Decoy Fm.
Fen Fm.
NORTH KESTEVEN
LINCOLN DISTRICT
LINCOLN
RELIEF ROAD A46
ROAD
Wiseholme Holt
Skellingthorpe Moor
SKELLINGTHORPE ROAD
FEN PLANTATION
Foal Close
Playing Field
Hartsholme Lake
B.1378 ROAD
White Br.
HARTSHOLME COUNTRY PARK
O.A.P. Home
Swanholme Lakes
Black Bridge
DODDINGTON PARK
INDUSTRIAL ESTATE
DODDINGTON ROAD
B1190
Museum
Broomhill Fm.
Supers Retail Park
MOORLAND CENTRE
Lancaster Ist. Sch.
The Birchwood Centre
Birchwood Leisure Cnt.
Ch.
Sch.
Lib.
BIRCHWOOD AVENUE
WOODFIELD AVE
JASMIN RD.
NIGHTINGALE CRES.
FULMER WAY
BRANT ROAD
AVENUE
HARTSHOLME DR.
1 BLYTON CL.
2 BLYTON GR.
3 KELSTERN CL.
KINLOSS CL
BENSON CL
WATERLOO LANE
STATION FIELD
LAPWING CL.
WOODPECKER CL.
SWALLOW CL.
GOLDFINCH CL.
THE DENE
DENE RD.
VICARAGE DR.
HAMILTON GR.
LIVERPOOL CL.
WOODLAND AVE.
WISEHOLME RD.
FARRINGTON CL.
FARRINGTON CR.
ETON CL.
ROCHESTER DR.
CHELSEA CT.
EUSTON CL.
GROSVENOR AV.
SHAFTESBURY AV.
CHALGROVE WY.
ROXBOROUGH CL.
BELGRAVIA CL.
LANDMERE GR.
BURGHLEY RD.
HADDON CL.
BURGHLEY CL.
DENBY DALE CL.
ULDALE CL.
DURHAM CL.
RYDAL CL.
TEESDALE CL.
WASDALE CL.
GRASMERE WAY
BUTTERMERE CL.
RINGWOOD CL.
MALHAM CL.
HICKORY RD.
REGENT AV.
WHITETHORN GR.
WHEATFIELD ROAD
CAMWOOD CL.
EBONY GR.
EASTLEIGH CL.
CHIVENOR CL.
SUNFIELD CRE.
PEAR TREE CL.
LANCEWOOD GS.
MEADOWLAKE CL.
MEADOWLAKE CR.
STONES PL.
GOLDCREST CL.
MALLARD CL.
SHEARWATER RD.
SHEARWATER CL.
OLD POND CL.
BITTERN WY.
KINGFISHER CL.
REDWING CL.
FINCH CL.
KESTREL CL.
PLOVER GR.
HERON VW.
LINNET CL.
SPILSBY CL.
ELSHAM CL.
STRUBBY CL.
HARRIER CT.
SYCAMORE CL.
LIME TREE CL.
ASH CL.
ST. CLAIRES CT.
RIDGEWELL CL.
BOTTESFORD CRE.
FOLKINGHAM CL.
MELBOURNE RD.
CAISTOR RD.
FALDINGWORTH CL.
METHERINGHAM CL.
WEDGEWOOD CL.
WEDGEWOOD RD.
ACER CL.
BAKER CR.
HIGGINS CL.
WORCESTER CL.
HIBALDSTOW RD.
WINTHORPE RD.
WINTHORPE GR.
BOXHILL GR.
SHERATON CL.
ADAM CL.
CHIPPENDALE CL.
TUDOR RD.
SANDTOFT CL.
JACOBEAN RD.
WIGSLEY RD.
WITTERING CL.
LEEMING CL.
FINNINGLEY CL.
FROME CL.
SWAYTHLING CL.
COTTESMORE RD.
WOODVALE AV.
ABINGDON AV.
BOSCOMBE CL.
PERSHORE AVE.
WITCHFORD CL.
WITCHFORD RD.
WALTHAM CL.
ELVINGTON CL.
LISSETT CL.
WYTTON CL.
SWAITHE GR.
TRURO DR.
EPSOM CL.
STAVERTON CRE.
MILDENHALL DR.
HALTON CL.
HENLOW CL.
ALNESS CL.
ABERPORTH DR.
KEMBLE CL.
COSFORD CL.
ANDOVER CL.
MARHAM CL.
BAWTRY CL.
LYNEHAM CL.
SNETTERTON CL.
ALDERGROVE CR.
ALDERGROVE CL.
BROOKLANDS WY.
MALLORY CL.
WENWORTH CL.
BROCKENHURST CLOSE
BRECON CL.
GREENOCK WAY
KINGSDOWN RD
TURNBURY CL.
SALIX APR.
SPIREA AP.
SYRINGA GN.
SORREL CT.
SNOWBERRY GS.
CLEMATIS AP.
LILAC CL.
CYDONIA AP.
CASSIA GN.
LARCHWOOD CRES.
HAZELWOOD AV.
ROSEWOOD CL.
OAK WOOD
KEADBY CL.
ROXBY CL.
BELTON AV.
REVESBY CL.
SCAMPTON AV.
GUNBY AV.
BARDNEY CL.
ANDERBY DR.
ANDERBY CL.
ASHBY AVENUE
PARK AVENUE
JARVIS CL.
FOSTON CRE.
MORTON CL.
CROXTON DR.
WYVILLE WK.
DAWSON
MOORLAND WY.
HADLEIGH DR.
PARKSGATE AVE.
ASHWORTH CL.
SWANHOLME CL.
ROSEUM CL.
LOW MOOR RD.
PYKE RD.
HARRISON PL.
WHISBY WAY
WAINER CL.
FARRIER RD.
EARLSFIELD CL.
SADLER ROAD
KINGSLEY ROAD
CHESHIRE RD.
RUNCORN RD
WEAVER RD

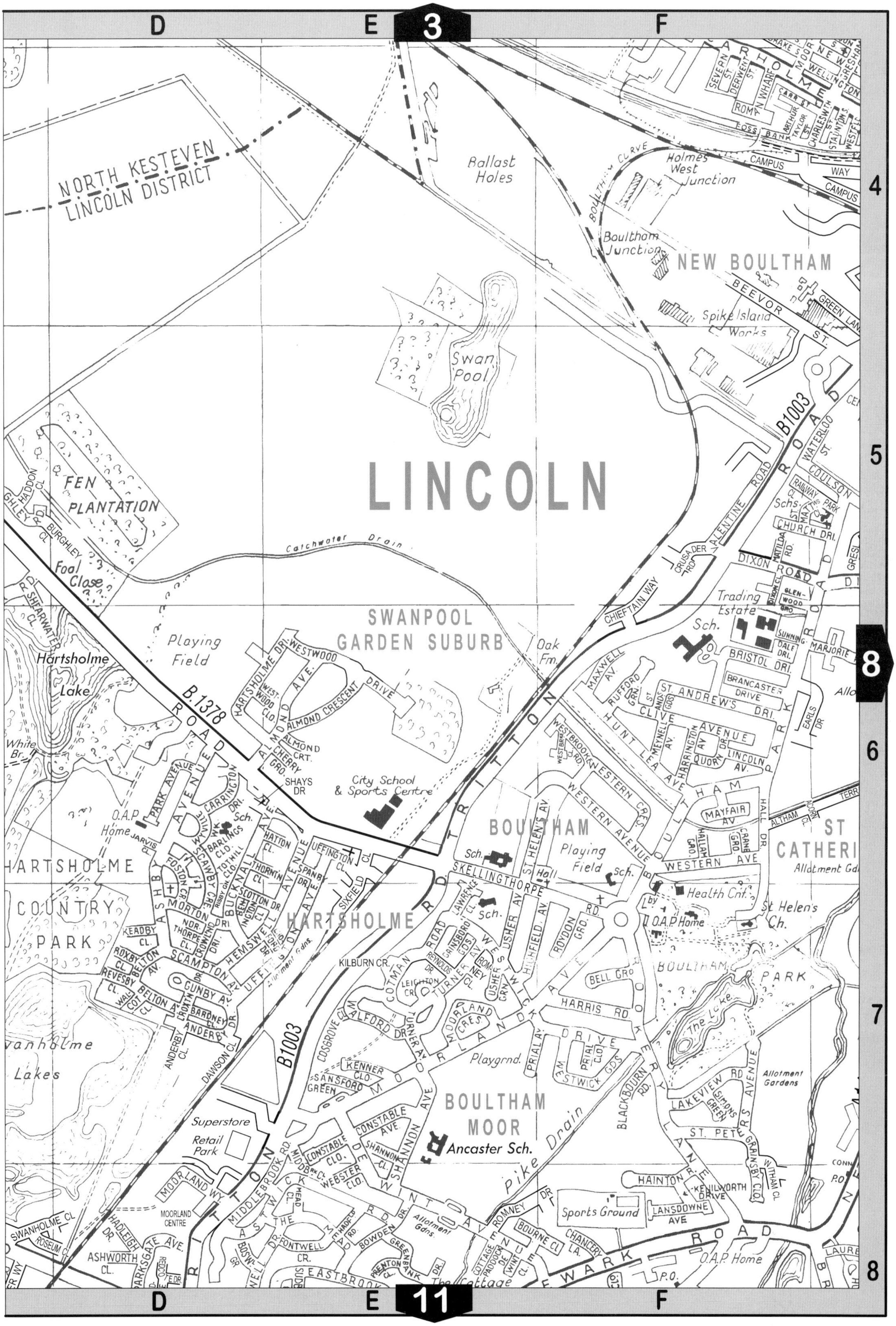
D
E
3
F
4
5
8
6
7
8
11
NORTH KESTEVEN
LINCOLN DISTRICT
Ballast Holes
Holmes West Junction
Boultham Junction
BOULTHAM CURVE
NEW BOULTHAM
CAMPUS WAY
BEEVOR ST.
GREEN LANE
Spike Island Works
Swan Pool
LINCOLN
FEN PLANTATION
Foal Close
Catchwater Drain
B1003
VALENTINE ROAD
WATERLOO ST.
COULSON
RAILWAY PARK
Schs.
CHURCH DRI.
DIXON ROAD
CRUSADER RD.
CHIEFTAIN WAY
Trading Estate
SWANPOOL GARDEN SUBURB
Playing Field
Hartsholme Lake
WESTWOOD DRIVE
ALMOND AVE.
ALMOND CRESCENT
Oak Fm.
B.1378 ROAD
BRISTOL DRI.
BRANCASTER DRIVE
ST. ANDREW'S DRI.
MAXWELL AV.
RUFFORD GRN.
CLIVE AVENUE
HUNT LEA AVE
HARRINGTON AV.
QUORN DR.
LINCOLN AV.
EARLS DR.
BIRCHWOOD
PARK AVENUE
CARRINGTON DRI.
O.A.P. Home
City School & Sports Centre
SHAYS DR
WESTBROOKE RD.
WESTERN CRES.
WESTERN AVENUE
BOULTHAM
MAYFAIR AV.
HALL DR.
ST CATHERI
Allotment Gdns.
HARTSHOLME COUNTRY PARK
HARTSHOLME
ASHBY AVENUE
UFFINGTON CL.
SKELLINGTHORPE RD.
ST. HELEN'S AV.
Health Cnt.
St Helen's Ch.
O.A.P. Home
SCAMPTON AV.
GUNBY AV.
BELTON AV.
ANDERBY CL.
KILBURN CR.
COTMAN ROAD
LAWRENCE CL.
USHER AV.
HIGHFIELD AV.
ROYDON GRO.
BELL GRO.
HARRIS RD.
BOULTHAM PARK
The Lake
MOORLAND CRES.
PRIAL AV.
MOORLAND AVE
DRIVE
WESTWICK GDNS.
Playgrnd.
Swanholme Lakes
DAWSON CL.
KENNER CLO.
SANSFORD GREEN
BOULTHAM MOOR
Ancaster Sch.
Pike Drain
BLACKBOURN RD.
COOKERY LANE
LAKEVIEW RD
ST. PETERS AVENUE
Allotment Gardens
Superstore Retail Park
CONSTABLE AVE.
SHANNON AVE
MIDDLEBROOK RD.
MOORLAND WY.
MOORLAND CENTRE
WEBSTER CLO.
DE WINT AV.
HAINTON RD.
KENILWORTH DRIVE
WITHAM CL.
Sports Ground
LANSDOWNE AVE
SWANHOLME CL.
ROSEUM CL.
HADLEIGH DR.
ASHWORTH CL.
PARKSGATE AVE.
FONTWELL CR.
BOWDEN DR.
GREENBANK DR.
EASTBROOK
ROMNEY DR.
BOURNE CL.
CHANCERY LA.
NEWARK ROAD
O.A.P. Home
P.O.
The Cottage

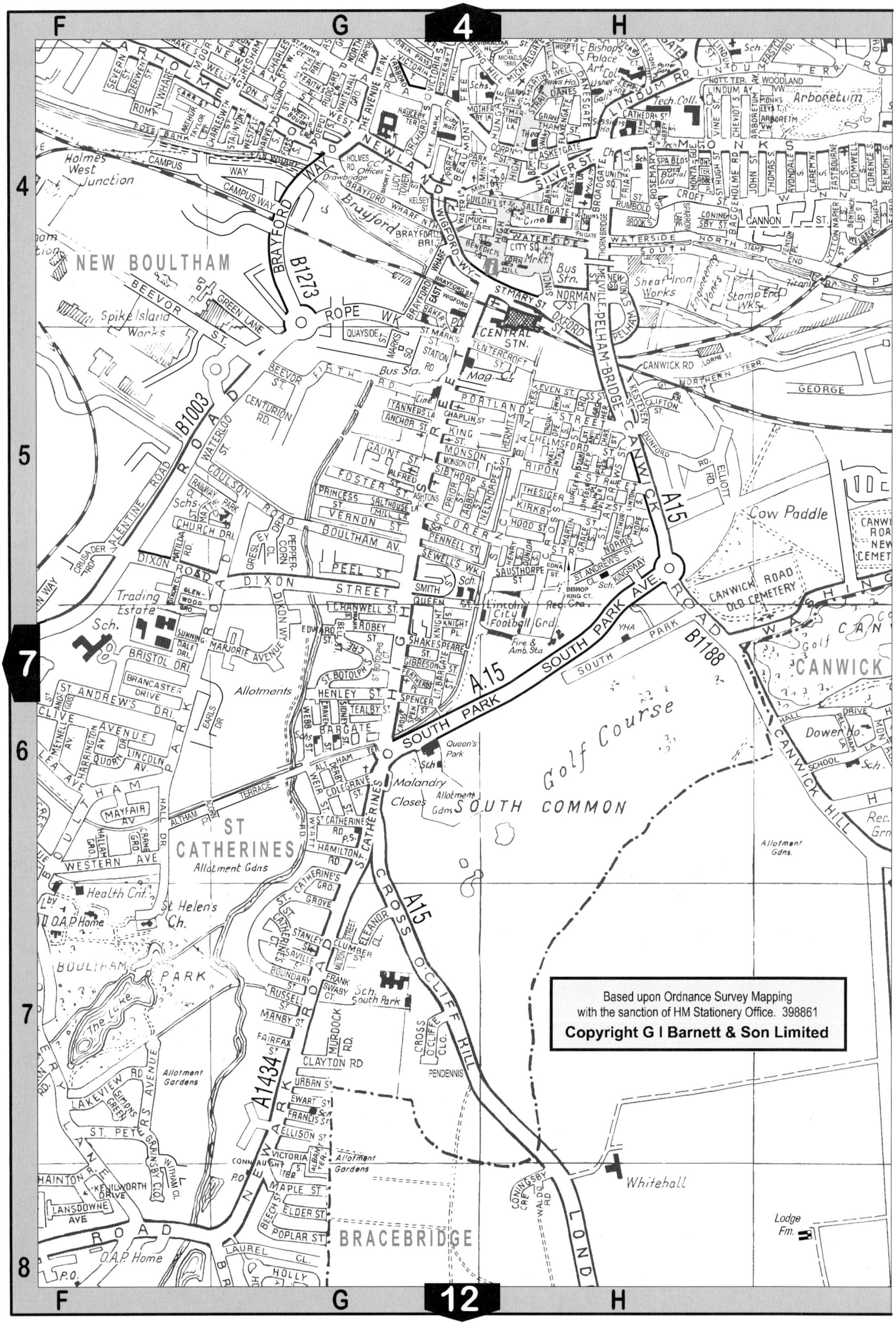
F
G
4
H
4
5
6
7
8
7
12
NEW BOULTHAM
Holmes West Junction
CAMPUS WAY
BRAYFORD WAY
B1273
Brayford
BRAYFORD WHARF NTH
Spike Island Works
BEEVOR ST.
GREEN LANE
ROPE WK
QUAYSIDE
CENTRAL STN.
ST MARY ST
Bus Stn.
NORMAN ST.
OXFORD ST.
MELVILLE ST.
PELHAM BRIDGE
Sheaf Iron Works
Engineering Works
Stamp End Wks
WATERSIDE SOUTH
WATERSIDE NORTH
CANWICK RD
NORTHERN TERR.
GEORGE
CLIFTON ST.
CITY SQ.
Mrkt.
SALTERGATE
SILVER ST.
CLASKETGATE
BROADGATE
LINDUM RD
Tech. Coll.
Arboretum
MONKS RD
CROFT ST.
RUMBOLD ST.
CANNON ST.
NEWLAND
B1003
WATERLOO ST.
CENTURION RD.
FIRTH RD
Bus Sta.
Mag. Ct.
TENTERCROFT ST.
PORTLAND ST.
CHAPLIN ST
KING ST.
MONSON ST.
GAUNT ST.
FOSTER ST.
ALFRED ST.
SIBTHORP ST.
PRINCESS ST.
VERNON ST.
BOULTHAM AV.
PEEL ST.
SCORER ST.
PENNELL ST.
SEWELLS WK.
RIPON ST.
THESIGER ST.
KIRKBY ST.
HOOD ST.
ST ANDREWS ST.
CHELMSFORD ST.
DUNFORD
ELLIOTT RD.
A15
Cow Paddle
CANWICK ROAD OLD CEMETERY
VALENTINE ROAD
COULSON ROAD
CHURCH DRI.
DIXON ROAD
DIXON STREET
CRUSADER RD
Trading Estate
Sch.
SMITH ST.
QUEEN ST.
Lincoln City Football Grd.
Fire & Amb. Sta.
SOUTH PARK AVE
SOUTH PARK
A.15
YHA
B1188
Golf
CANWICK
BRISTOL DRI.
BRANCASTER DRIVE
ST. ANDREW'S DRI.
MARJORIE AVENUE
Allotments
HENLEY ST.
BARGATE
SPENCER ST.
SHAKESPEARE ST.
GIBBESON ST.
CLIVE AVENUE
LINCOLN AV.
QUORN DR
HARRINGTON AV
MAYFAIR AV
ALTHAM TERRACE
HALL DR
ST CATHERINES
Allotment Gdns
WESTERN AVE
Health Cnt.
O.A.P. Home
St Helen's Ch.
Queen's Park
Malandry Closes
Allotment Gdns
SOUTH COMMON
Golf Course
ST. CATHERINES
HAMILTON RD.
ST CATHERINE'S GRO.
GROVE
CROSS O'CLIFF HILL
A15
STANLEY PL.
SAVILLE ST.
BOUNDARY ST.
RUSSELL ST.
MANBY ST.
FAIRFAX ST.
CLAYTON RD
URBAN ST.
EWART ST.
FRANCIS ST.
ELLISON ST.
VICTORIA TER.
MAPLE ST.
ELDER ST.
POPLAR ST.
BRACEBRIDGE
MURDOCK RD.
ELEANOR CL.
South Park
CROSS O'CLIFF CLO.
PENDENNIS
A1434
NEWARK ROAD
BOULTHAM PARK
The Lake
LAKEVIEW RD
Allotment Gardens
ST. PETERS AVENUE
GRAINSBY CL.
WITHAM CL.
KENILWORTH DRIVE
LANSDOWNE AVE
ROAD
O.A.P. Home
P.O.
LAUREL CL.
HOLLY
Allotment Gardens
CONINGSBY CRE
WALDO RD
LONDON
Whitehall
Lodge Fm.
Dower Ho.
SCHOOL
Rec. Grn
CANWICK HILL
Allotment Gdns.

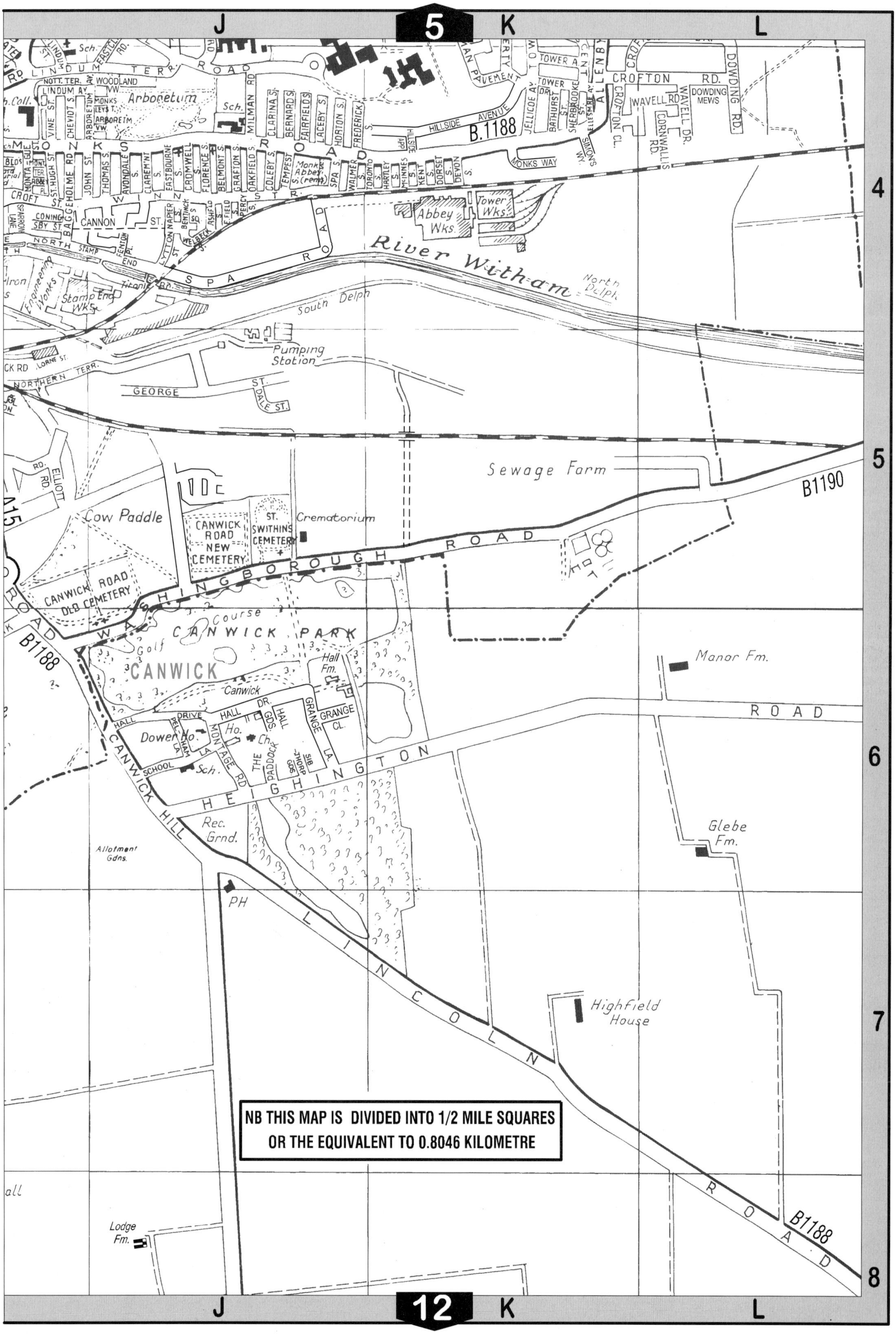
5
J
K
L
4
5
6
7
8
12
LINDUM TERR.
ROAD
WOODLAND VW.
NOTT. TER.
LINDUM AV.
Arboretum
Sch.
MILMAN RD
CLARINA S.
BERNARDS S.
FAIRFIELDS
LACEBY S.
HORTON S.
FREDERICK S.
HILLSIDE AVENUE
B.1188
TOWER AV.
TOWER DR.
JELLICOE AV.
BATHURST ST.
SHERBROOKE ST.
ALLENBY
CROFTON RD.
CROFTON CL.
WAVELL RD.
WAVELL DR.
DOWDING MEWS
DOWDING RD.
CORNWALLIS RD.
MONKS WAY
VINE ST.
CHEVIOT S.
ARBORETUM VW.
MONKS ROAD
ST.HUGH ST.
BAGGEHOLME RD
JOHN ST.
THOMAS S.
AVONDALE S.
CLAREMONT S.
EASTBOURNE S.
CROMWELL S.
FLORENCE S.
BELMONT S.
GRAFTON S.
OAKFIELD S.
COLEBY S.
TEMPEST S.
Monks Abbey (rems)
SPA S.
WALMER S.
TORONTO S.
HARTLEY S.
McINNES S.
KENT S.
DORSET S.
DEVON S.
CROFT ST.
CANNON ST.
CONINGSBY ST.
SPARROW LANE
NAPIER ST.
BENTINCK SQ.
ASHFIELD S.
Abbey Wks.
Tower Wks.
NORTH STAMP END
FENTON PL.
SPA ROAD
River Witham
North Delph
South Delph
Titanic Br.
Engineering Works
Iron
Stamp End Wks.
Pumping Station
LORNE ST.
NORTHERN TERR.
GEORGE ST.
DALE ST.
ELLIOTT RD.
A15
Cow Paddle
CANWICK ROAD NEW CEMETERY
ST. SWITHINS CEMETERY
Crematorium
Sewage Farm
B1190
WASHINGBOROUGH ROAD
CANWICK ROAD OLD CEMETERY
B1188
CANWICK ROAD
Golf Course
CANWICK PARK
CANWICK
Canwick
Hall Fm.
Manor Fm.
HALL DRIVE
HALL DR.
HALL GDS.
GRANGE LA.
GRANGE CL.
Dower Ho.
PELHAM LA.
MONTAGUE RD.
Ho.
Ch.
THE PADDOCK
SIBTHORP GDS.
SCHOOL LA.
Sch.
HEIGHINGTON ROAD
CANWICK HILL
Rec. Grnd.
Allotment Gdns.
PH
LINCOLN ROAD
Glebe Fm.
Highfield House
B1188
Lodge Fm.
NB THIS MAP IS DIVIDED INTO 1/2 MILE SQUARES
OR THE EQUIVALENT TO 0.8046 KILOMETRE

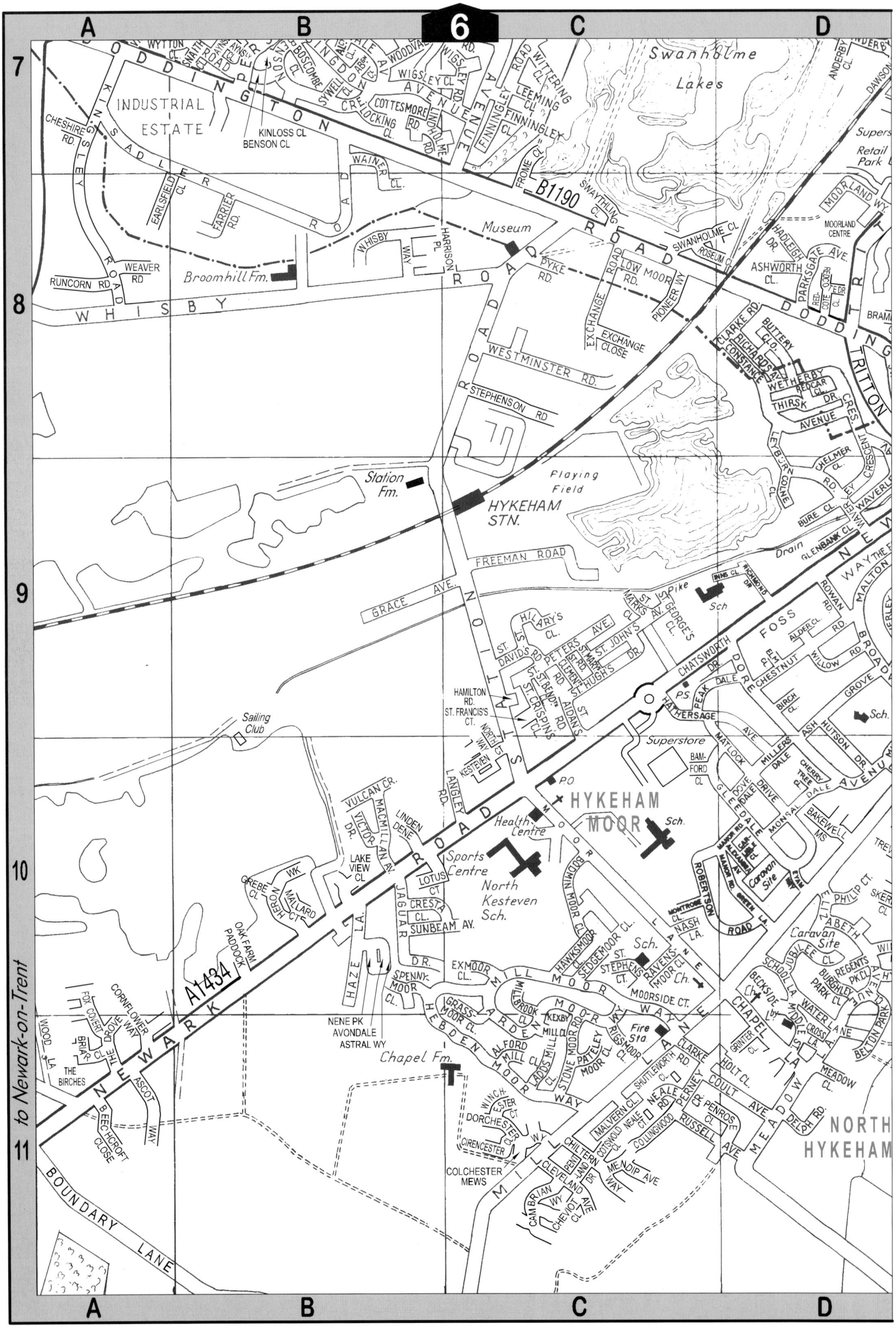
A
B
6
C
D
7
8
9
10
11
Swanholme Lakes
INDUSTRIAL ESTATE
DODDINGTON ROAD
KINLOSS CL
BENSON CL
CHESHIRE RD.
KINGSLEY RD.
SADLER ROAD
EARLSFIELD CL
FARRIER RD.
WAINER CL.
COTTESMORE RD.
FINNINGLEY CL.
FINNINGLEY RD.
LEEMING CL
WITTERING CL
FROME CL
B1190
SWAYTHLING CL
Museum
WHISBY WAY
HARRISON PL
WEAVER RD
RUNCORN RD
Broomhill Fm.
WHISBY ROAD
PYKE RD.
EXCHANGE ROAD
LOW MOOR RD.
PIONEER WY
EXCHANGE CLOSE
SWANHOLME CL
ROSEUM CL
HADLEIGH DR.
ASHWORTH CL.
PARKSGATE AVE.
MOORLAND CENTRE
MOORLAND WY.
Supers
Retail Park
ANDERBY CL
DAWSON
WESTMINSTER RD.
STEPHENSON RD
CLARKE RD
BUTTERY CL
RICHARDSON
CONSTANCE
WETHERBY
REDCAR CL.
THIRSK DR
AVENUE
CRES
LEYBURN CL
CHELMER CL.
CRESCENT
TRITTON
Station Fm.
HYKEHAM STN.
Playing Field
BURE CL.
GLENBANK CL
Drain
FREEMAN ROAD
GRACE AVE.
STATION ROAD
Pike
Sch
ST. MARKS AV.
ST GEORGE'S CL.
ST. HILARY'S CL.
ST. PETERS AVE.
ST. JOHN'S DR.
ST. DAVID'S RD
ST. HUGH'S DR.
ST. CRISPINS CL.
ST. AIDAN'S RD.
HAMILTON RD.
ST. FRANCIS'S CT.
NORTH WAY
KESTEVEN CT
CHATSWORTH DR
PEAK DALE
DORE AVE
HATHERSAGE AVE
FOSS
ROWAN RD
ALDER CL.
CHESTNUT
WILLOW RD
BIRCH CL
MALTON
GROVE
BROADWAY
ASH
HUTSON DR.
Sch.
Superstore
BAMFORD CL
MATLOCK
MILLERS DALE
CHERRY TREE CL
DOVEDALE
GLEE DALE
DRIVE
MONSAL DALE
BAKEWELL MS
Sailing Club
VULCAN CR.
MACMILLAN AV.
VICTOR DR.
LINDEN DENE
LANGLEY RD.
LAKE VIEW CL
P.O
HYKEHAM MOOR
Health Centre
Sch.
Sports Centre
North Kesteven Sch.
LOTUS CT
CRESTA CL.
SUNBEAM AY.
JAGUAR DR.
BODMIN MOOR CL
ROBERTSON ROAD
MONTROSE CL.
NASH LA.
Caravan Site
PHILIP CT.
ELIZABETH
JUBILEE CL
Caravan Site
GREBE CL
HERON WK
MALLARD CT
OAK FARM PADDOCK
A1434
NEWARK ROAD
HAZE LA.
SPENNY MOOR CL.
EXMOOR CL.
MILL MOOR WAY
HAWKSMOOR
SEDGEMOOR CL.
ST. STEPHENS CT.
RAVENS MOOR CL
MOORSIDE CT.
Ch.
Sch.
LANE
SCHOOL LA.
BECKSIDE
REGENTS PK
BURGHLEY PARK CL
WATER LANE
BELTON PARK
MIDDLE ST.
CROSS LA.
MEADOW CL.
NENE PK
AVONDALE
ASTRAL WY
GRASSMOOR CL.
ARDEN MOOR
MILLBROOK CL
EXBY
MILL CL
ALFORD MILL CL
LADDS MILL
STONE MOOR
PATELEY MOOR CL.
RIGSMOOR CL.
Fire Sta.
HEBDEN MOOR WAY
Chapel Fm.
SHUTTLEWORTH CL
CLARKE RD
CHAPEL LA
GRINTER CL
HOLT CL.
COULT AVE
MEADOW
DELPH RD.
NORTH HYKEHAM
to Newark-on-Trent
WOOD LA
FOX COVERT
BRIAR CL
THE DROVE
CORNFLOWER WAY
THE BIRCHES
ASCOT WAY
BEECHCROFT CLOSE
WINCHESTER CT
DORCHESTER CL
CIRENCESTER
COLCHESTER MEWS
MALVERN CL.
COTSWOLD
NEALE CT
NEALE RD
PERNEY CR
PENROSE CL
RUSSELL AVE
COLLINGWOOD
CHILTERN DR
PENTLAND DR
MENDIP AVE
MENDIP WAY
CLEVELAND AVE
CAMBRIAN WY
CHEVIOT CL
MILL LANE
BOUNDARY LANE

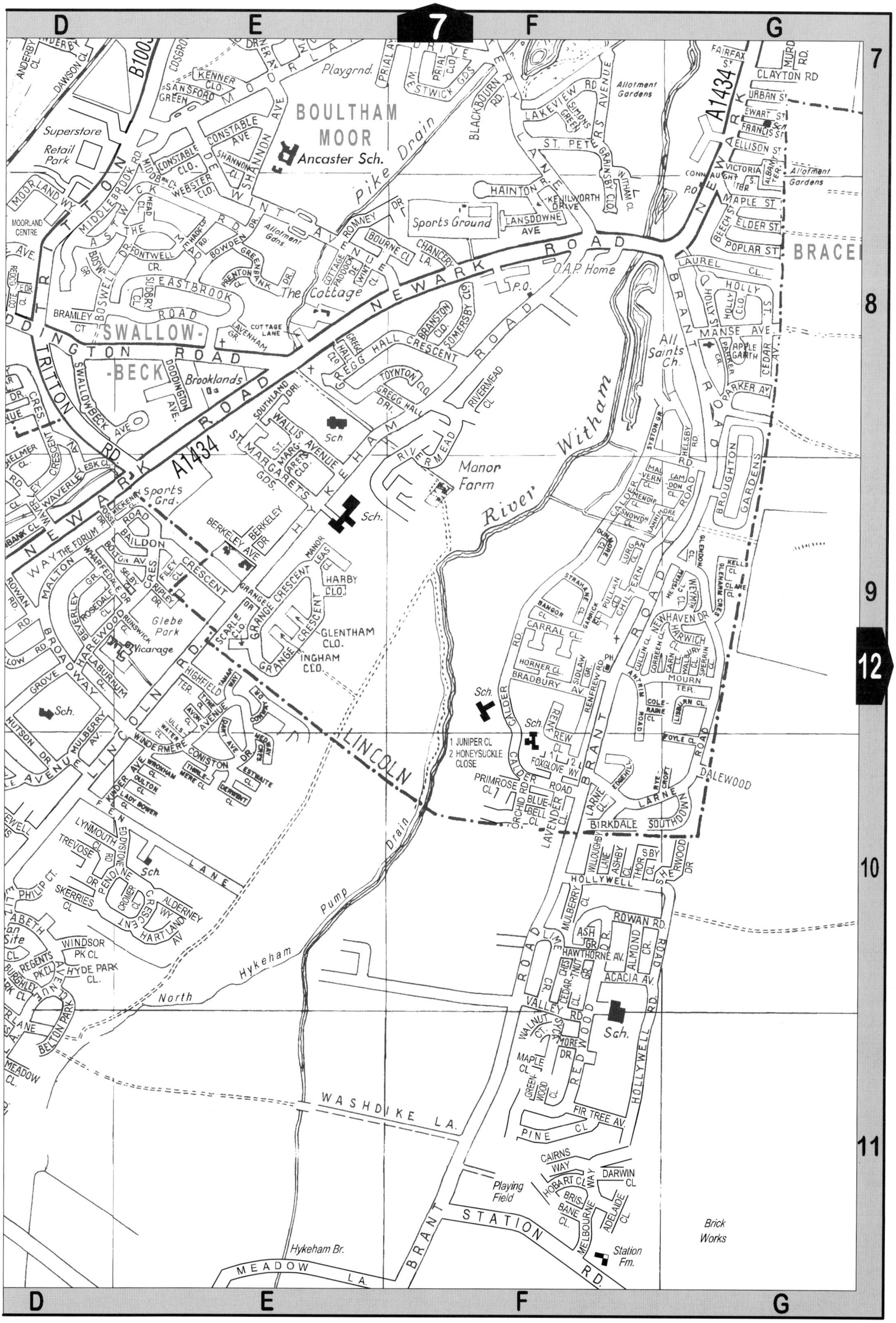
7
D
E
F
G
8
9
10
11
12
BOULTHAM MOOR
Ancaster Sch.
Playgrnd.
Pike Drain
Superstore
Retail Park
MOORLAND CENTRE
SWALLOW-BECK
Brooklands
The Cottage
Sports Ground
O.A.P. Home
P.O.
Allotment Gdns.
Allotment Gardens
BRACE
All Saints Ch.
River Witham
Manor Farm
Sch.
Sports Grd.
Glebe Park
Vicarage
LINCOLN
North Hykeham Pump Drain
WASHDIKE LA.
Playing Field
Brick Works
Station Fm.
Hykeham Br.
MEADOW LA.
BRANT
STATION RD.
NEWARK ROAD
A1434
DODDINGTON ROAD
TRITTON ROAD
B1003
HYKEHAM ROAD
BRANT ROAD
LINCOLN RD.
1 JUNIPER CL
2 HONEYSUCKLE CLOSE
CLAYTON RD
URBAN ST
EWART ST
FRANCIS ST
ELLISON ST
VICTORIA TER
ALBANY TER.
MAPLE ST
ELDER ST
POPLAR ST
LAUREL CL.
HOLLY ST
MANSE AVE
CEDAR AV.
PARKER AV.
BROUGHTON GARDENS
LAKEVIEW RD
ST. PETERS AVENUE
HAINTON RD
KENILWORTH DRIVE
LANSDOWNE AVE
CONSTABLE AVE.
SHANNON AVE
KENNER CLO.
SANSFORD GREEN
DEWINT AVE
ROMNEY DR.
BOURNE CL.
CHANCERY LA.
GREGG HALL CRESCENT
TOYNTON CLO.
SOMERSBY CLO.
BRANSTON CLO.
RIVERMEAD
SOUTHLAND DRI.
WALLIS AVENUE
ST. MARGARET'S GDS.
BERKELEY AVE
BERKELEY DR
GRANGE CRESCENT
HARBY CLO.
GLENTHAM CLO.
INGHAM CLO.
SCARLE CLO.
MANOR LEAS CL.
EASTBROOK ROAD
BRAMLEY CT
BOSWELL DR.
FONTWELL CR.
SUDBURY CL.
BOWDEN DR.
GREENBANK DR.
SWALLOWBECK AVE
WAVERLEY CRESCENT
THE FORUM
MALTON WAY
ROWAN RD.
BAILDON CRESCENT
RIPLEY DR.
FILEY CL.
ROSEDALE CL.
HAREWOOD CRES.
BROADWAY
GROVE
MULBERRY AV.
HUTSON DR
WINDERMERE
CONISTON AVENUE
HIGHFIELD TER.
ESTWAITE CL.
DERWENT CL.
KINDER AVE
LADY BOWER CL.
LYNMOUTH CL.
TREVOSE DR.
PENDINE CRESCENT
ALDERNEY WY
HARTLAND AV
SKERRIES CL.
PHILIP CT.
WINDSOR PK CL
REGENTS PK CL
HYDE PARK CL.
BELTON PARK
MEADOW CL.
CALDER RD.
BANGOR CL.
CARRAL CL.
HORNER CL.
BRADBURY AV.
SIDLAW GR.
RENFREW RD.
PRIMROSE CL.
ORCHID RD.
BLUEBELL CL.
LAVENDER CL.
FOXGLOVE WY.
BIRKDALE
SOUTHDOWN
LARNE CL.
DALEWOOD
MOURN TER.
COLERAINE CL.
FOYLE CL.
NEWHAVEN DR.
HARWICH
CHILTERN
HELSBY RD.
WILLOUGHBY LANE
ASHBY CL.
THORESBY CL.
SHERWOOD DR
HOLLYWELL CL.
ROWAN RD.
MULBERRY CL.
ASH GR.
HAWTHORNE AV.
ALMOND CR.
ACACIA AV.
LIME CR.
CEDAR CL.
VALLEY RD.
WALNUT CT.
MAPLE CL.
GREENWOOD CL.
REDWOOD DR.
HOLLYWELL RD.
FIR TREE AV.
PINE CL.
CAIRNS WAY
DARWIN CL.
HOBART CL.
BRISBANE CL.
MELBOURNE WAY
ADELAIDE CL.

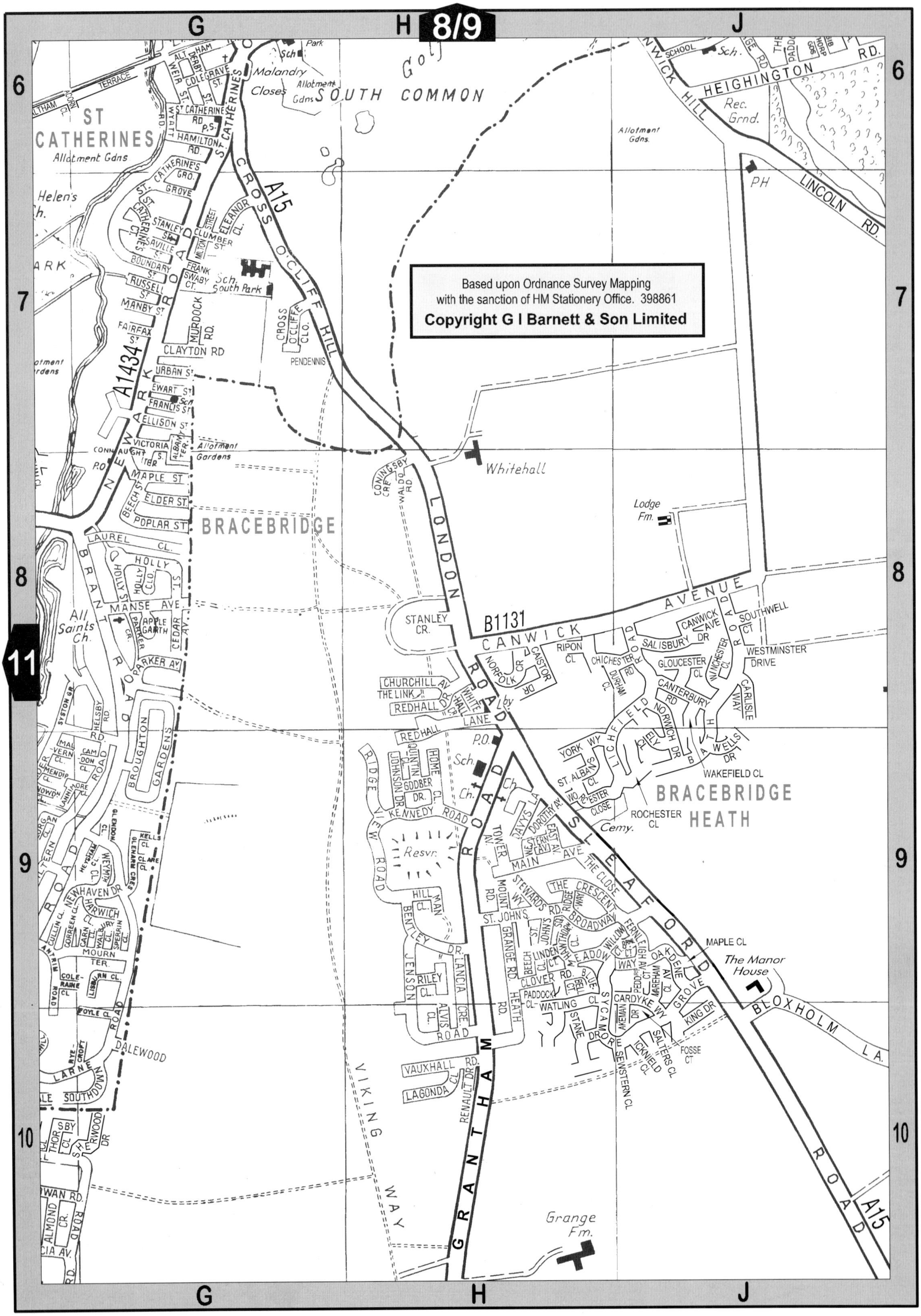
G
H
8/9
J
6
7
8
9
10
11
ST CATHERINES
Allotment Gdns
Helen's
SOUTH COMMON
Malandry Closes
Allotment Gdns
Park
Sch.
Golf
COLEGRAVE ST.
ST. CATHERINES RD
HAMILTON RD.
ST. CATHERINES
ST. CATHERINE'S GRO.
GROVE
STANLEY ST.
SAVILLE ST.
BOUNDARY ST.
RUSSELL ST.
MANBY ST.
FAIRFAX ST.
A1434
NEWARK ROAD
CLUMBER ST.
MILTON STREET
ELEANOR CL.
FRANK SWABY CT.
Sch. South Park
MURDOCK RD.
CLAYTON RD
URBAN ST.
EWART ST.
FRANCIS ST.
ELLISON ST.
VICTORIA TER.
ALBANY TER.
CONNAUGHT TER.
P.O.
MAPLE ST.
BEECH ST.
ELDER ST.
POPLAR ST.
Allotment Gardens
BRACEBRIDGE
CROSS O'CLIFF HILL
A15
CROSS O'CLIFF CLO.
PENDENNIS
Allotment Gdns.
HEIGHINGTON RD.
SCHOOL
Sch.
CANWICK HILL
Rec. Grnd.
PH
LINCOLN RD.
Whitehall
Lodge Fm.
CONINGSBY CRE.
WALDO RD
LONDON ROAD
LAUREL CL.
HOLLY ST.
HOLLY CLO.
MANSE AVE.
APPLE GARTH
PARKER AV.
CEDAR AV.
BRANT ROAD
All Saints Ch.
STANLEY CR.
B1131
CANWICK AVENUE
NORFOLK CR.
CAISTOR DR.
RIPON CL.
CHICHESTER RD.
DURHAM CL.
SALISBURY DR.
CANWICK AVE.
GLOUCESTER CL.
WINCHESTER CL.
SOUTHWELL CT.
WESTMINSTER DRIVE
CARLISLE WAY
CANTERBURY RD.
NORWICH DR.
LICHFIELD CL.
ELY CL.
BATH RD.
WELLS DR.
WAKEFIELD CL
YORK WY
ST. ALBANS CL
WORCESTER CLOSE
ROCHESTER CL
BRACEBRIDGE HEATH
Cemy.
CHURCHILL AV.
THE LINK
REDHALL DR.
WHITEHALL CR.
REDHALL LANE
P.O.
Sch.
Ch.
QUINTIN CL.
JOHNSON DR.
HOME CL.
GODBER DR.
KENNEDY ROAD
RIDGE VIEW ROAD
Resvr.
BROUGHTON GARDENS
SYSTON GR.
HELSBY RD.
ROAD
CAMDON CL.
NEWHAVEN DR.
HARWICH CL.
MOURN TER.
DALEWOOD
SOUTHDOWN
THORSBY CL.
SHERWOOD DR.
TOWER AV.
DAVYS LA.
DOROTHY AV.
WESTERN AV.
EAST AV.
MAIN AVE
THE CLOSE
STEWARDS WY
MOUNT RD.
THE CRESCENT
RIDGE WAY
BROADWAY
ST. JOHNS RD.
GRANGE RD.
HILLMAN CL.
BENTLEY DR.
JENSON
RILEY CL.
LANCIA CRE.
ALVIS CL.
ROAD
BEECH CL.
LINDEN CT.
MEADOW
CLOVER RD.
PADDOCK CL.
WATLING CL.
STANE DR.
SYCAMORE DR.
WILLOW CT.
FERN CT.
WAY
OAKDENE AV.
GROVE
MAPLE CL
The Manor House
BLOXHOLM LA.
KING DR
FOSSE CT
SALTERS CL
ICKNIELD CL
SEWSTERN CL
CARDYKE WY
HEATH RD.
VAUXHALL RD.
LAGONDA CL.
RENAULT DR.
GRANTHAM ROAD
VIKING WAY
SLEAFORD ROAD
ROAD
A15
Grange Fm.
ALMOND CR.
WAN RD.
CIA AV.

Abbey Place H.4
Abbot Street G.5
Aberporth Drive A.6
Abingdon Avenue B.7
Abingdon Close B.7
Acacia Avenue F.10
Acer Close C.6
Acer Court C.6
Acorn Close F.6
Adam Close C.7
Addison Drive J.2
Adelaide Close F.11
Aisne Close G.2
Albany Terrace G.7
Albany Street G.3
Albert Crescent G.3
Albion Close F.2
Alconbury Close B.6
Alder Close D.9
Aldergrove Close B.6
Aldergrove Crescent B.6
Aldermans Walk F.3
Aldernay Way E.10
Alexandra Avenue D.10
Alexandra Terrace G.3
Alford Mill Close C.11
Alfred Street G.5
Allandale Close G.1
Allandale View G.1
Allenby Road K.4
Allison Place G.3
Allison Street G.3
Almond Avenue E.6
Almond Court E.6
Almond Crescent F.10
Almond Crescent
Swan Pool
Garden Suburb E.6
Almond Grove (Inset) A.3
Alness Close B.6
Altham Terrace F.6
Altham Terrace G.6
Alvis Close H.10
Amble Close G.1
Ancaster Avenue J.3
Anchor Street G.5
Anderby Close D.7
Anderby Drive D.7
Anderson Lane H.2
Andover Close B.6
Anson Close (Inset) A.3
Antrim Road F.9
Anzio Close G.2
Anzio Crescent G.2
Anzio Terrace G.2
Anzio Walk G.2
Apley Close H.1
Apple Garth G.8
Arboretum Avenue J.4
Arboretum View J.4
Archer Street H.5
Arden Moor Way C.11
Arabis Close K.1
Arrras Close G.2
Arthur Street H.5
Arthur Taylor Street F.4
Ash Close C.6
Ash Grove F.10
Ash Grove
Hykeham Moor D.9
Ash Lin Grove G.3
Ashby Avenue D.7
Ashby Close F.10
Ashfield Street J.4
Ashtons Court G.5
Ashworth Close D.8
Aster Close K.1
Asterby Close H.1
Astral Way B.10
Astwick Road D.8
Atwater Close L.2
Atwater Court L.1
Atwater Grove L.2
Auborn Avenue H.2
Auden Close J.3
Auston Walk K.2
Avocet Close C.6
Avon Close E.9
Avondale B.10
Avondale Street J.4
Aynsley Close B.7
Aynsley Road B.7
Azalea Road K.1

Badgers Close (Inset) A.2
Baggeholme Road H.4
Baoldon Crescent E.9
Bailgate H.3
Bain Street G.1
Baker Crescent C.6
Baker Street G.4
Bakewell Mews D.10
Bamford Close C.10
Bangor Close F.9
Bank Street H.4
Bardney Close D.7
Bargate G.6
Barkston Gardens J.1
Barlings Close D.6
Barratts Close H.3
Bassingham Crescent H.2
Bath Road J.9
Bathurst Street K.4
Bawtry Close B.6
Baywood Close B.5
Beaufort Close L.1
Beaufort Road L.1
Beaumont Fee G.4
Beaver Close (Inset) A.3
Beckside Close D.10
Bedford Street G.3
Beech Close H.9
Beech Street G.8
Beechcroft Close A.11
Beevor Street G.5
Belgravia Close C.5
Bell Grove F.7
Bell Street G.6
Belle Vue Road G.3
Belle Vue Terrace G.3
Bellflower Close K.1
Belmont Street J.4
Belton Avenue D.7
Belton Park Close D.11
Belvedere House H.1
Belvoir Close F.10
Benington Close D.7
Benson Close B.7
Benson Crescent B.7
Bentinck Square J.4
Bentick Street J.4
Bentley Drive H.9
Berkeley Avenue E.9
Berkeley Drive E.9
Berilldon Drive F.2
Bernard Street J.4
Beswick Close C.6
Betula Grove C.6
Beverley Drive D.9
Beverley Grove D.9
Bilsby Close J.1
Binbrook Close B.6
Birch Close D.9
BIRCHWOOD C.6
Birchwood Avenue B.6
Birds Holt (Inset) A.4
Birds Holt Close A.4
Birkdale F.10
Bishop King Court H.5
Bishops Road K.3
Bittern Way C.6
Blackbourn Road F.7
Blackthorn Close K.1
Blackney Crescent H.1
Blenheim Close (Inset) A.3
Blenheim Road F.3
Bloxholm Lane J.10
Bluebell Close F.10
Bluebell Court H.9
Blyton Close B.7
Blyton Grove B.7
Blyton Road B.7
Bodmin Moor Close C.10
Bolton Avenue D.9
Boscombe Close B.7
Boswell Drive D.8
Boswell Grove D.8
Bottespurd Close C.6
BOULTHAM E.6
BOULTHAM MOOR E.7
Boultham Avenue G.5
Boultham Park Road F.6
Boundary Lane A.11
Boundary Street G.7
Bourne Close E.8
Bowden Drive E.8
BRACEBRIDGE F.7
BRACEBRIDGE HEATH J.9
Bramley Court D.8
Brancaster Drive F.6
Branston Close F.8
Brant Road G.8
Bradbury Avenue F.9
Brattleby Crescent H.1
Brayford Bridge G.4
Brayford Street G.4
Brayford Way G.4
Brayford Wharf East G.4
Brayford Wharf North G.4
Breedon Drive G.1
Briar Close A.11
Brigg Close B.7
Brigg Grove B.7
Brisbane Close F.11
Bristol Drive F.6
Broadgate H.4
Broadway H.2
Broadway Bracebridge
Heath H.9
Broadway Hykeham Moor D.9
Broadway Close H.2
Brookfield Close (Inset) A.3
Brook Street H.4
Brooklands Close B.6
Brooklands Way B.6
Broomhill B.6
Brough Close B.7
Broughton Gardens G.9
Browning Drive J.2
Broxholme Gardens H.1
Bruce Close H.2
Bruce Road H.2
Buchanan Street G.1
Buckfast Road H.2
Buckingham House H.1
Bucknall Avenue D.7
Burn Moor Close B.5
Bullingham Road K.2
Bunkers Hill K.2
Bure Close D.9
Burghley Close D.5
Burghley Park Close D.10
Burghley Road C.5
Burneside Close J.1
Burns Gardens K.2
Burton Bridge G.2
Burton Road G.1
Burwell Close J.1
Butchery Court H.4
Buttermere Close C.5
Buttery Close D.8
Byron Avenue J.2

Cabourne Avenue J.2
Cabourne Court J.2
Cadwell Close B.6
Caenby Street G.2
Cairns Way F.11
Caistor Close B.6
Casitor Drive H.8
Caistor Road B.6
Calder Road F.9
Cambrian Way C.11
Cambridge Avenue G.3
Camdon Close G.9
Campus Way G.4
Camwood Crescent B.5
Canberra Way (Inset) A.3
Cannon Street J.4
Canterbury Road J.8
CANWICK J.6
Canwick Avenue J.8
Canwick Hill J.6
Canwick Road H.5
Cardinal Close K.3
Carholme Road F.4
Carline Road G.3
Carlisle Close D.10
Carlisle Way J.8
Carlton Boulevard K.3
Carlton Grove H.1
Carlton Street G.3
Carlye Walk J.2
Carn Close G.9
Carr Street F.4
Carral Close F.9
Carram Way F.2
Carrington Drive D.6
Carrisbrooke Close G.2
Cassia Green B.6
Castle Hill H.3
Castle Lane G.3
Castle Street G.3
Cathedral Street H.4
Cedar Avenue G.8
Cedar Close F.10
Cecil Street H.3
Centurion Road G.5
Chalgrove Way C.5
Chancery Lane F.8
Chapel Lane H.3
Chapel Lane
North Hykeham D.10
Chaplin Street G.5
Charles Street H.5
Charles Street West G.4
Charlesworth Street G.4
Chatsworth Close K.1
Chatsworth Drive C.9
Chatterton Avenue G.1
Chaucer Drive J.2
Chedburgh Close B.7
Chedworth Close K.2
Chedworth Road K.1
Chelmer Close D.9
Chelmsford Street H.5
Chelsea Court C.4
Cherry Grove E.6
Cherry Tree Close D.10
Cheshire Road A.7
Chesney Road L.2
Chestnut Grove F.10
Chestnut Road D.9
Chestnut Street G.3
Cheviot Close C.11
Cheviot Street H.4
Chichester Road H.8
Chieftain Way F.5
Chiltern Road F.9
Chiltern Way C.11
Chippendale Close C.7
Chippendale Road C.7
Chivenor Close A.5
Christ's Hospital Terrace H.3
Church Drive F.5
Church Lane H.3
Church Road A.3
Churchill Avenue H.8
City Square H.4
Clare Close G.9
Claremont Street J.4
Clarence Street G.2
Clarendon Gardens G.1
Clarendon View G.1
Clarina Street J.4
Clarke Road
Hykeham Moor C.11
Clarke Road
Swallow Beck D.8
Clasket Gate H.4
Clayton Road G.7
Clematis Approach B.6
Cleveland Avenue C.11
Clive Avenue F.6
Clifton Grove H.5
Clifton Street H.5
Clover Road H.9
Clumber Street G.7
Coalport Close C.6
Coleby Street J.4
Colegrave Street G.6
Colenso Terrace G.3
Coleraine Close F.9
Coleridge Gardens J.2
Coleridge Green K.2
College Close H.2
Collingwood C.11
Coline Close D.9
Coningsby Crescent H.8
Coningsby Street H.4
Coniston Drive E.10
Connaught Terrace G.7
Constable Close E.7
Constance Avenue D.8
Conway Drive E.9
Coopers Holt Close A.4
Cornflower Way A.11
Cornhill H.4
Cornwallis Road L.4
Corporation Street H.4
Correen Close F.9
Cosford Close B.6
Cosgrove Close E.7
Cotman Road E.7
Cotswold Close C.11
Cottage Lane E.8
Cottage Paddock E.8
Cottesford Place H.3
Cottesmore Road B.7
Cottingham Drive J.2
Coult Avenue C.11
Coulson Road G.5
Cowper Drive K.2
Crane Grove F.6
Cranwell Street G.6
Craven Street G.6
Cresta Close B.10
Croft Street H.4
Crofton Close K.4
Crofton Drive K.4
Crofton Road K.4
Cromer Close E.10
Cromwell Street J.4
Cross O'Cliff Close G.7
Cross O'Cliff hill G.7
Cross lane D.11
Cross Street H.5
Cross Spencer Street G.6
Crowland Drive D.7
Croxton Drive D.7
Crusader Road F.5
Cullin Close F.9
Curle Avenue J.3
Cydonia Approach B.6

Dales Street J.5
Daleswood G.10
Danesgate H.4
Danes Terrace H.4
Dart Avenue E.9
Darwin Close F.11
Davy's Lane H.9
Deacon Road K.3
Dean Road K.3
Dellfield Avenue B.5
Dellfield Close B.5
Dellfield Court B.5
Delph Road D.11
Denby Dale Close B.5
Dene Close A.4
Dene Road A.4
Denzlingen Close B.10
Depot Street G.4
Derby Street G.6
Derwent Close E.10
Derwent Street F.4
Devon Street K.4
De Wint Avenue E.7
De Wint Close E.8
Digby Close B.6
Dixon Close F.5
Dixon Road F.5
Dixon Street G.5
Dixon Way G.5
Doddington Avenue E.8
DODDINGTON PARK A.7
Doddington Road A.7
Dore Avenue D.9
Dorothy Avenue H.9
Dorset Street K.4
Doulton Close C.6
Dove Dale D.10
Dowding Mews L.4
Dowding Road L.4
Drake Street F.3
Drury Lane H.3
Dryden Avenue J.2
Dunford Road H.5
Dunholme Court J.1
Dunkirk Road G.2
Dunlop Street H.5
Dunmore Close F.9
Dunston Close H.1
Durham Close B.5

Earls Drive F.6
Earlsfield Close A.8
East Avenue H.9
East Liberty K.3
Eastbright H.3
Eastbourne Street J.4
Eastbrook Road E.8
Eastcliffe Road J.4
Eastfield Street J.4
Eastgate H.3
Eastgate Close H.3
Eastleigh Close B.5
Ebony Grove B.5
Eddystone Road E.10
Edendale Gardens G.1
Edendale View G.1
Edgehill F.10
Edlington Close H.1
Edna Street H.5
Edward Street G.6
Egerton Road J.3
Egret Grove C.6
Elder Street G.8
Eleanor Close G.7
Elizabeth Avenue D.10
Elleshere Avenue K.4
Elliot Road H.5
Ellison Street G.7
Elm Close D.9
Elmwood Close B.5
Elsham Close C.6
Elsham Crescent C.6
Elvin Close H.2
Elvington Close A.7
Elvington Road A.7
Ely Close J.9
Ely Street G.3
Ennerdale Close B.5
Epsom Close A.6
Epsom Road A.7
Epworth View G.1
Ermine Close H.1
Ernest Terrace H.3
Escombe View G.1
Esk Close D.9
Estwaite Close E.10
Eton Close C.4
Euston Close C.4
Euston Close C.4
Ewart Street G.7
Exchange Close C.8
Exchange Road C.8
Exchequer Gate H.3
Exmoor Close C.10
Eyam Way D.10

Fairfax Street G.7
Fairfield Street J.4
Falcon View B.6
Faldingworth Close B.6
Falklands Close G.1
Far Wharf G.4
Farrier Road B.8
Farrington Close B.4
Farrington Crescent C.4
Fawsley Close L.2
Featherby Place G.6
Fen Lane D.10
Fenton Place J.45
Fernleigh Avenue J.9
Ferry Lane (Inset) A.3
Fir Tree Avenue F.11
Firtree Avenue
Birchwood B.5
Filey Close E.9
Finch Close C.6
Finningley Close C.6
Finningley Road C.7
Firth Road G.5
Fiskerton Drive H.1
Flaxengate H.4
Fleet Street F.3
Florence Street J.4
Folkingham Close C.6
Fontwell Crescent E.8
Foss Bank F.4
Foss Street G.4
Foss Way D.9
Fosse Court J.10
Fosse Drive D.9
Foster Street G.5
Foston Crescent D.6
Fox Covert A.10
Foxfield (Inset) A.3
Foxglove Way F.10
Foyle Close G.10
Francis Street H.3
Francis Street
St. Catherines G.7
Frank Street G.6
Frank Swaby Court G.7
Frank Wright Close K.2
Frederick Street J.4
Free School Lane H.4
Freeman Road C.9

Friars Lane H.4
Frome Close C.8
Fulmer Road,
Birchwood B.6
Fulmer Road,
Doddington Park C.7
Fulstow Road J.1
Furndown Court B.7

Gainsborough Gardens E.7
Gardenfield A.4
Garfield Close G.1
Garfield View F.1
Garmstone Street H.4
Garrick Close F.9
Gaunt Street G.5
Gayton Close J.1
Geneva Avenue J.2
George Street J.5
Geralds Close J.3
Gibbeson Street G.6
Gibralter Hill H.3
Gibson House J.10
Gleedale D.10
Glenarm Crescent G.9
Glenbank Close D.9
Glendon Close G.9
Glentham Close E.9
Glenwood Grove F.5
Gloucester Close J.8
Glynn Road G.1
Glynn View G.1
Godber Drive H.9
Goldcrest Close C.5
Goldfinch Close A.4
Goldsmith Walk K.1
Good Lane H.3
Gordan Road H.3
Gothic Close C.7
Goxhill Close C.7
Goxhill Grove B.7
Grace Avenue B.9
Grace Street H.5
Grafton Street J.4
Grainsby Close F.7
Grange Close J.6
Grange Crescent E.9
Grange Drive E.9
Grange Lane J.6
Grange Road H.9
Grantham Road H.11
Grantham Street H.4
Grasmere Way C.5
Grassmoor Close C.10
Gravely Close B.7
Gray Street G.3
Great Northern Terrace H.5
Grebe Close B.10
Green Lane G.4
Green Lane
Hykeham Moor D.10
Green Lane (Inset) B.3
Greenbank Drive E.8
Greenhome Close J.1
Greenock Way B.6
Greenwood Close F.11
Greestone Place H.3
Greetwell Close J.3
Greetwell Place J.3
Greetwell Road J.3
Gretwell Gate H.3
Gregg Hall Close E.8
Gregg Hall Crescent E.8
Gregg Hall Drive F.8
Gresham Street G.4
Gresley Drive G.5
Greyling Close G.1
Greyling View G.1
Grinter Close C.11
Grosvenor Avenue C.4
Guildhall Street H.4
Gunby Avenue D.7
Gynewell Grove K.2

Hackthorn Place H.1
Haddon Close C.5
Hadfield Road E.8
Hadleigh Drive D.8
Haffenden Road H.2
Hainton Road F.8
Hale Close L.1
Halifax Close (Inset) A.3
Hall Drive, Boultham F.6
Hall Drive, Canwick J.6
Hallam Grove F.6
Halton Close B.6
Harby Close E.9
Hardwick Place H.1
Hareshaw Close G.8
Harewood Crescent D.9
Harloxton Close B.7
Harloxton Drive B.7
Harmston Close J.1
Harpswell Road H.2
Harrier Court C.6
Harrington Avenue F.6
Harris Road F.7
Harrison Court C.6
Harrison Place G.3
Hartland Avenue E.10
Hartley Street K.4
HARTSHOLME E.7
Hartsholme Drive D.6
Harvey Street G.4
Harwich Close G.9
Hamilton Close A.4
Hamilton Road G.6
Hamilton Road C.9
Hampden Close (Inset) A.3
Hanover House H.1
Harewood House H.1
Hatcliffe Gardens H.1
Hathersage Avenue C.9
Halton Close E.6
Hawkshead Grove J.1
Hawks Moor Close C.10
Hawthorn Chase L.2
Hawthorn Close H.9
Hawthorn Road L.2
Hawthorne Avenue F.10
Haydor Avenue J.1
Haze Lane B.10
Hazelwood Avenue B.5
Heath Road H.9
Hebden Moor Way C.11
Heighington Road L.6
Helsby Road G.8
Hemswell Avenue B.5
Henley Street G.6
Henlow Close A.6
Henry Street H.5
Hereward Street H.3
Hermit Street H.5
Heron View C.6
Heron Walk B.10
Hewson Road F.3
Heysham Close G.9
Hibaldstow Close B.7
Hibaldstow Road B.6
Hickory Road B.5
Higgins Close C.7
High Bridge H.4
High Street H.4
High Street
St. Catherines G.6
High Street
Skellingthorpe (Inset) A.3
Highfield Avenue E.7
Highfield Terrace E.9
Higson Road G.2
Hilman Close H.9
Hillside Approach K.4
Hillside Avenue K.4
Hobart Close F.11
Hodson Close A.3
Holdenny Close L.1
Holdenny Road L.1
Holly Close G.8
Holly Street G.8
Hollywell Road F.10
Holms Road G.4
Holt Close D.11
Holyrood House H.1
Home Close H.9
Honington Crescent G.1
Honnington Approach G.1
Hood Street H.5
Hope Street H.5
Horner Close F.9
Horton Street J.4
Howard Street F.3
Hungate H.4
Hunt Lea Avenue F.6
Hurn Close B.6
Hurstwood Close K.1
Hutson Drive D.9
Hyde Park Close D.10
HYKEHAM MOOR C.10
Hykeham Road E.9

Icknield Close J.10
Ingham Close E.9
Ingleby Crescent H.1
Inns Close D.9

Jacobean Road C.7
Jaguar Drive B.10
James Street H.3
Jarvis Close D.6
Jasmin Road B.6
Jellicoe Avenue K.4
Jenson Road H.9
Jerusalem Road (Inset) A.4
Jesmond View G.1
John Street J.4
Johnson Drive H.9
Jubilee Close D.10

Keadby Close D.7
Keats Close K.1
Keddington Avenue H.1
Kells Close G.9
Kelstern Close B.7
Kelstern Road B.7
Kemble Close B.6
Kenneth Street H.2
Kenilworth Drive F.8
Kennedy Road H.9
Kenner Close E.7
Kent Street K.4
Kershaw View G.1
Kesteven Court C.10
Kesteven Street H.5
Kestral Close C.6
Kexby Mill Close C.11
Kilburn Crescent E.7
Kinder Avenue E.10
King Street G.5
Kingfisher Close C.6
Kingsdown Road B.7
Kingsley Road A.7
Kingsley Street G.3
Kingsway H.5
Kinloss Close B.7
Kipling Close J.2
Kirkby Street H.5
Kirmington Close b.7
Knight Place G.6
Knight Street G.6

Laburnham Close D.9
Laceby Street J.4
Ladds Mill Close C.11
Lady Bower E.10
Lagonda Close H.10
Lake View Close B.10
Lakeview Road F.7
Lamb Gardens J.2
Lancaster Place H.5
Lancaster Way (Inset) A.3
Lancewood Gardens C.5
Lancia Crescent H.9
Landmere Grove C.5
Laney Close K.2
Langdale Close J.1
Langley Road C.10
Langton Close J.1
Langor Close B.7
Langworthgate H.3
Lannimore Close F.9
Lansdowne Avenue F.8
Lapwing Close A.4
Larchwood Crescent B.6
Larkspur Road K.1
Larne Close F.10
Larne Road F.10
Latham Place G.3
Laughton Crescent J.10
Laughton Way J.1
Laughton Way North H.1
Laurel Close G.8
Lavender Close F.10
Lavenham Grove E.8
Lawn Court G.3
Lawrence Close E.7
Leconfield Close B.7
Leconfield Road B.7
Lee Road J.3
Leeming Close C.7
Legbourne Close G.1
Leighton Crescent E.7
Lenton Green J.1
Lewis Street H.5
Leyburn Road D.8
Lichfield Road H.9
Lievelsley Road G.2
Lilac Close B.6
Lilford Court L.1
Lilford Road L.2
Lillys Road H.3
Lime Crescent F.10
Lime Kiln Way K.3
Lime Tree Close C.6
Limelands J.3
Lincoln Avenue F.6
Lincoln Relief Road A.7
Lincoln Road, Canwick J.7
Lincoln Road,
Hykeham Moor D.10
Lincoln Road,
Skellingthorpe A.3
Lincoln Road
St. Giles K.1
Linden Court H.9
Lindholme Road B.7
Lindum Avenue H.4
Lindum Road H.4
Lindum Terrace H.4
Linton Street H.5
Little Bargate Street G.6
Lisburn Close G.9
Lissett Close A.7
Lissington Close H.1
Liverpool Close B.4
Locking Close B.7
London Road H.8
Long Dales Road H.2
Long Leys Road E.2
Longland Walk L.2
Longssdale Place H.5
Low Moor Road C.8
Lower Church
Road (Inset) A.3
Lucy Tower Street G.4
Ludford Drive E.7
Lumley Place H.5
Lupin Road K.1
Lurgan Close F.9
Luton Close B.5
Lydd Close B.7
Lyneham Close B.6
Lynmouth Close D.10
Lytton Street J.4
Macaulay Drive J.2
Macmillan Avenue B.10
Magpie Close A.4
Maidment Drive F.2
Main Avenue H.9
Mainwaring Road H.3
Malham Close B.5
Malham Drive B.5
Mallard Close C.5
Mallard Court B.10
Mallory Close B.6
Malton Road D.9
Malvern Close F.9
Malvern Close C.11
Manby Street G.7
Manor Close H.3
Manor Grounds (Inset) A.3
Manor Leas Close E.9
Manor Road H.3
Manor Road,
North Hykeham D.10
Manse Avenue G.8
Manton Road H.2
Maple Close J.9
Maple Close F.11
Maple Street G.8
Marham Close B.6
Marigold Close K.1
Marjorie Avenue G.6
Marlborough Close K.1
Marlowe Drive J.2
Marne Gardens G.2
Martin Close (Inset) A.4
Martin Street H.5
Massey Road J.3
Matilda Road F.5
Matlock Drive D.10
Maxwell Avenue F.6
May Crescent G.3
Mayfair Avenue F.6
McInnes Street K.4
Mead Close E.8
Meadow Close D.11
Meadow Lane D.11
Meadow Lane E.11
Meadow Way H.9
Meadowlake Close C.5
Meadowlake Crescent C.5
Medway Crescent E.10
Melbourne Close B.6
Melbourne Road B.6
Melbourne Way F.11
Melville Street H.4
Mendip Avenue C.11
Mendip Close F.9
Metheringham Close C.6
Meynell Avenue F.6
Michaelgate H.4
Middle Street D.10
Middlebrook Close E.7
Middlebrook Road D.8
Middletons Field H.3
Midville Close G.1
Mildenhall Drive A.6
Mildmay Street G.2
Mill Court G.3
Millbeck Court J.10
Mill Lane,
New Boultham G.5
Mill Lane,
North Hykeham C.11
Mill Moor Way C.10
Mill Road C.3
Mill Row G.2
Millbrook Close C.10
Millers Dale D.10
Milman Road J.4
Milton Street G.7
Minster Yard H.3
Minting Close G.1
Mint Lane H.4
Mint Street H.4
Mitchell Close (Inset) A.3
Monks Ley Terrace J.4
Monks Manor Drive J.3
Monks Road H.4
Monks Way K.4
Mons Road G.2
Monsal Dale D.10
Monson Court H.5
Monson Park (Inset) A.3
Monson Street G.5
Montage Road J.6
Montague Terrace H.4
Montaigne Close K.2
Montaigne Crescent K.2
Montaigne Garden K.1
Montrose Close C.10
Moor Lane C.10
Moorland Centre D.8
Moor Street C.6
Moorby Close H.1
Moorland Avenue E.7
Moorland Crescent E.7
Moorland Way D.8
Moorside Court C.10
Morton Drive D.7
Motherby Hill G.4
Motherby Lane H.4
Mount Road H.9
Mount Street G.2
Mourn Terrace G.9
Much Lane G.4
Mulberry Avenue D.10
Mulberry Close F.10
Murdock Road g.7

Naam Green G.3
Naam Place G.3
Napier Street J.4
Nash Lane C.10
Natal view G.1
Neale Court C.11
Neale Road C.11
Neile Close K.2
Nelson Street G.4
Nelthorpe Street H.5
Nene Park B.10
Nene Road G.1
Nettleham Close H.2
Nettleham Road H.3
Newark Road D.9
NEW BOULTHAM F.4
Newhaven Drive F.9
Newland G.4
Newland Street West G.4
Newport H.3
Newsums Villas F.3
Newton Street H.4
Nightingale Crescent C.6
Nocton Drive H.1
Norfolk Crescent H.8
Norfolk Street F.3
Norman Street H.4
Norris Street H.5
NORTH HYKEHAM D.11
North Parade G.4
North Way C.10
Northgate H.3
Northgate Close D.7
Nottingham Terrace H.4
Norwich Drive J.8
Nursery Fields F.10
Nursery Green J.2
Nurses Lane A.3

Oakdene Avenue J.9
Oakfield Street J.4
Oakleigh Drive F.2
Oakleigh Terrace F.2
Oakwood Avenue B.6
Occupation Road G.3
Old Chapel Road (Inset) A.3
Old Pond Close C.6
Old Wood B.5
Olive Street G.2
Orchard Street G.4
Orchid Road F.10
Osborne Close G.2
Oulton Close E.10
Outer Circle Drive J.1
Outer Circle Green K.2
Outer Circle Road K.2
Oval Approach J.2
Oxen Park Close H.1
Oxford Street H.4

Paddock Close
Bracebridge Heath H.9
Palmer Street H.5
Park Avenue D.6
Park Road F.6
Park Street G.4
Parker Avenue G.8
Parker Crescent G.8
Parksgate Avenue D.8
Pateley Moor Close C.11
Peak Dale C.9
Peartree Close B.5
Peddars Court J.9
Peel Street G.5
Pelham Bridge H.4
Pelham Lane J.6
Pelham Street H.5
Pendennis G.7
Pendine Crescent D.10
Pennell Street G.5
Pennycress Close K.1
Penrose Close C.11
Pentland Drive C.11
Peppercorn Close G.5
Percy Street J.4
Perney Crescent C.11
Pershore Way B.7
Petersfield Close A.6
Philip Court D.10
Pietermartiz Street G.1
Pietermartiz View G.1
Pine Close F.11
Pine Close, Ermine H.1
Pioneer Way C.8
Plover Grove C.6
Poachers Brook (Inset) A.3
Poplar Street G.8
Portland Street G.5
Pottergate H.3
Prenton Close E.8
Preswick Close B.5
Prial Avenue E.7
Prial Close F.7
Primrose Close F.10

Princess Royal Close H.3
Princess Street G.5
Prior Street G.5
Priorygate H.3
Proctors Road K.3
Pullan Close F.9
Pyke Road C.8

Quayside G.5
Queen Elizabeth Road G.1
Queen Mary Road G.1
Queen Street G.5
Queens Crescent G.3
Queensway J.3
Queensway (Inset) A.4
Quintin Close H.9
Quorn Drive F.6

Railway Park Close F.5
Rasen Lane G.3
Rauceby Terrace G.4
Ravendale Drive H.2
Ravensmoor Close C.10
Redbourne Drive J.1
Redcar Close D.8
Redcote Close D.8
Redcote Drive D.8
Redhall Drive H.8
Redhall Lane H.9
Redwing Close (Inset) A.4
Redwing Grove C.6
Redwood Drive F.11
Regent Avenue B.5
Regents Park Close D.10
Remigius Grove K.2
Renault Drive H.10
Renfrew Road F.9
Reservoir Street G.3
Retief Close G.1
Retief View G.1
Revesby Close D.7
Reynolds Drive E.7
Richards Avenue D.8
Richmond Drive D.9
Richmond Grove G.3
Richmond Road G.3
Ridge View G.1
Ridge View Road H.9
Ridgeway H.9
Ridgewell Close B.6
Rigsmoor Close C.11
Riley Close H.9
Ringwood Close B.5
Ripely Drive E.9
Ripon Close H.8
Ripon Street H.5
Riseholme Road H.1
Risby Green D.7
Rivermead F.8
Rivermead Close F.8
Riverton Close G.1
Riverton View G.1
Robertson Road C.10
Robert Tressell Walk K.2
Robey Street G.6
Rochester Drive C.4
Rolleston Close H.2
Roman Pavement K.3
Roman Wharf F.4
Romney Close E.7
Romney Drive E.8
Rookery Lane F.7
Rope Walk G.5
Rosebery Avenue F.3
Rosedale Close D.9
Rosemary Lane H.4
Roseum Close C.8
Rosewood Close B.5
Rothwell Road H.2
Roughton Court J.1
Rowan Road F.10
Rowan Road
Hykeham Moor D.9
Roxborough Close C.5
Roxby Close D.7
Roydon Grove F.7
Ruckland Avenue G.1
Rudgard Lane G.4
Rufford Green F.6
Runcorn Road A.8
Runswick Close E.9
Ruskin Avenue J.2
Ruskin Green J.2
Rusland Close J.1
Russell Avenue C.11
Russell Street G.7
Rydal Close B.5
Ryecroft F.10

St. Adian's Road C.9
St. Albans Close H.9
St. Andrew's Close H.5
St. Andrew's Drive F.6
St. Andrews Gardens F.6
St. Andrew's Place H.5
St. Andrews Street H.5
St. Anne's Close J.3
St. Anne's Bedehouses J.3
St. Anne's Road J.3
St. Benedicts Close C.9
St. Benedicts Square H.4
St. Botolphs Court G.6
St. Botolph's Crescent G.6
ST. CATHERINES G.6
St. Catherine's G.6
St. Catherine's Court G.7
St. Catherine's Grove G.7
St. Catherine's Road G.6
St. Claires Court B.6
St. Clements Road C.9
St. Crispin's Close C.9
St. David's Road C.9
St. Faith's Court G.4
St. Faith's Street G.4
St. Francis's Court C.9
ST. GILES J.2
St. George's Close C.9
St. Giles Avenue H.3
St. Helen's Avenue E.6
St. Hilary's Close C.9
St. Hugh's Drive C.9
St. Hughs Street H.4
St. John's Avenue C.9
St. Johns Road H.2
St. John's Road
Bracebridge Heath H.9
St. John's Square H.9
St. Leonard's Lane H.3
St. Margaret's Close E.8
St. Margaret's Gardens E.8
St. Marks Close C.9
St. Marks Square G.5
St. Marks Street G.5
St. Martins Street H.4
St. Martins Lane H.4
St. Mary Street H.4
St. Mary's Road C.9
St. Matthews Close F.5
St. Michaels Terrace H.4
St. Nicholas Street H.3
St. Paul's Lane H.3
St. Peters Avenue
Boultham F.7
St. Peter's Avenue
Hykeham Moor C.9
St. Rumbold Street H.4
St. Stephen's Court C.10
St. Swithins Square H.4
Sadler Road A.7
Salisbury Drive J.8
Salix Approach B.5
Saltergate H.4
Salters Close J.10
Salters Close J.10
Salthouse Lane G.5
Sanders Close G.1
Sanders View G.1
Sandtoft Close B.7
Sandwell Drive B.5
Sansford Green E.7
Satinwood Close B.5
Sausthorpe Street H.5
Saville Street G.7
Saxilby Road A.2
Saxon Street H.3
Scampton Avenue D.7
Scarle Close E.9
Scawby Crescent D.6
Scopwick Place H.1
Scopwick Place H.1
Scorer Street G.5
Scotton Drive D.7
Scott Gardens K.2
School Lane, Canwick J.6
School Lane,
North Hykeham D.10
Searby Road J.1
Sedgebrook Close H.1
Sedgemoor Close C.10
Selby Close E.9
Severn Street F.4
Sewell Road J.3
Sewell's Walk G.5
Sewstern Close J.10
Shaftesbury Avenue C.5
Shakespeare Street G.6
Shannon Avenue E.8
Shannon Close E.7
Shawbury Close B.7
Shearwater Close C.5
Shearwater Road C.6
Shelley Drive J.2
Sheraton Close C.7
Sherbrooke Street K.4
Sheridon Close K.2
Sherwood Drive F.10
Short Lane G.4
Shuttleworth Close C.11
Sibthorp Gardens J.6
Sibthorp Street G.5
Sidlaw Grove F.9
Sidney Street G.6
Silver Street H.4
Simons Green F.7
Simon's Way K.4
Sincil Bank H.5
Sincil Street H.4
SKELLINGTHORPE A.3
Skellingthorpe Road D.6
Skellingthorpe Road B.4
Skerries Close D.10
Sleaford Road H.9
Smith Street G.5
Snaith Close B.7
Snetterton Close B.6
Snowberry Gardens B.6
Snowden Close F.9
Sobraon Barracks G.2
Somersby Close F.8
Somerset House H.1
Sorrel Court B.6
South Parade G.4
South Park H.6
South Park Avenue H.6
Southdown F.10
Southland Drive E.8
Southwell Court J.8
Spa Buildings H.4
Spa Street J.4
Spa Road J.4
Spanby Drive E.6
Sparrow Lane H.4
Spencer Street G.6
Spennymoor Close B.1
Sperrin Close G.9
Spilsby Close C.6
Spirea Approach B.6
Spital Street H.2
Spring Hill H.4
Staffordshire Crescent C.7
Stainton Gardens G.1
Stamp End J.4
Stanley Crescent H.8
Stanley Place H.5
Stanley Street G.7
Stapleford Avenue H.1
Station Field A.4
Station Road C.10
Station Road F.11
Station Road G.5
Staunton Street G.4
Staverton Crescent A.6
Steep Hill H.3
Steeping Court G.1
Stenigot Close B.7
Stenigot Grove B.7
Stephenson Road C.8
Stewards Way H.9
Stirling Way (Inset) A.3
Stonebow H.4
Stonefield Avenue H.3
Stone Moor Road C.11
Stones Place C.5
Stoney Yard A.3
Strahane Close F.9
Strait H.4
Strubby Close C.6
Sturgate Close B.7
Sturton Close H.1
Sudbrooke Drive H.1
Sudbury Close E.8
Sunbeam Avenue B.10
Sunderland Close (Inset) A.3
Sunfield Crescent C.5
Sunningdale Drive F.6
Swaby Close H.1
Swalow Avenue A.4
SWALLOW-BECK E.8
Swallowbeck Avenue D.8
Swan Street H.4
Swanholme Close C.8
SWANPOOL
GARDEN SUBURB E.6
Swayne Close L.1
Swaythling Close C.8
Swift Gardens J.2
Swift Green J.2
Sycamore Close C.6
Sycamore Crescent C.6
Sycamore Drive F.11
Sycamore Grove H.9
Syd Wilson Court G.2
Sympson Close L.2
Syringa Green B.5
Syston Grove F.8
Sywell Close B.7

Tamar Way E.9
Tanners Lane G.5
Tealby Street G.6
Teesdale Close B.5
Tempest Street J.4
Temple Gardens H.4
Temple Street H.4
Tennyson Street G.3
Tentercroft Street H.5
Tetney Close H.1
The Avenue G.4
The Birches A.11
The Close H.9
The Crescent H.9
The Dene A.4
The Drove A.11
The Forum D.9
The Grove H.3
The Hill (Inset) A.3
The Link H.8
The Mead E.8
The Oval J.2
The Paddock (Inset) A.3
The Paddock J.6
The Park G.4
Theodore Street G.3
Thesigner Street H.5
Thirlemere Close E.10
Thirlmere Way B.5
Thirsk Drive D.8
Thistle Close K.1
Thomas Street J.4
Thonock Close H.2
Thoresway Drive H.1
Thorn Bridge H.4
Thorngate H.4
Thornton Close D.6
Thorpe Avenue G.1
Thorsby Close F.10
Thurlby Crescent J.1
Thurlow Court L.1
Tobruck Close G.1
Toronto Street K.4
Torrington Road H.1
Tothill close D.6
Tower Avenue K.4
Tower Avenue,
Bracebridge Heath H.9
Tower Crescent K.4
Tower Drive K.4
Tower Gardens K.3
Toynton Close F.8
Trelawney Crescent G.1
Trevose Drive D.10
Tritton Road D.8
Trollope Street H.5
Troutbeck Close J.1
Truro Drive A.6
Tudor House J.10
Tudor Road C.7
Turnbury Close B.6
Turner Avenue E.7
Turner Street G.3
Tyne Close E.9

Uffington Avenue D.7
Uffington Close E.6
Uldale Close B.5
Ullswater Close E.9
Union Road G.3
Unity Square H.4
Upper Avenue G.4
Upper Lindum Street H.3
Upper Long Leys Road G.3
Upper Saxon Street G.3
Urban Street G.7
Usher Avenue E.7
Usher Green E.7

Valentine Road F.5
Valley Road F.10
Vauxhall Road H.10
Verdon Close G.1
Vere Street H.2
Vernon Street G.5
Vicarage Drive B.4
Vicars Court H.3
Victor Drive B.10
Victoria Passage G.3
Victoria Street G.4
Victoria Street,
Bracebridge G.7
Victoria Terrace G.4
Vine Street H.4
Vulcan Crescent B.10

Waddingworth Grove H.1
Wainer Close B.7
Wain Well Mews H.3
Wake Street G.3
Wakefield Close J.8
Walbury Close G.9
Walcot Close D.7
Waldeck Street G.3
Waldo Road H.8
Walford Drive E.7
Wallis Avenue E.8
Walmer Street J.4
Walnut Court F.11
Walnut Place H.5
Waltham Close B.7
Waltham Road B.7
Wasdale Close B.5
Washdike Lane E.11
Washingborough Road J.6
Wash Lane,
New Boultham G.4
Water Lane,
North Hykeham D.10
Waterloo Lane A.4
Waterloo Street G.5
Waterside North H.4
Waterside South H.4
Watling Close H.10
Wavell Drive L.4
Wavell Road L.4
Waverley Avenue D.9
Weaver Road A.8
Webb Street G.6
Webstar Close E.8
Wedgewood Close C.6
Wedgewood Grove C.6
Wedgewood Road C.6
Weir Street G.6
Wellbeck Street J.4
Welbourne Gardens H.1
Well Lane H.4
Welland Road G.1
Wellingore Road H.1
Wellington Close (Inset) A.3
Wellington Street G.4
Wells Drive J.9
Welton Gardens H.1
West Bourne Grove C.4
West Parade G.3
Westbight H.3
Westbrooke Close F.6
Westbrooke Road F.6
Westcliff Street G.2
Western Avenue,
Boultham F.6
Western Avenue,
Bracebridge heath H.9
Western Crescent F.6
Western Lane (Inset) A.3
Westfield Street G.4
Westgate H.3
Westholm Close K.1
Westminster Drive J.8
Westminster House H.1
Westminster Road C.8
Westwick Drive E.7
Westwick Gardens F.7
Westwood Close E.6
Westwood Drive E.6
Wetherby Crescent D.8
Weymouth Close G.9
Wharfedale Drive D.9
Wheatfield Road B.5
Whisby Road A.8
Whisby Way B.8
Whitehall Crescent H.8
Whitehall Grove G.4
Whitethorn Grove B.5
Whitley Close (Inset) A.3
Wickenby Close E.9
Wickenby Crescent H.1
Wigford G.4
Wigford Way G.4
Wigsley Close B.7
Wigsley Road C.7
Williamson Street H.3
Willingham Avenue H.1
Willis Close G.3
Willow Close (Inset) A.4
Willow Close A.4
Willow Court H.9
Willow Road D.9
Willoughby Lane F.10
Willowtree Close B.6
Wilson Street G.3
Winchester Close J.8
Windermere Avenue E.10
Windermere Road K.1
Windmill View G.3
Windsor Park Close D.10
Wingrave Street G.2
Winn Street J.4
Winniffe Gardens K.2
Winnowsty Lane H.3
Winster Close H.1
Winthorpe Close B.7
Winthorpe Grove C.7
Winthorpe Road B.7
Wiseholme Road A.4
Witchford Close B.7
Witchford Road B.7
Wittering Close C.7
Woburn Avenue G.2
Wolsey Way K.1
Wood Bank (Inset) A.3
Wood Lane A.11
Wood Vale Close B.7
Woodburn Close H.1
Woodburn View H.1
Woodfield Avenue A.6
Woodfield Court B.5
Woodhall Drive H.1
Woodland Avenue A.4
Woodland View J.4
Woodpecker Close A.4
Woodrush Road K.1
Woodstock Road F.3
Woodvale Avenue B.7
Worcester Close C.6
Worcester Close
(BRACEBRIDGE HEATH) H.9
Wordsworth Street H.3
Wragby Road H.3
Wrights Way K.3
Wroxham Close E.10
Wyatt House J.2
Wyatt Road G.6
Wytton Close A.7
Wyville Walk D.6

Yarborough Crescent G.2
Yarborough Road G.3
Yarborough Terrace G.3
York Avenue G.3
York Way H.9

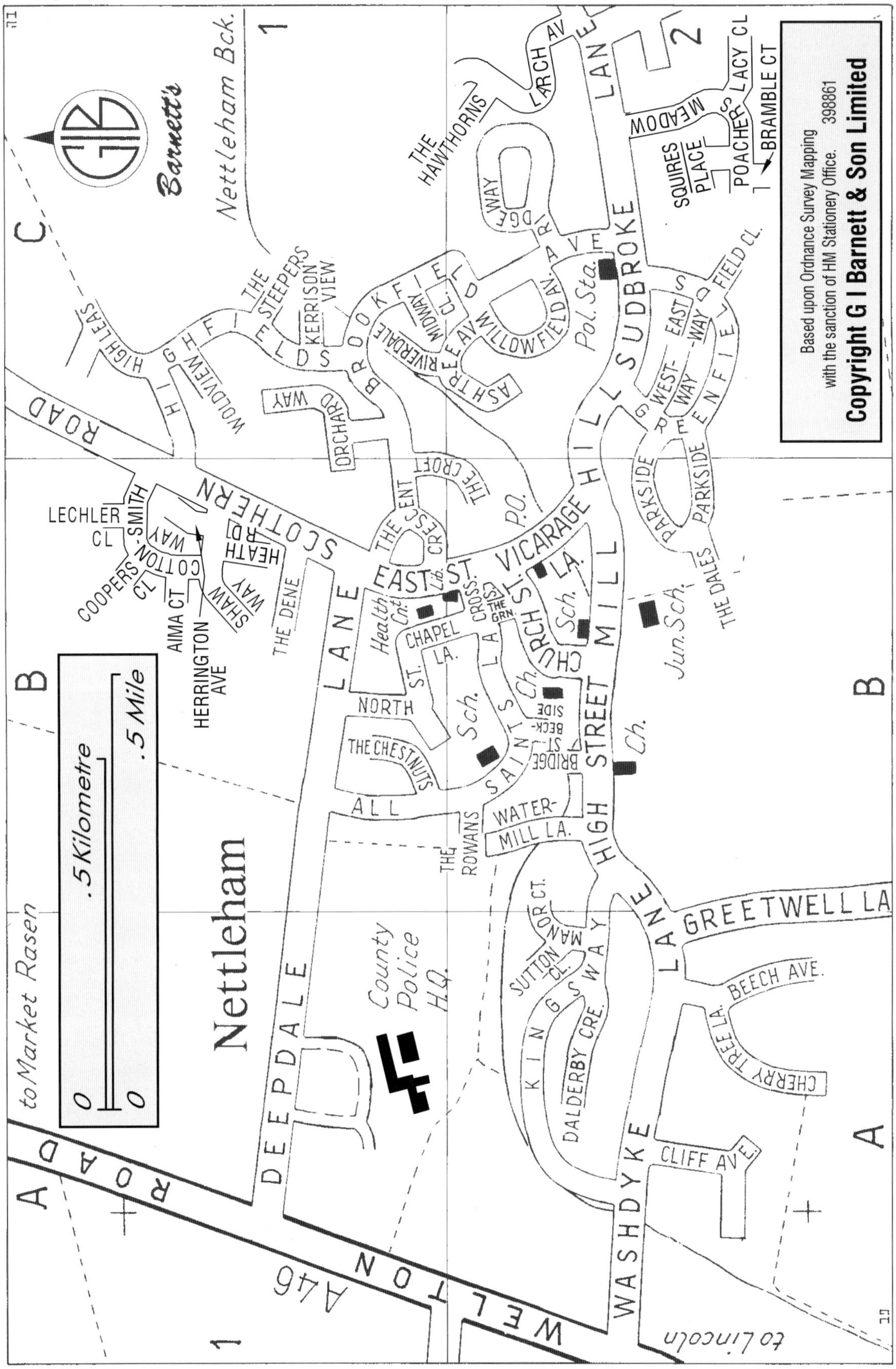

NETTLEHAM INDEX TO STREETS

Aima Court B.1
All Saints Lane B.1
Ash Tree Avenue C.2

Beech Avenue A.2
Bridge Street B.2
Beckside B.2
Brookfield Avenue C.1

Cotton-Smith Way B.1
Chapel Lane B.1
Cherry Tree Lane A.2
Church Street B.2
Cliff Avenue A.2
Coopers Close B.1

Cross Street B.2
Dalderby Crescent A.2
Deepdale Lane A.1

East Street B.1
East Way C.2

Field Close C.2

Greenfields C.2
Greenwell Lane A.2

Heath Road B.1
Hetherington Avenue B.1
High Leas C.1

High Street B.2
Highfields C.1
Kerrison View C.1
Kingsway A.2

Larch Avenue C.2
Lecher Close B.1

Manor Court A.2
Midway Close C.1
Mill Hill B.2

North Street B.1

Orchard Way C.1

Parkside B.2
Poachers Meadow C.2

Ridgeway C.2
Riverdale C.1

Scothern Road B.1
Shaw Way B.1
Squires Place C.2
Sudbroke Lane C.2
Sutton Close A.2

The Chestnuts B.1
The Crescent B.1
The Croft B.2

The Dales B.2
The Dene B.1
The Hawthorns C.2
The Rowans B.2
The Steepers C.1

Vicarage Lane B.2

Washdyke Lane A.2
Watermill Lane A.2
Welton Road B.2
West Way A.2
Willowfield Avenue C.2
Woldview C.1

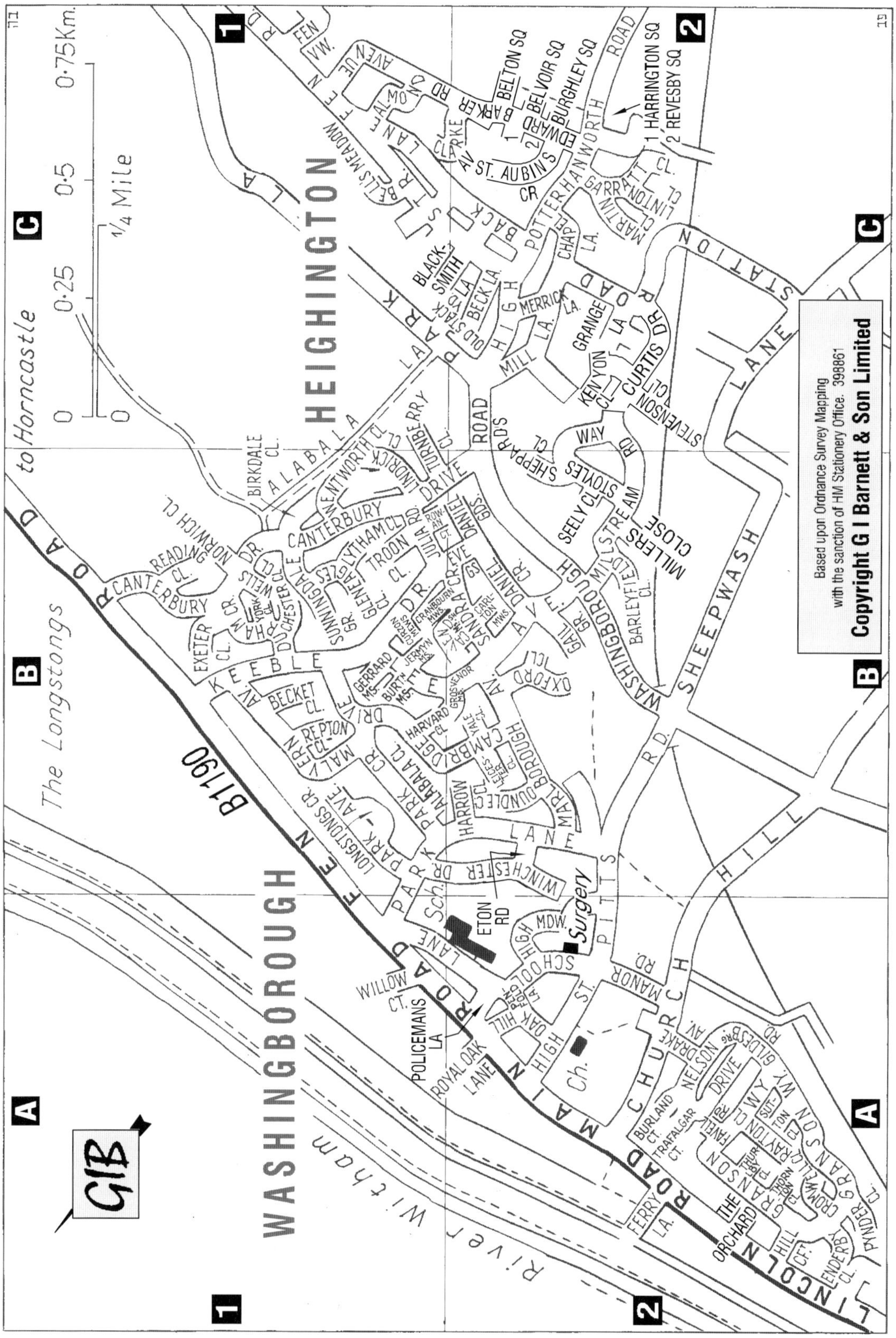

WASHINGBOROUGH INDEX TO STREETS

Alabala Close B.1
Alabala Lane B.1
Almond Avenue C.1

Back Lane C.2
Barleyfield Close B.2
Beck Lane C.2
Becket Close B.1
Bell's Meadow C.1
Belton Square C.2
Belvoir Square C.2
Birkdale Close B.1
Blacksmith Lane C.1
Burghley Square C.2
Buryland Court A.2
Burton Mews B.1

Cambridge Drive B.2
Canterbury Drive B.1
Carlton Mews B.2
Cavendish Mews B.2
Chapel Lane C.2
Chester Close B.1
Church Hill A.2
Clarke Avenue C.2
Cranbourn Mews B.1
Cromwell Close A.2
Curtis Drive C.2
Curzon Mews B.1

Daniel Crescent B.2
Daniel Gardens B.2
Drake Avenue A.2
Durham Crescent B.1

Edward Barker Road C.2
Enderby Close C.2
Eton Road B.2
Eve Gardens B.2
Exeter Close B.1

Favell Road A.2
Fen Road, Heighington C.1
Fen Road, Washingborough B.1
Fen View C.1
Ferry Lane A.2
Gail Grove B.2
Garratt Close C.2
Gerrard Mews B.1
Gildesbridge Road A.2
Gleneagles Close B.1
Grange Lane (Private Road) C.2
Granson Way A.2
Grosvenor Mews B.2

Harrington Square C.2
Harrow Close B.2
Harvard Close B.1
HEIGHINGTON C.1
High Meadow A.2
High Street, Heighington C.2
High Street, Washingborough ..A.2
Hill Croft A.2

Jermyn Mews B.1
Julia Road B.1

Keeble Drive B.1
Kenyon Close C.2
Lee Avenue B.1
Leicester Close B.2
Lincoln Road A.2
Lindrick Close B.1
Linton Close C.2
Longstongs Crescent B.1
Lytham Close B.1

Main Road A.2
Malvern Avenue B.1
Manor Road A.2
Marlborough Avenue B.2
Martin Close C.2
Merrick Lane C.2
Mill Lane C.2
Millers Close B.2
Millstream Road B.2

Nelson Drive A.2
Norwich Close B.1

Oak Hill A.2
Old Stack Yard C.2
Oundle Close B.2
Oxford Close B.2

Park Avenue B.1
Park Crescent B.1
Park Lane, Heighington C.1
Park Lane, Washingborough B.1
Penfold Lane A.2
Pitts Road A.2
Policemans Lane A.2
Potterhanworth Road C.2
Pynder Close A.2

Rayton Close A.2
Reading Close B.1
Repton Close B.1
Revesby Square C.2
Rowan Court B.1
Royal Oak Lane A.2

St. Aubins Crescent C.2
Sandra Crescent B.2
School Lane A.2
Seely Close B.2
Sheepwash Lane B.2
Sheppard's Close B.2
Station Road C.2
Stevenson Close C.2
Stoyles Way B.2
Sunningdale Grove B.1
Sutton Close A.2

The Orchard A.2
Thornton Close A.2
Thurlby Close A.2
Trafalgar Court A.2
Troon Close B.1
Turnberry Close B.1

Washingborough Road B.2
Wells Close B.1
Wentworth Close B.1
Willow Court A.1
Winchester Drive B.2

Yale Close B.2
York Close B.1

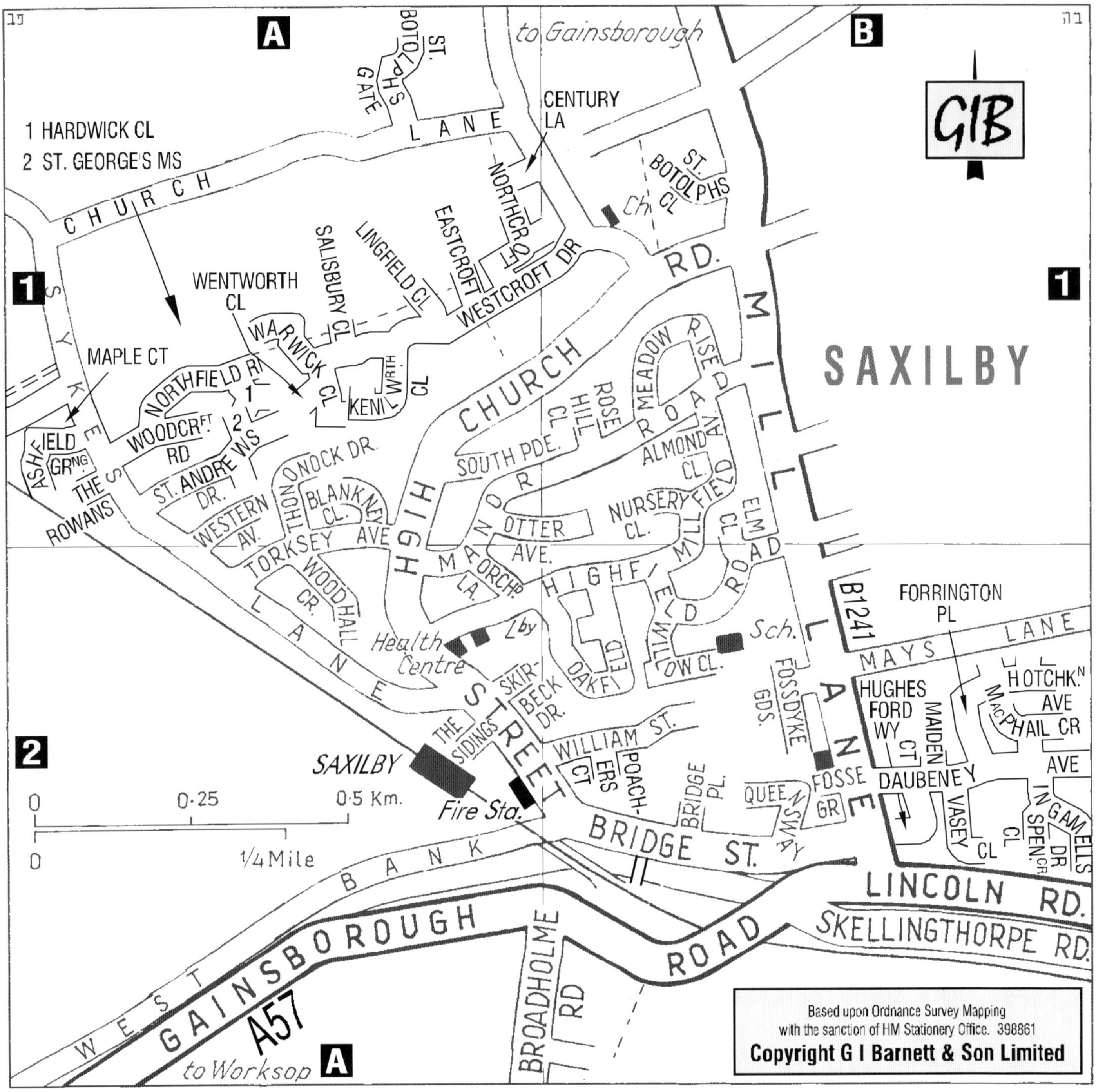

SAXILBY INDEX TO STREETS

Almond Close B.1
Ashfield Grange A.1

Bridge Place B.2
Blankney Close A.1
Bridge Street B.2
Broadholme Road A.2

Century Lane A.1
Church Lane A.1
Church Road A.1

Daubeney Avenue B.2

Eastcroft A.1
Elm Close B.1

Forrington Place B.2
Fossdyke Gardens B.2
Fosse Green B.2

Gainsborough Road A.2

Hardwick Close A.1
High Street A.1
Highfield Road B.2
Hotchkin Avenue B.2
Hughes Ford Way B.2

Ingamells Drive B.2

Kenilworth Close A.1

Lincoln Road B.2
Lingfield Close A.1

Macpahail Crescent B.2
Maiden Court A.1
Manor Road A.2
Maple Court A.1
Mays Lane B.2
Meadow Rise B.1
Mill Lane B.1
Millfield Avenue B.1

Northcroft A.1
Northfield Rise A.1
Nursery Close B.1

Oakfield B.2
Orchard Lane A.2
Otter Avenue A.1

Poachers Court B.2

Queensway B.2

Rose Hill Close B.1

St. Andrews Drive A.1
St. Botolphs Close B.1
St. Botolphs Gate A.1
St. George's Mews A.1
Salisbury Close A.1
Skelling Thorpe Road B.2
Skirbeck Drive A.2
South Parade A.2
South Parade A.1
Spencer Close B.2
Sykes Lane A.1

The Rowans A.1
The Sidings A.2
Thononock Drive A.1
Torksey Avenue A.2

Vasey Close B.2

Warwick Close A.1
Wentworth Close A.1
West Bank A.2
Westcroft Drive A.1
Western Avenue A.1
William Street B.2
Willow Close B.2
Woodcroft Road A.1
Woodhall Crescent A.2

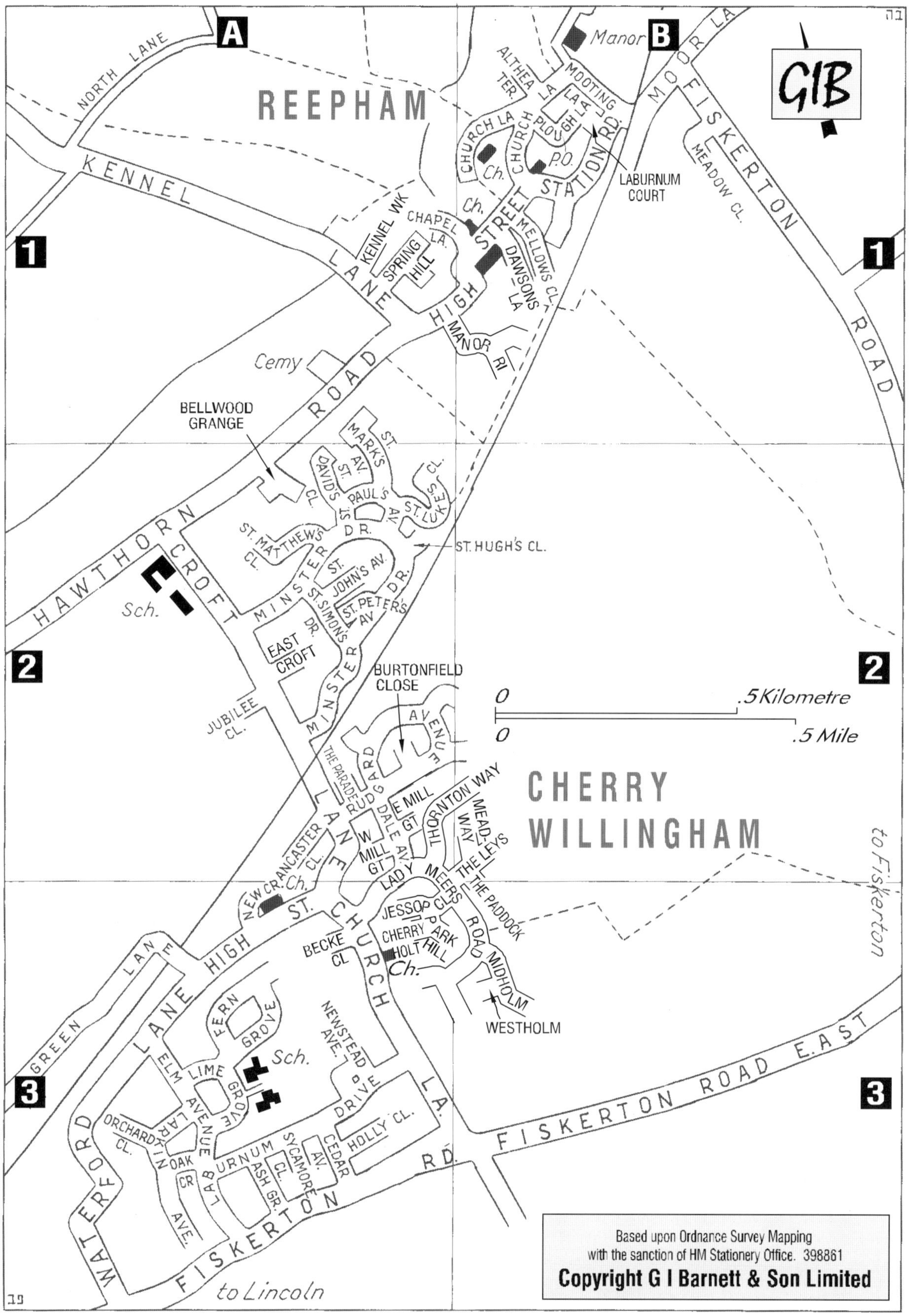

CHERRY WILLINGHAM INDEX TO STREETS

Althea Terrace B.1
Ancaster Close A.2
Ash Grove A.3

Becke Close A.3
Bellwood Grange A.2
Burtonfield Close A.2

Chapel Lane A.1
Cherry Holt A.3
Cedar Avenue A.3
Church Lane,
 Cherry Willingham A.3
Church Lane, Reepham B.1
Croft Lane A.2

Dale Avenue A.2
Dawsons Lane B.1

East Croft A.2
East Mill Gate A.2
Elm Avenue A.3

Fern Grove A.3
Fiskerton Road,
 Cherry Willingham B.3
Fiskerton Road, Reepham B.1

Green Lane A.3

Holly Close A.3
Hawthorn Road A.2
High Street,
 Cherry Willingham A.3
High Street, Reepham A.1

Jessop Close A.3

Jubilee Close A.2

Kennel Lane A.1
Kennel Walk A.1

Laburnum Court B.1
Laburnum Drive A.3
Lady Meers Road A.3
Larkin Avenue A.3
Lime Grove A.3

Manor Rise B.1
Meadow Close B.1
Meadway B.2
Mellows Close B.1
Midholm B.3
Minster Drive A.2
Moor Lane B.1

Mooting Lane B.1

New Cross A.2
Newstead Avenue B.1

Oak Crescent A.3
Orchard Close A.3

Park Hill A.3
Plough Lane B.1

REEPHAM A.1
Rudgard Avenue A.2

St. David's Close A.2
St. Hugh's Close B.2
St. John's Avenue A.2
St. Luke's Close A.2

St. Mark's Avenue A.1
St. Matthew's Close A.2
St. Paul's Avenue A.2
St. Peter's Avenue A.2
St. Simon's Drive A.2
Spring Hill A.1
Station Road B.1
Sycamore Close A.3

The Leys B.2
The Paddock B.3
The Parade A.2
Thornton Way A.2

Waterford Lane A.3
West Mill Gate B.3
Westholm B.3

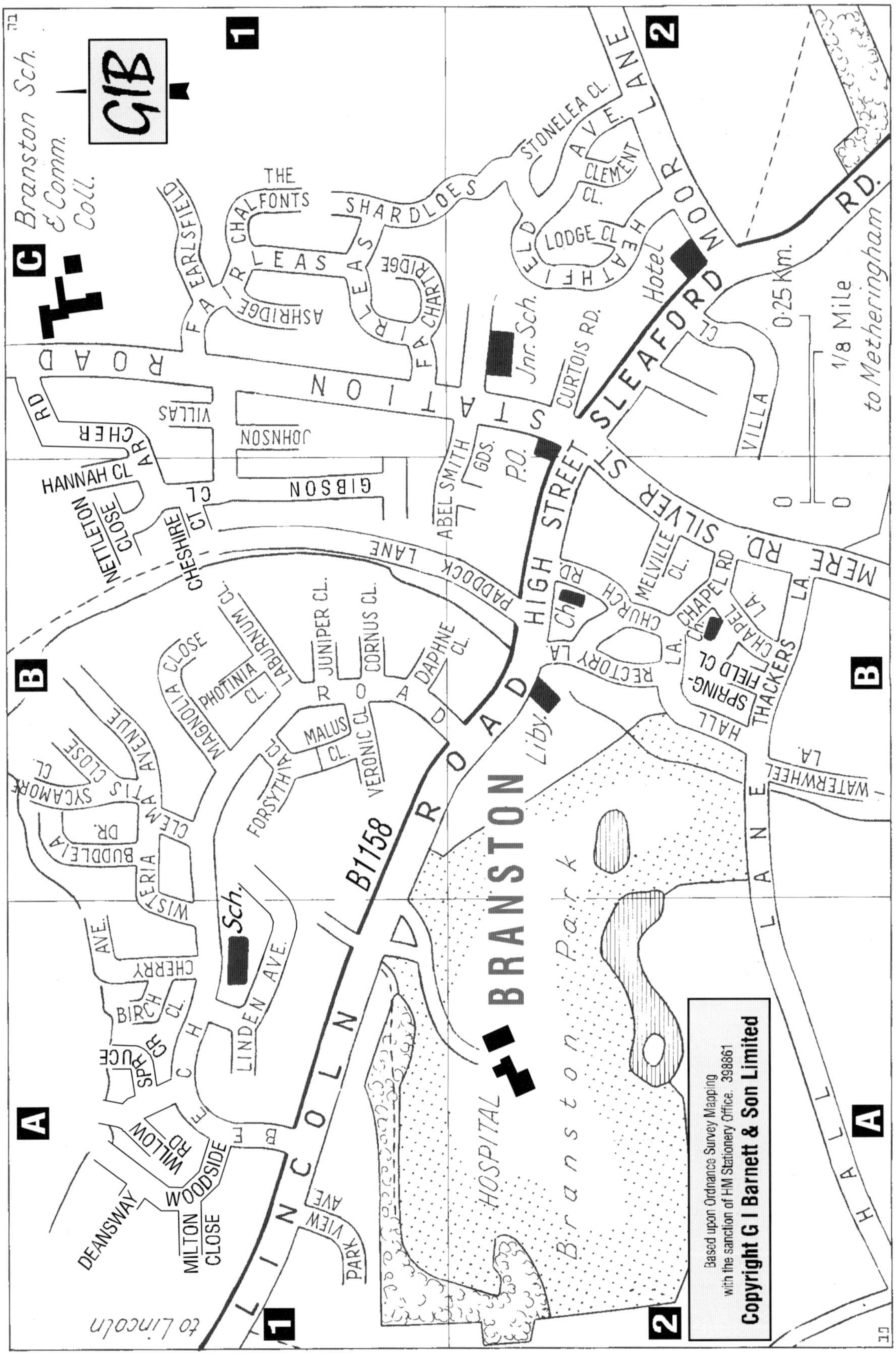

BRANSTON INDEX TO STREETS

Abel Smith Gardens B.1
Archer Road B.1
Ashridge C.1

Beech Road A.1
Birch Close A.1
Buddleia Drive B.1

Chapel Lane B.2
Chapel Road B.2
Chartridge C.1
Cherry Avenue A.1
Cheshire Court B.1
Church Road B.2
Clematis Close B.1
Clement Close C.2

Cornus Close B.1
Curtois Road C.2

Daphne Close B.1
Deansway A.1

Earlsfield C.1

Fairleas C.1
Forsythia Close B.1

Gibson Close B.1

Hall Lane B.2
Hannah Close B.1
Heathfield Avenue C.2

High Street B.2

Johnson Villas C.1
Juniper Close B.1

Laburnum Close B.1
Lincoln Road A.1
Linden Avenue A.1
Lodge Close C.2

Magnolia Close B.1
Malus Close B.1
Melville Close B.2
Mere Road B.2
Milton Close A.1
Moor Lane C.2

Nettleton Close B.1

Paddock Lane B.2
Park View Avenue A.1
Photinia Close B.1

Rectory Lane B.2

Shardloes C.1
Silver Street B.2
Sleaford Road C.2
Springfield Close B.2
Spruce Crescent A.1
Station Road C.2
Stonelea Close C.2
Sycamore Close B.1

Thackers Lane B.2
The Chalfonts C.1

Veronic Close B.1
Villa Close C.2

Waterwheel Lane B.2
Willow Road A.1
Wisteria Avenue A.1

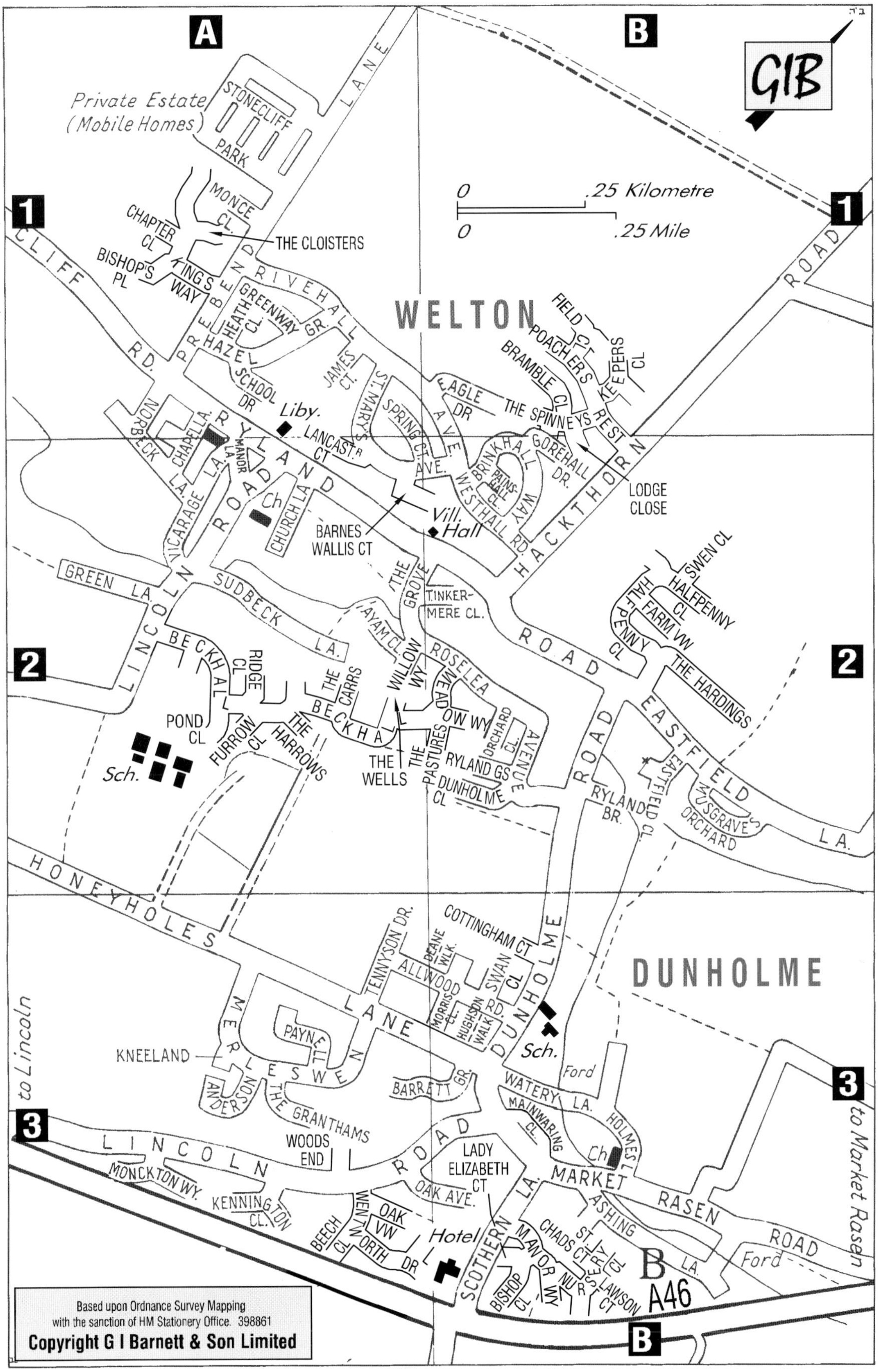

WELTON & DUNHOLME INDEX TO STREETS

Allwood Road A.3
Anderson A.3
Ashing Lane B.3
Ayam Close A.2

Barnes Wallis Court ..A.2
Barrett Grove A.3
Beck Hall A.2
Beech Close A.3
Bishop's Place A.1
Bramble Close B.1
Brinkhall Way B.2

Chapel Lane A.2
Chapter Close A.1
Church Lane A.2
Cliff Road A.1
Cottingham
Court B.3
Deane Walk B.3
DUNHOLME B.3
Dunholme Close B.2
Dunholme Road B.3

Eagle Drive B.1
Eastfield Close B.2
Eastfield Lane B.2

Farm View B.2
Field Close B.1
Furrow Close A.1

Gorehall Drive B.2
Green Lane A.2
Greenway A.1

Hackthorn Road B.2
Halfpenny Close B.2
Hazel Grove A.1
Heath Close A.1
Holmes Lane B.3
Honeyholes Lane A.2
Hughson Walk B.3

James Court A.1
Keepers Close B.1
Kennington Close A.3
Kings Way A.1
Kneeland A.3

Lady Elizabeth Court B.3
Lancaster Court A.2
Lawson Court B.3
Lincoln Road,
Dunholme A.3
Lincoln Road, Welton A.2
Lodge Close B.2

Mainwaring Close B.3
Manor Lane A.2
Manor Way b.3
Market Rasen Road B.3
Meadow Way B.2
Merleswen A.3
Monce Close A.1
Monckton Way A.3
Morris Close B.3
Musgraves Orchard ..B.2

Norbeck Lane A.1
Nursery Close B.3

Ryland Road A.1

St. Chads Court B.3
St. Mary's Avenue A.1
School Drive A.1
Scothern Lane B.3
Spring Court A.1
Stonecliff Park A.1
Studbeck Lane A.2
Swan Close B.3
Swen Close B.2

Tennyson Drive A.3
The Carrs A.2
The Cloisters A.1
The Granthams A.3
The Grove A.2
The Harrows A.2
The Pastures B.2
The Spinneys B.1
Tinkermere Close B.3

Vicarage Lane A.2

Watery Lane A.2
WELTON B.1
Wentworth Drive A.3
Westhall Road B.2
Willow Way A.2
Woods End A.3

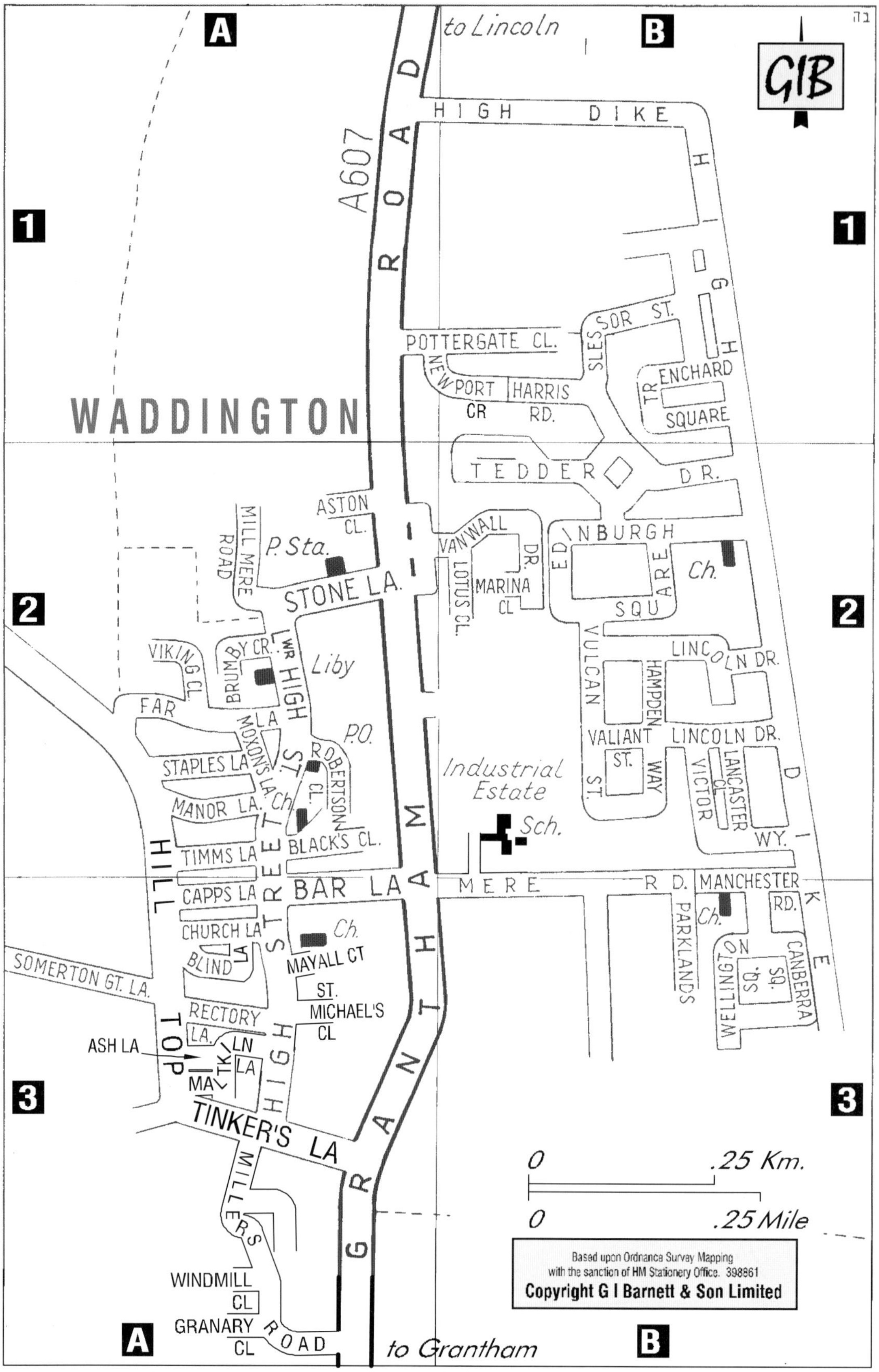

WADDINGTON INDEX TO STREETS

Ash Lane A.3
Aston Close A.2

Bar Lane A.3
Black's Close A.2
Blind Lane A.3
Brumby Crescent A.2

Canberra Square B.3
Capps Lane A.3
Church Lane A.3

Edinburgh Square B.2

Far Lane A.2

Granary Close A.3

Grantham Road A.3

Hampden Way B.2
Harris Road B.1
High Dike B.1
High Street A.3
Hill Top A.2

Lancaster Close B.2
Lincoln Drive B.2
Lotus Close B.2
Lower High Street A.2

Maltkiln Lane A.3
Manchester Road B.3
Manor Lane A.2
Marina Close B.2
Mayall Court A.3

Mere Road b.3
Mill Mere Road A.2
Millers Road A.3
Moxon's Lane A.2

Newport Crescent B.1

Parklands B.3
Pottergate Close A.1

Rectory Lane A.3
Robertson Close A.2

St. Michael's Close A.3
Slessor Street B.1
Somerton Great Lane A.3
Staples Lane A.2
Stone Lane A.2

Tedder Drive B.2
Timms Lane A.2
Trenchard Square B.1

Valiant Street B.2
Vanwall Drive B.2
Victor Way B.2
Viking Close A.2
Vulcan Street B.2

Wellington Square B.3
Windmill Close A.3

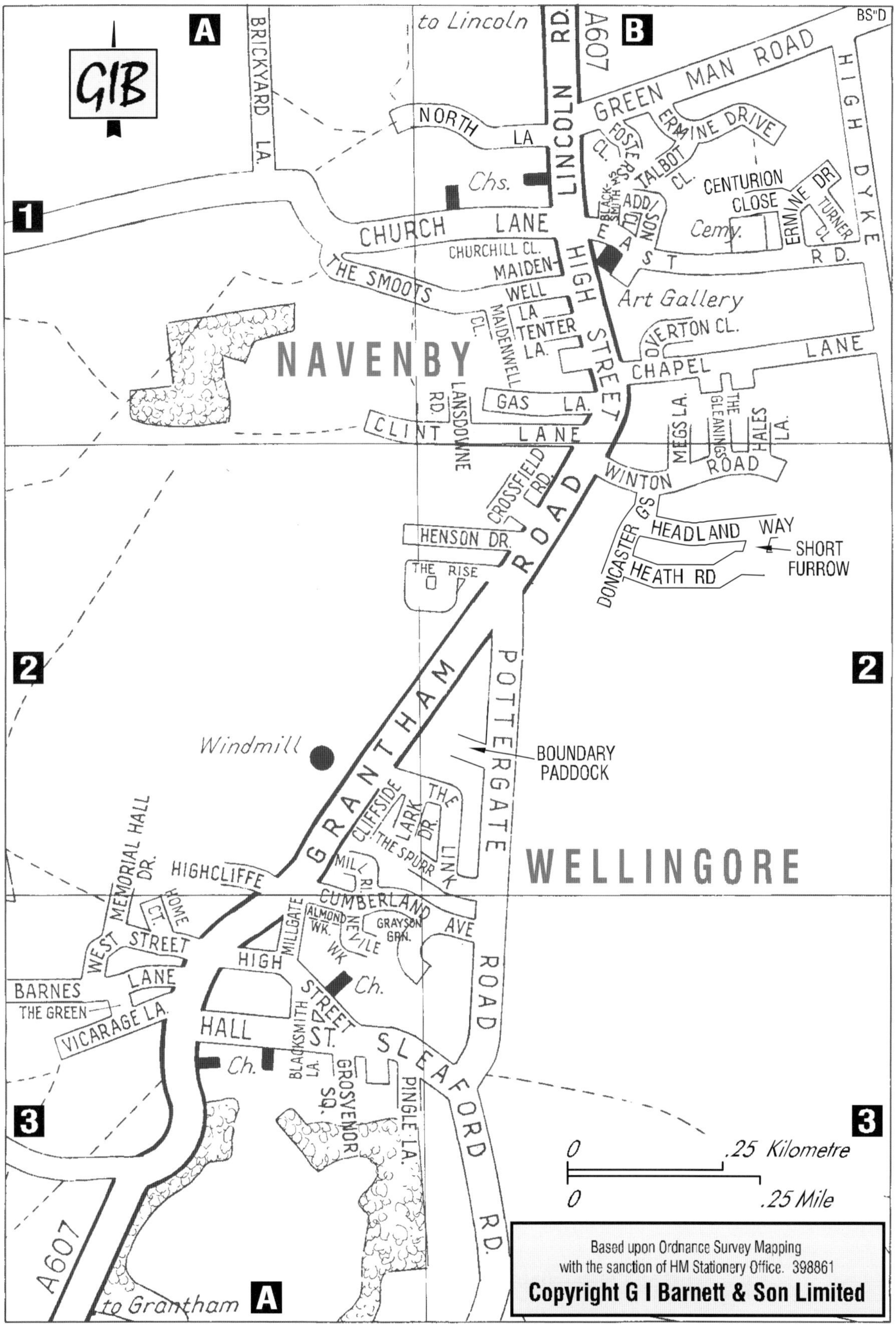

NAVENBY/WELLINGORE INDEX TO STREETS

Addison Close B.1
Almond Walk A.3

Barnes Lane A.3
Blacksmith Lane A.3
Blacksmith Mews B.1
Boundary Paddock B.2
Brickyard Lane A.1

Centurion Close B.1
Chapel Heath B.2
Chapel Lane B.1
Churchill Close B.1
Church Lane A.1
Cliffside A.2
Clint Lane A.1
Crossfield Road B.2

Cumberland Avenue A.3

Doncaster Gardens B.2

East Road B.1
Ermine Drive B.1

Fosters Close B.1

Gas Lane B.1
Grantham Road A.2
Grayson Green A.3
Green Man Road B.1
Grosvenor Square A.3

Hales Lane B.1

Hall Street A.3
Headland Way B.2
Heath Road B.2
Henson Drive B.2
Highcliffe A.2
High Dyke B.1
High Street, Nevenby B.1
High Street, Wellingore A.3
Home Court A.3

Lansdowne Road B.1
Lark Drive A.2
Lincoln Road B.1

Maidenwell Close B.1
Maidenwell Lane B.1
Megs Lane B.2

Memorial Hall Drive A.3
Millgate A.3
Mioll Rise A.2

NAVENBY A.1
Nevile Walk A.3
North Lane B.1

Overton Close B.1

Pingle Lane A.3
Pottergate Road B.2

Short Furrow B.2
Sleaford Road A.3

Talbot Close B.1

Tenter Lane B.1
The Gleanings B.1
The Green A.3
The Link B.2
The Rise B.2
The Smoats A.1
The Spurr A.2
Turner Close B.1

Vicarage Lane A.3

WELLINGORE B.2
West Street A.3
Winton Road B.2

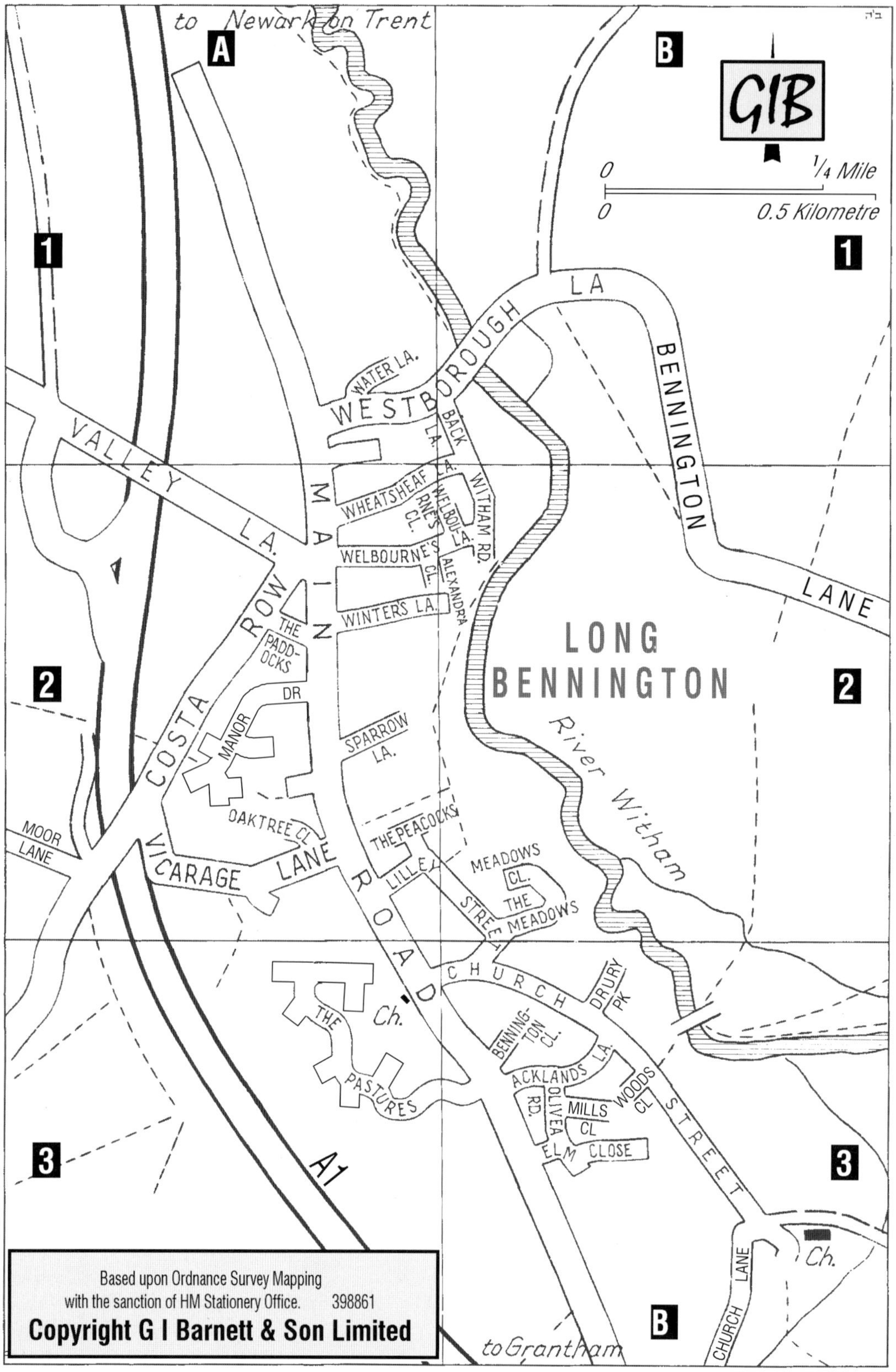

LONG BENNINGTON INDEX TO STREETS

Acklands Lane B.3
Alexandra Close A.2

Back Lane B.1
Bennington Close B.3
Bennington Lane................B.1

Church Lane B.3
Church Street B.3
Costa Row A.2

Drury Park..........................B.3

Elm Close B.3
Lilley Street A.2

Main Road A.2
Manor Drive A.2
Meadows Close B.2
Mills Close B.3
Moor Lane...........................A.2

Oak Tree Close A.2
Olivea Road B.3

Sparrow Lane A.2

The Meadows B.2
The Paddocks A.2
The Pastures A.3
The Peacocks A.2

Water Lane A.1
Welbourne's Close B.2
Welbourne's Lane A.2
Westborough Lane A.1
Wheatsheaf Lane A.2
Winter's Lane A.2
Witham Road B.2
Woods Close B.3

Valley Lane A.1
Vicarage Lane A.2

Abbey-Dale Crescent D.2
Abraham Close C.1
Acorn Close E.2
Adam-Styles A.4
Agnes Street D.4
Aire Road C.5
Albert Street E.6
Albion Place D.3
Albion Street D.3
Alexandra Road C.5
Alford Street D.3
Alma Park Close G.3
ALMA PARK
INDUSTRIAL ESTATE G.2
Alma Park Road G.3
Almond Grove E.3
Ambergate Walk C.5
Applewood Drive D.2
Arnold Avenue C.2
Ascot Drive E.2
Ash Green F.2
Ashley Drive C.2
Avenue Road D.4
Aviary Close E.3
Avon Close C.5

Balmoral Drive B.3
Barnwell Terrace C.5
Barrowdale Way D.1
BARROWBY A.4
Barrowby Gate B.4
Barrowby Road A.3
Bath Street D.4
Baysdale Grove D.1
Beacon Lane E.4
Beacon Road E.4
Beaumont Drive C.1
Bedford Close G.3
Beechcroft Road B.5
Bell Close C.2
Belmont Green F.3
Belton Avenue E.3
Belton Green E.2
Belton Lane D.3
Belton Lane, Manthorpe D.1
Belvoir Avenue C.6
Belvoir Avenue,
Spitalgate Airfield G.6
Belvoir Gardens A.1
Berkleley Avenue C.3
Berkshire Drive F.2
Birchwood Close C.2
Birkdale Close F.2
Birmingham Close B.4
Bishopsdale Close D.1
Blackburn Close B.4
Blenheim Avenue F.5
Bluegate D.4
Bowling Green Lane E.5
Bradford close B.4
Braemar Close E.2
Brading Avenue C.4
Bramblewood Close D.2
Brecon Close B.2
Brendon Close B.2
Brewery Hill D.5
Briarwood Close D.2
Bridge End Grove E.6
Bridge End Road E.5
Bridge Street E.5
Bristol close B.4
Brittain Drive E.4
Broad Street D.4
Brook Street D.4
Broomwood Close D.2
Brownlow Road E.4
Buckminster Gardens C.6
Burleigh Close G.3
Burns Close G.3

Calder Close C.5
Camarthen Close C.3
Cambrian Close B.2
Cambridge Street D.5
Campbell Close C.4
Canberra Crescent F.2
Canterbury Close F.2
Carlisle Close B.4
Castlegate D.4
Cecil Street E.5
Cedarwood Close C.2
Central Place F.3
Chambers Street D.3
Chapel Street D.4
Chatsworth Avenue G.3
Chelmsford Drive C.4
CHERRY ORCHARD
ESTATE F.3
Cherrywood Drive C.2
Chester Gardens B.4
Chestnut Grove B.5
Cheviot Close C.2
Chichester Close C.4
Chiltern Close C.2
Christchurch Road F.2
Church Lane B.1
Church Street D.4
Church View B.1

Cliff Road C.2
Clyde Court B.5
Cochran Close C.2
Coldharbour Lane E.5
College Street D.5
Colne Court C.5
Commercial Street D.5
Conduit Lane D.4
Cornwall Close E.2
Corfe Close C.3
Cotswold Drive B.2
Cottesmore Close E.3
Coventry Close B.4
Covill Close B.1
Cowes Road C.4
Cox's Walk B.1
Croft Drive E.5
Crossgill Close G.3

Dale Road D.2
Darleydale Crescent D.2
Denton Avenue C.6
Denton Close C.6
Derby Close C.4
Derwent Road C.5
Dickens Road F.3
Dovedale Close D.2
Dover Close C.3
Dryden Close F.3
Dudley Road E.4
Durham Close B.4
Dysart Road B.5

Earlesfield Lane C.5
East Avenue C.5
East Street D.4
Eastwood Drive F.5
Edinburgh Road F.3
Edward Street E.5
Elliot Close F.3
Elm Grove E.3
Elms View B.1
Elmer Street North D.4
Elmer Street South D.4
Elton Street D.5
Ely Way C.4
Emminson Way B.1
Ermine Close F.3
Eskdale Road D.2
Eton Street E.5
Exeter Close B.3

Falcon Court C.5
Farndale Crescent D.2
Fifth Avenue G.3
Finkin Street D.4
Fircroft E.6
First Avenue G.3
Fletcher Street D.5
Formby Close E.2
Foston Road C.5
Fourth Avenue G.3
Fulford Close F.2

Gannet Court C.5
Gasworks Lane C.5
George Street D.4
Gladstone Terrace D.3
Gleneagles E.2
Gloucester Road B.4
Goldsmith Road F.3
GONERBY HILL FOOT C.2
Gonerby Road B.1
Goodliff Road C.5
Goodman Close C.1
Gorse Lane C.7
Gorse Rise E.3
Gorse Road F.3
Grampion Way B.2
Grange Gardens D.4
Granta Crescent E.2
Grantham By-Pass A.1
Grantley Street D.5
Granville Street E.5
GREAT GONERBY B.1
Great North Road E.6
Green Hill Road C.4
Green Lane E.2
Green Street B.1
Greenwoods Row D.4
Gresley Court C.6
Greyfriars D.4
Grimsthorpe Close B.3
Grizedale Close D.2
Grove End Road E.4
Guildford Close C.4
Guildhall Street D.4

Hall Drive E.4
Hall Road G.4
Hamilton Road F.3
Harby Close C.6
Harlaxton Road C.6
Harrow Street E.5
Harrowby Close E.3
Harrowby Crescent F.6
Harrowby Lane E.3
Harrow Road E.4

Hatcliffe Close D.1
Hawksdale Close D.2
Hawthorn Court B.6
Hazelwood Drive C.2
Heathfield Road B.5
Hereford Way C.4
Hever Close C.3
Hickling Close C.6
Highcliffe Road D.2
High Meadow B.4
High Street, Grantham D.4
High Street,Great Gonerby B.1
Hill Avenue E.3
Hill View Close C.5
Hillingford Way C.5
Hillside Crescent F.5
Hillside Drive F.5
Hobart Road F.2
Hodder Close C.5
Holden Way C.1
Hollis Road C.5
Holly Close E.6
Hollywood Close C.2
Hornsby Road C.6
Houghton Road E.5
Huntingtower Road D.5
Huntlea Avenue C.6
Hurst Crescent A.4

Inner Street E.5
Ipswich Gardens B.4
Isaac Newton Centre D.4
Isaac Newton Way G.3
Ivatt Close C.6

John Foster Close F.2
Jubilee Avenue E.3

Keats Avenue F.3
Kelham Road B.1
Kempton Way C.5
Kenilworth Road G.3
Kenwick Drive E.4
Kestrel Court C.5
Killarney Close F.2
Kimberley Terrace C.2
Kindulton Court C.6
Kingscliffe Road D.2
Kingston Avenue C.4
Kintore Drive E.4
Kipling Close F.3
Kitty Briggs Lane C.6

Laburnam Close E.3
Lady's Walk F.4
Ladysmith Terrace C.2
Lancaster Gardens F.5
Langdale Crescent D.1
Larch Close B.6
Launder Terrace D.5
Leicester Green B.4
Leys Close A.4
Lichfield Close C.4
Lilac Wood Drive C.2
Lime Grove E.3
Lincoln Close B.4
Lindisfarne Way B.3
Lindrick Close F.2
Lodge Way D.3
London Road D.5
London Thorpe Lane F.2
Long Street B.1
Longcliffe Road D.2
Lord Drive C.1
Low Road, Barrowby A.5
Low Road, Manthorpe E.2
Lymn Court C.5
Lynden Avenue C.2
Lytham Close F.2

Mallard Court C.5
Market Place D.4
Malim Way C.2
Malvern Drive B.2
Manchester Way B.4
Manners Street D.3
Manor Close B.1
Manor Drive B.1
MANTHORPE E.1
Manthorpe Road D.3
Maplewood Close C.2
Marretts Lane B.1
Meadow Dale Crescent D.2
Meadow End F.6
Melbourn Road F.2
Mendip Close B.2
Meres Road A.5
Merrick Close B.1
Middlemore yard D.4
Montrose Close F.2
Moortown Close F.2
Mossdale Close D.1
Mount Street D.3
Mount Street D.4
Muirfield E.2
Muston Road C.6

Nene Court B.5

New Beacon Road E.4
New Row C.2
NEW SOMERBY E.5
New Street D.3
Newcastle Close B.4
Newport Avenue B.4
Newton Lodge C.3
Newton Road D.4
Ninth Avenue G.3
Northcliffe Road D.2
North Parade D.3
North Street D.4
Northings A.4
Norton Street D.5
Norwich Way C.4

Oak-Dale Close D.2
Oakham Close C.3
Oakhurst Close F.5
Oakleigh Road B.5
Old Wharf Road D.5
Orangewood Close C.2
Orchard Close C.2
Ostler Close C.2
Oxford Street D.5

Palmwood Close D.2
Park Road D.3
Pasture Close F.6
Peachwood Close C.2
Peascliffe Drive D.2
Penine Way B.2
Pennine Way B.3
Peterborough Close C.4
Pinewood Drive C.2
Pond Street B.1
Ponton Avenue G.6
Portrush Drive F.2
Portsmouth Close C.4
Premier Close D.4
Prestwick Close F.2
Pretoria Close C.2
Primrose Way F.6
Princess Drive E.2
Prospect Place D.3
Purcell Close F.3

Queen Street D.5
Queensway E.2

Railway Terrace D.5
Range Road E.4
Ravendale Close D.1
Redcliffe Road D.2
Redcross Street D.3
Reedings Close A.4
Reedings Road A.4
Regency Gardens F.3
Riber Close C.3
Richmond Drive C.3
Rippon Close C.4
Riverside E.4
Riverside E.4
Robertson Road C.4
Rochester Drive C.4
Rosedale Drive D.2
Rosemary Crescent C.6
Rossetti Court F.3
Rowanwood Drive D.2
Rushcliffe Road D.2
Ruston Road G.3
Ryde Avenue C.4
Ryedale Close E.1
Ryecroft D.5

St. Albans Close B.4
St. Andrews F.2
St. Anne's Street E.5
St. Catherine's Road D.4
St. Edmond's Court B.4
St. Georges Way F.2
St. Helens Close B.4
St. Peter's Hill D.4
St. Peter's Place D.4
St. Vincent's Road E.5
Salisbury Close B.4
Saltersford Road F.6
Saltersford Grove F.6
Sandcliffe Road D.2
Sandon Close E.4
Sandon Road E.4
Sandringham Drive G.3
Sankt Augustin Way D.4
Scotney Drive G.3
Second Avenue G.3
Seventh Avenue G.3
Shakespeare Avenue F.3
Shanklin Drive C.4
Sharpe Road E.3
Shaw Road B.6
Sheep Wash Lane A.4
Shelley Avenue F.3
Sherwell Close B.4
Sidney Street D.3
Signal Road E.3
Sixth Avenue G.3
Slate Mill Place D.3
Somerby Grove F.6

Somerby Hill E.5
Somerby Place G.6
South Parade E.5
Southlands Drive E.4
Southwell Close B.4
SPITALGATE AIRFIELD G.6
Spring End B.1
Spring Gardens D.5
Springfield Road C.6
Stamford Street D.6
Station Road D.4/D.5
Stephenson Avenue C.2
Stirling Court C.6
Stonebridge Road E.4
Stonemasons Court E.4
Stour Court C.5
Stuart Street E.5
Sturrock Court C.6
Sunningdale F.2
Swadales Close C.1
Swinegate D.4
Swingbridge Road B.6
Sycamore Court B.6

Tamar Court C.5
Tattershall Close B.3
Teesdale Road D.2
Tennyson Avenue F.3
Thames Road C.5
The Avenue B.5
The Avenue,Great Gonerby B.1
The Belfry F.2
The Drive B.5
The Grove B.5
The Haverlands C.2
The Knoll B.1
The Lindens D.6
The Maltings C.2
Third Avenue G.3
Toll Bar Road E.5
Tollemache Road (North) E.7
Treadgold Avenue C.1
Trent Road B.5
Troon Close F.2
Truro Close C.4
Turnberry Close F.2
Turnor Crescent E.3
Turnpike Close B.6
Tyndal Road C.4
Tyson Close E.3

Union Street D.4
Uplands Drive F.3

Vale Road C.2
Valley Road B.4
Ventnor Avenue C.4
Venture Way B.5
Vernon Avenue C.1
Victoria Street D.6
Vine Street D.4
Vivien Close C.1

Wakefield Close B.4
Walton Gardens D.6
Walton Heath Close F.2
Wardour Drive G.3
Warren Way G.2
Warwick Close b.4
Watergate D.4
Webster Way C.2
Welby D.4
Welby Gardens D.3
Welham Street D.4
Welland Court C.5
Wellington Drive f.5
Wells Close B.3
Welwyn Close C.6
Wensleydale Close D.1
Wentworth Drive F.2
West Avenue B.5
Westbourne Place C.4
Westerdale Road D.2
Westgate D.4
Westminster Way C.4
Westside Avenue B.7
Wharf Road D.5
William Street D.5
Willow Lane C.6
Winchester Road b.4
Windsor Drive G.3
Witham Brook Park G.2
Witham Place E.5
Witham Road D.4
Woburn Drive G.3
Woffindi Close C.1
Wong Row D.4
Woodland Drive G.2
Woodlands Drive E.4
Worcester Road B.4
Wordsworth Close F.3
Wroxall Drive B.4
Wulfram Drive G.6
Wyndham Close E.3
Wyville Road B.7

Yarmouth Avenue B.4
York Way B.4

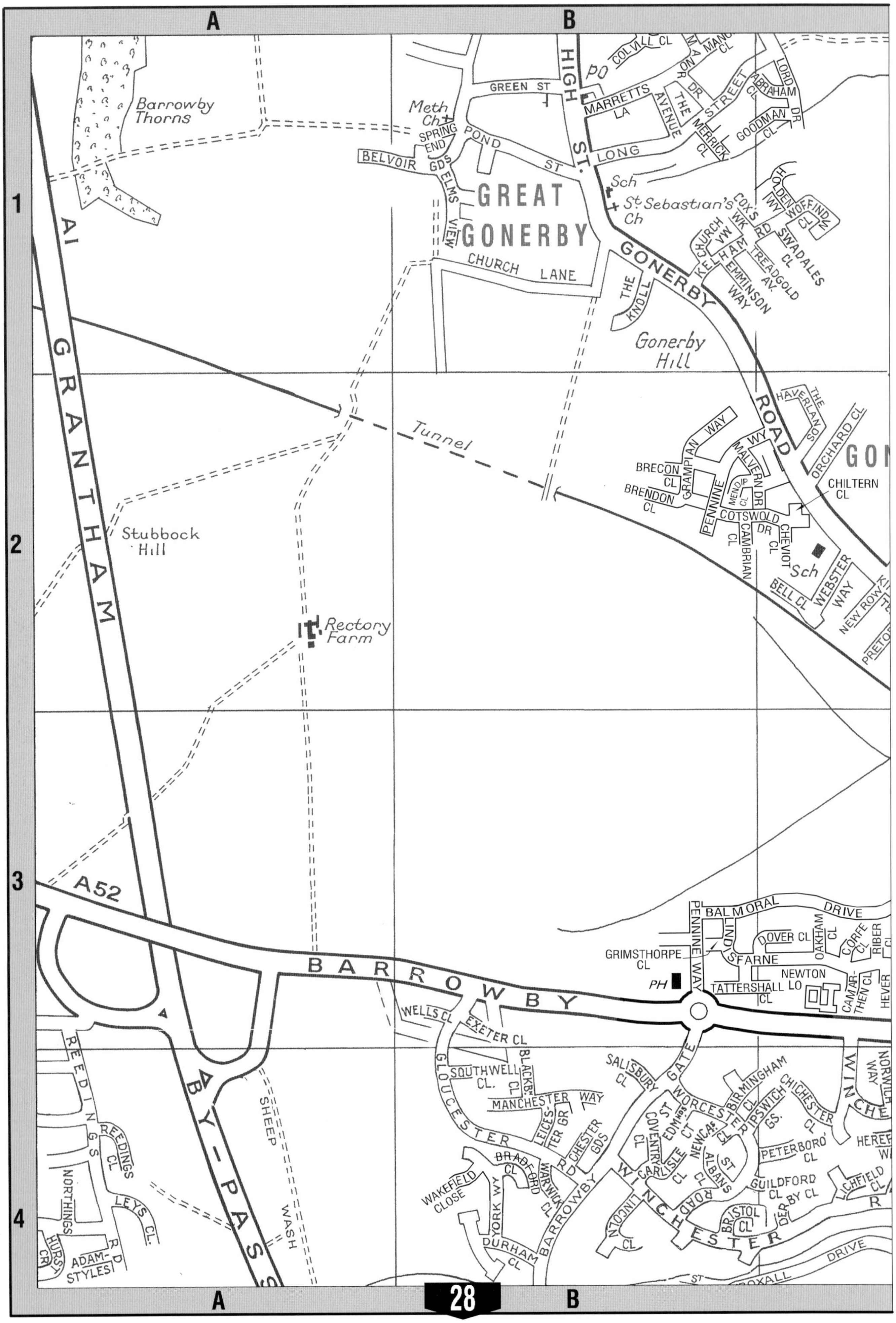
A
B
1
2
3
4
Barrowby Thorns
A1
GRANTHAM
Meth Ch
GREEN ST
HIGH ST.
PO
COLVILL CL
MANOR DR
MARRETTS LA
THE AVENUE
THE MERRICK
STREET
ABRAHAM
LORD DR
GOODMAN CL
LONG
SPRING END
POND ST
BELVOIR GDS
ELMS VIEW
GREAT GONERBY
Sch
St Sebastian's Ch
CHURCH LANE
GONERBY ROAD
THE KNOLL
CHURCH VW
KELHAM
COX'S WK
RD
SWADALES CL
WOFFINDEN CL
TREADGOLD AV.
EMMINSON WAY
Gonerby Hill
Tunnel
THE HAVERLANDS
ORCHARD CL
GON
GRAMPIAN WAY
BRECON CL
BRENDON CL
MALVERN DR
MENDIP CL
PENNINE
COTSWOLD DR
CAMBRIAN CL
CHEVIOT CL
CHILTERN CL
Sch
BELL CL
WEBSTER WAY
NEW ROW
Stubbock Hill
Rectory Farm
A52
BARROWBY
BALMORAL DRIVE
PENNINE WAY
LINDISFARNE
DOVER CL
OAKHAM CL
CORFE CL
RIBER CL
GRIMSTHORPE CL
NEWTON LO
TATTERSHALL CL
CAMARTHEN CL
HEVER
PH
WELLS CL
EXETER CL
GLOUCESTER
SOUTHWELL CL.
BLACKBURN CL
MANCHESTER WAY
LEICESTER GR
CHESTER GDS
SALISBURY CL
GATE
WORCESTER CL
BIRMINGHAM CL
ST EDMUNDS CT
COVENTRY CL
NEWCASTLE CL
IPSWICH GS.
CHICHESTER CL
WINCHESTER
NORWICH WAY
PETERBORO' CL
HEREF
ST ALBANS CL
CARLISLE CL
ROAD
LINCOLN CL
BRISTOL CL
GUILDFORD CL
DERBY CL
LICHFIELD CL
BRADFORD CL
WARWICK CL
RD
WAKEFIELD CLOSE
YORK WY
DURHAM CL
BARROWBY
REEDINGS
REEDINGS CL
NORTHINGS
LEYS CL.
HURST CR
ADAM-STYLES RD
BY-PASS
SHEEP WASH
DRIVE
ST
28

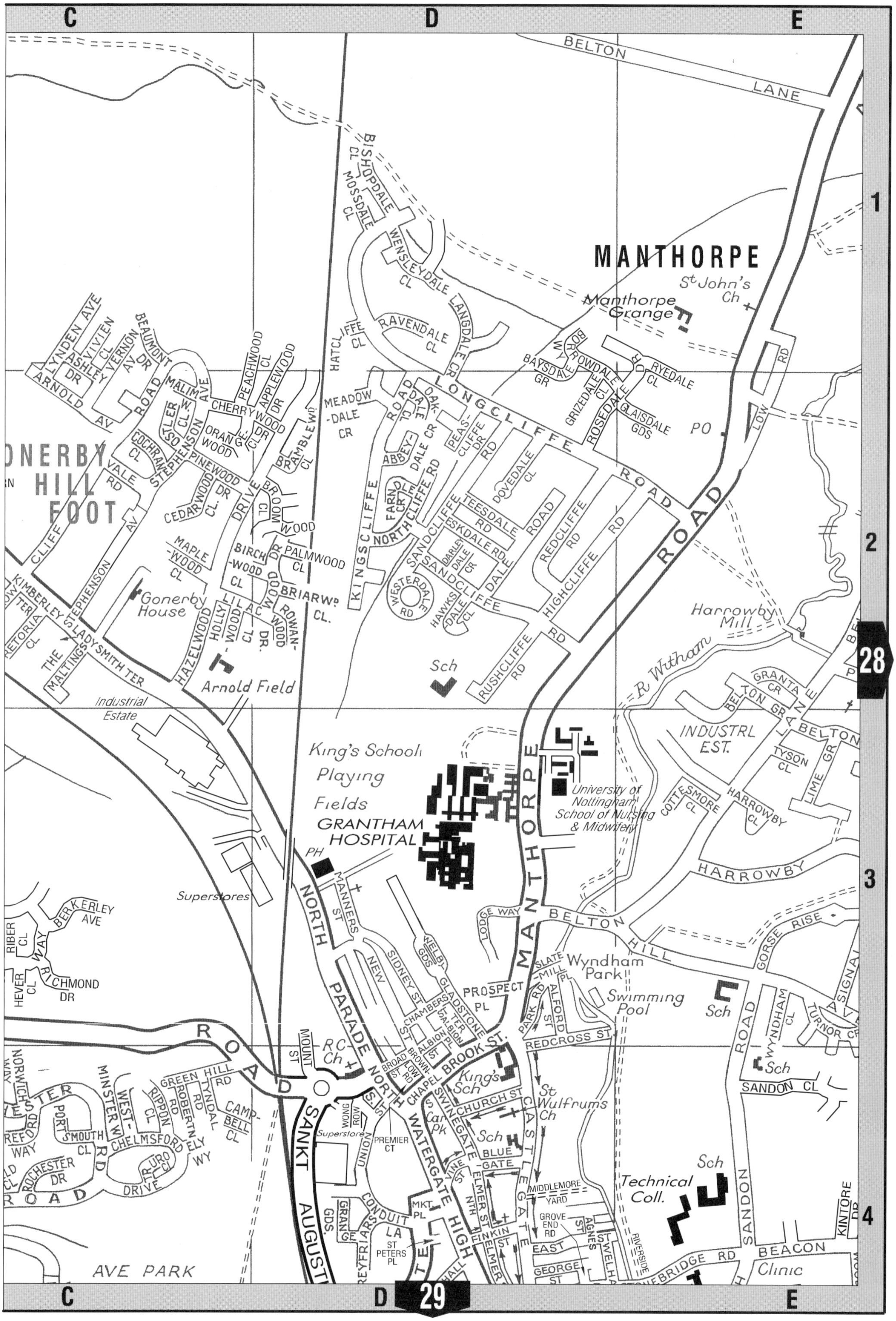
C
D
E
1
2
3
4
28
29
BELTON LANE
MANTHORPE
St John's Ch
Manthorpe Grange
BISHOPDALE CL
MOSSDALE CL
WENSLEYDALE CL
LANGDALE CR
RAVENDALE CL
HATCLIFFE CL
BAYSDALE GR
BORROWDALE WAY
GRIZEDALE CL
ROSEDALE CL
RYEDALE CL
GLAISDALE GDS
LOW RD
PO
LONGCLIFFE ROAD
MEADOW-DALE CR
OAKDALE CL
ABBEY-DALE CR
PEASCLIFFE DR
NORTHCLIFFE RD
FARNDALE CR
KINGSCLIFFE
DOVEDALE CL
TEESDALE RD
ESKDALE RD
SANDCLIFFE
DARLEY DALE CR
WESTERDALE RD
HAWKSDALE CL
REDCLIFFE RD
HIGHCLIFFE RD
RUSHCLIFFE RD
MANTHORPE ROAD
Harrowby Mill
R. Witham
GRANTA CR
BELTON GR
BELTON LANE
INDUSTRL EST.
TYSON CL
LIME GR
COTTESMORE CL
HARROWBY CL
HARROWBY
GONERBY HILL FOOT
LYNDEN AVE
VIVIEN CL
ASHLEY DR
VERNON AV
BEAUMONT DR
ARNOLD AV
MALIM W.
MILLER CL
STEPHENSON
CHERRYWOOD DR
PEACHWOOD CL
APPLEWOOD DR
ORANGEWOOD
BRAMBLEWOOD CL
COCHRANE CL
VALE RD
PINEWOOD DR
CEDARWOOD CL.
DRIVE
BROOMWOOD CL
MAPLEWOOD CL
BIRCHWOOD CL
PALMWOOD CL
BRIARWD CL.
LILAC
HOLLY-WOOD
HAZELWOOD
ROWAN-WOOD
CLIFF AV
KIMBERLEY TER
PRETORIA CL
STEPHENSON AV
LADYSMITH TER
THE MALTINGS
Gonerby House
Arnold Field
Sch
Industrial Estate
King's School Playing Fields
GRANTHAM HOSPITAL
PH
University of Nottingham School of Nursing & Midwifery
Superstores
MANNERS ST
NORTH PARADE
NEW
SIDNEY ST
NELBY GDS
GLADSTONE TER
CHAMBERS ST
ALBION TER
PROSPECT PL
LODGE WAY
BELTON HILL
Wyndham Park
Swimming Pool
SLATE MILL PL
PARK RD
ALFORD ST
REDCROSS ST
GORSE RISE
SIGNAL AVE
TURNOR CR
WYNDHAM CL
SANDON CL
SANDON ROAD
BERKERLEY AVE
RIBER CL
WAY
RICHMOND DR
HEVER CL
ROAD
NORWICH WAY
WESTER
PORTSMOUTH CL
HEREFORD WAY
ROCHESTER DR
WESTMINSTER RD
RIPPON CL
ROBERTSON RD
GREEN HILL RD
TYNDAL
CAMPBELL CL
CHELMSFORD
ELY WY
TRURO DRIVE
MOUNT ST
RC Ch
BROAD ST
BROWNLOW RD
CHAPEL ST
BROOK ST.
King's Sch
CHURCH ST
SWINEGATE
St Wulfrums Ch
Car pk
Sch
BLUE GATE
VINE ST
ELMER ST
CASTLEGATE
MIDDLEMORE YARD
GROVE END RD
AGNES ST
WELHAM
RIVERSIDE
EAST ST
GEORGE ST
FINKIN ST
WONG ROW
UNION
Superstore
PREMIER CT
WATERGATE
HIGH
CONDUIT LA
MKT PL
ST PETERS PL
GREYFRIARS
GRANGE
GDS.
SANKT AUGUSTI
AVE PARK
Technical Coll.
Sch
STONEBRIDGE RD
BEACON
Clinic
KINTORE DR

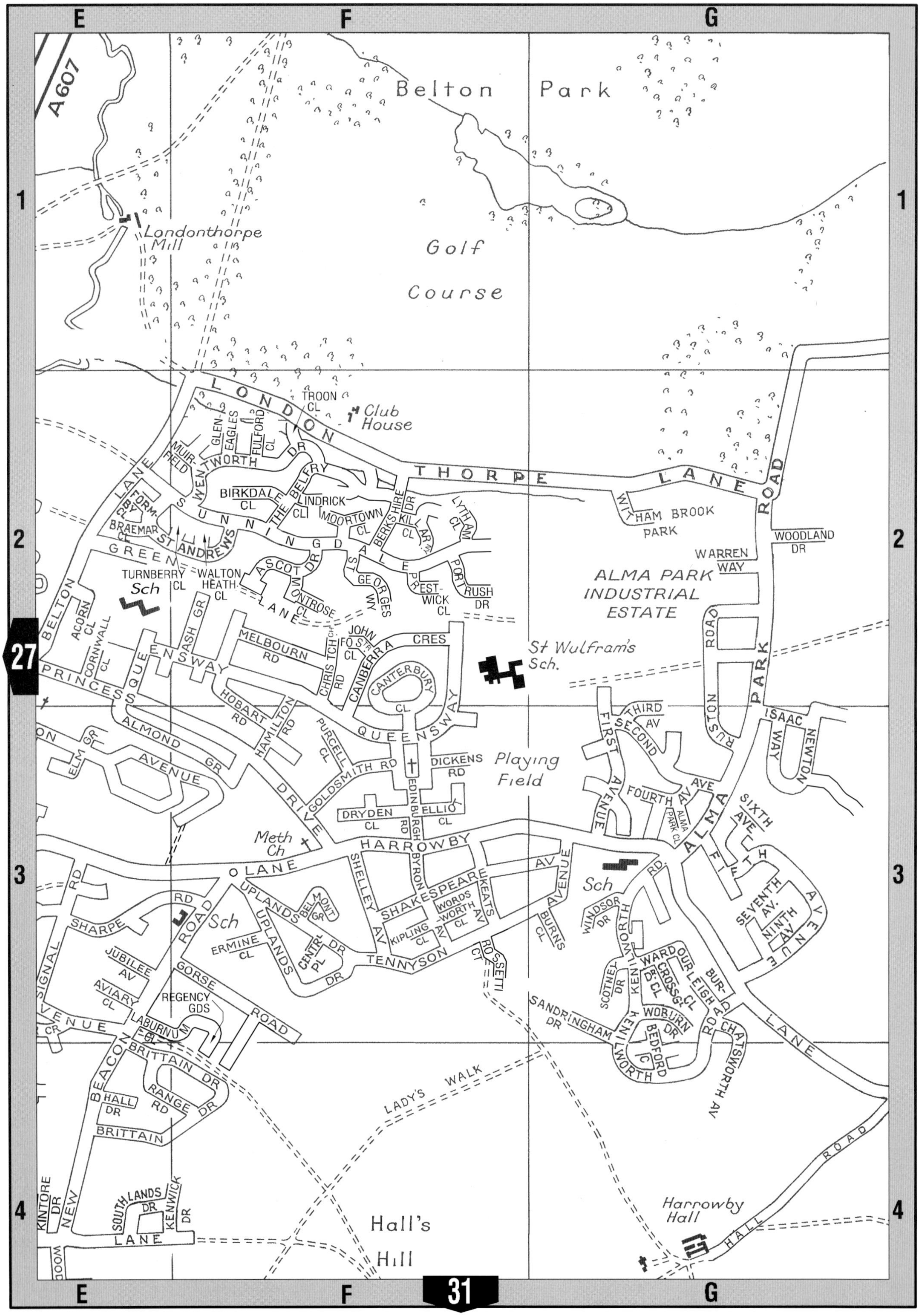
E
F
G
1
2
3
4
27
31
A607
Belton Park
Londonthorpe Mill
Golf Course
TROON CL
Club House
LONDON
THORPE LANE
ROAD
GLEN-EAGLES
FULFORD CL
MUIR-FIELD
WENTWORTH DR
BIRKDALE CL
THE BELFRY
LINDRICK CL
MOORTOWN CL
BERKSHIRE DR
KILLARNEY CL
LYTHAM CL
WYTHAM BROOK PARK
WOODLAND DR
WARREN WAY
ALMA PARK INDUSTRIAL ESTATE
LANE
FORMBY CL
BRAEMAR CL
ST ANDREWS
SUNNINGDALE
GREEN
TURNBERRY CL
WALTON HEATH CL
ASCOT DR
MONTROSE CL
ST GEORGES WAY
PRESTWICK CL
PORTRUSH DR
Sch
BELTON LANE
ACORN CL
CORNWALL CL
ASH GR
QUEENSWAY
MELBOURN RD
CHRISTCHURCH RD
JOHN FOSTER CL
CANBERRA CRES
CANTERBURY CL
St Wulfram's Sch.
RUSTON ROAD
PARK
PRINCESS
HOBART RD
HAMILTON RD
PURCELL CL
ALMOND GR
ELM GR
AVENUE
DRIVE
GOLDSMITH RD
DICKENS RD
Playing Field
FIRST AVENUE
SECOND AV
THIRD AV
FOURTH AV
ALMA PARK CL
ISAAC NEWTON WAY
AVE
ALMA
SIXTH AVE
FIFTH
DRYDEN CL
EDINBURGH RD
ELLIOT CL
Meth Ch
HARROWBY LANE
SHELLEY AV
BYRON
SHAKESPEARE AV
WORDSWORTH CL
KEATS AV
AVENUE
Sch
RD
WINDSOR DR
SEVENTH AV.
NINTH AV
AVENUE
RD
SHARPE RD
ROAD
Sch
UPLANDS DR
UPLANDS DR
BELMONT GR
CENTRAL PL
ERMINE CL
KIPLING CL
TENNYSON
ROSSETTI CT
BURNS CL
KENILWORTH
SCOTNEY DR
WARD CL
DR. CL
CROSSG
BURLEIGH CL
BURLEIGH ROAD
SIGNAL
JUBILEE AV
AVIARY CL
GORSE ROAD
REGENCY GDS
AVENUE
CR
LABURNUM CL
SANDRINGHAM DR
WOBURN DR
BEDFORD CL
KENILWORTH
CHATSWORTH AV
LANE
BEACON
BRITTAIN DR
RANGE RD
HALL DR
DR
BRITTAIN
LADY'S WALK
ROAD
KINTORE DR
NEW
SOUTHLANDS DR
KENWICK DR
LANE
Hall's Hill
Harrowby Hall
HALL
DOOM

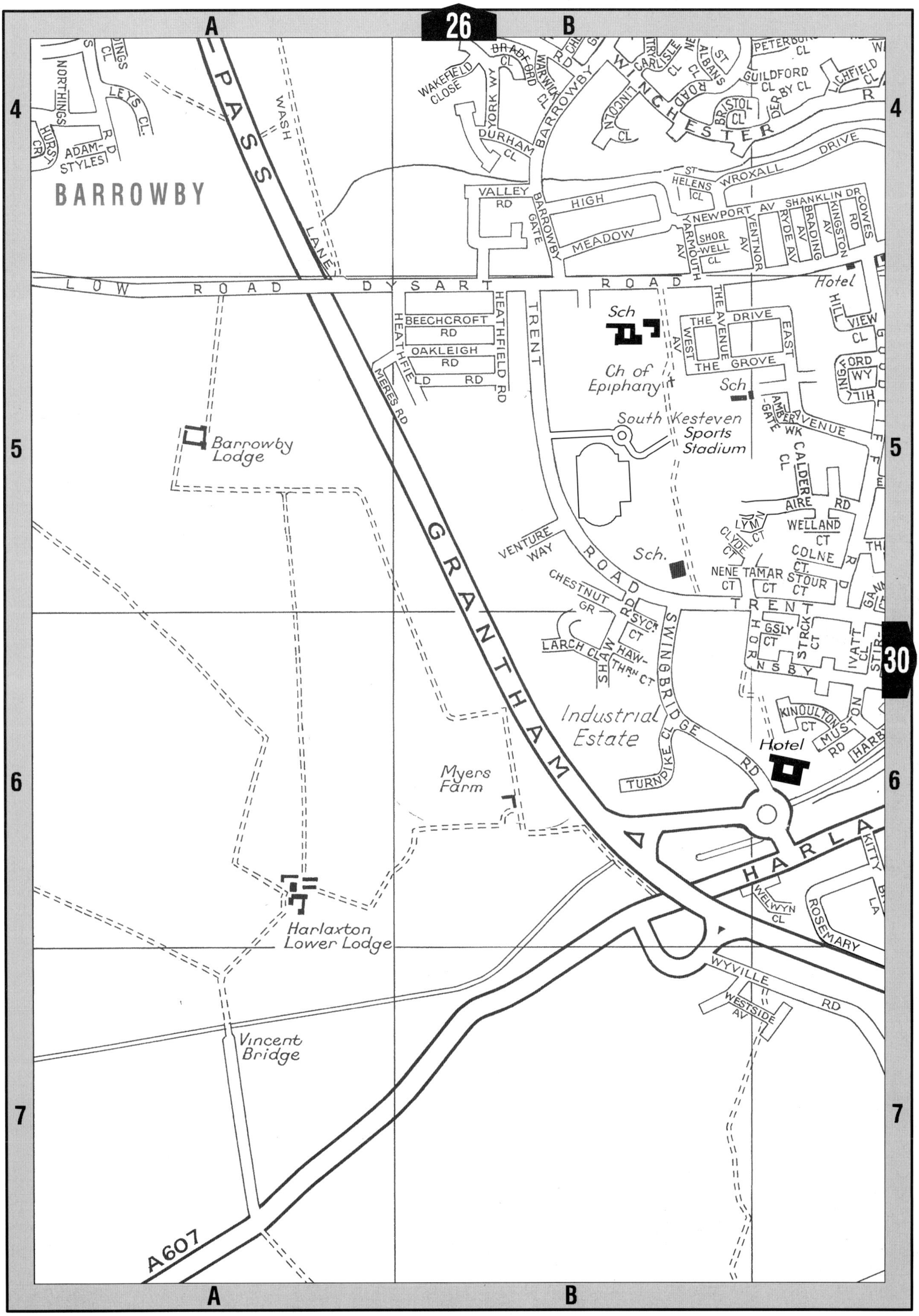
26
30
A
B
4
5
6
7
BARROWBY
NORTHINGS
HURST CRT
ADAM-STYLES RD
LEYS CL
WASH
LANE
PASS
WAKEFIELD CLOSE
YORK WY
DURHAM CL
BRADFORD CL
WARWICK CL
BARROWBY RD
LINCOLN CL
CARLISLE CL
ST ALBANS RD
WINCHESTER RD
PETERBOROUGH CL
GUILDFORD CL
DERBY CL
BRISTOL CL
LICHFIELD CL
VALLEY RD
BARROWBY GATE
HIGH MEADOW
ST HELENS CL
WROXALL DRIVE
NEWPORT AV
SHANKLIN DR
SHOR-WELL CL
YARMOUTH AV
VENTNOR AV
RYDE AV
BRADING AV
KINGSTON RD
COWES RD
LOW ROAD
DYSART ROAD
Hotel
HILL VIEW CL
BEECHCROFT RD
OAKLEIGH RD
HEATHFIELD RD
MIERES RD
TRENT ROAD
Sch
Ch of Epiphany
WEST AV
THE AVENUE
THE DRIVE
EAST
THE GROVE
Sch
AMBER GATE
AVENUE
WK
South Kesteven Sports Stadium
Barrowby Lodge
CALDER CL
AIRE RD
WELLAND CT
COLNE CT
STOUR CT
TAMAR CT
NENE CT
CLYDE CT
LYM CT
VENTURE WAY
GRANTHAM
Sch.
CHESTNUT GR
LARCH CL
SHAW RD
SYC CT
HAW-THRN CT
SWINGBRIDGE RD
TRENT
HORNSBY
GSLY CT
STRCK CT
IVATT CL
Industrial Estate
TURNPIKE CL
KINOULTON CT
MUSTON RD
Hotel
Myers Farm
HARLAXTON
Harlaxton Lower Lodge
WELWYN CL
ROSEMARY
KITTY
LA
WYVILLE RD
WESTSIDE AV
Vincent Bridge
A607

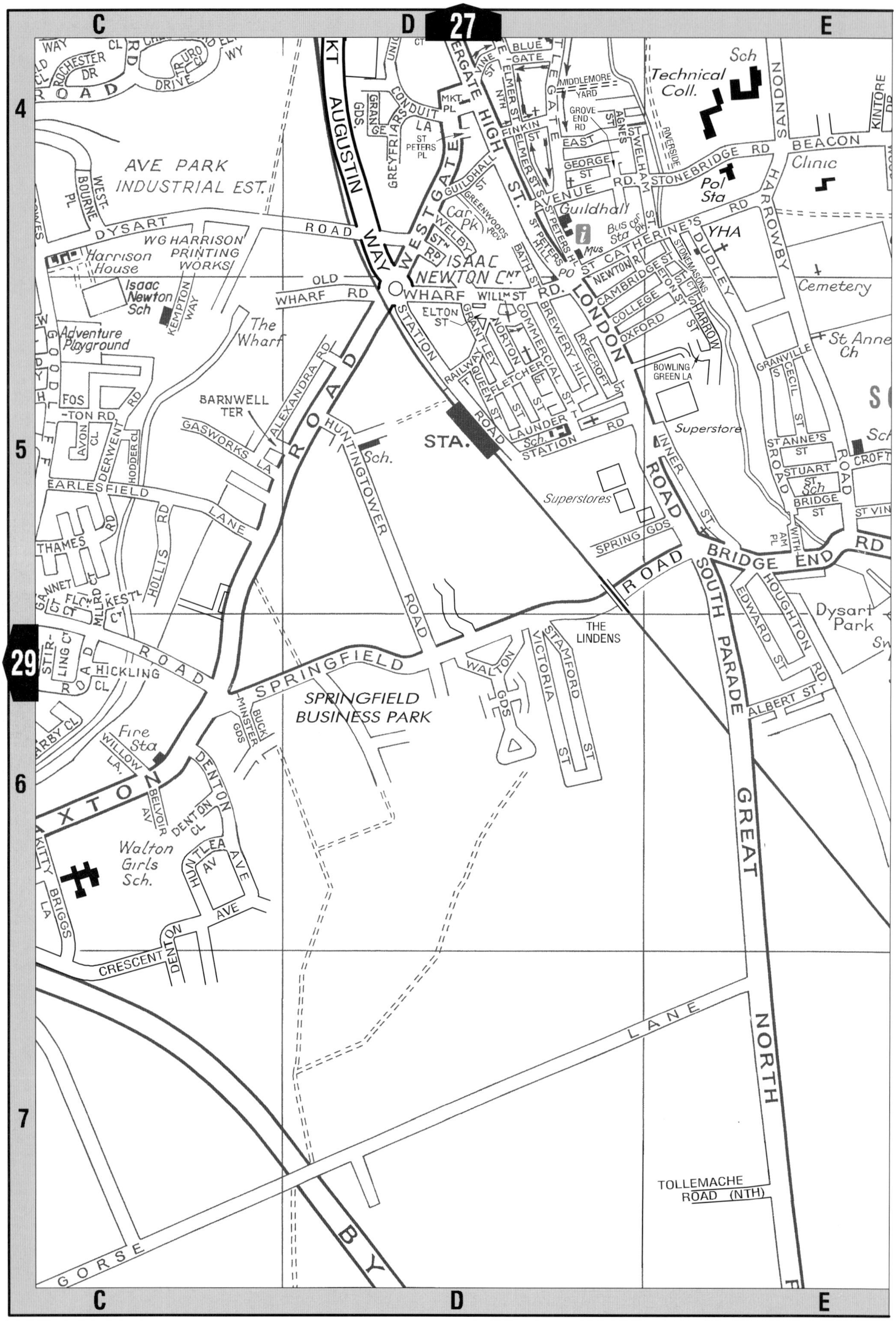

C
D
27
E
4
5
6
7
29
AVE PARK INDUSTRIAL EST.
DYSART ROAD
WG HARRISON PRINTING WORKS
Harrison House
Isaac Newton Sch
KEMPTON WAY
OLD WHARF RD
Adventure Playground
The Wharf
BARNWELL TER
GASWORKS LA
ALEXANDRA RD
ROAD
HUNTINGTOWER ROAD
Sch.
STA.
FOSTON RD
AVON CL
DERWENT RD
HODDER CL
EARLESFIELD LANE
THAMES
HOLLIS RD
HICKLING CL
ROAD
STIRLING CT
SPRINGFIELD RD
SPRINGFIELD BUSINESS PARK
MINSTER GDS
BUCK
WALTON GDS
VICTORIA ST
STAMFORD ST
THE LINDENS
Fire Sta
WILLOW LA.
DENTON AVE
BELVOIR AV
DENTON CL
HUNTLEA AV
Walton Girls Sch.
KITTY BRIGGS LA
CRESCENT
DENTON
LANE
GORSE
BY
TOLLEMACHE ROAD (NTH)
GREAT NORTH
SOUTH PARADE
ALBERT ST
EDWARD ST
HOUGHTON RD.
Dysart Park
BRIDGE END RD
SPRING GDS
Superstores
INNER ST.
Superstore
BOWLING GREEN LA
ST ANNE'S ST
STUART ST
Sch
BRIDGE ST
CROFT
WITHAM PL
GRANVILLE ST
CECIL ST
St Anne Ch
Cemetery
HARROWBY ROAD
DUDLEY RD
YHA
STONEBRIDGE RD
BEACON
Clinic
Pol Sta
KINTORE DR
SANDON
Technical Coll.
Sch
RIVERSIDE
WELHAM ST
AGNES ST
GROVE END RD
MIDDLEMORE YARD
EAST ST
GEORGE ST
AVENUE RD.
Guildhall
Mus
Bus Sta
ST CATHERINE'S RD
NEWTON
CAMBRIDGE ST
COLLEGE ST
OXFORD
ELTON ST
STONEMASONS CT
HARROW ST
LONDON RD.
RYECROFT ST
BREWERY HILL
COMMERCIAL ST
NORTON
GRANTLEY
FLETCHER ST
QUEEN ST
RAILWAY
LAUNDER ST
STATION RD
Sch.
ELTON ST
WHARF RD
WILLM ST
ISAAC NEWTON CNT
ST PETERS HILL
BATH ST
GREENWOODS ROW
WELBY ST
GUILDHALL ST
Car Pk
WESTGATE
HIGH ST.
WATERGATE
VINE ST
ELMER ST NTH
ELMER ST
FINKIN ST
BLUE GATE
MKT PL
CONDUIT LA
ST PETERS PL
GREYFRIARS
GRANGE GDS.
AUGUSTIN WAY
STATION RD
ROCHESTER DR
DRIVE
ROAD
WY
GOODLIFF
LA
BOURNE PL
WEST

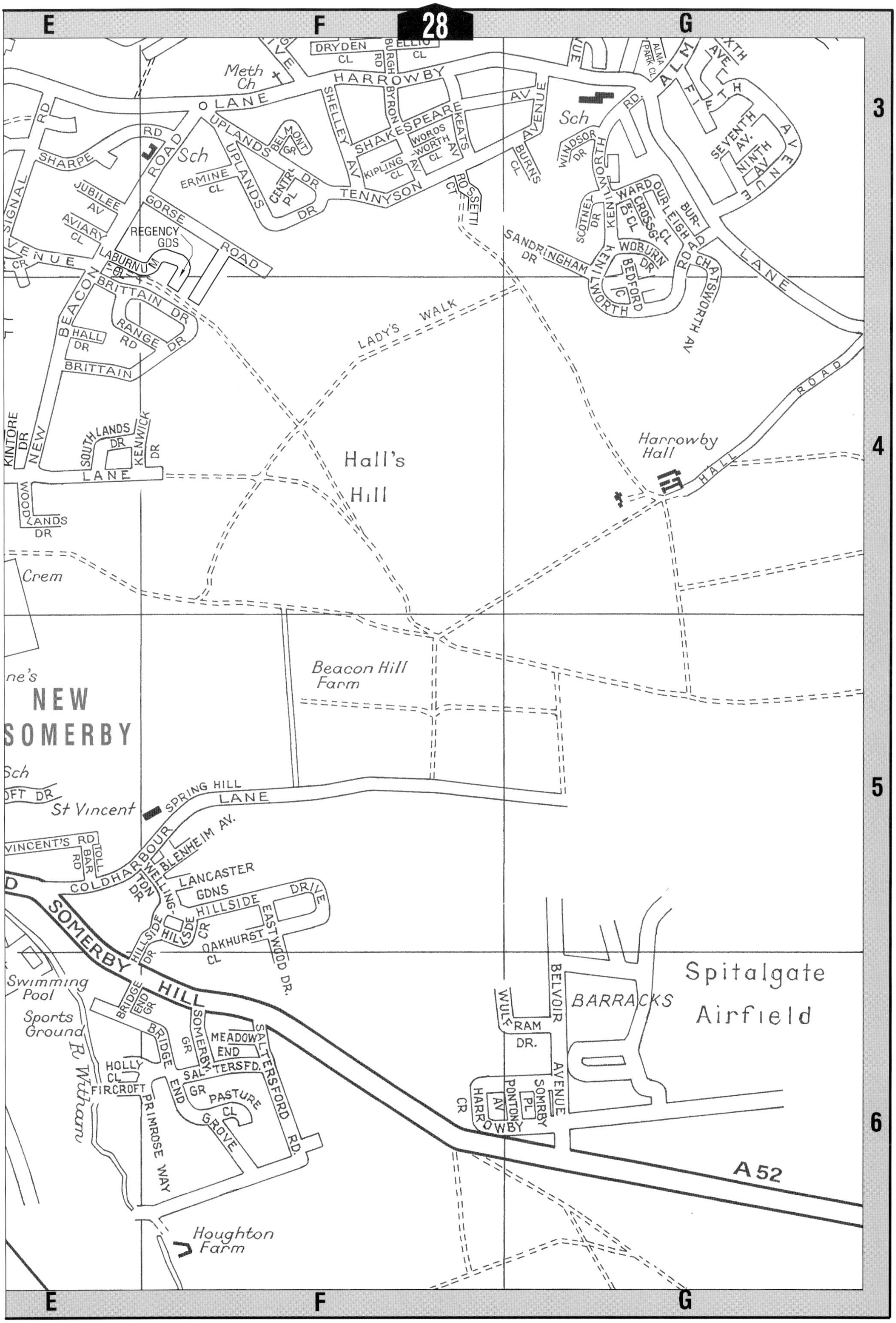
E
F
28
G
3
4
5
6
Meth Ch
DRYDEN CL
HARROWBY
LANE
SHELLEY AV
BYRON RD
SHAKESPEARE
WORDS-WORTH CL
KEATS AV
KIPLING CL
TENNYSON
AVENUE
BURNS CL
Sch
WINDSOR DR
KENILWORTH
UPLANDS DR
BELMONT GR
CENTRAL PL
ERMINE CL
SHARPE RD
ROAD
GORSE ROAD
JUBILEE AV
AVIARY CL
REGENCY GDS
SIGNAL
AVENUE
LABURNUM CL
BEACON
BRITTAIN DR
RANGE RD
HALL DR
BRITTAIN
LADY'S WALK
SANDRINGHAM DR
WARD CL
CROSSGATE
WOBURN DR
BEDFORD
SCOTNEY DR
BURLEIGH ROAD
CHATSWORTH AV
LANE
FIFTH
SEVENTH AV.
NINTH AV
AVENUE
ROAD
KINTORE DR
NEW LANE
SOUTHLANDS DR
KENWICK DR
Hall's Hill
Harrowby Hall
HALL
WOODLANDS DR
Crem
Beacon Hill Farm
NEW SOMERBY
Sch
St Vincent
SPRING HILL LANE
BLENHEIM AV.
VINCENT'S RD
TOLL BAR RD
COLDHARBOUR
WELLINGTON DR
LANCASTER GDNS
HILLSIDE DRIVE
EASTWOOD DR.
OAKHURST CL
HILLSIDE DR
SOMERBY HILL
Swimming Pool
Sports Ground
R. Witham
BRIDGE END GR
BRIDGE END GR
SOMERBY GR
MEADOW END
SALTERSFORD RD.
SALTERSFD. GR
PASTURE CL
GROVE
HOLLY CL
FIRCROFT
PRIMROSE WAY
Houghton Farm
BELVOIR AVENUE
WULFRAM DR.
BARRACKS
Spitalgate Airfield
HARROWBY CR
PONTON AV
SOMERBY PL
A52

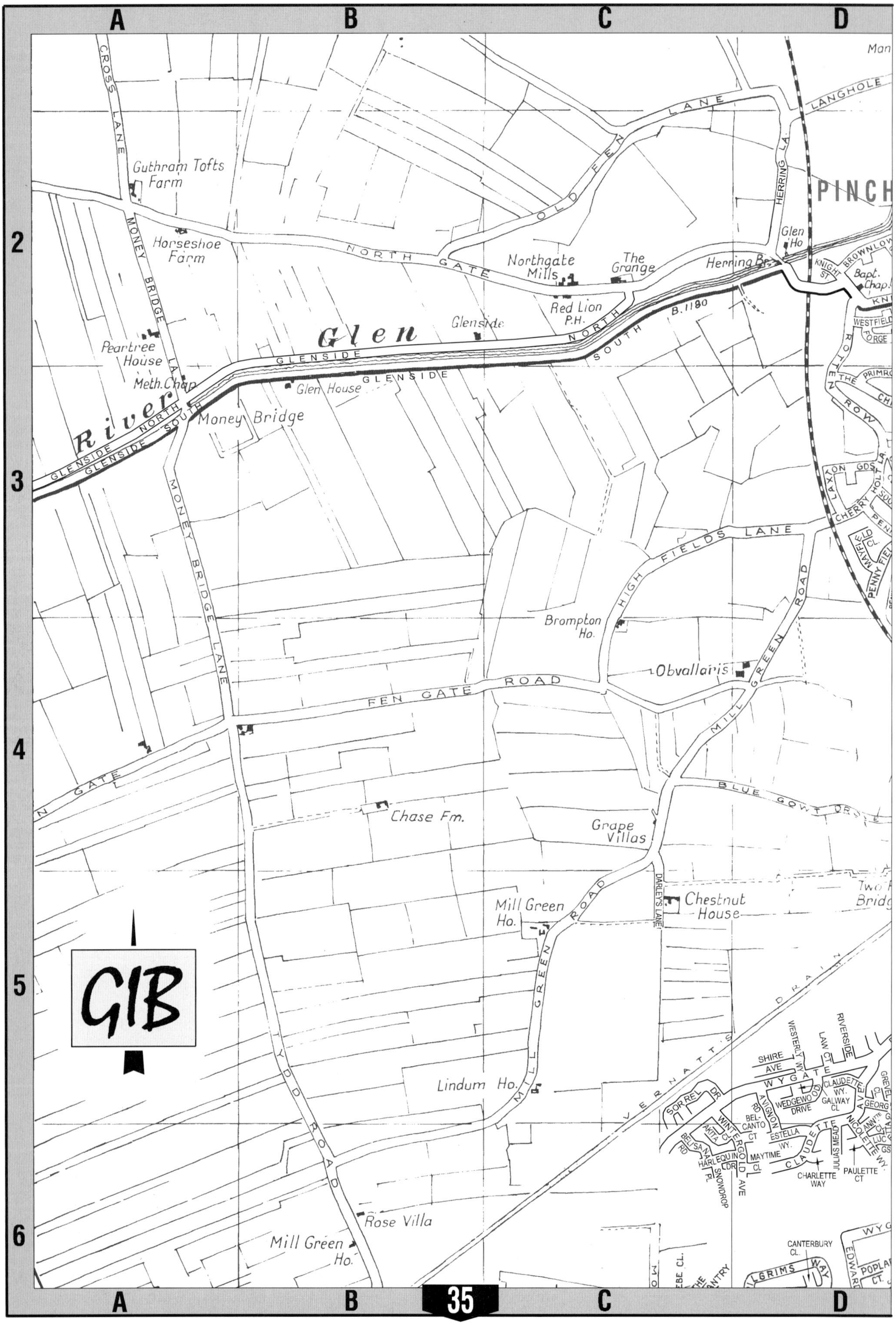
A
B
C
D
2
3
4
5
6
CROSS LANE
Guthram Tofts Farm
MONEY BRIDGE LA.
Horseshoe Farm
NORTH GATE
OLD FEN LANE
LANGHOLE
HERRING LA.
PINCH
Glen Ho
Northgate Mills
The Grange
Herring Br.
Red Lion P.H.
B.1180
Glenside
Glen
River
GLENSIDE NORTH
GLENSIDE SOUTH
Peartree House
Meth.Chap.
Glen House
Money Bridge
KNIGHT ST
BROWNLOW
Bapt. Chap.
WESTFIELD
FORGE
ROTTEN ROW
THE PRIMROSE
LAXTON GDS
CHERRY HOLT LA.
MAYFIELD CL.
PENNY
MONEY BRIDGE LANE
HIGH FIELDS LANE
Brompton Ho.
MILL GREEN ROAD
Obvallaris
FEN GATE ROAD
GATE
BLUE GOWT DROVE
Chase Fm.
Grape Villas
DARLEY'S LANE
Chestnut House
Mill Green Ho.
Two Bridge
VERNATTS DRAIN
MILL GREEN ROAD
Lindum Ho.
TYDD ROAD
Rose Villa
Mill Green Ho.
SHIRE AVE
WESTERLY WY.
LAW CT
RIVERSIDE
WYGATE
CLAUDETTE AVE
WY.
GALWAY CL
GEORGE
WEDGEWOOD DRIVE
AVIGNON RD
SORREL DR
BEL-CANTO CT
ESTELLA WY.
WINTERGOLD AVE
AKITA CL
BELVISA RD
HARLEQUIN DR
MAYTIME CL
CLAUDETTE
JULIAS MEAD
NICOLETTE WY.
CHARLETTE WAY
PAULETTE CT
SNOWDROP PL
CANTERBURY CL.
PILGRIMS WAY
EDWARD
POPLAR CT.
THE CHANTRY
GLEBE CL.
Man
GIB
35

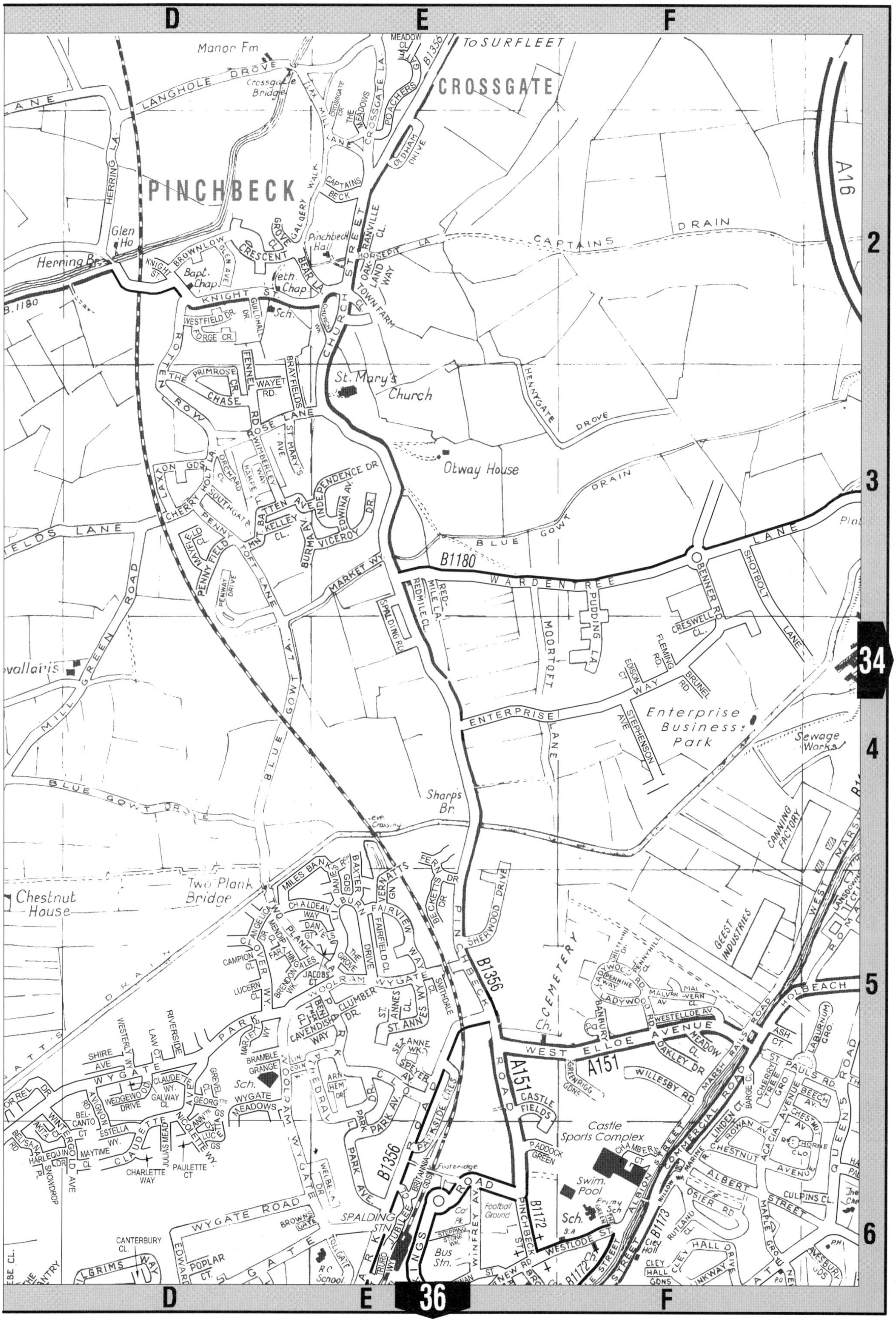
D
E
F
To SURFLEET
CROSSGATE
PINCHBECK
Manor Fm
LANGHOLE DROVE
Crossgate Bridge
HERRING LA.
Glen Ho
Herning Br.
B.1180
KNIGHT ST.
BROWNLOW
Bapt. Chap.
Meth. Chap.
Sch.
Pinchbeck Hall
CRESCENT
CHURCH ST.
CAPTAINS BECK
GALLERY WALK
OLDHAM DRIVE
POACHERS GA.
B1356
A16
CAPTAINS DRAIN
HORSESHOE LA.
TOWN FARM
WESTFIELD DR.
FORGE CR.
ROTTEN ROW
THE CHASE
PRIMROSE CR.
FENNEL
WAYET RD.
BRAYFIELDS
St. Mary's Church
ROSE LANE
HENNYGATE DROVE
Otway House
DRAIN
BLUE GOWT
INDEPENDENCE DR.
BATTEN AVE
KELLEY CL.
EDWINA AV.
VICEROY
BURMA AV.
LAXTON GDS.
CHERRY HOLT LA.
SOUTHGATE
PENNY TOFT LANE
PENNY FIELD
MAYFIELD CL.
FIELDS LANE
GREEN ROAD
MILL GREEN ROAD
MARKET WY.
PENWAY DRIVE
B1180
WARDENTREE LANE
LANE
SHOTBOLT LANE
BENNER RD.
CRESWELL CL.
PUDDING LA.
MOORTOFT
REDMILE CL.
REDMILE LA.
SPALDING RD.
FLEMING RD.
EDISON CT.
BRUNEL RD.
WAY
ENTERPRISE
STEPHENSON AVE
Enterprise Business Park
Sewage Works
BLUE GOWT LA.
BLUE GOWT DROVE
Sharps Br.
CANNING FACTORY
GEEST INDUSTRIES
WEST MARSH
Chestnut House
Two Plank Bridge
MILES BANK
DANE'S RD.
BAXTER GDS.
VERNATTS GN.
FERN DR.
BECKETTS DR.
SHERWOOD DRIVE
PINCHBECK RD.
CHALDEAN WAY
FAIRVIEW WAY
FAIRFIELD CL.
THE GROVE
JACOBS CT.
WOOLRAM WYGATE
CAMPION CL.
LUCERN CL.
CLUMBER DR.
ST. ANNES CL.
ST. ANNES WY.
SMITHDALE CL.
B1356
CEMETERY
Ch.
LADYWOOD
PENNINE WAY
MALVERN AV.
WESTELLOE AV.
WEST ELLOE AVENUE
A151
MEADOW CL.
OAKLEY DR.
WILLESBY RD.
HOLBEACH
ASH CT.
LABURNUM GRO.
ST. PAULS RD.
BEECH AV.
QUEEN'S ROAD
RIVERSIDE
LAW CT.
SHIRE AVE
WESTERLY WY.
PARK RD.
WYGATE
BRAMBLE GRANGE
Sch.
CLAUDETTE WY.
GALWAY CL.
WEDGEWOOD DRIVE
WYGATE MEADOWS
SPEYER AV.
PARKSIDE CRES.
PARK AV.
CASTLE FIELDS
Castle Sports Complex
PADDOCK GREEN
Swim. Pool
Sch.
CHAMBERS CT.
ALBION STREET
COMMERCIAL ROAD
LINDEN CT.
ROWAN AV.
CHESTNUT AV.
ALBERT
OSIER RD.
CULPINS CL.
MAPLE GRO.
CHARLETTE WAY
PAULETTE CT.
MAYTIME
ESTELLA
HARLEQUIN
WYGATE ROAD
CANTERBURY CL.
PILGRIMS WAY
POPLAR CT.
EDWARD
BROWNS GATE
RC School
SPALDING STN.
Footbridge
Car Pk.
Football Ground
Bus Stn.
WINFREY AV.
B1172
WESTLODE ST.
KINGS ROAD
CLEY HALL GDNS
Cley Hall
HALL DRIVE
INKWAY
B1173
AVESBURY GDS.
34
36
2
3
4
5
6

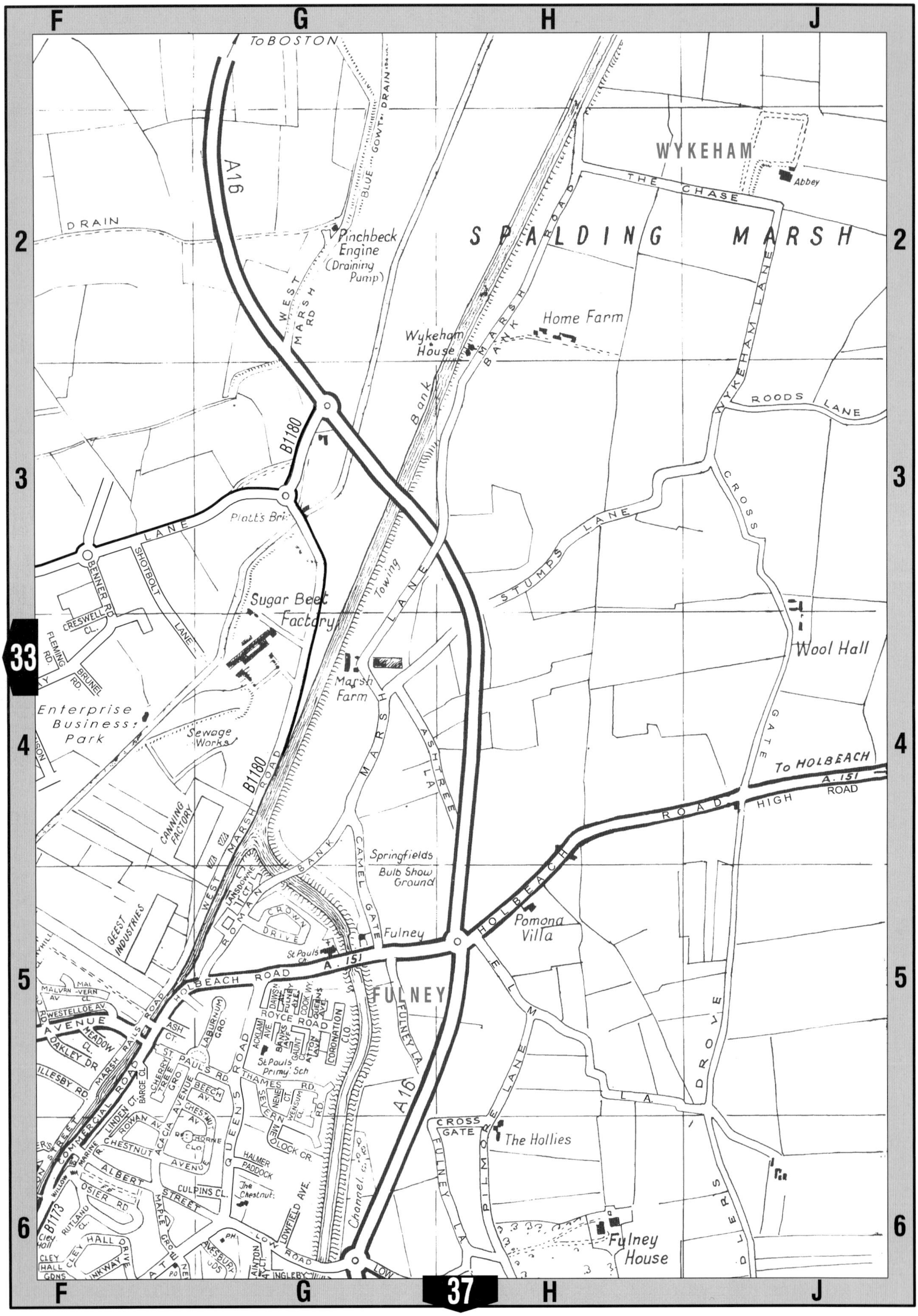
F
G
H
J
2
3
4
5
6
33
37
To BOSTON
BLUE GOWT DRAIN
A16
DRAIN
Pinchbeck Engine (Draining Pump)
WEST MARSH RD
WYKEHAM
THE CHASE
Abbey
SPALDING MARSH
ROAD
MARSH BANK
Home Farm
Wykeham House
Bank
WYKEHAM LANE
ROODS LANE
B1180
CROSS
LANE
Platt's Bri.
STUMPS LANE
BENNER RD
SHOTBOLT LANE
CRESWELL CL.
Sugar Beet Factory
Towing
LANE
FLEMING RD.
BRUNEL RD.
Marsh Farm
Wool Hall
Enterprise Business Park
Sewage Works
MARSH
ASHTREE LA
GATE
To HOLBEACH
A.151
HIGH ROAD
ROAD
CANNING FACTORY
WEST MARSH ROAD
BANK
CAMEL GATE
Springfields Bulb Show Ground
HOLBEACH
ROMAN
LANSDOWNE CT.
CROWN DRIVE
Fulney
Pomona Villa
GEEST INDUSTRIES
St Pauls Ct.
HOLBEACH ROAD
FULNEY
MALVERN AV
MAL-VERN CL.
WESTELLOE AV
AVENUE
MEADOW CL.
DAKLEY DR
ROYCE ROAD
ACKLAM AVE.
CORONATION CLO.
FULNEY LA.
ELM
ASH CT.
LABURNUM GRO.
ST PAUL'S RD
St Pauls Primy. Sch
DROVE
MARSH RAILS ROAD
ILLESBY RD.
CHERRY TREE GRO.
BEECH AV.
THAMES RD.
COMMERCIAL ROAD
LINDEN CT.
BARGE CL.
NENE CT.
WENSUM CL.
SEVERN
MEDLOCK CR.
A16
PILMORE LANE
LA.
CROSS GATE
The Hollies
ROWAN AV.
ACACIA AVENUE
CHESTNUT AV
HORNE CLO.
CHESTNUT
AVENUE
QUEEN'S ROAD
HALMER PADDOCK
The Chestnut
ALBERT STREET
CULPINS CL.
LOWFIELD AVE.
Channel
FULNEY LA.
PILMORE LANE
SLADLERS
B1173
OSIER RD.
MAPLE GRO.
RUTLAND CL.
HALL DRIVE
Fulney House
Cley Hall
CLEY HALL GDNS
LINKWAY
AYLESBURY GDS
LOW ROAD
AINTON CT.
INGLEBY
LOW
PO
PH

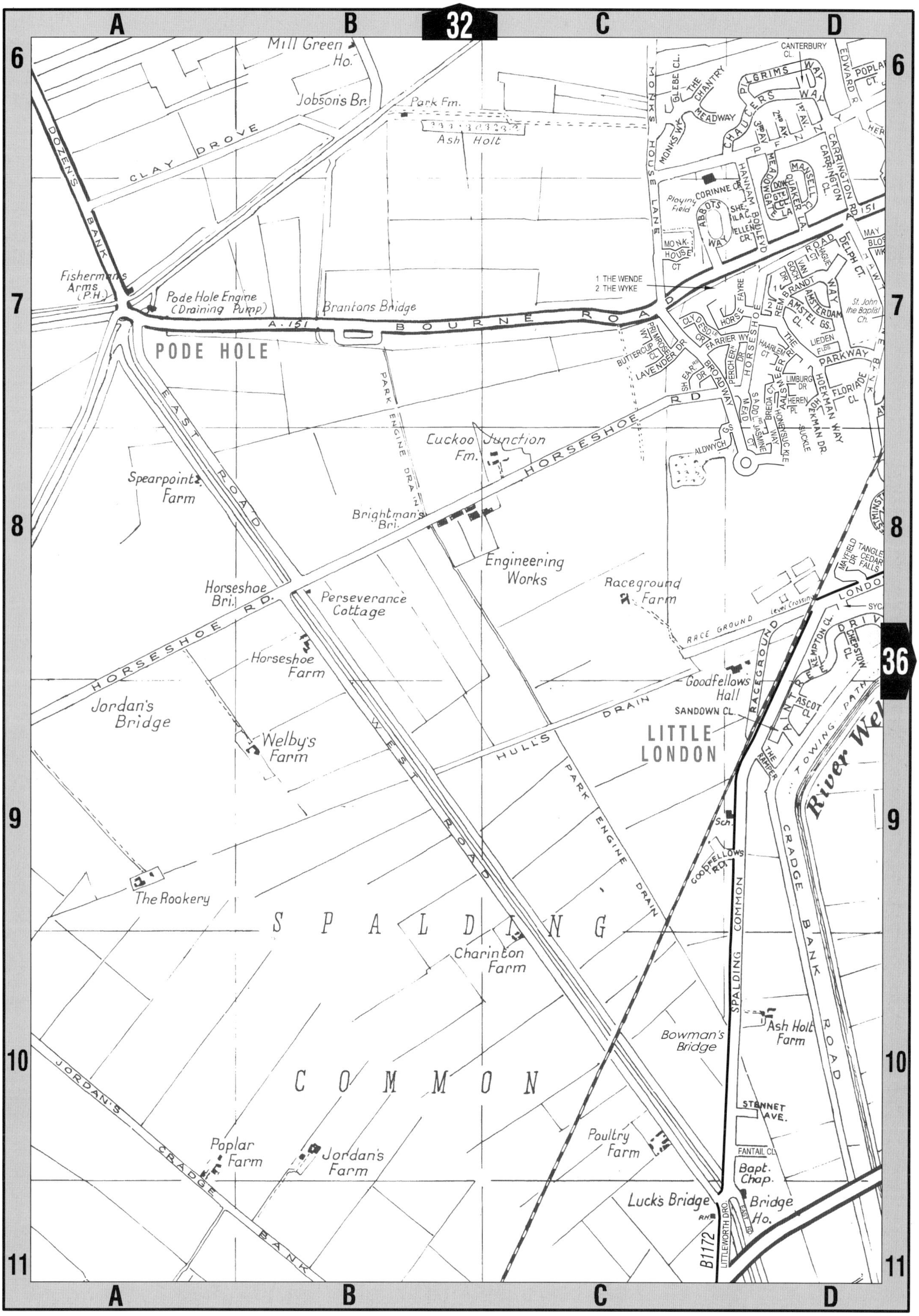
A
B
32
C
D
6
7
8
9
10
11
Mill Green Ho.
Jobson's Br.
Park Fm.
Ash Holt
CLAY DROVE
DOZEN'S BANK
Fishermans Arms (P.H.)
Pode Hole Engine (Draining Pump)
Brantons Bridge
A.151
BOURNE ROAD
PODE HOLE
PARK ENGINE DRAIN
EAST ROAD
Spearpoint Farm
Cuckoo Junction Fm.
HORSESHOE RD.
Brightman's Bri.
Engineering Works
Horseshoe Bri.
Perseverance Cottage
Raceground Farm
RACE GROUND
Horseshoe Farm
Jordan's Bridge
Welby's Farm
WEST ROAD
HULLS DRAIN
Goodfellows Hall
SANDOWN CL.
LITTLE LONDON
The Rookery
SPALDING
COMMON
Charinton Farm
Bowman's Bridge
Ash Holt Farm
JORDAN'S CRADGE BANK
Poplar Farm
Jordan's Farm
Poultry Farm
Luck's Bridge
Bapt. Chap.
Bridge Ho.
B1172
LITTLEWORTH DRO.
SPALDING COMMON
CRADGE BANK ROAD
STENNET AVE.
FANTAIL CL.
GOODFELLOWS RD.
Sch.
River Welland
TOWING PATH
RACEGROUND
THE RAMPER
ASCOT CL.
KEMPTON CL.
CHEPSTOW CL.
MONKS HOUSE LANE
GLEBE CL.
THE CHANTRY
MEADWAY
MONKS WK.
PILGRIMS WAY
CANTERBURY CL.
CHAUCERS WAY
EDWARD RD.
POPLAR CT.
CARRINGTON RD.
CARRINGTON CL.
MANSELL CL.
QUAKER LA.
HANNAM BOULEVARD
CORINNE CR.
Playing Field
ABBOTS WAY
MONK HOUSE CT.
1 THE WENDE
2 THE WYKE
DELPH CT.
St. John the Baptist Ch.
AMSTERDAM GS.
AMSTEL CL.
REMBRANDT WAY
LIEDEN FLDS.
PARKWAY
HORSESHOE RD.
FARRIER WY.
PERCHERON
HAARLEM CT.
LIMBURG DR.
HEREN PL.
FLORIADE CL.
HOEKMAN WAY
HOEKMAN DR.
BROADWAY
LAVENDER DR.
BUTTERCUP WAY
PRIMROSE CL.
SHEAR DR.
ALDWYCH
HONEYSUCKLE
MAYFIELD DR.
TANGLE
CEDAR FALLS
LONDON RD.
36
A151

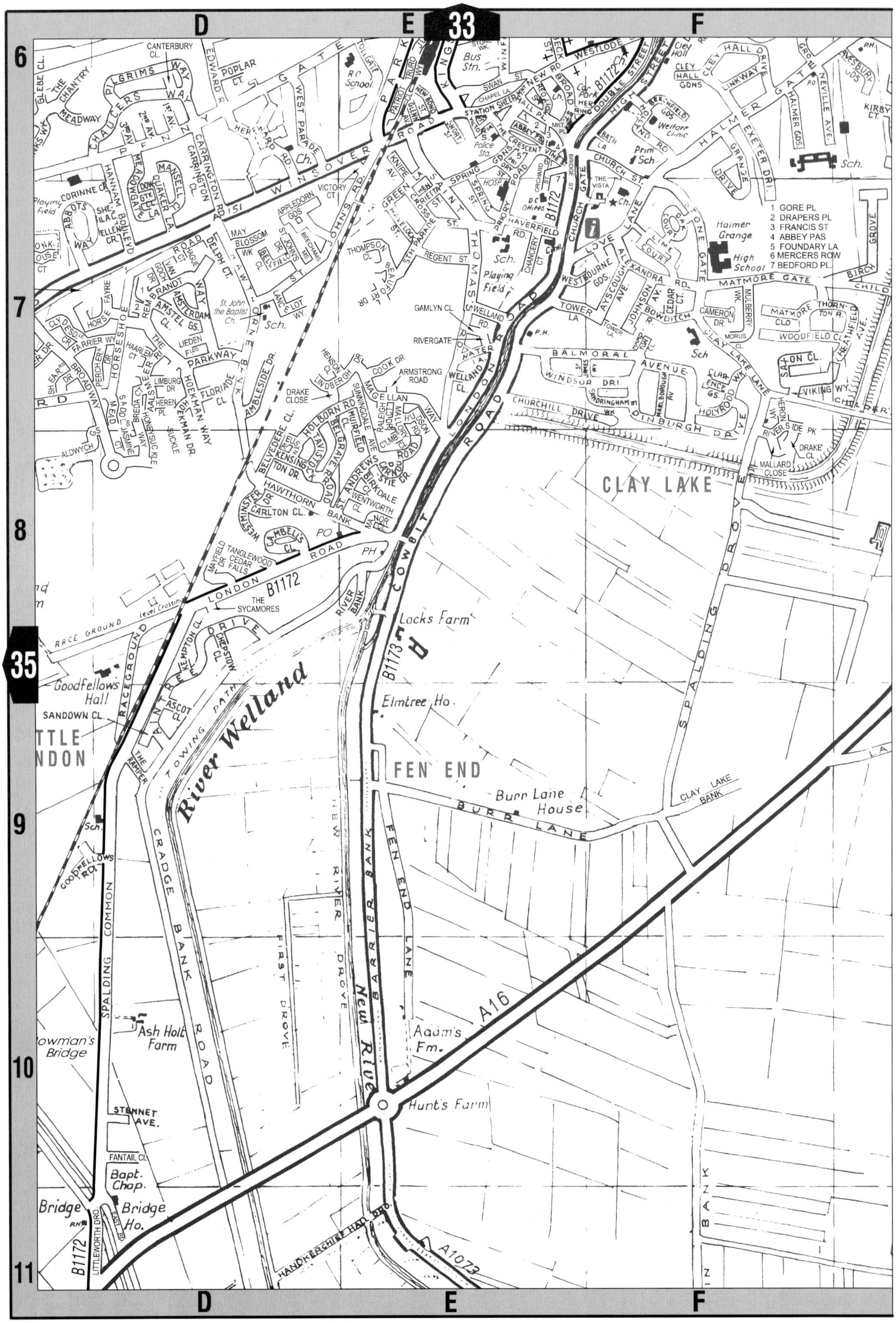
D
E
33
F
6
7
8
9
10
11
35
CANTERBURY CL.
GLEBE CL.
THE CHANTRY
PILGRIMS WAY
CHAUCERS WAY
MEADWAY
EDWARD RD.
POPLAR CT.
GATE
WEST PARADE
RC School
TOLLGATE
PARK RD.
TRURO WY
KING ST.
Bus Stn.
SWAN ST.
WINFREY AV.
STATION SHEEP MKT
NEW RD.
BROAD ST.
Car Park
HERRING LA
WESTLODE ST.
DOUBLE ST.
HIGH STREET
B1172
Cley Hall
CLEY HALL DRIVE
CLEY HALL GDNS
LINKWAY
BEECHFIELD GDS
Welfare Clinic
Prim Sch
HALMER GATE
EXETER DRI.
GRANGE DRIVE
HALMER GDS
NEVILLE AVE.
AYLESBURY GDS
KIRBY CT.
Sch.
HANNAM BOULEVARD
CARRINGTON RD.
CARRINGTON CL.
MANSELL CT.
QUAKER LA
MEADOWGATE
CORINNE CL.
Playing Field
ABBOTS WAY
A151 WINSOVER ROAD
VICTORY CT
ST. JOHN'S RD.
APPLEDORN GDS
MAY BLOSSOM WK
DELPH CT.
HEREWARD RD.
Ch.
KNIPE AV.
GREEN LA
HAVELOCK ST.
HENRIETTA ST.
ST. THOMAS RD.
SPRING GDNS.
HOSP.
Police Sta.
PRIORY ROAD
HAVERFIELD RD.
DC Offices
B1172
CHURCH GATE
BRIDGE ST.
CHURCH ST.
THE VISTA
LOVE LANE
CHANCERY CT.
THOMPSON CL.
REGENT ST.
STH PARADE
BEAUFORT DR
Sch.
Playing Field
WESTBOURNE GDS.
AYSCOUGH AVE.
ALEXANDRA RD.
JOHNSON AV.
CEDAR CT.
BOWDITCH R.
TOWER LA
Halmer Grange
High School
1 GORE PL
2 DRAPERS PL
3 FRANCIS ST
4 ABBEY PAS
5 FOUNDARY LA
6 MERCERS ROW
7 BEDFORD PL
MATMORE GATE
GROVE
BIRCH
CAMERON DR
MULBERRY WK.
MORUS CL.
MATMORE CLO
THORNTON R.
WOODFIELD CL.
HEATHFIELD AVE.
SAXON CL.
VIKING WY
CLAY LAKE LANE
Sch
HORSE FAYRE
REMBRANDT WAY
AMSTERDAM GS.
AMSTEL CL.
HAARLEM CT
LIEDEN F'LDS
PARKWAY
FLORIADE CL
FARRIER WY
BROADWAY
HORSESHOE
St. John the Baptist Ch.
Sch.
GAMLYN CL.
RIVERGATE
WELLAND RD.
WATER
WELLAND CL.
P.H.
BALMORAL AVENUE
WINDSOR DRI.
SANDRINGHAM WK
MARLBOROUGH AV
HOLYROOD
CLARENCE GS.
CHURCHILL DRIVE
EDINBURGH DR.
HERON WAY
RIVERSIDE PK
DRAKE CL
MALLARD CLOSE
CLAY LAKE
HENSON CL.
LINDBERGH
COOK DR.
ARMSTRONG ROAD
DRAKE CLOSE
MAGELLAN WAY
RALEIGH
HUDSON RD
BELVEDERE CL.
HOLBORN RD
SUNNINGDALE
MUIRFIELD
BELGRAVE ROAD
KENSINGTON DR.
TAVISTOCK
ST. ANDREWS
BIRKDALE
WENTWORTH CL.
HAWTHORN BANK
CARLTON CL.
WESTMINSTER DR
CAMBELLS CL
PO
ROAD
PH
CEDAR FALLS
TANGLEWOOD
LONDON B1172
THE SYCAMORES
AMBLESIDE DR.
ALDWYCH
HOEKMAN WAY
HOEKMAN DR.
LIMBURG DR
SADDLERS MEAD
BREDA CT
JASMINE CT
HONEYSUCKLE CT
RACE GROUND
Level Crossing
RACEGROUND
KEMPTON CL.
DRIVE
CHEPSTOW CL
Goodfellows Hall
SANDOWN CL.
ASCOT CL
LITTLE LONDON
THE KAMPER
TOWING PATH
River Welland
RIVER BANK
COWBIT ROAD
Locks Farm
B1173
Elmtree Ho.
FEN END
Burr Lane House
BURR LANE
CLAY LAKE BANK
SPALDING DROVE
Sch.
GOODFELLOWS RD.
SPALDING COMMON
CRADGE BANK ROAD
FIRST DROVE
NEW RIVER DROVE
BARRIER BANK
FEN END LANE
New River
A16
Adam's Fm.
Hunt's Farm
Ash Holt Farm
Bowman's Bridge
STENNET AVE.
FANTAIL CL
Bapt. Chap.
Bridge
Bridge Ho.
LITTLEWORTH DRO.
EAST RD.
B1172
HANDKERCHIEF HALL DRO.
A1073
BANK
D
E
F

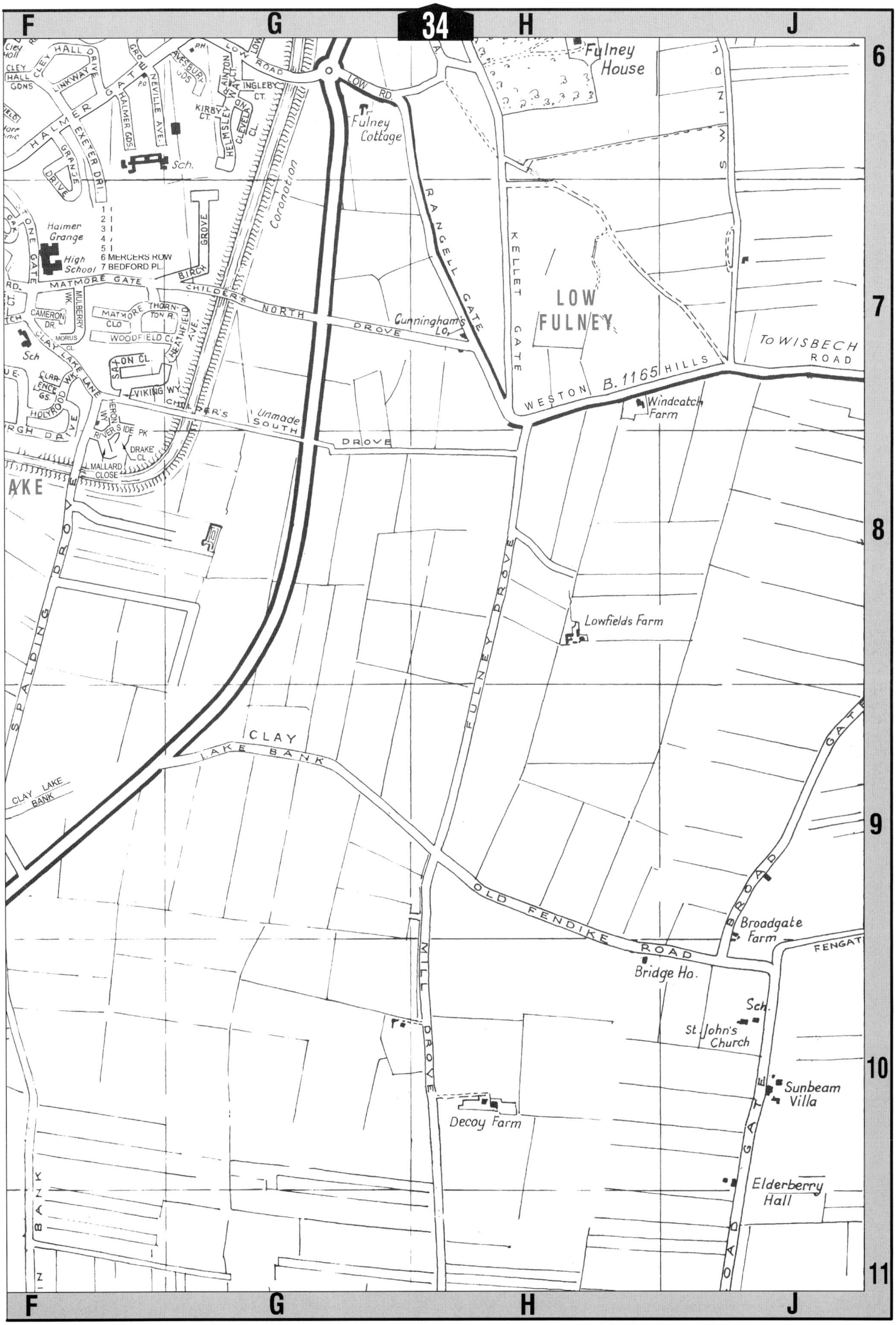
F
G
34
H
J
6
7
8
9
10
11
Fulney House
Fulney Cottage
LOW ROAD
LOW RD.
HALL DRIVE
CLEY HALL GDNS
LINKWAY
HALMER GATE
HALMER GDS.
NEVILLE AVE.
AYLESBURY GDS
KIRBY CT.
HELMSLEY WAY
RAINTON CT.
CLEVELAND CL.
INGLEBY CT.
EXETER DRI.
GRANGE DRIVE
Sch.
Halmer Grange
High School
6 MERCERS ROW
7 BEDFORD PL.
BIRCH GROVE
Coronation
RANGELL GATE
KELLET GATE
SWINDL
MATMORE GATE
CHILDER'S NORTH DROVE
Cunningham's Lo.
LOW FULNEY
MULBERRY WK.
CAMERON DR.
MORUS CL.
MATMORE CLO
THORNTON R.
HEATHFIELD AVE.
WOODFIELD CL.
SAXON CL.
VIKING WY.
CLARENCE GS.
CLAY LAKE LANE
HOLYROOD WK.
Sch
HERON WY.
RIVERSIDE PK
DRAKE CL
MALLARD CLOSE
CHILDER'S SOUTH DROVE
Unmade
WESTON HILLS
B.1165
To WISBECH ROAD
Windcatch Farm
SPALDING DROVE
FULNEY DROVE
Lowfields Farm
CLAY LAKE BANK
OLD FENDIKE ROAD
BROADGATE
Broadgate Farm
FENGATE
Bridge Ho.
MILL DROVE
Sch.
St John's Church
Sunbeam Villa
Decoy Farm
Elderberry Hall
BANK

SPALDING INDEX TO STREETS

Aalsmeer Rise D.7
Abbey Passage E.6
Abbot's Way C.7
Acacia Avenue F.6
Acklam Avenue G.5
Aintree Drive D.8
Akita Close C.6
Albert Street F.6
Albion Street F.6
Aldwych Gardens C.8
Alexandra Road F.7
Ambleside Drive D.7
Amstel Close D.7
Amsterdam Gardens D.7
Angelica Drive D.5
Annette Close D.6
Appledorn Gardens D.7
Armstrong Road E.7
Arnhem Drive B.5
Ascot Close D.8
Ash Court F.5
Ashtree Lane G.4
Atton Avenue G.5
Avesbury Gardens G.6
Avignon Road D.5
Ayscough Avenue F.7

Balmoral Avenue E.7
Banbury Close F.5
Banks Avenue G.5
Barge Close F.5
Barrier Bank E.10
Bath Lane F.6
Baxter Gardens E.5
Bear Lane D.2
Beaufort Drive E.7
Beckett Drive E.5
Bedford Place E.6
Beech Avenue G.5
Beecham Mews D.7
Beechfield Gardens F.6
Belcanto Court D.6
Belgrave Road D.8
Belisana Road C.6
Bellfield Close D.7
Belvedere Close D.8
Benner Road F.3
Bentinck Close E.5
Birch Grove G.7
Birkdale Close E.8
Blue Gowt Drain E.3
Blue Gowt Drove C.4
Blue Gowt Lane D.4
Bourne Road E.7
Bowditch Road F.7
Bramble Grange D.5
Brayfields D.3
Breda Court D.7
Brendon Walk D.5
Bridge Street E.6
Britannia Gardens E.6
Broad Gate J.11
Broad Street E.6
Broadway C.7
Brownlow Crescent D.2
Browns Gate D.6
Brunel Road F.4
Burma Avenue D.3
Burr Lane E.9
Buttercup Close C.7

Camel Gate G.4
Cameron Drive F.7
Campbell's Close D.8
Campion Close D.5
Canterbury Close D.6
Captains Beck E.2
Captains Drain E.2
Carlton Close D.8
Carnoustie Crescent E.8
Carrington Close D.6
Carrington Road D.6
Castle Fields E.5
Cathedral Drive E.5
Cavendish Way D.5
Cedar Court F.7
Chaldean Way D.5
Chamber's Court F.6
Chancery Court E.7
Chapel Lane E.6
Charlette Way D.6
Chaucers Way C.6
Chepstow Close D.8
Cherry Holt Lane D.3
Cherry Tree Grove F.5
Chestnut Avenue F.5
Childers South Drove G.7
Childers North Drove G.7
Chiltern Drive F.5
Church Gate E.7
Church Street,
Pinchbeck E.2
Church Street, Spalding F.6
Church Walk E.2
Churchill Drive E.7
Clarence Gardens F.7
Claudette Avenue D.6
Claudette Way D.5
Clay Drove A.6
CLAY LAKE F.8
Clay Lake Bank F.9
Clay Lake Lane F.7
Cleveland Close G.6
Cley Hall Drive F.6
Cley Hall Gardens F.6
Clover Way D.5
Clumber Drive E.5
Clydesdale Crescent C.7
Columbus Close E.8
Commercial Road F.6
Cook Drive E.7
Cook Way G.5
Corinne Crescent D.7
Coronation Close G.5
Cowbitt Road E.8
Cradge Bank Road D.9
Creswell Close F.4
Cross Gate H.6
Cross Gate J.3
Cross Lane A.1
Cross Street E.7
CROSSGATE E.1
Crossgate Crescent E.2
Crossgate Lane E.2
Crown Drive G.5
Culpins Close G.6

Daniels Gate D.5
Daniels Reach E.5
Darley's Lane C.5
Dawson Avenue G.5
Delph Court D.7
Double Street F.6
Dowgate Close D.7
Dozen's Bank A.6
Drake Close D.7
Drake Close F.8
Drapers Place E.6
Drian Bank F.11

East Road A.7
East Road(Luck's Bridge) D.11
Edinburgh Drive F.7
Edison Court F.4
Edward Road D.6
Edwina Avenue E.3
Ellen Crescent D.7
Elm Lane H.5
Enterprise Way E.4
Estella Way D.6
Euston Avenue D.8
Exeter Drive F.6

Fairfield Close E.5
Fairview Way E.5
Fantail Close D.10
Farrier Way C.7
Farthingales D.5
FEN END E.9
Fen End Lane E.9
Fen Gate A.4
Fen Gate Road B.4
Fengate Drive J.10
Fennel Road D.3
Fern Drive E.4
First Avenue D.6
First Drove D.10
Flax Mill Lane E.1
Gleming Road F.4
Floriade Close D.7
Forge Crescent D.2
Foundry Lane E.6
Francis Street E.6
FULNEY G.5
Fulney Avenue G.5
Fulney Drove H.9
Fulney Lane G.5

Gallery Walk D.2
Galway Close D.5
Gamlyn Close E.7
Gaunt Close G.5
Georgette Gardens D.5
Glebe Close C.6
Glen Avenue D.2
Glenn Avenue E.6
Glenside North A.3
Glenside South A.3
Goodfellow Road C.9
Gore Lane E.6
Grange Drive F.6
Green Lane E.7
Greenrigg Gardens F.5
Grevel Close D.5
Grove Close D.2
Guildhall Drive D.2

Haarlem Court D.7
Hague Court D.7
Handkerchief Hall Drove D.11
Hall Place E.6
Halmer Gardens F.6
Halmer Gate F.6
Halmer Paddock G.6
Hampton Close F.7
Hannam Boulevard D.6
Harlequin Drive C.6
Harpe Close D.3
Havelock Street E.7
Haverfield Road E.7
Hawthorn Bank D.8
Heathfield Avenue G.7
Helmsley Way G.6
Hennygate Drove E.3
Henrietta Street E.7
Henson Close D.7
Heren Place D.7
Hereward Road D.6
Heron Way F.7
Herring Lane D.2
Herring Lane E.6
High Fields Lane C.3
High Road (East) J.4
High Street F.6
Hoekman Drive D.7
Hoekman Way D.7
Holbeach Road F.5
Holborn Road D.7
Holland Road F.6
Holyrood Walk F.7
Honeysuckle Way D.7
Horse Fayre C.7
Horsepit Lane E.2
Horseshoe Road A.8
Hudson Road E.7
Hull's Drain C.9

Independence Drive E.3
Ingleby Court G.6

Jacobs Court D.5
Jasmine Court D.8
Johnson Avenue F.7
Jordan's Cradge
Bank Road A.10
Jubilee Close E.6
Juliasmead D.6

Kellet Gate H.7
Kelly Close D.3
Kempton Close D.8
Kensington Drive D.8
Kings Road E.6
Kirby Court G.6
Knight Street D.2
Knipe Avenue E.6

Laburnum Grove G.5
Ladywood Road F.5
Lancelot Way D.7
Langhole Drove D.1
Lansdowne Court G.5
Lavender Drive C.7
Law Court D.5
Laxton Gardens D.3
Lieden Fields D.7
Lilburn Drive E.5
Limberg Drive D.7
Lime Court F.7
Lincoln Way D.5
Lindbergh Drive D.7
Linden Court F.6
Linkway F.6
London Road,
(Little London) D.8
London Road E.7
Littleworth Drove C.11
Love Lane F.7
Lowfields Avenue G.6
LOW FULNEY H.7
Low Road G.6
Lucerne Close D.5
Lucette Way D.6

Magellan Way E.7
Mallard Close F.8
Mallory Drive E.7
Malvern Avenue F.5
Malvern Close F.5
Manor Close E.8
Mansell Close D.6
Manor Close E.8
Maple Grove F.6
Marine Road F.6
Market Place E.6
Market Way E.3
Marlborough Avenue F.7
Marsh Rails Road F.5
Marsh Road G.4
Maryette Way D.5
Matmore Close F.7
Matmore Gate F.7
May Blossom Walk D.7
Mayfair Drive D.8
Mayfield Close D.3
Maytime Close D.6
Meadow Close E.1
Meadow Close F.5
Meadway C.6
Meadowgate Lane D.6
Medlock Crescent G.6
Mendip Close D.5
Mercers Row E.6
Miles Bank E.4
Mill Green Road C.5
Mill Drove H.10
Money Bridge Lane A.3
Monkhouse Court C.7
Monks House Lane C.6
Monks Walk C.6
Moortoft Lane E.4
Morus Close F.7
Mountbatten Avenue D.3
Muirfield Close E.7
Mulberry Walk F.7

Nene Court G.5
Neville Avenue F.6
New Bond Street E.6
New River Drove D.9
New Road E.6
Nicolette Way D.6
North Gate B.2

Oak Court F.7
Oakland Way E.2
Oakley Drive F.5
Old Fendike Road H.9
Old Fen Lane C.2
Oldham Drive E.2
Orchard Street E.7
Osier Road F.6

Paddock Green E.6
Park Avenue E.5
Park Close E.5
Park Engine Drain B.7
Park Lane E.6
Park Road E.6
Parkside Crescent E.6
Patriot Close E.6
Paulette Court D.6
Pennine F.5
Penny Gate D.6
Penny Toft Lane D.3
Pennyfield D.3
Pennyhill Close F.5
Penway Drive D.3
Percheron Drive D.7
Pilgrims Way D.6
Pilmore Lane H.6
PINCHBECK D.2
Pinchbeck Road E.5
Pinchbeck Street E.6
Poachers Gate E.2
PODE HOLE A.7
Poplar Court D.6
Primrose Crescent D.3
Primrose Way C.7
Priory Road E.7
Prior Street E.6
Pudding Lane F.3
Pump Hole Drain F.11

Quaker Lane D.7
Queens Avenue G.5
Queens Road G.6

Raceground D.9
Rainton Court G.6
Raleigh Court E.7
Rangell Gate H.7
Ranville Close E.2
Red Lion Street E.6
Redmile Close E.3
Redmile Lane E.3
Redthorne Close F.6
Regent Street E.7
Rembrandt Way D.7
Rivergate E.7
River Bank E.8
Riverside D.5
Riverside Park F.7
Roman Bank G.5
Rood's Lane J.3
Rose Lane D.3
Rotten Row D.2
Rowan Avenue F.6
Royce Road G.5
Rutland Close F.6

St. Andrews Road E.8
St. Annes Close E.5
St. Annes Way E.5
St. James Way F.7
St. Johns Drive D.7
St. Johns Road D.7
St. Mary's Avenue D.3
St. Pauls Road F.5
Saddlers Mead D.7
Saint Thomas's Road E.7
Sandown Close D.9
Sandringham Walk F.7
Saxon Close F.7
Second Avenue D.6
Severn Road G.5
Sezanne Walk E.5
Shearers Drive D.7
Sheep Market E.6
Sheila Crescent D.7
Sherwood Drive E.5
Shire Avenue D.5
Short Street E.6
Shotbolt Lane F.3
Smithdale Close E.5
Snowdrop Place C.6
Sorrel Drive C.5
South Parade E.7
Southgate D.3
Spalding Common D.10
Spalding Grove F.9
Spalding Road E.3
Speyer Avenue E.5
Spring Gardens E.6
Spring Street E.7
Station Approach E.6
Station Street E.6
Stennet Avenue D.10
Stephenson Avenue F.4
Steppingstone Walk E.6
Stone Gate F.7
Stumps Lane H.4
Sunningdale Avenue E.8
Swan Street E.6
Swindlers Drove J.6

Tanglewood Cedar Falls D.8
Tavistock Road D.8
Thames Road G.5
The Cantry C.6
The Chase D.3
The Chase H.2
The Crescent E.6
The Green F.6
The Grove E.5
The Meadows E.2
The Parkway D.7
The Ramper D.9
The Sycamores D.8
The Wende D.7
The Wyke D.7
Third Avenue D.6
Thompson Close E.7
Thornton Road F.7
Tollgate E.6
Tower Lane F.7
Town Farm Close E.2
Truro Way E.6
Two Plank Lane D.5
Tydd Road B.5

Van Goch Drive D.7
Vernatts Green E.5
Viceroy Drive E.3
Victoria Street E.6
Victory Court E.6
Viking Way F.7
Vine Street E.6

Wardentree Lane E.3
Water Lane E.7
Wavet Road D.3
Wedgewood Drive D.5
Welbeck Drive E.6
Welland Close E.7
Wellands E.7
Wensum Close G.5
Wentworth Close E.8
West Elloe Avenue E.5
West Marsh Road G.5
West Parade D.6
West Road B.9
Westbourne Gardens E.7
Westelloe Avenue F.5
Westerly Way D.5
Westfield Drive D.2
Westlode Street F.6
Westminster Drive D.8
Weston Hills Road H.7
Willesby Road F.5
Willow Walk F.6
Wimberley Way D.3
Windsor Drive E.7
Winfrey Avenue E.6
Winsover Road D.7
Wintergold Avenue C.5
Woodfield Close F.7
Woolram Wygate D.5
WYKEHAM H.2
Wykeham Lane J.3
Wygate Park D.5
Wygate Road D.6
Wyngate Meadows D.5

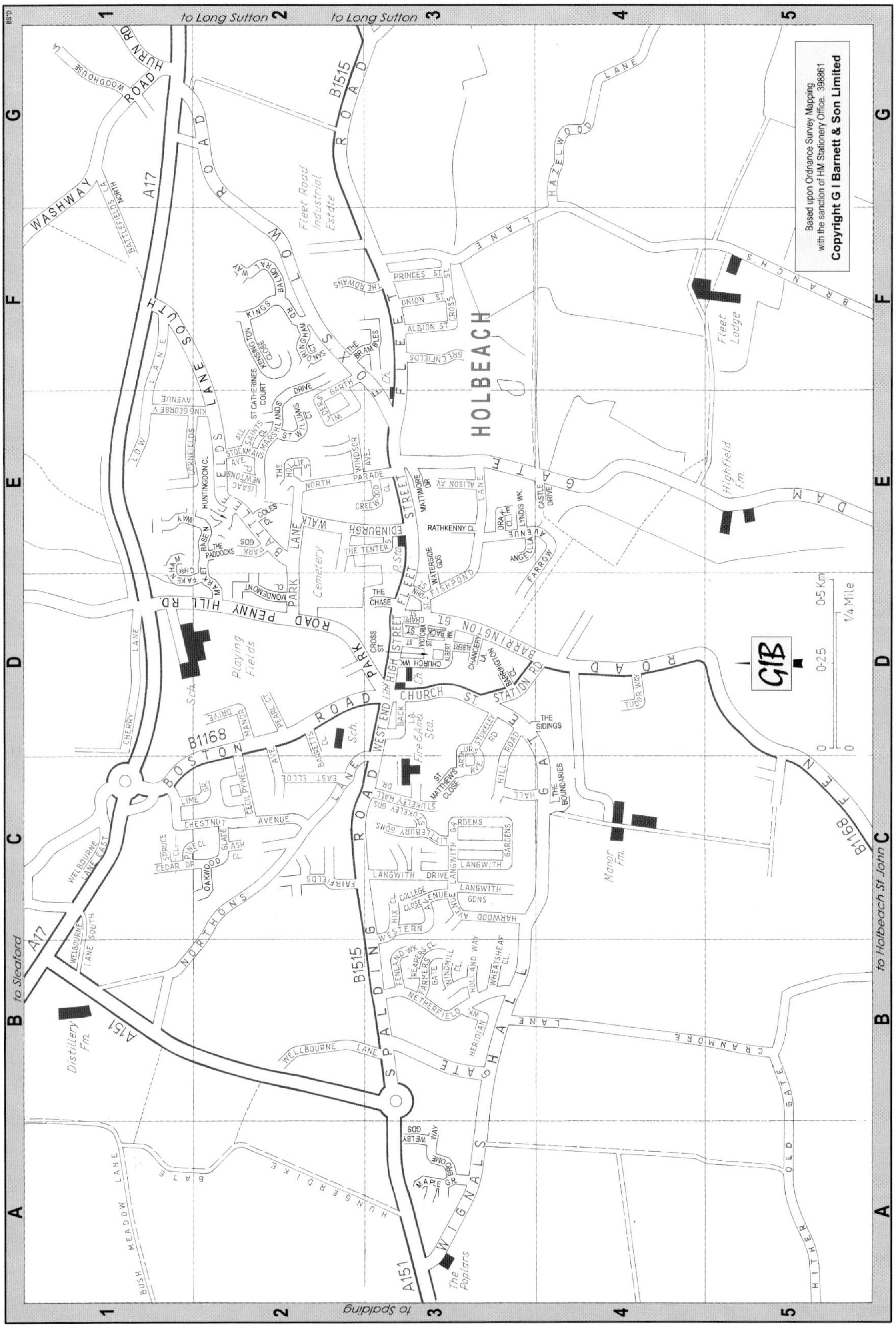

HOLBEACH INDEX TO STREETS

Albert Street D.3
Albert Walk D.3
Albion Street F.3
Alison Avenue E.3
All Saints Close E.2
Angell Lane E.3
Arthurs Avenue C.3
Ash Close C.2

Back Lane D.3
Back Street D.3
Balmoral Way F.2
Barretts Close C.2
Barrington Close D.3
Barrington Gate D.3
Battlefields Lane North F.1
Battlefields Lane South E.2
Boston Road C.1
Branch's Lane F.5
Broome Way A.3
Bush Meadow Lane A.1

Castle Drive E.4
Cecil Pywell C.2
Cedar Drive C.1
Chancery Lane D.3
Chapel Street D.3
Cherry Lane D.1
Chestnut Avenue C.1
Church Street D.3
Church Walk D.3
Coles Close E.2
College Close C.3
Cornfields E.1
Cranmore Lane B.5
Creewood Close E.2
Cross Street D.3
Cross Street F.3

Dam Gate E.5
Drakes Close E.3

East Elloe Avenue C.2
Edinburgh Walk E.3

Fairfields C.2
Fakenham Chase D.2
Farmers Gate B.3
Farrow Avenue D.3
Fenland Walk B.3
Fen Road C.5
Fishpond Lane D.3
Fleet Road F.3
Fleet Street D.3
Fox's Low Road F.2

Greenfields F.3

Hall Gate B.3
Hall Hill Farm C.3
Harwood Avenue C.3
Hazelwood Lane G.4
Heridian Walk B.3
High Street D.3
Hither Old Gate A.5
Hix Close C.3
Holland Way B.3
Hungerdike Gate A.3
Huntingdon Close E.2
Hurn Road G.1

Isaac Newton's Close E.2

Kensington Close F.2
King George V Avenue E.2
Kings Road F.2

Langwith Drive C.3
Langwith Gardens C.3
Lime Grove C.1
Littlebury Gardens C.3
Low Lane E.1
Lyndis Walk E.3

Market Rasen Way D.2
Manor Drive D.2
Marshlands Drive E.2
Maple Grove A.3
Mondemont Close D.2

Netherfield B.3
Northon's Lane B.1
North Parade E.2

Oakwood Glade C.2

Park Gardens E.2
Park Lane D.2
Park Road D.2
Pearl Court D.2
Penny Hill Road D.2
Pine Close C.1
Princes Street F.3

Rathkenny Close E.3
Reapers Close B.3

St. Catherines Court F.2
St. John Street D.3
St. Matthew's Close C.3
St. Williams Court E.2
Sandringham Court F.2
Spalding Road B.3
Spruce Close C.1
Station Road D.3
Stockmans Avenue E.2
Stukeley Gardens C.3
Stukeley Hall Drive C.3
Stukeley Road D.3

The Boundaries C.4
The Brambles F.2
The Chase D.3
The Hollies E.2
The Paddocks E.2
The Rowans F.3
The Sidings C.5
The Tenters E.2
Tudor Way D.4

Union Street F.3

Victoria Street D.3

Washway Road F.1
Waterside Gardens D.3
Welbourne Lane East C.1
Welbourne Lane South B.1
Welbourne Lane B.2
Welby Gardens A.3
West Road D.3
Western Avenue C.3
Wheatsheaf Close B.3
Wignals Gate A.3
Wilders Garth E.2
Windmill Close B.3
Windsor Avenue E.2
Woodhouse Lane G.1

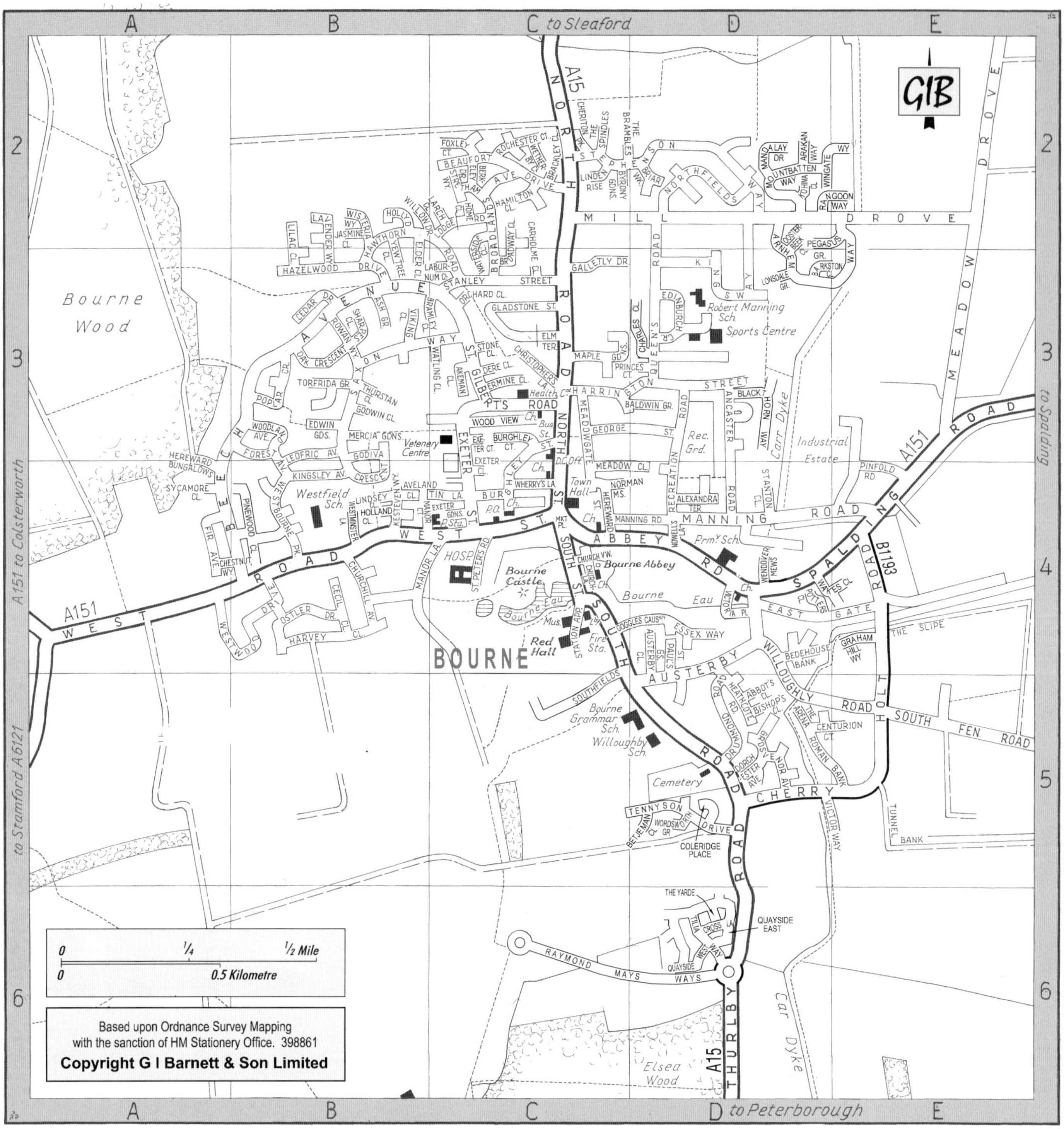

BOURNE INDEX TO STREETS

Abbey Road C.4
Abbot's Close D.5
Akeman Close C.3
Alexandra Terrace D.4
Ancaster Road D.3
Arnhem Way D.2
Ash Grove B.3
Austerby D.5
Austerby Close D.4
Aveland Close B.4

Baldwin Grove D.3
Barkston Close D.3
Beaufort Drive C.2
Bedehouse Bank D.4
Beech Avenue A.4
Berkeley Drive C.2
Bishop's Close D.5
Blackthorn Way D.3
Bourne Abbey C.4
Bourne Castle C.4
Bourne Hospital D.6
Brackley Close C.2
Bramley Close C.3
Briar Walk D.2
Broadlands Avenue . . . C.3
Broadway Close C.3
Burgheley Court C.3
Burghley Street C.4
Byrony Gardens C.2

Carholme Close C.2
CAWTHORPE B.1
Cecil Close B.4
Cedar Drive B.3
Centurion Court D.5
Charles Close D.3
Cheriton Park C.2
Cherry Holt Road E.5
Chestnut Way A.4
Christopher's Lane C.3
Church Lane C.4
Church View C.4
Churchill Avenue B.4
Cross Lane D.6

Dere Close C.3
Dorchester Avenue D.5
Drummond Road D.5

East Gate D.4
Edinburgh Crescent . . . D.3
Edwin Gardens B.3
Elder Close B.2
Elm Terrace C.3
Ermine Close C.3
Essex Way D.4
Exeter Close C.3
Exeter Court C.3
Exeter Gardens C.4
Exeter Street C.3

Fir Avenue A.4
Forest Avenue B.3
Foxley Court C.2
Galletly Drive C.3
George Street C.3
Gladstone Street C.3
Godiva Crescent B.3
Godwin Close B.3
Goggles Causeway D.4
Grosvenor Avenue D.5

Hamilton Close C.2
Harrington Street C.3
Harvey Close B.4
Hawthorn Road B.3
Hazelwood Drive B.3
Heathcote Road D.5
Hereward Bungalows . . . A.3
Hereward Street C.4
Holland Close B.4
Holly Drive B.2
Home Close C.2

Jasmine Close B.2

Kesteven Way B.4
Kingsley Avenue B.4
Kingsway D.3

Laburnum Close C.3
Larch Close C.2
Lavender Way B.2
Leofric Avenue B.3
Lilac Close B.2
Linden Rise C.2
Lodge Road C.2
Lonsdale Grove D.3
Lyndsey Close B.4

Manning Road D.4
Manor Court B.4
Manor Lane B.4
Maple Garden C.3
Market Place C.4
Meadow Close C.4
Meadow Drove E.3
Meadowgate C.3
Mercia Gardens B.3
Mill Drove C.2

Norman Mews C.4
North Road C.2
North Street C.3
Northfields D.2
Nowell's Lane D.4

Oak Crescent B.3
Oosterbeek Close D.2
Orchard Close C.3
Ostler Drive B.4

Pegasus Grove D.2
Pinewood Close B.4
Pinfold Road E.4
Poplar Crescent B.3
Potters Close D.4
Princes Court C.3

Queen's Road D.3
Quayside East D.6
Quayside West D.6

Raymond Mays Way . . . D.6
Recreation Road D.4
Rochester Court C.2
Roman Bank D.5
Rowan Way B.3

St. Gilbert's Road C.3
St. Paul's Gardens D.4
St. Peter's Road C.4
Saxon Way B.3
Sharpes Close B.3
South Fen Road E.5
South Road C.4
South Street C.4
Southfields C.5
Spalding Road D.4
Stanley Street C.3
Stanton Close D.4
Station Approach C.4
Stephenson Way C.2
Stone Close C.3
Stretham Way C.2
Sycamore Close A.4

The Arena D.5
The Brambles C.2
The Slipe E.4
The Spindles C.2
The Yarde D.6
Thurlby Road D.6
Thurstan Close B.3
Tilia Way D.6
Tin Lane C.4
Torfrida Grove B.3
Tunnel Bank E.5

Victor Way E.5
Victoria Place D.4
Viking Close B.3

Waterside Close C.3
Watling Close C.3
Wendover Mews D.4
West Road A.4
West Street B.4
Westbourne Park B.4
Westminster lane B.4
Westwood Drive A.4
Wetherby Close C.2
Wherry's Lane C.4
Willoughby Road D.4
Willow Drive B.2
Wisteria Way B.2
Wood View C.3
Woodland Avenue B.3

Yew Tree Close B.2

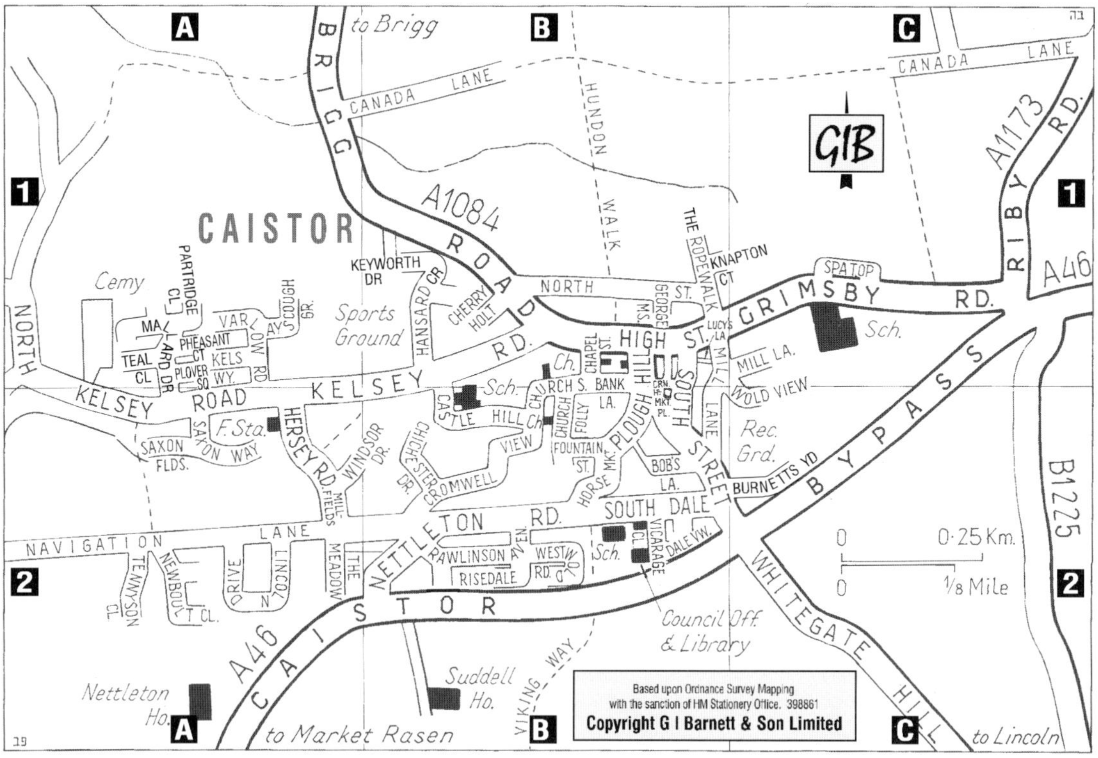

CAISTOR INDEX TO STREETS

Ayscough Grove ..A.1

Bank Lane B.1
Bob's Lane B.2
Brigg Road A.1
Burnetts yard C.2

Caistor By-Pass ..A.2
Canada Lane B.1
Castle Hill B.2
Chapel Street B.1
Cherry Holt B.1
Chichester Drive ..B.2
Church Folly B.2
Church Street B.2
Cornhill B.1
Cromwell View B.2

Dale View B.2

Fountain Street B.2

George Mews B.1
Grimsby Road C.1

Hasard Crescent ..B.1
Hersey Road A.2
High Street B.1
Horse Market B.2
Hundon Walk B.1

Kelsey Road A.2
Keis Way A.1
Keyworth Drive B.1
Knapton Court B.1

Lincoln Drive A.2
Lucy's Lane A.2

Mallard Drive A.1

Market Place B.2
Mill Lane B.1
Millfields A.2

Navigation Lane ..A.2
Nettleton Road B.2
Newboult Close A.2
North Kelsey Road A.1
North Street B.1

Patridge Close A.1
Pheasant Court A.1
Plough Hill B.2
Plover Square A.1

Rawlinson Avenue B.2
Riby Road C.1
Risedale B.2

Saxon Fields A.2
Saxon Way A.2
South Dale B.2
South Street B.1
Spa Top C.1

Teal Close A.1
Tennyson Close ..A.2
The Meadow A.2
The Ropewalk B.1

Varlow Road A.1
Vicarage Close B.2
Viking Way B.2

Westwood Road ..B.2
Whitegate Hill C.2
Windsor Drive A.2
Wold View C.2

MARKET DEEPING INDEX TO STREETS

Allen Close D.2
Althorpe Close B.3
Ascendale E.2

Back Lane E.2
Beaufort Avenue C.2
Beech Close B.2
Bell Lane D.3
Belton Close B.3
Belvoir Close A.2
Black Prince Avenue B.2
Blackthorn Close C.1
Blenheim Way B.1
Bluebells C.2
Bramley Road C.2
Bridge Street D.3
Broadgate Lane E.2
Brownlow Drive D.3
Bryony Way C.2
Burchall Close C.1
Burchnall Close C.2
Burghley Close E.3
Burnside Avenue B.2
Buttercup Court C.1

Campion Drive C.1
Cedar Close B.3
Chatsworth Close A.2
Cherry Grove C.2
Chestnut Way B.2
Church Gate E.2
Church Street, Deeping St. James D.3
Church Street, Market Deeping B.2
Clover Road C.2
Cowslip Drive C.1
Cromwell Way A.2
Crowfields E.2
Crowson Way C.2
Curlew Walk C.2

Deeping, St. James Road D.3
Deene Close A.2
Dixons Road C.3
Douglas Road C.3
Dovecote Road B.2

Eastfield C.2
Eastgate...............................E.3
Elm Close C.2
Ermine Way D.2
Exeter Close D.2

Fairfax Way D.3
Fenely Close D.2
Florence Way C.2
Forge Court B.2
Foxgloves C.2
Fraser Close C.2
Frognall E.1

Glebe View B.2
Godseys Crescent C.2
Godseys Lane B.2
Green Walk B.2
Grimsthorpe Close B.3

Halfleet A.2
Hall Farm B.2
Hall Meadow Road E.1
Hawthorne Close B.2
Hereward Way E.3
High Street C.3
Holland Close A.2
Holly Way D.2
Horsegate D.2

John Eve Way B.2
Joan Wake Close B.2

Kesteven Close C.2
Kesteven Drive A.2
Knight Close D.2

Lady Margarets Avenue C.2
Lamport Close A.2
Lancaster Drive B.1
Lark Rise C.2
Limetree Avenue A.2
Linchfield Close D.2
Linchfield Road C.1
Lincoln Close A.2
Lincoln Road C.3
Lindsey Avenue A.2

Linnet Close C.2

Manor Way C.2
Marigolds C.2
Maxey Close A.3
Maxey View C.3
Millfield Road, Deeping St. James D.2
Millfield Road, Market Deeping A.2

New Row D.3
Nightingales C.2
North Field Road A.1

Oak Grove B.2
Orchard Close D.3
Osbourne Way A.2

Panton Close D.2
Park Drive B.2
Park Estate D.2
Park Road D.2
Pawlett Close D.2
Peakirk Road D.3
Pendlebury Drive C.2
Peterborough Road A.1
Petworth Close A.2
Prestland B.2
Primroses C.2
Priory Close E.2

Queens Avenue C.2

Riverbank Close E.3
Riverside D.3
Robin Close C.2
Rockingham Close A.2
Rosemary Avenue C.2
Ryecroft Avenue E.2
Ryecroft Close E.2

St. Gulthlacs Avenue B.2
Sandringham Way A.2
Sewell Close D.2
Shackelton Close B.1
Sorrel Close C.1

Spalding Road D.2
Speedwell Court C.2
Stamford Close B.3
Stamford Road A.3
Stephens Way E.3
Still Close B.2
Stirling Way B.1
Suttons Lane C.3
Swallow Walk C.2
Sweet Close C.2
Swift Close D.2

Tattershall Drive A.2
Teasles C.2
Thackers Way C.2
The Avenue B.2
The Brambles C.1
The Grove B.2
The Lees D.2
The Meadows C.2
The Meadway B.2
The Orchard B.2
The Paddocks A.2
The Parslins E.2
The Pasture C.2
The Precincts C.3
The Spinney B.2
The Woodlands B.3
Thyme Close C.2
Towngate East A.2
Towngate Outgang B.1
Towngate West A.2
Towning Close D.2
Tyghes Close E.2

Wade Park Avenue C.2
Waterton Close D.3
Welland Way D.3
Wellington Way B.1
Whitley Way B.1
Willoughby Avenue C.2
Woburn Close A.2
Woodcroft Close A.3
Wren Close C.2

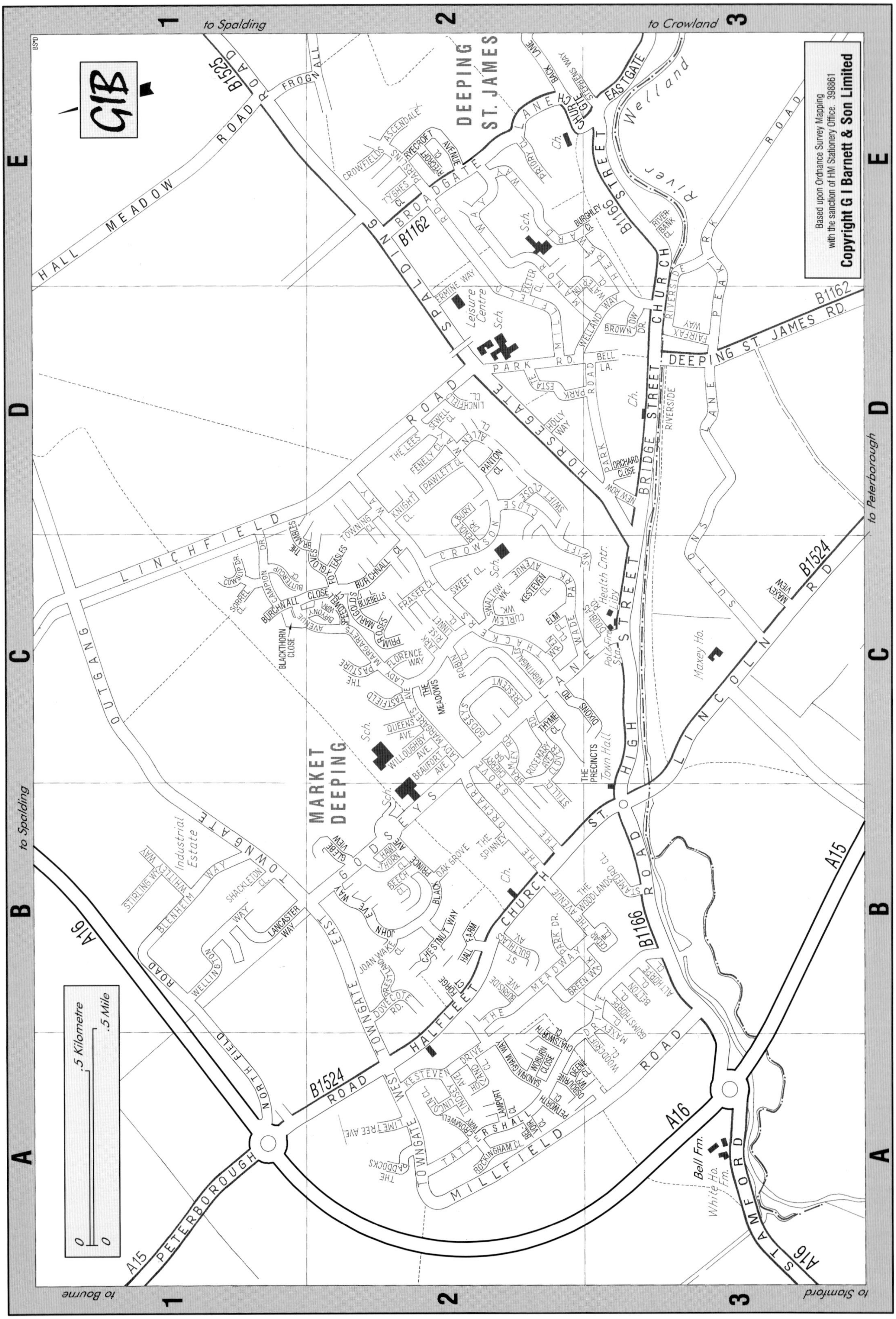

to Spalding
to Crowland
to Peterborough
to Stamford
to Bourne
DEEPING ST. JAMES
MARKET DEEPING
Based upon Ordnance Survey Mapping with the sanction of HM Stationery Office. 398861
Copyright G I Barnett & Son Limited
.5 Kilometre
.5 Mile
Industrial Estate
Leisure Centre
Health Cntr.
Library
Police Sta.
Fire Sta.
Town Hall
Maxey Ho.
Bell Fm.
White Ho. Fm.
River Welland
HALL MEADOW ROAD
LINCHFIELD ROAD
SPALDING GATE
HORSEGATE
BROADGATE
EASTGATE
CHURCH STREET
BRIDGE STREET
HIGH STREET
DEEPING ST. JAMES RD.
LINCOLN RD.
STAMFORD ROAD
PETERBOROUGH ROAD
MILLFIELD ROAD
HALFLEET
TOWNGATE
TOWNGATE EAST
TOWNGATE WEST
OUTGANG
GODSEYS LANE
NORTHFIELD ROAD
PARK RD.
PEAKIRK ROAD
SUTTONS LANE
A15
A16
B1162
B1166
B1524
B1525

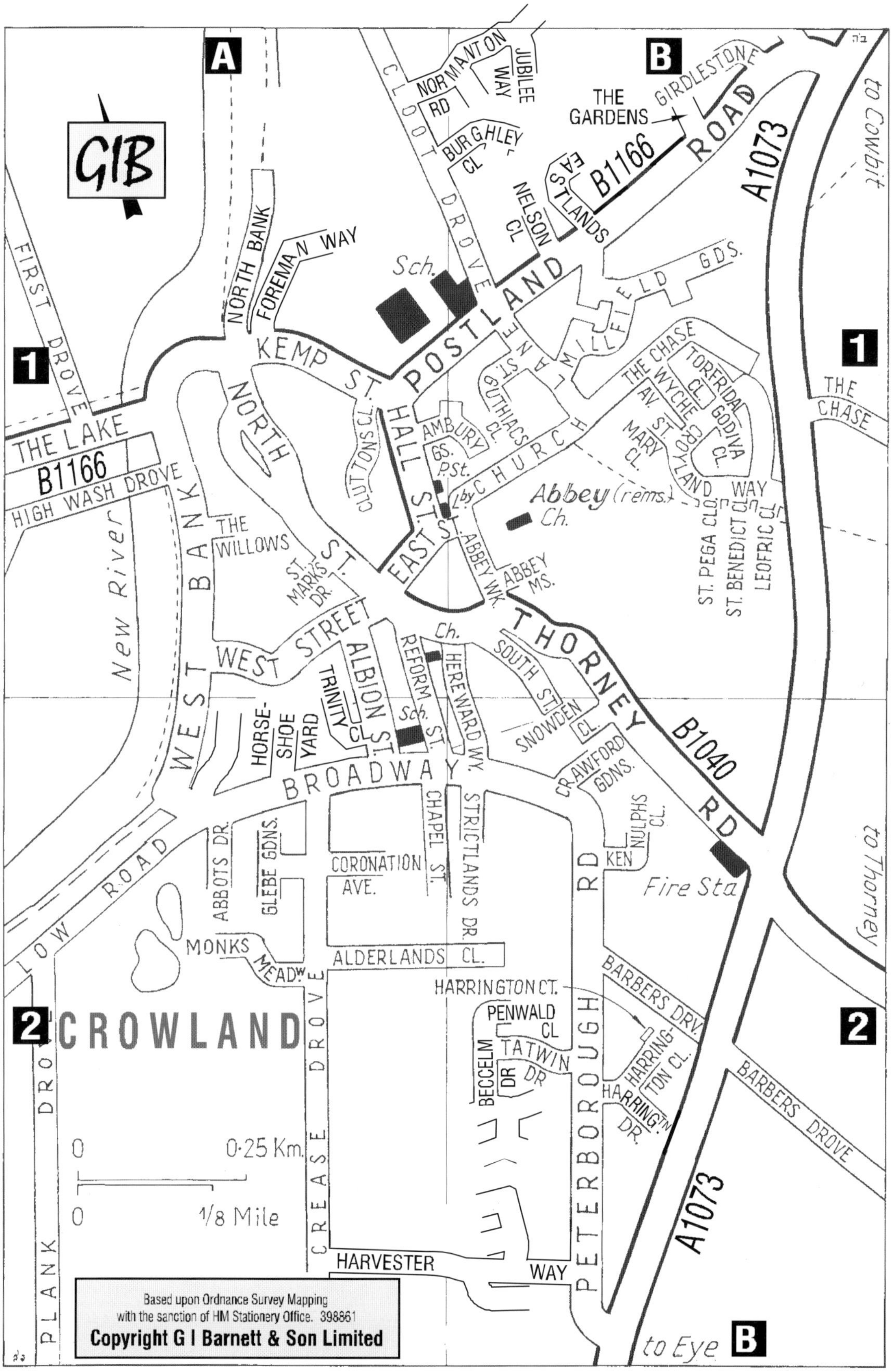

CROWLAND INDEX TO STREETS

Abbey Mews B.1
Abbey Walk B.1
Abbots Drive A.2
Albion Street A.1
Alderlands Close A.2
Ambury Gardens A.1

Barbers Drove B.2
Beccelm Drive B.2
Broadway A.2
Burghley Close B.1

Chapel Street A.2
Church Lane B.1
Cloot Drove A.1
Cluttons Close A.1
Coronation Avenue A.2
Crawford Gardens B.2
Crease Drove A.2
Croyland Way B.1

East Street A.1
Eastlands B.1

First Drove A.1
Foreman Way A.1

Girdlestone B.1
Glebe Gardens A.2
Godiva Close B.1

Hall Street A.1
Harrington Close B.2
Harrington Court B.2
Harrington Drive B.2
Harvester Way A.2
Hereward Way B.1
High Wash Drove A.1
Horseshoe Yard A.2

Jubilee Way B.1

Kemp Street A.1
Ken Nulphs Close B.2

Leofric Close B.1
Low Road A.2

Millfield Gardens B.1
Monks Meadow A.2
Nelson Close B.1
Normanton Road A.1
North Bank A.1
North Street A.1

Penwald Close B.2
Peterborough Road B.2
Plank Drove A.2
Postland Road A.1

Reform Street A.1

St. Benedict Clost B.1
St. Guthiacs Close B.1
St. Mark's Drive A.1
St. Mary Close B.1
St. Pega Close B.1
Snowden Close B.2
South Street B.1
Strictlands Drive B.2

Tatwin Drive B.2
The Chase B.1
The Gardens B.1
The Lake A.1
The Willows A.1
Thorney Road B.1
Torfridal Close B.1
Trinity Close A.2

West Bank A.2
West Street A.1
Wyche Avenue B.1

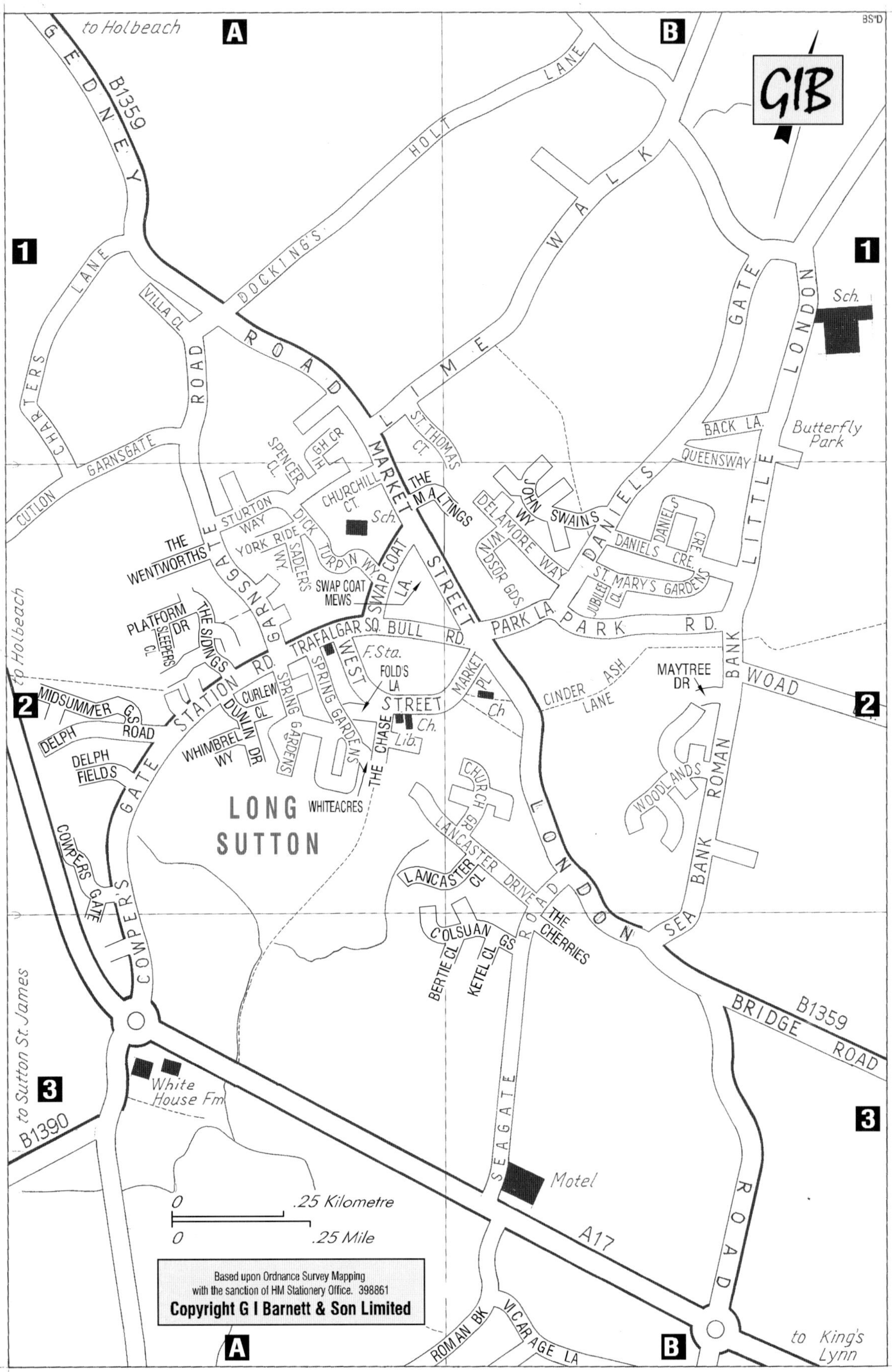

LONG SUTTON INDEX TO STREETS

Back Lane ... B.1
Bertie Close ... B.3
Bridge Road ... B.3
Bull Road ... A.2

Charters Lane ... A.1
Church Green ... B.2
Churchill Court ... A.2
Cinder Ash Lane ... B.2
Colsuan Gardens ... B.3
Cowper's Gate ... B.3
Curlew Close ... A.2
Culton Garnsgate ... A.2

Daniels Crescent ... B.2
Daniels Gate ... B.2
Delamore Way ... B.2
Delph Fields ... A.2
Delph Road ... A.2
Dick Turpin Way ... A.2
Docking's Holt Lane ... A.1
Dunlin Drive ... A.2

Fold's Lane ... A.2

Garnsgate Road ... A.2
Gadney Road ... A.1

High Crescent ... A.1

John Swains Way ... B.2
Jubilee Close ... B.2

Ketel Close ... B.3

Lancaster Close ... A.2
Lancaster Drive ... B.2
Lane Walk ... A.1
Little London ... B.2
London Road ... B.2

Market Place ... A.1
Market Street ... A.1
Maytree Drive ... B.2
Midsummer Gardens ... A.2

Park Lane ... B.2
Park Road ... B.2
Platform Drive ... A.2

Queensway ... B.1

Roman Bank ... A.3
Roman Bank ... B.2

St. Mary's Gardens ... B.2
St. Thomas Court ... A.1
Sadler's Way ... A.2
Sea Bank ... B.3
Seagate Road ... B.3
Sleepers Close ... A.2
Spencer Close ... A.1
Spring Gardens ... A.2
Station Road ... A.2
Sturton Way ... A.2
Swap Coat Lane ... A.2
Swap Coat Mews ... A.2

The Chase ... A.2
The Cherries ... B.3
The Maltings ... A.2
The Sidings ... A.2
The Wentworths ... A.2
Trafalgar Square ... A.2

Vicarage Lane ... B.3
Villa Close ... A.1

West Street ... A.2
Whimbrel Way ... A.2
Whiteacres ... A.2
Windsor Gardens ... B.2
Woad Lane ... B.2
Woodlands ... B.2

York Ride ... A.2

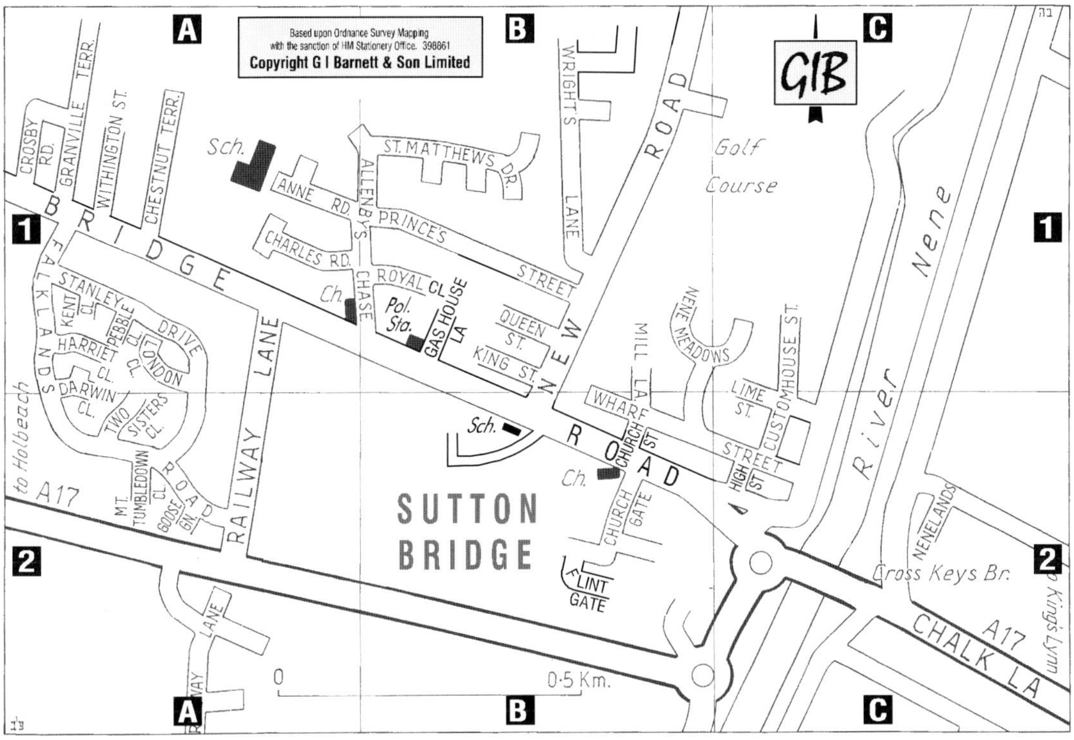

SUTTON BRIDGE INDEX TO STREETS

Allenbys Chase ..B.1
Anne Road A.1

Bridge Road A.1

Chalk Lane C.2
Charles Road A.1
Chestnut Terrace A.1
Church Gate B.2
Church Street C.2
Crosby Road A.1
Cross Keys Bridge C.2
Custom House Street C.2

Darwin Close A.2

Falklands Road ..A.1
Flint Gate B.2

Gas House Lane B.1
Goose Green A.2
Granville Terrace A.1

Harriet Close A.1

Kent Close A.1
King Street B.1

Lime Street C.2
London Close A.1

Mill Lane B.1
Mount Tumbledown Close A.2
Nene Meadows ..B.1
Nenelands C.2
New Road B.1

Pebble Close A.1
Prince's Street B.1

Queen Street B.1

Railway Lane A.2
Royal Close B.1

St. Matthews Drive B.1
Stanley Drive A.1

Two Sisters Close A.2

Wharf Street B.2
Withington Street A.1
Wright's Lane B.1

ALFORD INDEX TO STREETS

Ailby Lane A.1

Beechings Way A.2
Bilsby Road C.1
Bourne Road B.1

Candlehouse Lane B.1
Caroline Street ..B.1
Carr Lane B.1
Chapel Street B.1
Chauntry Road ..A.2
Christopher Road A.1
Church Street C.1
Coles Avenue A.1
Commercial Road B.1

Dashwood Road B.1
Dixon Drive A.1

East Street C.1
Evison Close A.1

Farlesthorpe Road B.2
Finsbury Street B.2

Hallam close A.1
Hamilton Road ..B.1
Hanby Lane C.2
Higgins Road A.1
High Street B.1
Holywell Road B.2

Kennedy Avenue A.2

Marbury Close ..B.2
Mill Close C.1
Mill Rundle Walk C.1
Millers Way C.1
Mountpleasant ..B.2

Nursery Gardens B.1

Old Bowling Green B.1

Park Lane B.1
Park Road B.1
Parsons Lane B.1
Ranters Row B.1
Rawnsley Close B.2
Robinson Avenue A.1

Seymour Lane ..B.2
South Market B.1
South Street B.2
Spanning Drive B.2
Spendluffe Avenue C.1
Station Road A.1
Staveley Road ..A.1
Stephenson Close A.1

Temple Close A.1
The Maltings C.1
Tothby Close A.1
Tothby Lane A.1
Tothby Meadows A.1

Waumsley Way A.1
West Street B.1
Westfields B.1
Willoughby Road B.2
Windmill Lane B.1
Wood Road B.2

ALFORD

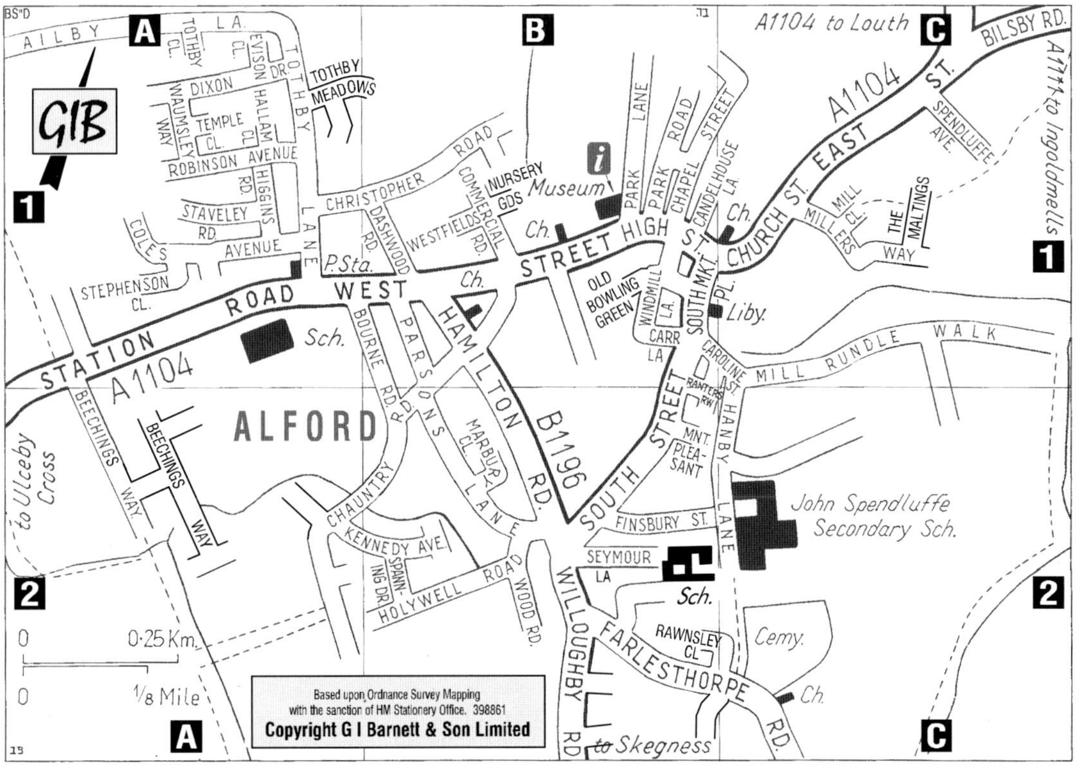

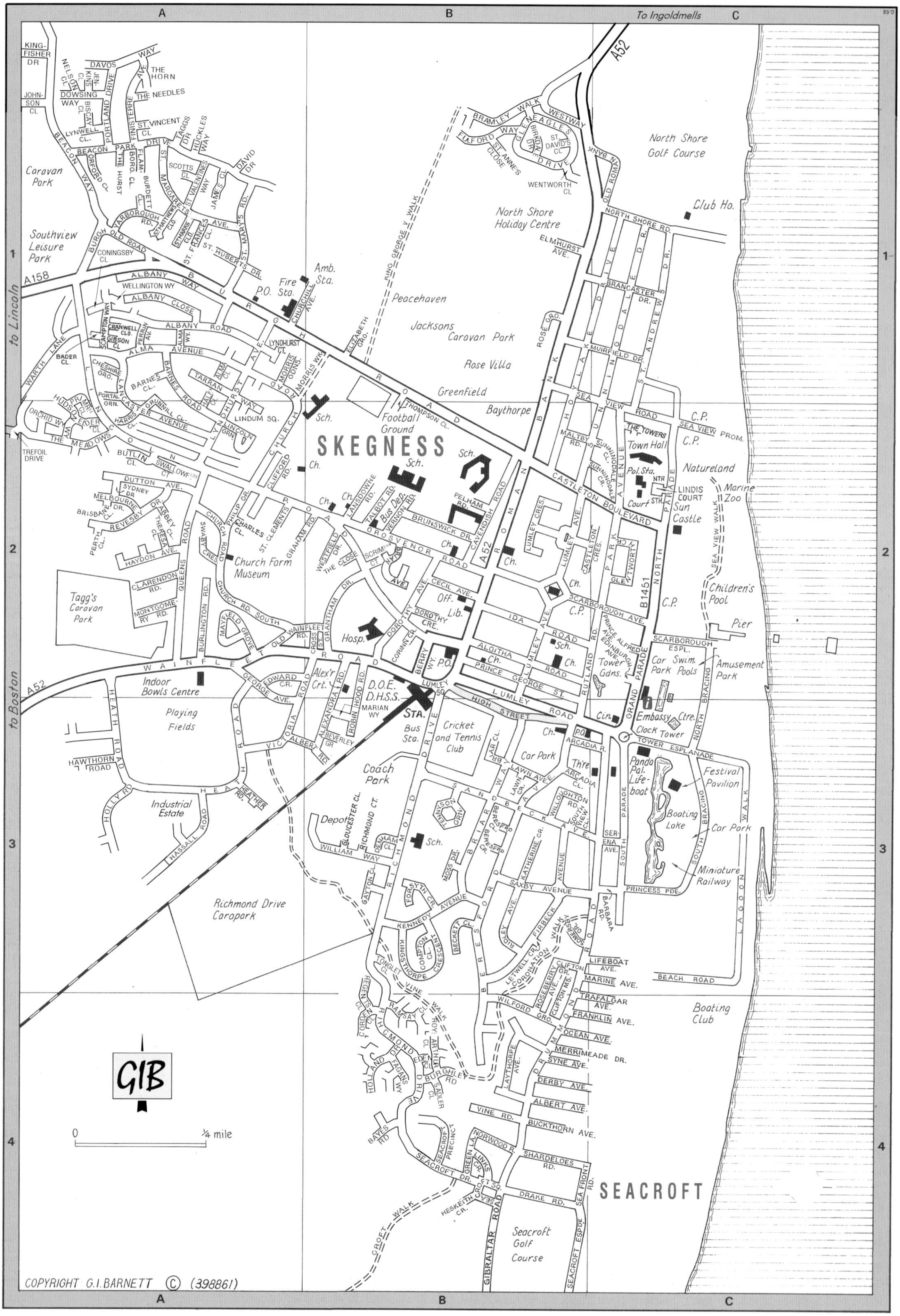
A
B
C
1
2
3
4
To Ingoldmells
A52
A158
to Lincoln
to Boston
SKEGNESS
SEACROFT
North Shore Golf Course
Club Ho.
North Shore Holiday Centre
Caravan Park
Southview Leisure Park
Peacehaven
Jacksons Caravan Park
Rose Villa
Greenfield
Baythorpe
Football Ground
Fire Sta.
Amb. Sta.
P.O.
Sch.
Ch.
Bus Dep.
Town Hall
Pol. Sta.
Court
Natureland
Marine Zoo
Sun Castle
Children's Pool
Pier
C.P.
Church Farm Museum
Tagg's Caravan Park
Hosp.
Off.
Lib.
Alex'r Crt.
D.O.E. D.H.S.S.
STA.
Bus Sta.
Cricket and Tennis Club
Car Park
Th're
Cin.
Embassy Ctre.
Clock Tower
Car Swim. Park Pools
Amusement Park
Tower Gdns.
Festival Pavilion
Panda Pal.
Life-boat
Boating Lake
Miniature Railway
Coach Park
Depot
Indoor Bowls Centre
Playing Fields
Industrial Estate
Richmond Drive Carapark
Boating Club
Seacroft Golf Course
ROMAN BANK
ROMAN BANK
NORTH PARADE
SOUTH PARADE
GRAND PARADE
HIGH STREET
LUMLEY ROAD
WAINFLEET ROAD
ALBANY ROAD
ALMA AVENUE
CASTLETON BOULEVARD
SCARBOROUGH AVE.
TOWER ESPLANADE
SEA VIEW ROAD
NORTH SHORE RD.
DRUMMOND ROAD
RICHMOND DRIVE
BERESFORD AVENUE
GIBRALTAR ROAD
SEA FRONT RD.
SEACROFT ESPDE.
GRAND PARADE
LIFEBOAT AVE.
MARINE AVE.
TRAFALGAR AVE.
FRANKLIN AVE.
OCEAN AVE.
MERRIMEADE DR.
SYNE AVE.
DERBY AVE.
ALBERT AVE.
BUCKTHORN AVE.
SHARDELOES RD.
DRAKE RD.
BEACH ROAD
SAXBY AVENUE
KENNEDY AVENUE
WILLIAM WAY
HEATH ROAD
HAWTHORN ROAD
HOLLY RD.
HASSALL ROAD
HEATHER RD.
PRINCESS PDE.
ROSE GRO.
BRANCASTER DR.
MUIRFIELD DR.
BRAMLEY WALK
FULFORD WAY
GLENEAGLES DR.
WESTWAY
WENTWORTH CL.
ELMHURST AVE.
CROFT WALK
KING GEORGE V WALK
SEA VIEW WALK
LAGOON WALK
BURGH ROAD
COPYRIGHT G.I.BARNETT © (398861)
0
¼ mile
GIB

SKEGNESS INDEX TO STREETS

Abbey Close ... A.2
Albany Close ... A.1
Albany Road ... A.1
Albany Way ... B.4
Albert Avenue ... B.4
Albert Road ... A.3
Alexandra Court ... B.3
Alexandra Road ... B.3
Algitha Road ... B.2
Alma Avenue ... A.1
Alma Close ... S.1
Alma Way ... A.1
Arcadia Close ... B.3
Arcadia Road ... B.3

Bader Way ... A.1
Barbara Road ... C.3
Barnes Close ... A.1
Bayes Road ... B.4
Beach Road ... C.3
Beacon Way ... A.1
Beckett Close ... B.3
Beresford Avenue ... B.3
Beresford Close ... B.3
Beresford Crescent ... B.3
Berry Way ... B.2
Beverley Grove ... B.3
Birkdale Drive ... B.1
Biscay Close ... A.1
Bramley Walk ... B.1
Brancaster Drive ... C.1
Brian Avenue ... B.2
Briar Close ... B.3
Briar Way ... B.3
Brisbane Way ... B.3
Brisbane Close ... A.2
Brunswick Drive ... B.2
Buckthorn Avenue ... B.4
Burdett Close ... A.1
Burgh Old Road ... A.1
Burgh Road ... A.1
Burghley Road ... B.4
Burlington Road ... A.2
Butlin Close ... A.2

Castleton Boulevard ... B.2
Castleton Crescent ... B.2
Cavendish Road ... B.2
Cecil Avenue ... B.2
Cheshire Grove ... A.1
Church Road ... A.2
Church Road South ... A.2
Churchill Avenue ... B.1
Clarendon Road ... A.2
Clifford Road ... A.2
Clifton Grove ... B.4
Clifton Mews ... B.4
Compton Close ... B.3
Coningsby Close ... A.1
Cordon Close ... B.4
Corinn Crescent ... B.2
Coronation Walk ... B.3
Cranwell Close ... A.1
Croft Walk ... B.4
Cross Street ... B.2

David Drive ... A.1
Davos Way ... A.1
Denham Close ... B.3
Derby Avenue ... B.4
Dorothy Avenue ... B.2
Dorothy Crescent ... B.2
Dowsing Way ... A.1
Drake Road ... B.4
Drummond Road ... B.4
Dutton Avenue ... A.2

Eden Close ... B.4
Edinburgh Avenue ... C.2
Edward Crescent ... A.2
Elizabeth Grove ... B.1
Elder Close ... A.2
Elmhurst Avenue ... B.1

Fagans Way ... B.4
Finisterre Avenue ... A.1
Firbeck Avenue ... B.3
Flamboro Close ... A.1
Forsyth Crescent ... B.3
Franklin Avenue ... B.4
Fulford Way ... B.1
Gayton Close ... B.3
George Avenue ... A.2
Gibraltar Road ... B.4
Gibson Place ... A.1
Gleneagles Drive ... B.1
Glentworth Crescent ... C.2
Gloucester Close ... B.3
Graham Road ... A.2
Grand Parade ... C.3
Grantham Drive ... B.2
Green Lane ... B.4
Grosvenor Road ... B.2
Grunnill Close ... A.2

Halifax Close ... A.2
Harris Close ... A.2
Hassall Road ... A.3
Hawthorn Road ... A.3
Haydon Avenue ... A.2
Heath Road ... A.3
Heather Road ... A.3
Heskeith Crescent ... B.4
High Street ... B.3
Holland Drive ... B.3
Holly Road ... A.3
Hoylake Drive ... B.2
Huckles Way ... A.1
Hudson Way ... A.1

Ida Road ... B.2

James Close ... A.1
Jenkins Close ... A.1
Johnson Close ... A.1

Katherine Crescent ... B.3
Kennedy Avenue ... B.3
King George V Walk ... B.1
Kingfisher Drive ... A.1
Kingsthorpe Crescent ... B.3

Lagoon Walk ... C.3
Lancaster Avenue ... A.1
Lansdowne Road ... B.2
Lawn Avenue ... B.3
Lawn Crescent ... B.3
Laythorpe Avenue ... B.4
Letwell Crescent ... B.3
Lifeboat Avenue ... C.3
Lincoln Gardens ... A.2
Lincoln Road ... A.1
Lindis Court (Nth & Sth) ... C.2
Lindum Square ... A.2
Links Grove ... B.4
Longhurst Drive ... A.2
Lumley Avenue ... B.2
Lumley Crescent ... B.2
Lumley Road ... B.2
Lumley Square ... B.2
Lyndhurst Avenue ... A.2
Lyndhurst Court ... A.1
Lynwell Close ... A.1

Maltby Road ... B.2
Marian Way ... B.3
Marine Avenue ... B.3
Mayfield Grove ... A.2
Melbourne Drive ... A.2
Merrimeade Drive ... B.4
Montgomery Road ... A.2
Morris Gardens ... A.1
Morris Walk ... A.1
Moss Drive ... B.3
Muirfield Drive ... C.1

Nelson Close ... A.1
North Bracing ... C.3
North Parade ... C.2
North Shore Road ... C.1
Norwood Road ... B.4

Ocean Avenue ... B.4
Old Roman Bank ... C.1
Old Wainfleet Road ... A.2
Orchid Way ... A.2
Orford Close ... A.1

Park Avenue ... C.2
Pelham Road ... B.2
Perrin Avenue ... A.1
Perth Close ... A.2
Philip Grove ... A.2
Portal Gardens ... A.1
Portland ... A.1
Primrose Close ... A.1
Prince Alfred Avenue ... C.2
Prince George Street ... B.2
Princess Parade ... C.3

Queens Road ... A.2

Ramsay Close ... B.4
Regents Close ... B.4
Revesby Drive ... A.2
Richmond Court ... B.3
Richmond Drive ... B.4
Ridley Avenue ... B.3
Robin Hood Road ... B.3
Roman Bank ... B.2
Rose Grove ... B.1
Roseberry Avenue ... B.4
Royal Arthur Close ... B.4
Rutland Road ... B.2

Sadler Close ... B.4
St. Andrew's Drive ... C.1
St. Anne's Close ... B.1
St. Clements ... A.2
St. David's Close ... B.1
St. Frances Close ... A.1
St. Huberts Drive ... A.1
St. Margarets Avenue ... A.1
St. Marks Close ... A.1
St. Mary's Road ... A.1
St. Matthews Close ... A.1
St. Valentines Way ... A.1
St. Vincent Close ... A.1
Sandbeck Avenue ... B.3
Saxby Avenue ... B.3
Scampton Way ... A.1
Scarborough Avenue ... B.2
Scarborough Esplanade ... C.2
Scotts Close ... A.1
Scrimshaw Court ... B.2
Sea Front Road ... B.4
Sea View Promenade ... C.2
Sea View Road ... B.1
Seacroft Drive ... B.4
Seacroft Esplanade ... B.4
Seacroft Precinct ... B.4
Seacroft Square ... B.4
Serena Avenue ... C.3
Shardeloes Road ... B.4
Somersby Grove ... B.3
South Bracing ... C.3
South Parade ... C.3
South View Close ... B.3
Sunningdale Crescent ... C.2
Sunningdale Drive ... B.2
Swaby Crescent ... A.2
Swallowfields Court ... A.2
Sydney Drive ... A.2
Syne Avenue ... B.4

Taggs Drive ... A.1
Talbot Road ... B.2
Tarran Way ... A.1
Tennyson Green ... B.3
The Close ... B.2
The Horn ... A.1
The Hurst ... A.1
The Meadows ... A.2
The Needles ... A.1
The Towers ... C.2
Theresa Close ... A.2
Thompson Close ... B.2
Tonglet Close ... B.3
Tower Esplanade ... C.3
Trafalgar Avenue ... B.4
Trefoil Drive ... A.2

Vernon Road ... B.2
Victoria Road ... A.3
Vine Road ... B.4
Vine Walk ... B.4

Wainfleet Road ... A.2
Warth Lane ... A.1
Wellington Way ... A.1
Wentworth Close ... B.1
Westfield Drive ... B.2
Westway ... B.1
Wilford Grove ... B.4
William Way ... B.3
Willoughton Road ... B.3

Yarborough Road ... A.1

MABLETHORPE/SUTTON ON SEA INDEX TO STREETS

Admiralty Road ... C.3
Alexandra Park ... B.3
Alford Road, Mablethorpe ... A.3
Alford Road, Sutton on Sea ... A.7
Aqua Drive ... B.4
Arden Close ... C.4
Ashley Close ... C.5

Balmoral Close ... B.7
Beachside ... C.7
Bluestone Way ... B.8
Braemar Road ... B.7
Bray Avenue ... C.5
Brickyard Lane ... A.6
Broadway ... C.7
Brooke Drive ... C.4
Buckingham Close ... B.7
Bucknalls Meadow ... B.7
Byron Close ... C.2
Byron Road ... C.2

Cades Field Road ... B.7
Cambridge Road ... C.2
Camelot Gardens ... B.7
Cawkwell Close ... B.8
Chalfont Avenue ... C.2
Champion Way ... C.4
Chanctonbury Close ... B.7
Chanctonbury Way ... B.7
Charles Wright Close ... C.3
Church Close ... C.7
Church Lane ... B.4
Church Lane ... B.8
Church Park ... C.7
Church Road ... B.3
Cissbury Close ... C.7
Crabtree Lane ... A.8
Cromer Avenue ... C.7

De La Bere Avenue ... B.8
Dennor Close ... C.7
Drakes Close ... C.4
Dymoke Close ... C.8
Dymoke Road ... C.4

Eagle Close ... B.2
Edwalton Avenue ... C.4
Elm Avenue ... C.4
Enterprise Road ... B.2
Eton Road ... C.5

Fairway ... B.2
Fen Lane ... A.6
Fitzwilliam Street ... C.3
Foxe End ... C.3
Furlong Road ... C.7

George Street ... C.3
Gibraltar Road ... C.3
Golf Road ... B.3
Grange Road ... C.8
Green Lane ... A.2
Grift Bank ... C.4
Grosvenor Court ... B.3
Grosvenor Road ... B.3
Grove Road ... C.6

Hall Leas Drive ... C.6
Hamilton Road ... B.3
Hammond Court ... C.3
Hanson Drive ... B.7
Hardings Close ... B.6
Harlequin Drive ... B.4
Harris Boulevard ... C.4
Harrow Road ... B.3
Harrow Road ... B.3
Hawthorn Drive ... B.3
Henshaw Avenue ... B.8
High Gate ... B.6
High Street ... B.3
High Street, Sutton on Sea ... C.7
Highfield Avenue ... C.6
Highgate Close ... C.6
Hillside Avenue ... C.7
Hodgson Way ... C.7
Honeysuckle Close ... B.7
Hornby Drive ... C.8
Hotchin Road ... C.7
Huttoft Road ... B.8

Ings Road ... A.8
Ivel Close ... C.2
Ivel Grove ... C.2

Jacklin Crescent ... B.2
James Avenue ... C.5

Keats Close ... B.8
Kensington Gardens ... B.3
Kent Avenue ... A.1
King Street ... C.4
Kingsley Road ... B.3
Kipling Drive ... B.8
Kipling Drive ... B.8
Knowle Street ... C.3

Lancaster Road ... C.4
Lansdowne Close ... B.8
Lansdown Drive ... C.8
Lewis Avenue ... C.7
Links Avenue ... C.2
Links Close ... C.2
Locksley Road ... C.4
Long Acre ... C.2
Lyle Close ... B.2

MABLETHORPE ... C.3
Main Street ... A.6
Malvern Road ... B.3
Marian Avenue ... B.4
Marina Road ... C.4
Marine Avenue ... C.7
Marine Avenue West ... B.7
Marisco Court ... C.7
Marlborough Close ... B.3
Marlow Drive ... B.3
Martins Walk ... C.7
Masefield Drive ... B.8
Maxwell Drive ... B.3
Mayflower Way ... B.3
Medina Gardens ... C.4
Meers Bank ... B.1
Mile Lane ... A.5
Mill Field ... C.4
Moreland Avenue ... C.7
Morrison Close ... B.7

Nelson Road ... B.3
Newstead Road ... C.4
North Promenade ... C.3
North Road ... A.5

Oakham Avenue ... B.3
Ocean Court ... C.4
Orchard Close ... B.3
Orchard Way ... B.3
Oundle Road ... C.6

Park Avenue ... C.3
Park Road ... C.6
Park Road East ... C.6
Park Road West ... C.6
Park View ... C.6
Parkinsons Way ... C.5
Parklands ... B.3
Parry Road ... C.4
Phoenix Court ... B.3
Poplar Avenue ... C.2
Promenade ... C.4
Promenade, Sutton on Sea ... C.7

Quebec Road ... C.2
Queens Park Close ... C.4
Queens Road ... B.7
Queensway ... C.3

St. Andrews Road ... C.2
St. Clements Close ... B.3
St. Clements Close ... B.7
St. Francis Gardens ... B.8
St. Peter's Lane ... C.5
Sanders Close ... B.8
Sandhurst Court ... C.8
Sandhurst Road ... C.8
SANDILANDS ... C.8
Sandilands Close ... B.8
Sandringham Drive ... B.7
Sea Lane ... B.8
Seacroft Road ... C.3
Seaholme Road ... B.4
Sharmans Close ... B.8
Shelley Close ... B.8
Sherwood Road ... C.3
Somersby Avenue ... C.3
South Road ... C.6
Stain Lane ... A.2
Stanley Avenue ... B.3
Stanton Road ... C.7
Station Road ... B.3
Station Road, Sutton on Sea ... B.7
Strand Close ... B.3
Studio Court ... C.7
Surfside ... C.7
SUTTON ON SEA ... C.7
Sutton Road ... C.5

Tennyson Avenue ... C.3
Tennyson Close ... B.8
Tennyson Road ... C.3
The Boulevard ... C.3
The Crescent ... C.8
The Drive ... B.2
The Glande ... C.8
The Green ... B.2
The Meadows ... C.5
The Sidings ... B.7
The Strand ... B.3
Theddlethorpe Road ... A.3
THORPE ... A.6
Tower Close ... B.4
Trenchard Road ... B.3
TRUSTHORPE ... C.5
Trusthorpe Road ... C.6
Tudor Court ... C.4

Uppington Road ... B.6

Victoria Road, Sutton on Sea ... B.7
Victoria Road ... C.3
Vyner Close ... C.3

Walkington Way ... C.8
Waterloo Road ... C.3
Wellington Avenue ... C.3
Wellington Road ... C.3
White Row Lane ... B.6
Whitehead Close ... C.2
Willerton Close ... B.7
William Green Close ... B.7
William Tow Close ... B.7
Willoughby Road ... C.6
Wilmington Drive ... B.7
Wilyman Close ... C.8
Winchester Drive ... B.4
Windson Road ... C.3

York Road ... C.7
Youlgrave Road ... C.7

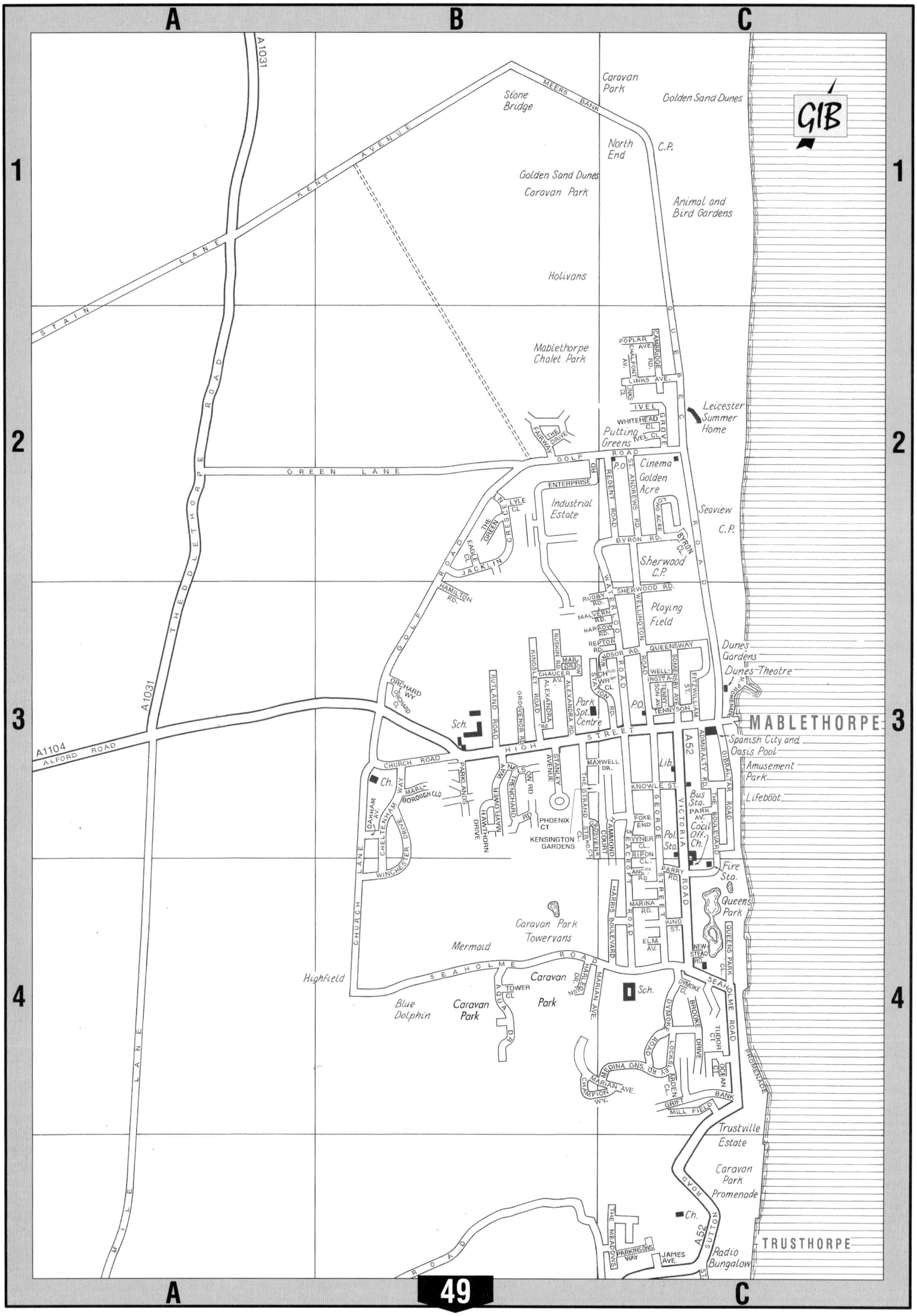
A
B
C
1
2
3
4
A1031
STAIN LANE
KENT AVENUE
MEERS BANK
Stone Bridge
Caravan Park
North End
C.P.
Golden Sand Dunes
GIB
Golden Sand Dunes Caravan Park
Animal and Bird Gardens
Holivans
QUEBEC ROAD
Mablethorpe Chalet Park
POPLAR AVE.
CAMBRIDGE RD.
CHALFONT AV.
LINKS AVE.
LINKS CL.
IVEL GROVE
WHITEHEAD CL.
IVEL CL.
Leicester Summer Home
Putting Greens
FAIRWAY
THE DRIVE
GOLF ROAD
GREEN LANE
THEDDLETHORPE ROAD
P.O.
Cinema
Golden Acre
ENTERPRISE RD
Industrial Estate
REGENT ROAD
ST. ANDREWS RD.
OLD ACRE
Seaview C.P.
LYLE CL.
THE GREEN
CRESCENT
EAGLE CL.
JACKLIN
BYRON RD.
BYRON CL.
Sherwood C.P.
HAMILTON RD.
SHERWOOD RD.
RUGBY RD.
MALVERN RD.
HARROW RD.
REPTON RD.
WATERLOO ROAD
WELLINGTON
Playing Field
GOLF ROAD
QUEENSWAY
Dunes Gardens
Dunes Theatre
ORCHARD WAY
ORCHARD CL.
RUSKIN RD.
MARLOW DR.
KINGSLEY ROAD
CHAUCER AV.
ALEXANDRA RD.
ALEXANDRA PK.
WINDSOR RD.
STATION RD.
STATION ROAD
WELLINGTON AV.
SOMERSBY AVE
TENNYSON
FITZWILLIAM ST.
PROMENADE
A1031
RUTLAND ROAD
GROSVENOR RD.
Park Spt. Centre
P.O.
MABLETHORPE
Sch.
A1104
ALFORD ROAD
HIGH STREET
A52
ADMIRALTY RD.
GIBRALTAR ROAD
Spanish City and Oasis Pool
Amusement Park
CHURCH ROAD
Ch.
MARLBOROUGH CLO
PARKLANDS
MAYFLOWER WAY
TRENCHARD RD
NELSON RD
STANLEY AVENUE
MAXWELL DR.
Lib.
KNOWLE ST.
Lifeboat
OAKHAM AV.
CHELTENHAM WAY
WINCHESTER DRIVE
HAWTHORN DRIVE
PHOENIX CT
KENSINGTON GARDENS
THE STRAND
STRAND CL.
STRAND CT.
GROSVENOR CT.
HAMMOND COURT
FOXE END
VYNER CL.
RIPON CL.
SACKVILLE ROAD
GEORGE STREET
Pol. Sta.
VICTORIA ROAD
Bus Sta.
PARK AV.
Cocil Off.
Ch.
THE BOULEVARD
Fire Sta.
PARRY RD.
HARRIS BOULEVARD
MARINA RD.
KING ST.
Queens Park
QUEENS PARK CL.
ELM AV.
NEWSTEAD RD.
CHURCH LANE
Caravan Park
Towervans
Mermaid
SEAHOLME ROAD
HARLEQUIN DR.
MARIAN AVE.
Highfield
Caravan Park
TOWER CL.
AQUA DR.
Blue Dolphin
Caravan Park
Sch.
DYMOKE CL.
DYMOKE ROAD
BROOKE DRIVE
SEAHOLME ROAD
TUDOR CT.
OCEAN CT.
PROMENADE
MEDINA GNS.
LOCKSLEY RD.
MARIAN AVE.
CHAMPION WY.
ARDEN CL.
GRIFT BANK
MILL FIELD
Trustville Estate
Caravan Park Promenade
ROAD
SUTTON ROAD
A52
Ch.
THE MEADOWS
PARKINSONS WAY
JAMES AVE.
Radio Bungalow
TRUSTHORPE
MILE LANE
ROAD
49

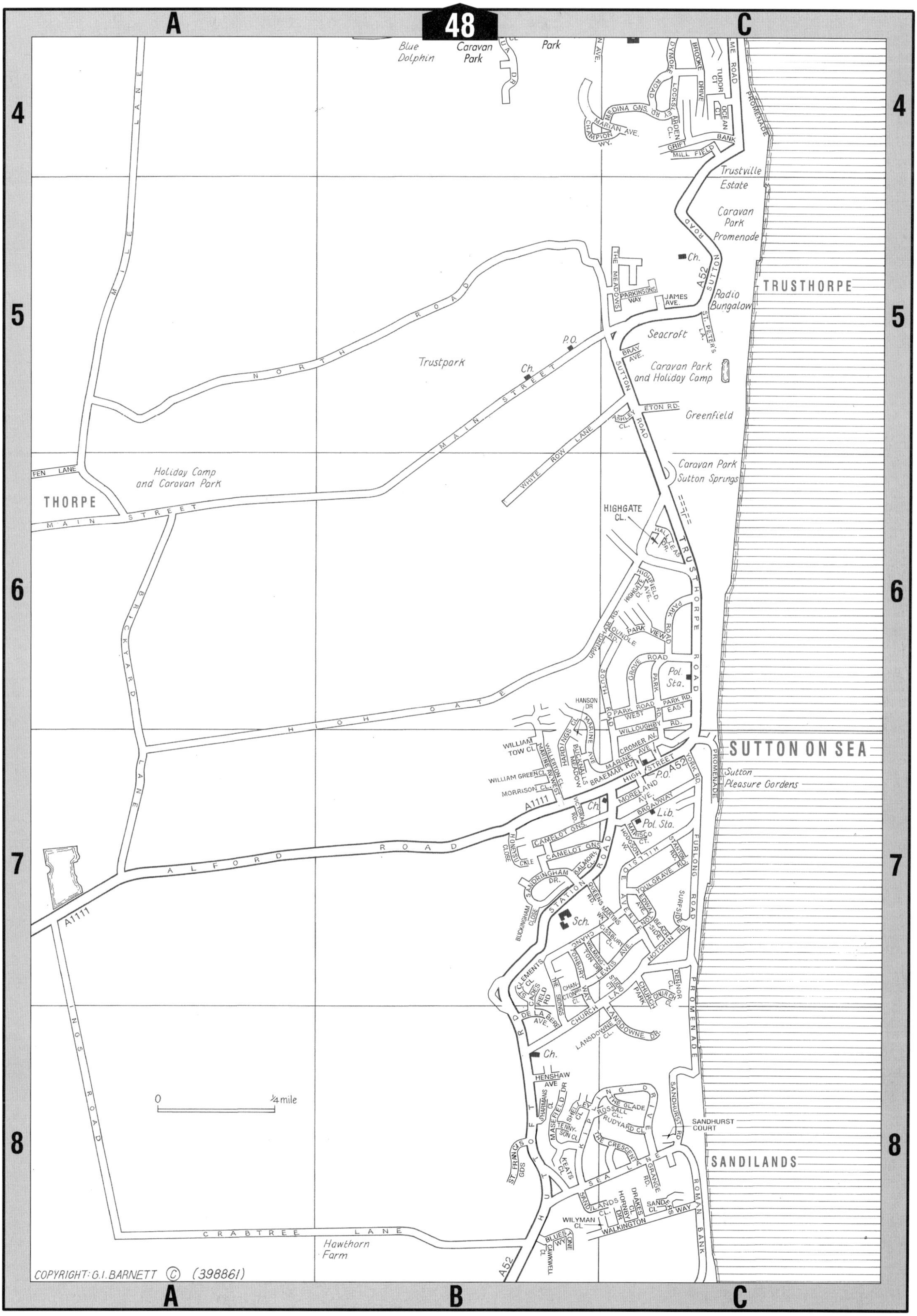
48
A
B
C
4
5
6
7
8
Blue Dolphin
Caravan Park
Park
Trustville Estate
Caravan Park Promenade
TRUSTHORPE
Radio Bungalow
Seacroft
Caravan Park and Holiday Camp
Trustpark
Greenfield
Caravan Park Sutton Springs
Holiday Camp and Caravan Park
THORPE
FEN LANE
MAIN STREET
NORTH ROAD
MILE LANE
WHITE ROW LANE
BRICKYARD LANE
HIGH GATE
ALFORD ROAD
A1111
A52
SUTTON ROAD
TRUSTHORPE ROAD
HIGHGATE CL.
SUTTON ON SEA
Sutton Pleasure Gardens
PROMENADE
FURLONG ROAD
SANDHURST COURT
SANDILANDS
ROMAN BANK
CRABTREE LANE
Hawthorn Farm
INGS ROAD
Sch.
Lib.
Pol. Sta.
P.O.
Ch.
0
¼ mile
COPYRIGHT: G.I. BARNETT © (398861)

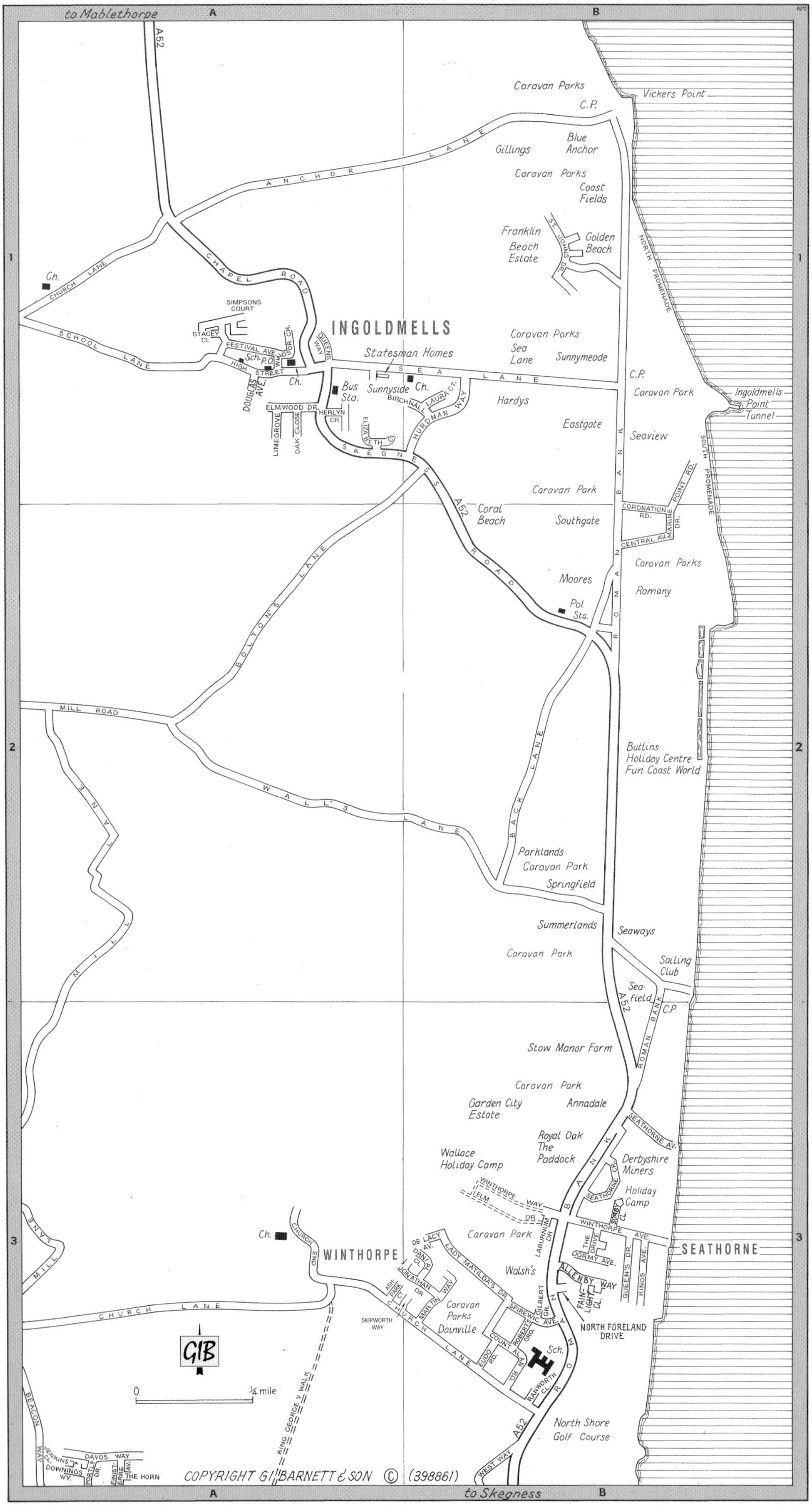

INGOLDMELLS INDEX TO STREETS

Allenby Way B.3
Anchor Lane A.1
Ashpark Court A.3

Back Lane B.2
Beacon Way A.3
Birchnall A.1
Bolton's Lane A.2

Central Avenue B.2
Chapel Road A.1
Church End A.3
Church Lane, Ingoldmells A.1
Church Lane, Winthorpe A.3
Coronation Road B.1
Count Alan Road B.3

Danial Close B.3
Davos Way A.3
De Lacy Avenue B.3
Dormy Avenue B.3
Douglas Avenue A.1
Downings Way A.3

Elizabeth Close A.1
Em Drive B.3
Elmwood Drive A.1
Eudo Road B.3

Fainlight Close B.3
Festival Avenue A.1
Finisterre Avenue A.3

Gilbert's Grove B.3

Herlyn Crescent A.1
High Street A.1
Hurdman Way B.1

Jenkins Close A.3
Jonathan Drive B.3

King George V Walk A.3
King's Avenue B.3

Lady Matilda's Drive B.3
Laura Court B.1
Laburnum Avenue B.3
Lime Grove A.1

Marine Drive B.2
Martin Way B.3
Mill Lane A.2
Mill Road A.2

North Foreland Drive B.3
North Promenade B.1

Oak Close A.1

Point Road B.1
Portland Drive A.3

Queen's Drive B.3
Queen's Way A.1

Ranworth Close B.3
Robert's Grove B.3
Roman Bank B.3

St. John's Drive B.1
School Lane A.1
Sea Lane B.1
SEATHORNE B.3
Seathorne Avenue B.3
Seathorne Crescent B.3
Skegness Road A.1
Skipworth Way B.3
Sorby Close B.3
South Promenade B.1
Spirewic Avenue B.3

The Drive B.3
The Horn A.3

Wall's Lane A.2
West Way B.3
Windsor Crescent A.1
WINTHORPE B.3
Winthorpe Avenue B.3
Winthorpe Way B.3

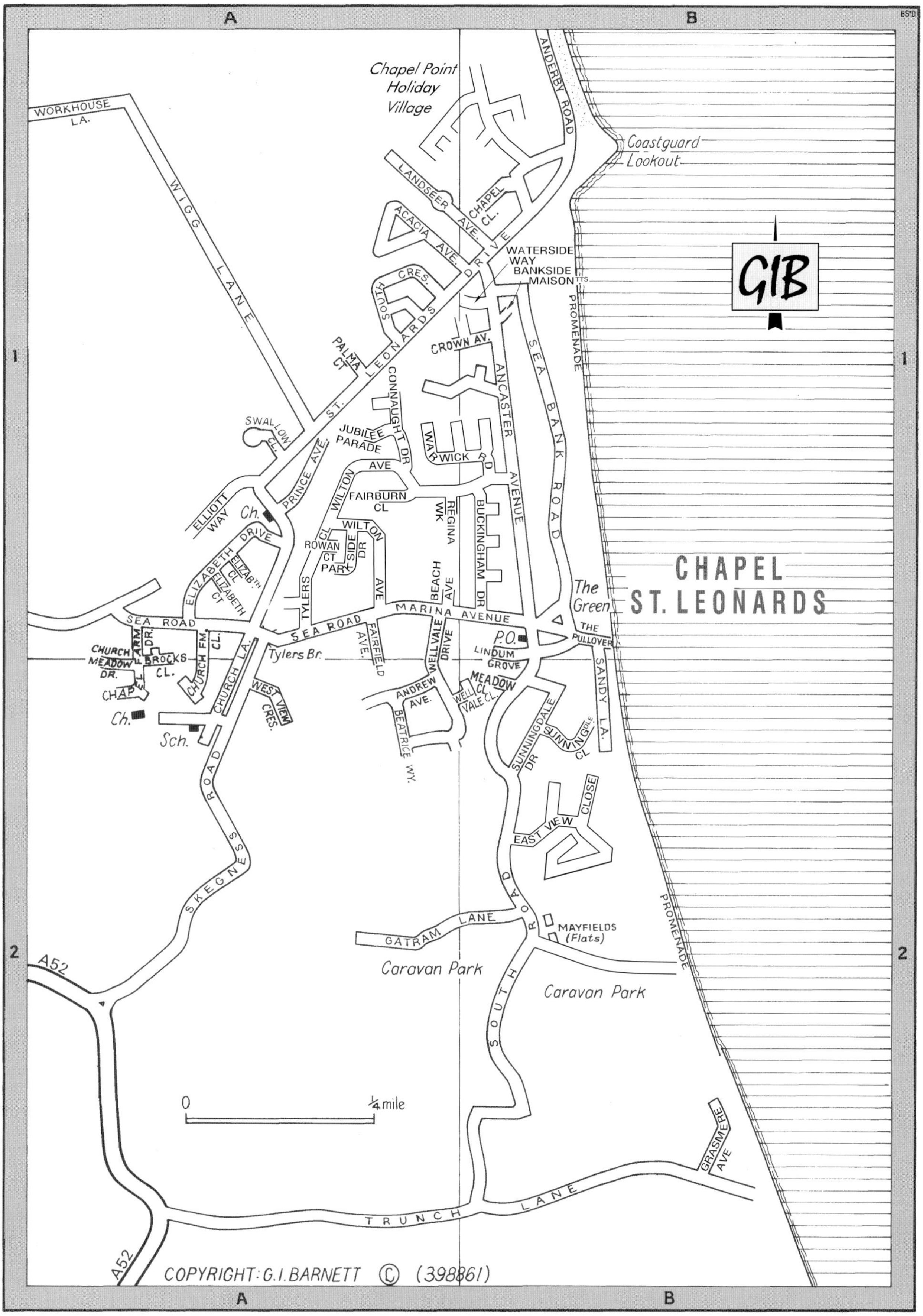

CHAPEL ST. LEONARDS INDEX TO STREETS

Acacia Avenue A.1
Ancaster Avenue B.1
Anderby Road B.1
Andrew Avenue A.2

Bankside Maisonettes B.1
Beach Avenue....A.1
Beatrice Way A.2
Brocks Close A.2
Buckingham Drive B.1

Chapel Close B.1
Chapel Farm Drive A.2
Church Farm Close A.2
Church Lane A.2
Church Meadow Drive A.2
Connaught Drive A.1
Crown Avenue A.1

East View Close B.2
Elizabeth Close....A.1
Elizabeth Court....A.1
Elizabeth Drive A.1
Elliott Way A.1

Fairburn Close A.1
Fairfield Avenue A.1

Gatram Lane A.2
Grasmere Avenue B.2
Jubilee Parade A.1

Landseer Avenue A.1
Lindum Grove B.1

Marina Avenue A.1
Mayfields B.2
Meadow Close B.2

Palma Court A.1
Parkside Drive A.1
Prince Avenue A.1
Promenade B.1
Regina Walk A.1
Rowan Court A.1

St. Leonard's Drive A.1
Sandy Lane B.2
Sea Bank Road B.1
Sea Road A.1
Skegness Road A.2
South Crescent A.1
South Road B.2
Sunningdale Close B.2
Sunningdale Drive B.2
Swallow Close A.1

The Green B.1
The Pullover B.1
Trunch Lane A.2
Tylers Bridge A.1
Tylers Close A.1

Warwick Road B.1
Waterside Way B.1
Well Vale Close A.2
Well Vale Drive A.1
West View Crescent A.2
Wigg Lane A.1
Wilton Avenue A.1
Workhouse Lane A.1

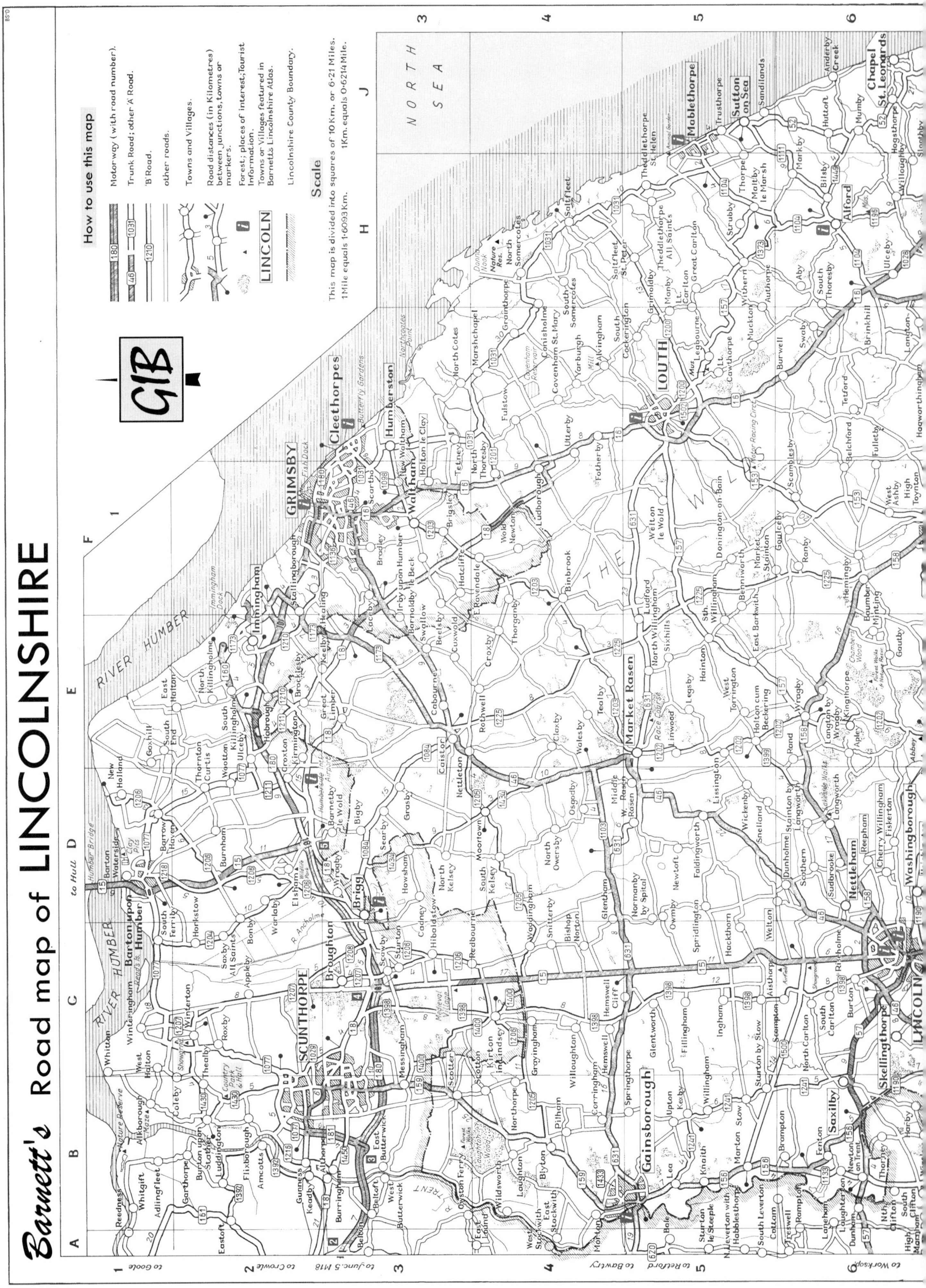
Barnett's Road map of LINCOLNSHIRE
How to use this map
Motorway (with road number).
Trunk Road; other 'A' Road.
'B' Road.
other roads.
Towns and Villages.
Road distances (in Kilometres) between junctions, towns or markers.
Forest; places of interest; Tourist Information.
Towns or Villages featured in Barnetts Lincolnshire Atlas.
Lincolnshire County Boundary.
Scale
This map is divided into squares of 10 Km. or 6·21 Miles.
1 Mile equals 1·6093 Km. 1 Km. equals 0·6214 Mile.
NORTH SEA
RIVER HUMBER
GRIMSBY
Cleethorpes
SCUNTHORPE
LINCOLN
LOUTH
Market Rasen
Gainsborough
Mablethorpe
Immingham
Brigg
Skegness

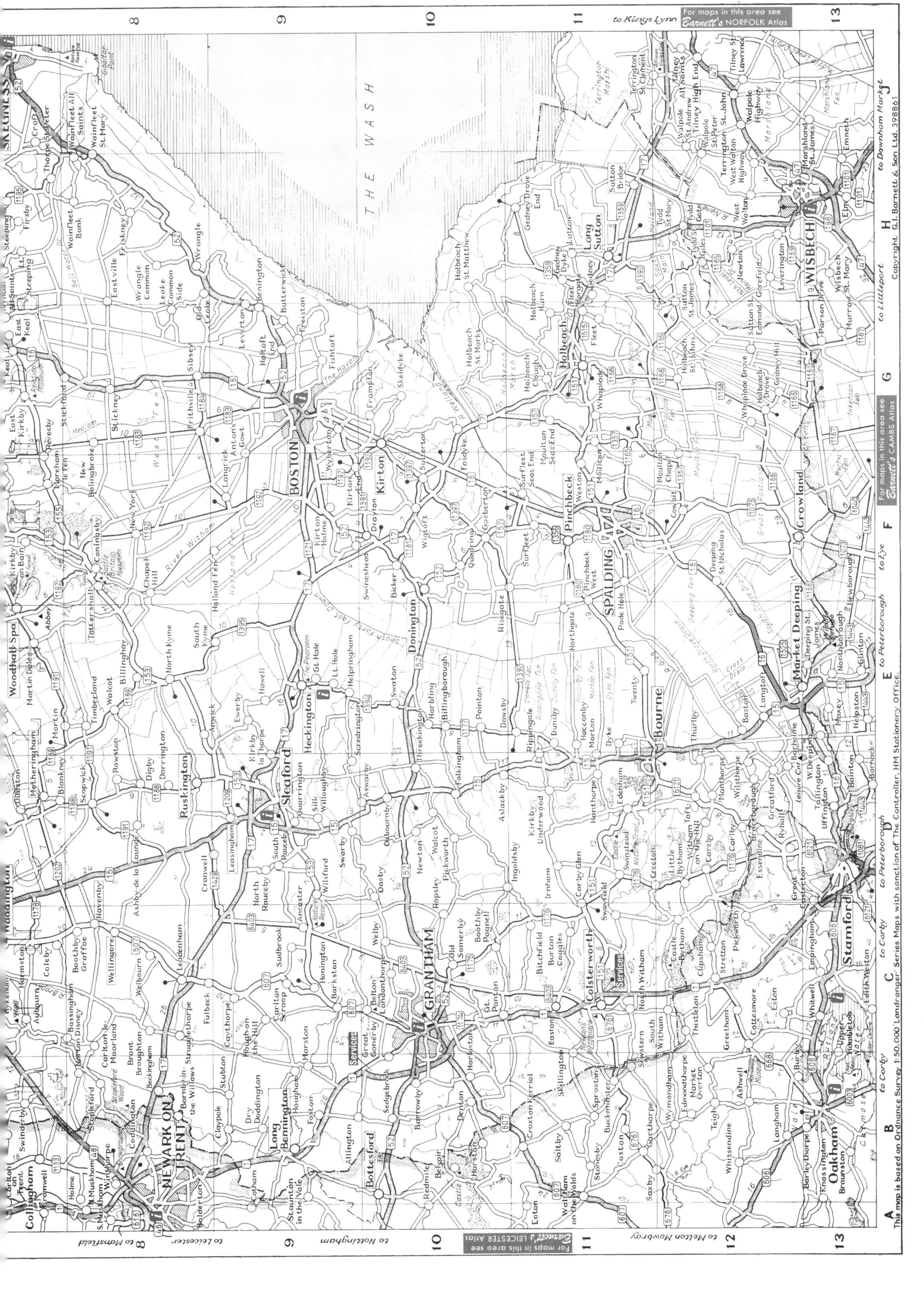

For maps in this area see Barnett's NORFOLK Atlas
For maps in this area see Barnett's CAMBS Atlas
For maps in this area see Barnett's LEICESTER Atlas
to Kings Lynn
to Downham Market
to Littleport
to Eye
to Peterborough
to Corby
to Melton Mowbray
to Nottingham
to Leicester
to Mansfield
THE WASH
SKEGNESS
BOSTON
SLEAFORD
GRANTHAM
SPALDING
HOLBEACH
LONG SUTTON
WISBECH
STAMFORD
NEWARK ON TRENT
Woodhall Spa
Coningsby
Kirton
Donington
Pinchbeck
Bourne
Market Deeping
Crowland
Heckington
Ruskington
Long Bennington
Bottesford
Colsterworth
Oakham
This map is based on Ordnance Survey 1:50,000 'Landranger' Series Maps with sanction of The Controller, HM Stationery Office.
Copyright G.I. Barnett & Son Ltd. 39886

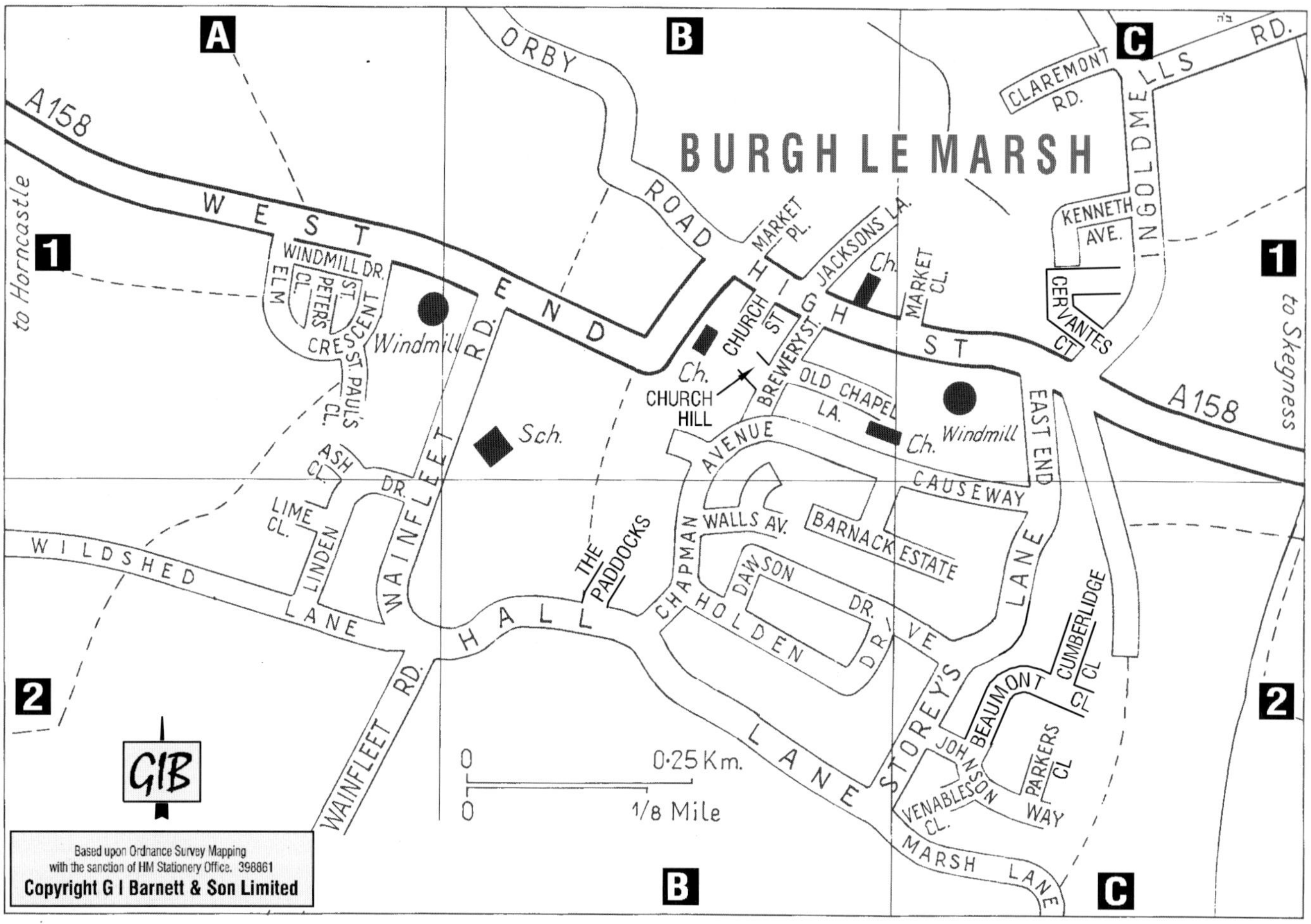

BURGH LE MARSH INDEX TO STREETS

Ash Close A.1

Barnack Estate B.2
Beaumont Close C.2
Brewery Street B.1

Causeway C.2
Cervantes Court C.1
Chapman Avenue B.2
Church Hill B.1
Church Street B.1

Claremont Road C.1
Cumberlidge Close C.2

Dawson Drive B.2

East End C.1
Elm Crescent A.1

Hall Lane B.2
High Street B.1
Holden Drive B.2

Ingoldmells Road C.1

Jacksons Lane B.1
Johnson Way C.2

Kenneth Avenue C.1

Lime Close A.2
Linden Drive A.2

Market Close C.1

Market Lane C.2
Market Place B.1

Old Chapel Lane B.1
Orby Road B.1

Parkers Close C.1

St. Peter's Close A.1
St. Paul's Close A.1
Storey's Lane C.2

The Paddocks.......................B.2

Venebles Close C.2

Wainfleet Road A.2
Walls Avenue B.2
West End A.1
Wildshed Lane A.2
Windmill Drive A.1

SPILSBY INDEX TO STREETS

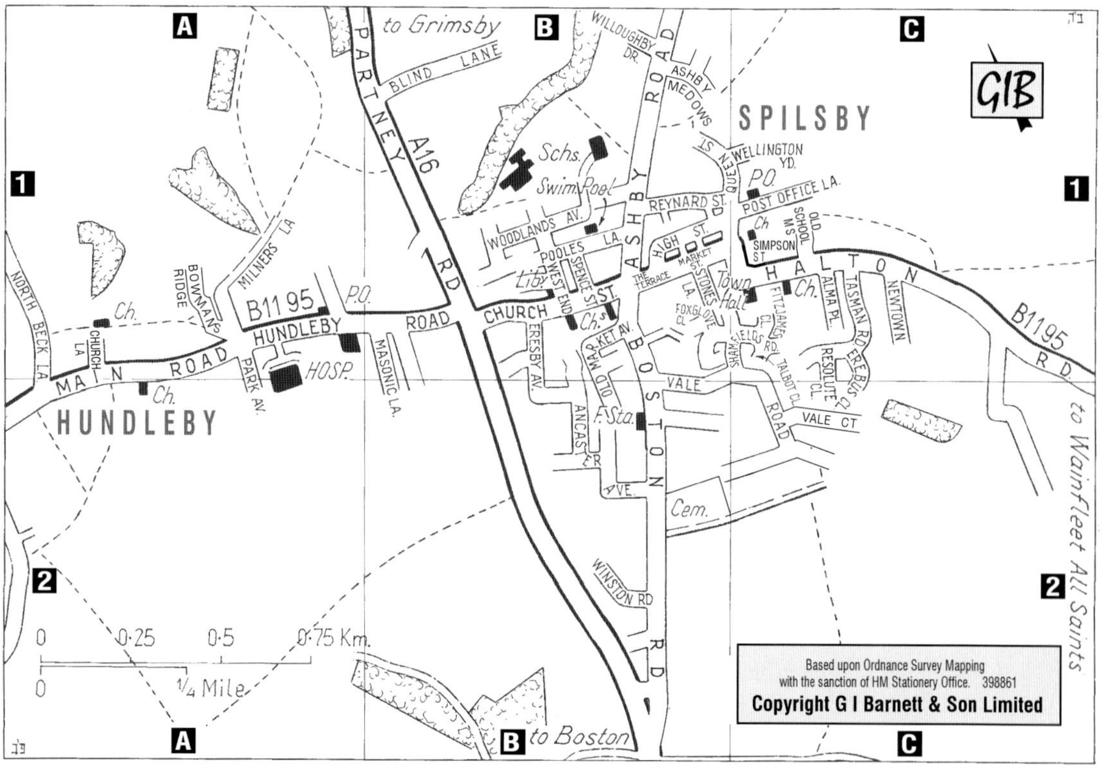

SPILSBY INDEX TO STREETS

Alma Place C.1
Ancaster Avenue B.2
Ashby Meadows B.1
Ashby Road B.1

Blind Lane B.1
Boston Road B.1
Bowmans Ridge A.1

Church Lane A.1
Church Street B.1

Erebus Close C.1
Eresby Avenue ..B.1

Fitzjames Close C.1
Foxglove Close ..B.1

Halton Road C.1
High Street B.1
HUNDLEBY A.2
Hundleby Road A.1

Main Road A.1
Market Street B.1
Masonic Lane B.1
Milners Lane A.1

Newtown C.1
North Beck Lane A.1

Old Market Avenue B.2

Old School Mews C.1

Park Avenue A.1
Partney Road B.1
Pooles Lane B.1
Post Office Lane C.1

Queen Street B.1

Resolute Close ..C.1
Reynard Street ..B.1

Shamfields Road C.1
Simpson Street ..C.1
Spence Street B.1
Stones Lane B.1

Talbot Close C.1
Tasman Road C.1
The Terrace B.1

Vale Court C.2
Vale Road B.2

Wellington Yard C.1
West End B.1
Willoughby Drive B.1
Winston Road B.2
Woodlands Avenue B.1

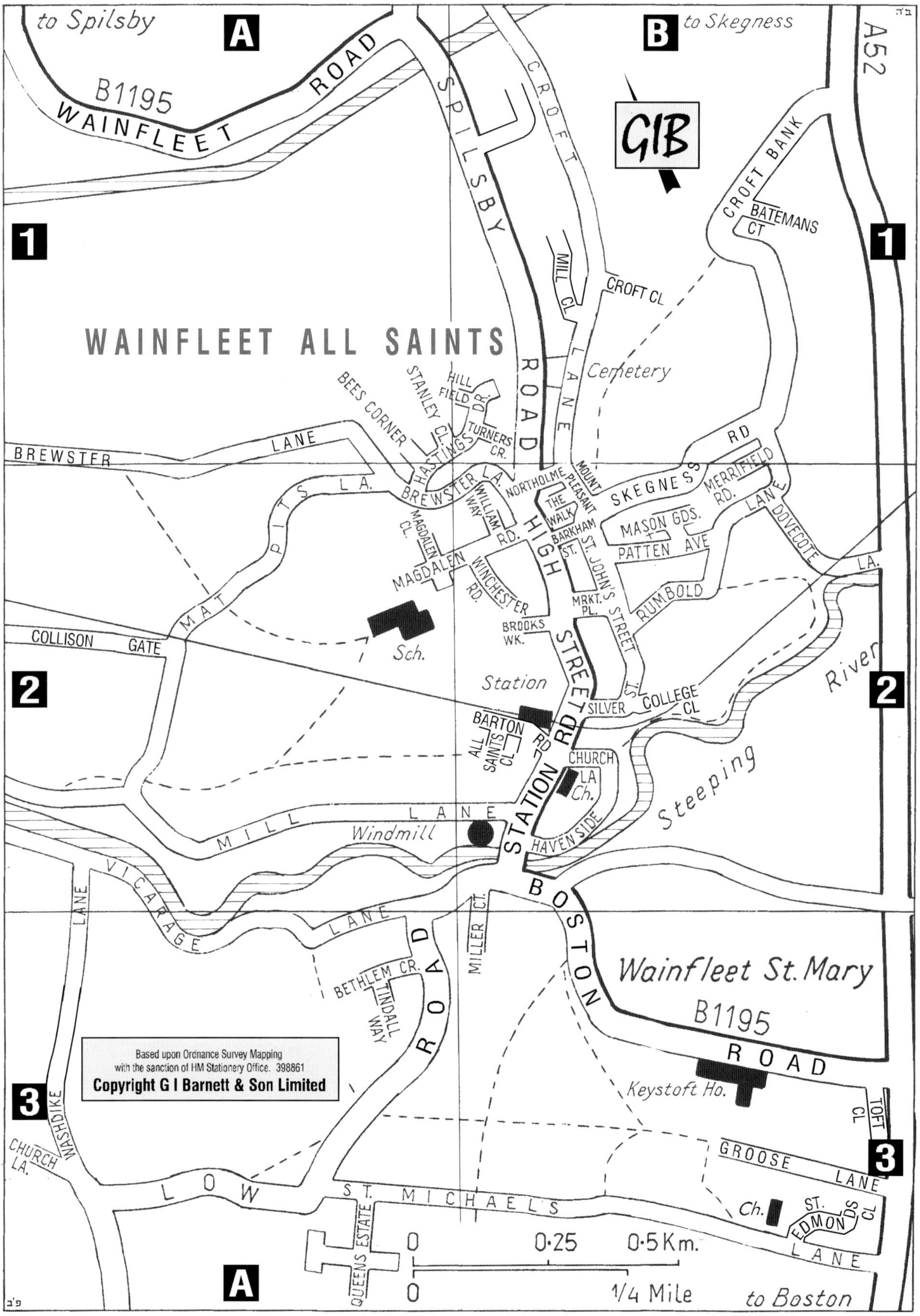

WAINFLEET ALL SAINTS INDEX TO STREETS

All Saints Close B.2
Barkham Street B.2
Barton Road B.2
Batemans Court B.1
Bees Corner A.1
Bethlem Crescent A.3
Boston Road..........................B.2
Brewster Lane A.2
Brooks Walk B.2
Church Lane A.3
Church Lane B.2
College Close.........................B.2
Collison Gate A.2
Croft Bank B.1
Croft Close B.1
Croft Lane B.1
Dovecote Lane B.2
Groose Lane...........................B.3
Hastings Drive A.2
Havenside b.2
High Street B.2
Hill Field B.1
Low Road A.3
Magdalen Close A.2
Magdalen Road A.2
Market Place B.2
Mason Gardens B.2
Mat Pits Lane A.2
Merrifield Road B.1
Miller Court b.2
Mill Close B.1
Mill Lane A.2
Mount Pleasant B.2
Northolme B.2
Patten Avenue B.2
Queen Estate A.3
Rumbold Lane B.2
St. Edmonds Close................B.3
St. Johns Street B.2
St. Michael's Lane A.3
Silver Street B.2
Skegness Road B.2
Spilsby Road B.1
Stanley Close A.1
Station Road..........................B.2
The Walk B.2
Tindall Way A.3
Toft Close B.3
Turners Crescent B.1
Vicarage Lane A.2
Wainfleet Road......................A.1
WAINSFLEET ALL SAINTS B.3
WAINSFLEET ST. MARY A.1
Washdike Lane A.3
William Way B.2
Winchester Road B.2

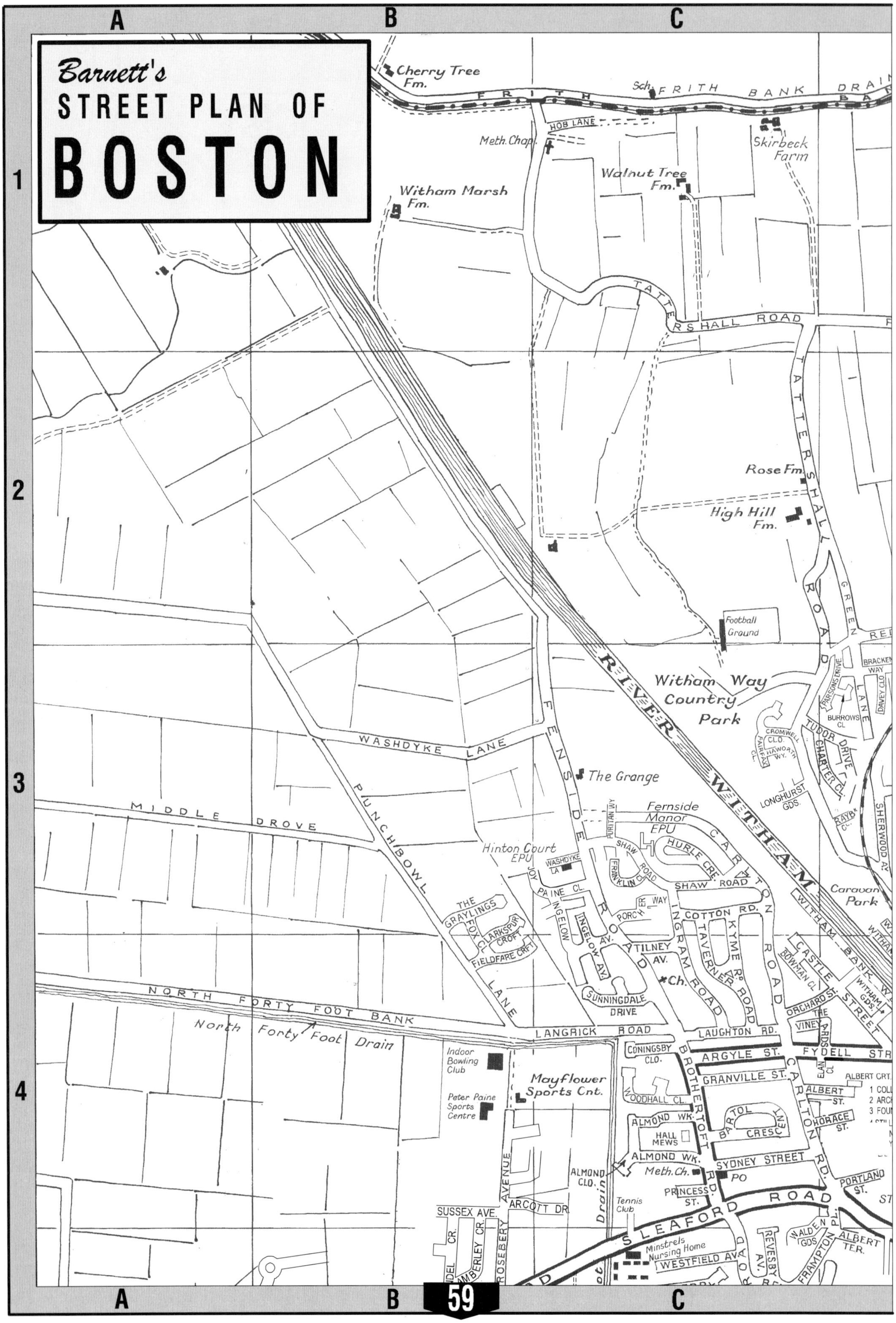
Barnett's
STREET PLAN OF
BOSTON
A
B
C
1
2
3
4
59
Cherry Tree Fm.
Sch.
FRITH BANK DRAIN
HOB LANE
Meth. Chap.
Skirbeck Farm
Walnut Tree Fm.
Witham Marsh Fm.
TATTERSHALL ROAD
TATTERSHALL ROAD
Rose Fm.
High Hill Fm.
GREEN LANE
Football Ground
RIVER WITHAM
Witham Way Country Park
BRACKEN WAY
PARSONS DRIVE
DAVEY CLO.
BURROWS CL.
CROMWELL CLO.
FAIRFAX CL.
HAWORTH WY.
TUDOR DRIVE
CHARTER CL.
LONGHURST GDS.
RAYBY CL.
SHERWOOD AV.
WASHDYKE LANE
FENSIDE ROAD
The Grange
MIDDLE DROVE
PUNCHBOWL LANE
PURITAN WY
Fernside Manor EPU
Hinton Court EPU
WASHDYKE LA
SHAW ROAD
HURLE CRES.
CARLTON ROAD
FRANKLIN CL.
JOY PAINE CL.
INGELOW AV.
PORCHER WAY
COTTON RD.
INGRAM ROAD
TAVERNER ROAD
KYME RD.
TILNEY AV.
Ch.
THE GRAYLINGS
FOX CL.
LARKSPUR CROFT
FIELDFARE CRFT
SUNNINGDALE DRIVE
Caravan Park
WITHAM BANK
WITHAM GDS.
CASTLE STREET
BOWMAN CL.
ORCHARD ST.
THE VINEYARDS
NORTH FORTY FOOT BANK
North Forty Foot Drain
LANGRICK ROAD
LAUGHTON RD.
CONINGSBY CLO.
ARGYLE ST.
FYDELL ST.
ELAN CL.
ALBERT CRT.
GRANVILLE ST.
ALBERT ST.
HORACE ST.
Indoor Bowling Club
Mayflower Sports Cnt.
Peter Paine Sports Centre
WOODHALL CL.
BROTHERTOFT RD.
BARTOL CRESCENT
ALMOND WK.
HALL MEWS
ALMOND WK.
Meth. Ch.
SYDNEY STREET
PO
ALMOND CLO.
PRINCESS ST.
PORTLAND ST.
Drain
Tennis Club
SLEAFORD ROAD
SUSSEX AVE.
ARCOTT DR.
AVENUE
ROSEBERY
AMBERLEY CR.
Minstrels Nursing Home
WESTFIELD AV.
REVESBY AV.
WALDEN GDS.
FRAMPTON PL.
ALBERT TER.
A
B
C

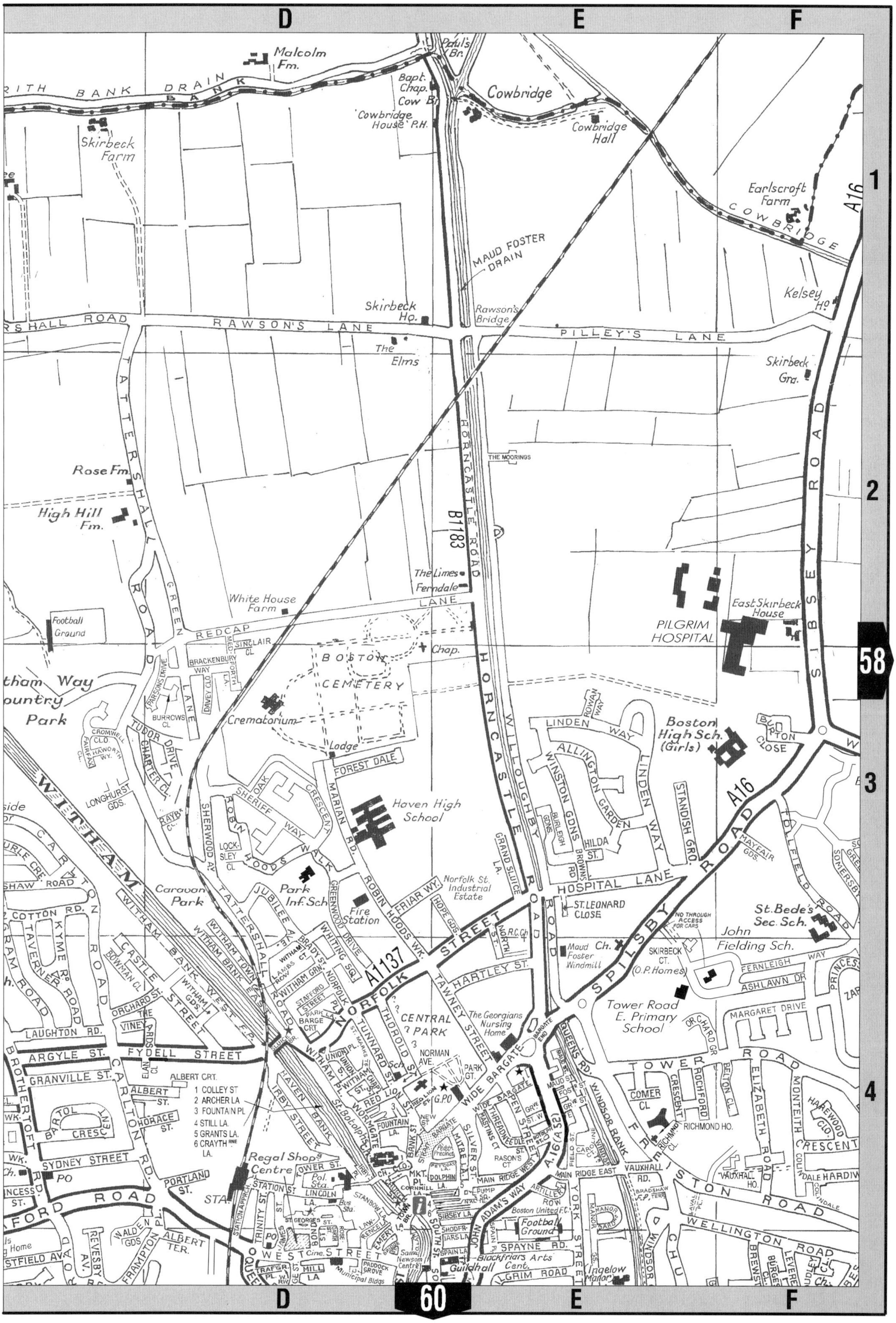
D
E
F
1
2
3
4
58
60
Malcolm Fm.
Skirbeck Farm
Paul's Br.
Bapt. Chap.
Cow Br.
'Cowbridge House' P.H.
Cowbridge
Cowbridge Hall
Earlscroft Farm
COWBRIDGE
A16
MAUD FOSTER DRAIN
Skirbeck Ho.
Rawson's Bridge
Kelsey Ho.
RAWSON'S LANE
PILLEY'S LANE
The Elms
Skirbeck Gra.
TATTERSHALL ROAD
HORNCASTLE ROAD
B1183
THE MOORINGS
Rose Fm.
High Hill Fm.
SIBSEY ROAD
The Limes
Ferndale
White House Farm
LANE
Football Ground
REDCAP
GREEN LANE
BOSTON CEMETERY
Chap.
PILGRIM HOSPITAL
East Skirbeck House
Witham Way Country Park
Crematorium
Lodge
WILLOUGHBY ROAD
LINDEN WAY
Boston High Sch. (Girls)
BURTON CLOSE
TUDOR DRIVE
FOREST DALE
Haven High School
ALLINGTON GARDEN
WINSTON GDNS
STANDISH GRO.
A16
MAYFAIR GDS.
WITHAM
SHERWOOD AV.
ROBIN HOODS WALK
MARIAN RD.
GRAND SLUICE LA.
HOSPITAL LANE
SPILSBY ROAD
Caravan Park
Park Inf. Sch.
Fire Station
Norfolk St. Industrial Estate
ST. LEONARD CLOSE
NO THROUGH ACCESS FOR CARS
St. Bede's Sec. Sch.
John Fielding Sch.
WITHAM BANK WEST F.P.
A1137
NORFOLK STREET
HARTLEY ST.
Maud Foster Windmill
SKIRBECK CT. (O.P. Homes)
FERNLEIGH WAY
ASHLAWN DR
Tower Road E. Primary School
MARGARET DRIVE
CENTRAL PARK
TAWNEY STREET
The Georgians Nursing Home
LAUGHTON RD.
ARGYLE ST.
FYDELL STREET
WIDE BARGATE
QUEENS RD.
TOWER ROAD
GRANVILLE ST.
ALBERT CRT.
1 COLLEY ST
2 ARCHER LA
3 FOUNTAIN PL
4 STILL LA
5 GRANTS LA
6 CRAYTH RNE LA.
G.P.O.
COMER CL
RICHMOND HO.
SYDNEY STREET
Regal Shop Centre
TOWER ST.
MAIN RIDGE EAST
VAUXHALL RD.
PORTLAND ST.
STA.
STATION ST
LINCOLN LA.
Bus Sta.
DOLPHIN LA.
JOHN ADAM'S WAY
Boston United F.C.
Football Ground
FRAMPTON PL.
ALBERT TER.
WEST STREET
Sam Newsom Centre
SPAYNE RD.
Blackfriars Arts Cent.
Guildhall
PILGRIM ROAD
Ingelow Manor
WELLINGTON ROAD
Municipal Bldgs

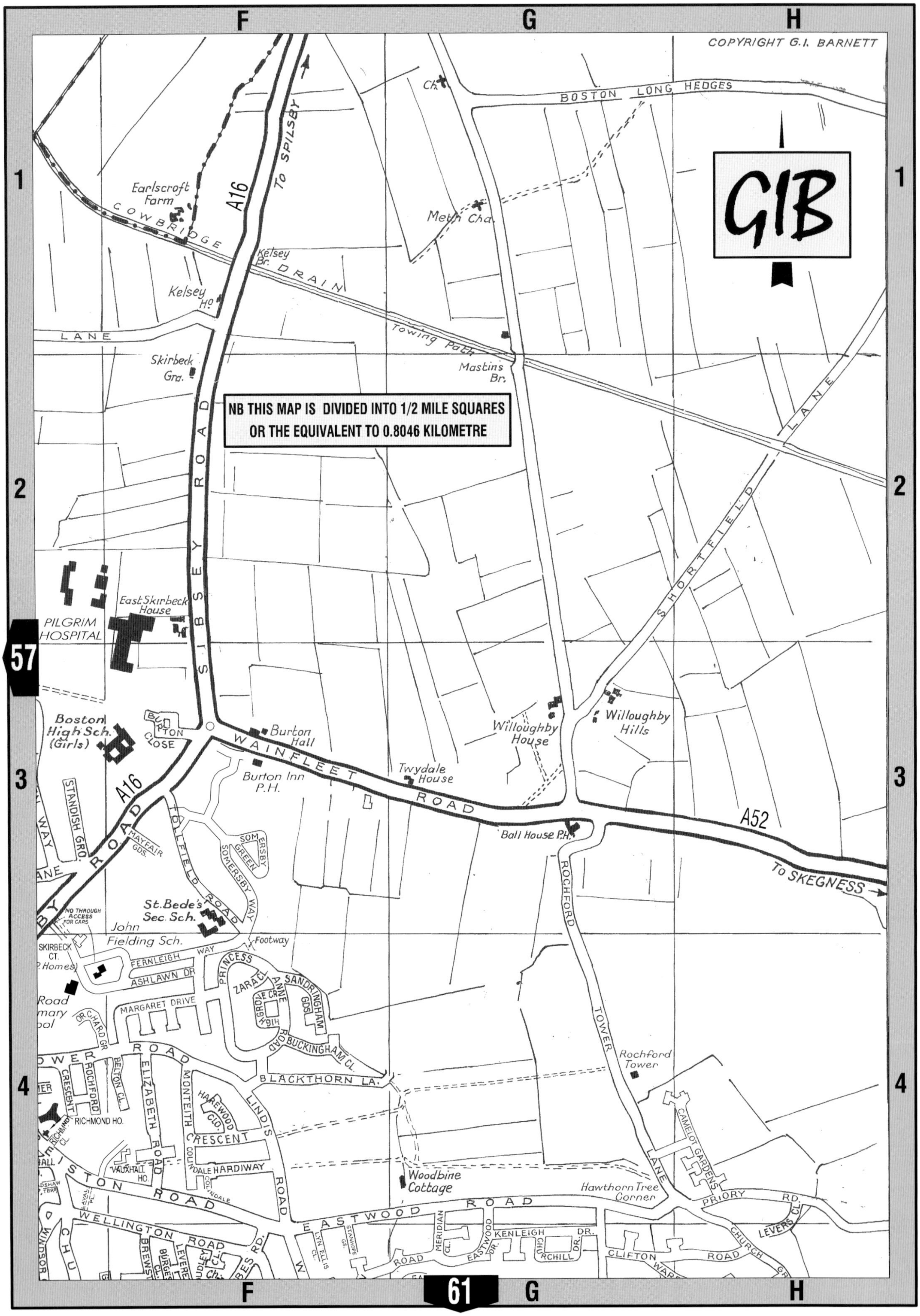

F
G
H
COPYRIGHT G.I. BARNETT
GIB
1
2
3
4
BOSTON LONG HEDGES
Earlscroft Farm
COWBRIDGE DRAIN
A16
To SPILSBY
Kelsey Br.
Kelsey Ho
Meth Cha
Towing Path
LANE
Skirbeck Gra.
Mastins Br.
NB THIS MAP IS DIVIDED INTO 1/2 MILE SQUARES
OR THE EQUIVALENT TO 0.8046 KILOMETRE
SIBSEY ROAD
SHORTFIELD LANE
East Skirbeck House
PILGRIM HOSPITAL
57
Boston High Sch. (Girls)
BURTON CLOSE
Burton Hall
WAINFLEET ROAD
Burton Inn P.H.
Twydale House
Willoughby House
Willoughby Hills
A52
Ball House P.H.
To SKEGNESS
STANDISH GRO.
MAYFAIR GDS.
TOLLFIELD ROAD
SOMERSBY GREEN
SOMERSBY WAY
St. Bede's Sec. Sch.
NO THROUGH ACCESS FOR CARS
John Fielding Sch.
Footway
ROCHFORD TOWER LANE
SKIRBECK CT.
FERNLEIGH WAY
ASHLAWN DR
PRINCESS ANNE ROAD
ZARA CL.
SANDRINGHAM GDS.
MARGARET DRIVE
ORCHARD GR.
BUCKINGHAM CL.
BLACKTHORN LA.
Rochford Tower
ROCHFORD CRESCENT
BELTON CL.
ELIZABETH ROAD
MONTEITH CRESCENT
HAREWOOD CLO.
LINDIS ROAD
RICHMOND HO.
RICHMOND CL.
CAMELOT GARDENS
VAUXHALL HO.
COLINDALE
HARDIWAY
Woodbine Cottage
Hawthorn Tree Corner
PRIORY RD.
EASTWOOD ROAD
WELLINGTON ROAD
LEVERS CL.
KENLEIGH DR.
CHURCHILL DR.
MERIDIAN CL.
EASTWOOD DR.
LYN ELLIS CL.
STANHOPE GS.
CLIFTON ROAD
CHURCH GR.
BREWSTER
BURGESS CL.
LEVERETT
DUDLEY CL.
Ch.
WINDSOR
61

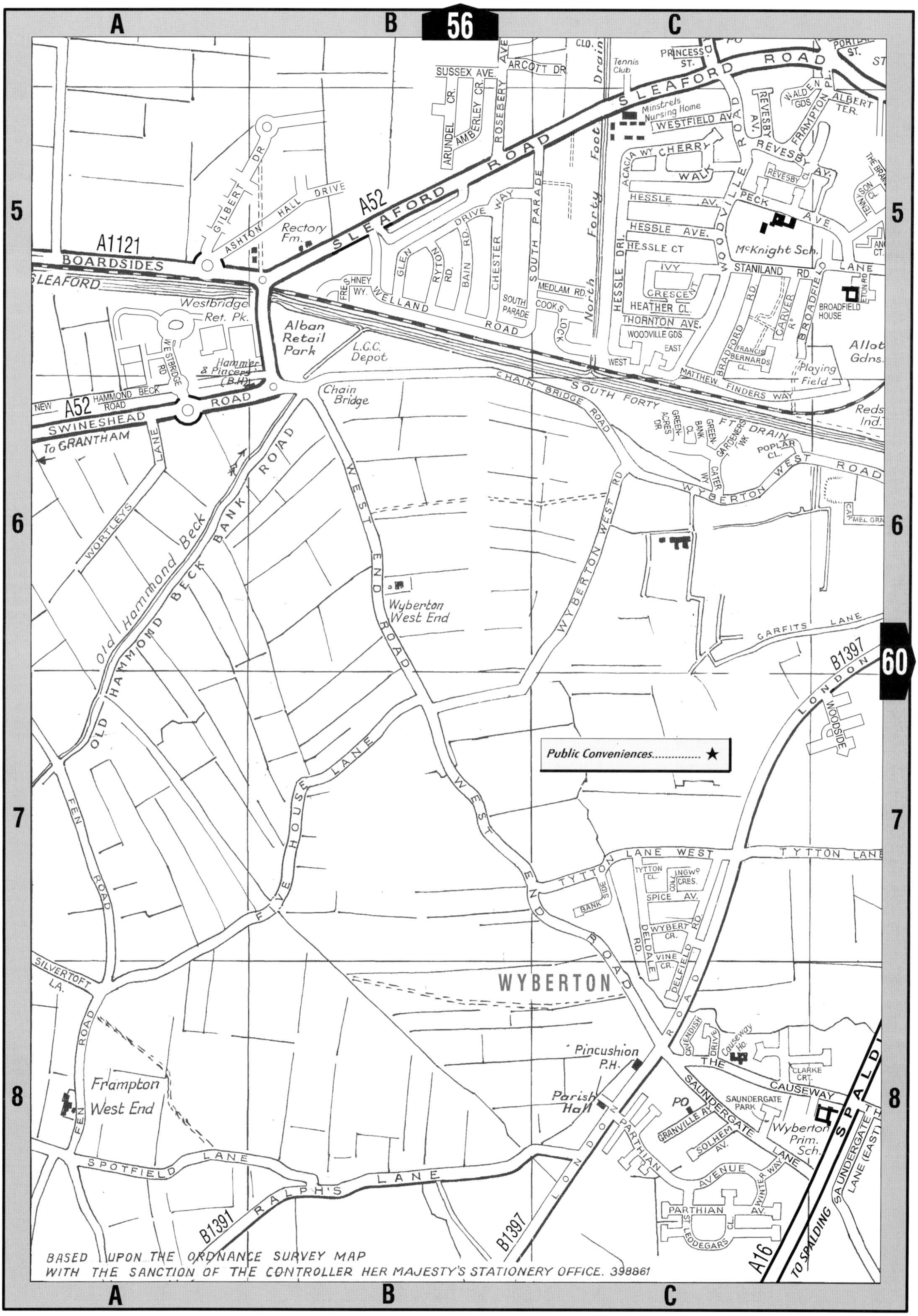
A
B
C
56
60
5
6
7
8
SLEAFORD ROAD
A52
A1121
BOARDSIDES
SLEAFORD
GILBERT DR
ASHTON HALL DRIVE
Rectory Fm.
Westbridge Ret. Pk.
WESTBRIDGE RD
Hammer & Pincers (B.H)
Alban Retail Park
L.C.C. Depot
Chain Bridge
HAMMOND BECK ROAD
NEW
SWINESHEAD ROAD
To GRANTHAM
LANE
WORTLEYS
Old Hammond Beck
BANK ROAD
OLD HAMMOND BECK
FEN ROAD
SILVERTOFT LA.
Frampton West End
SPOTFIELD LANE
RALPH'S LANE
B1391
B1397
LONDON ROAD
FIVE HOUSE LANE
WEST END ROAD
Wyberton West End
WYBERTON WEST RD
CHAIN BRIDGE ROAD
SOUTH FORTY FT. DRAIN
WYBERTON WEST ROAD
GARFITS LANE
Public Conveniences ★
TYTTON LANE WEST
TYTTON LANE
TYTTON CL.
INGWD CRES.
SPICE AV.
BANK SIDE
WYBERT CR.
DELDALE RD.
VINE CR.
DELFIELD RD.
WYBERTON
Pincushion P.H.
Parish Hall
PO
CAVENDISH DRIVE
Causeway Ho.
THE CAUSEWAY
CLARKE CRT.
SAUNDERGATE PARK
SAUNDERGATE LANE
GRANVILLE AV.
SOLHEM AV.
PARTHIAN AVENUE
WINTER WAY
PARTHIAN AV.
ST. LEODEGARS CL.
Wyberton Prim. Sch.
A16
SPALDING
TO SPALDING
SAUNDERGATE LANE (EAST)
WOODSIDE
SUSSEX AVE.
ARCOTT DR.
ARUNDEL CR.
AMBERLEY CR.
ROSEBERY AVE
CLO.
Drain
Tennis Club
PRINCESS ST.
North Forty Foot Drain
Minstrels Nursing Home
WESTFIELD AV.
ACACIA WY.
CHERRY WALK
HESSLE AV.
HESSLE AVE.
HESSLE CT
HESSLE DRI.
IVY CRESCENT
HEATHER CL.
THORNTON AVE.
WOODVILLE GDS.
WEST
EAST
WOODVILLE ROAD
REVESBY AV.
REVESBY AV.
REVESBY CL.
PECK AVE.
McKnight Sch.
STANILAND RD
LANE
BROADFIELD
BROADFIELD HOUSE
ETON RD
BRADFORD RD.
CARVER RD
FRANCIS BERNARDS CL.
MATTHEW FINDERS WAY
Playing Field
Allot. Gdns.
WALDEN GDS.
FRAMPTON PL.
ALBERT TER.
PORTLAND ST.
ST
TENNYSON CL.
ANC CT.
GLEN DRIVE
RYTON RD.
BAIN RD.
CHESTER WAY
SOUTH PARADE
MEDLAM RD.
COOKS LOCK
FRESHNEY WY.
WELLAND ROAD
GREEN ACRES DR
BANK CL.
GREEN GARDENERS WK
CATER WY
POPLAR CL.
CARMEL GRN
Reds Ind.
BASED UPON THE ORDNANCE SURVEY MAP
WITH THE SANCTION OF THE CONTROLLER HER MAJESTY'S STATIONERY OFFICE. 398861

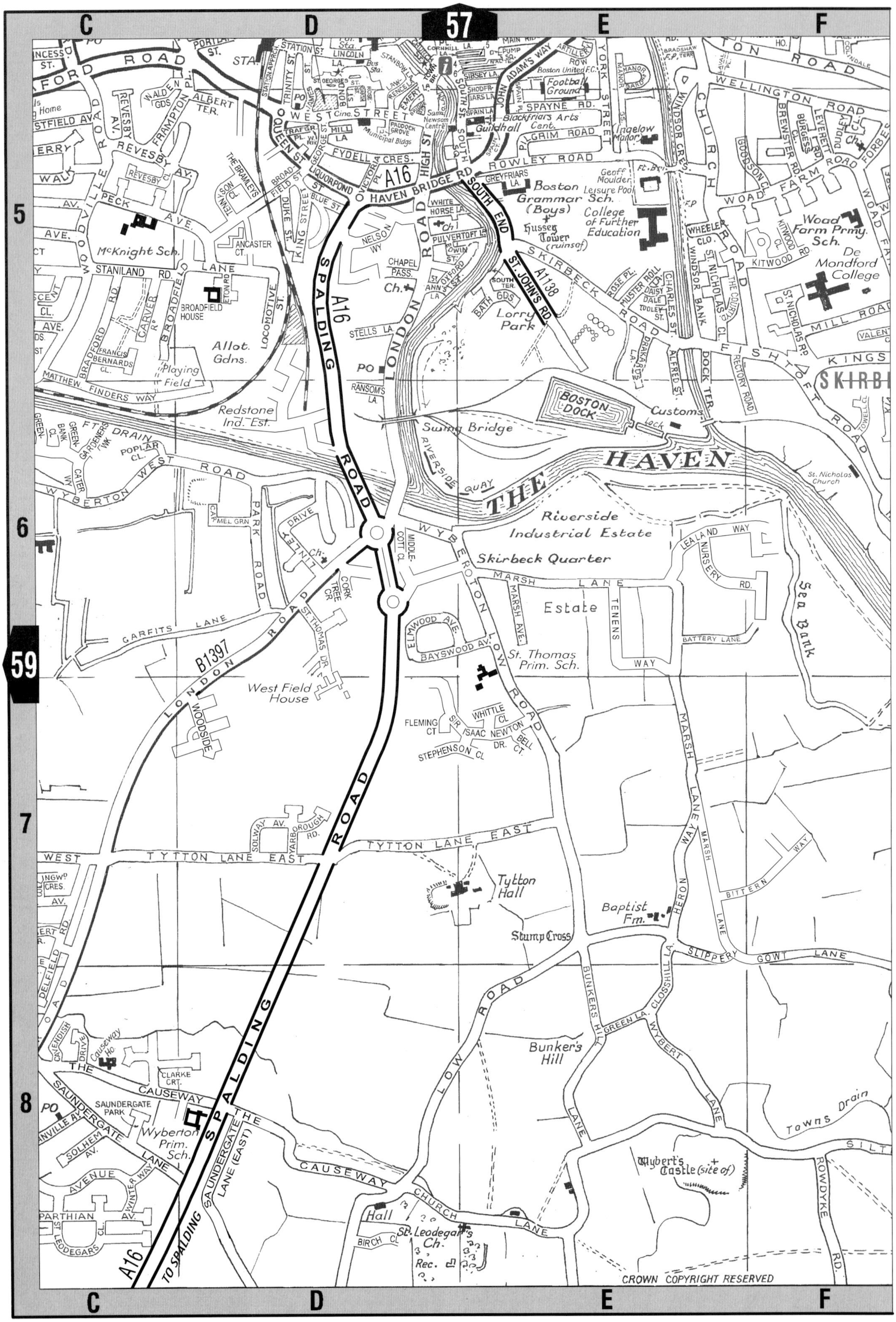
C
D
57
E
F
5
6
59
7
8
FRAMPTON PL.
ALBERT TER.
REVESBY AV.
REVESBY AV.
PECK AVE.
McKnight Sch.
STANILAND RD.
LANE
BROADFIELD HOUSE
BROADFIELD ST.
ANCASTER CT.
LOCOMOTIVE ST.
Allot. Gdns.
Playing Field
MATTHEW FINDERS WAY
Redstone Ind. Est.
STATION ST.
TRINITY ST.
QUEEN ST.
WEST STREET
FYDELL CRES.
LIQUORPOND ST.
BLUE ST.
DUKE ST.
KING STREET
HAVEN BRIDGE RD.
A16
HIGH ST.
SOUTH ST.
Guildhall
Blackfriars Arts Cent.
PILGRIM ROAD
SPAYNE RD.
Football Ground
Boston United F.C.
JOHN ADAM'S WAY
ARTILLERY ROW
YORK STREET
ROWLEY ROAD
GREYFRIARS LA.
SOUTH END
Boston Grammar Sch. (Boys)
Hussey Tower (ruins of)
College of Further Education
Geoff Moulder Leisure Pool
Ingelow Manor
WINDSOR CRES.
CHURCH ROAD
WELLINGTON ROAD
BREWSTER RD.
BURGESS RD.
LEVERETT RD.
FARM ROAD
WOAD
Wood Farm Prmy. Sch.
De Montfort College
KITWOOD RD.
WHEELER CLO.
ST. NICHOLAS CL.
MILL ROAD
KINGS
SKIRBECK
SPALDING ROAD
A16
NELSON WY
CHAPEL PASS.
Ch.
STELLS LA.
PO
RANSOM'S LA.
LONDON ROAD
WHITE HORSE LA.
PULVERTOFT LA.
ST. JOHN'S RD.
A1138
SKIRBECK ROAD
SOUTH TER.
BATH GDS.
Lorry Park
ROSE PL.
MUSTER ROLL LA.
DAISY DALE
TOOLEY ST.
CHARLES ST.
ALFRED ST.
DRAKARDS LA.
DOCK TER.
RECTORY ROAD
FISHTOFT ROAD
BOSTON DOCK
Customs
Lock
Swing Bridge
RIVERSIDE QUAY
THE HAVEN
St. Nicholas Church
Riverside Industrial Estate
Skirbeck Quarter
LEALAND WAY
NURSERY RD.
MARSH LANE
Estate
TENENS WAY
BATTERY LANE
Sea Bank
WYBERTON ROAD
MIDDLECOTT CL.
MARSH AVE.
ELMWOOD AVE.
BAYSWOOD AV.
St. Thomas Prim. Sch.
LOW ROAD
FLEMING CT
SIR ISAAC NEWTON DR.
WHITTLE CL.
BELL CT.
STEPHENSON CL.
POPLAR CL.
WYBERTON WEST ROAD
PARK ROAD
CARMEL GRN
LINLEY DRIVE
CORK TREE CR.
GARFITS LANE
LONDON ROAD
B1397
ST. THOMAS DR.
West Field House
WOODSIDE
SOLWAY AV.
YARBOROUGH RD.
TYTTON LANE EAST
WEST
Tytton Hall
Stump Cross
Baptist Fm.
HERON WAY
MARSH LANE
BITTERN
SLIPPERY GOWT LANE
BUNKERS HILL
CLOSSHILL LA.
GREEN LA.
WYBERT LANE
Bunker's Hill
LOW ROAD
LANE
Towns Drain
SILT
Wybert's Castle (site of)
ROWDYKE RD.
SPALDING ROAD
A16
TO SPALDING
SAUNDERGATE LANE (EAST)
THE CAUSEWAY
CLARKE CRT.
SAUNDERGATE PARK
Wyberton Prim. Sch.
SAUNDERGATE LANE
SOLHEM AV.
AVENUE
PARTHIAN AV.
ST. LEODEGARS CL.
CAVENDISH DRIVE
Causeway Ho.
Hall
BIRCH CL.
St. Leodegar's Ch.
Rec.
CHURCH LANE
CROWN COPYRIGHT RESERVED

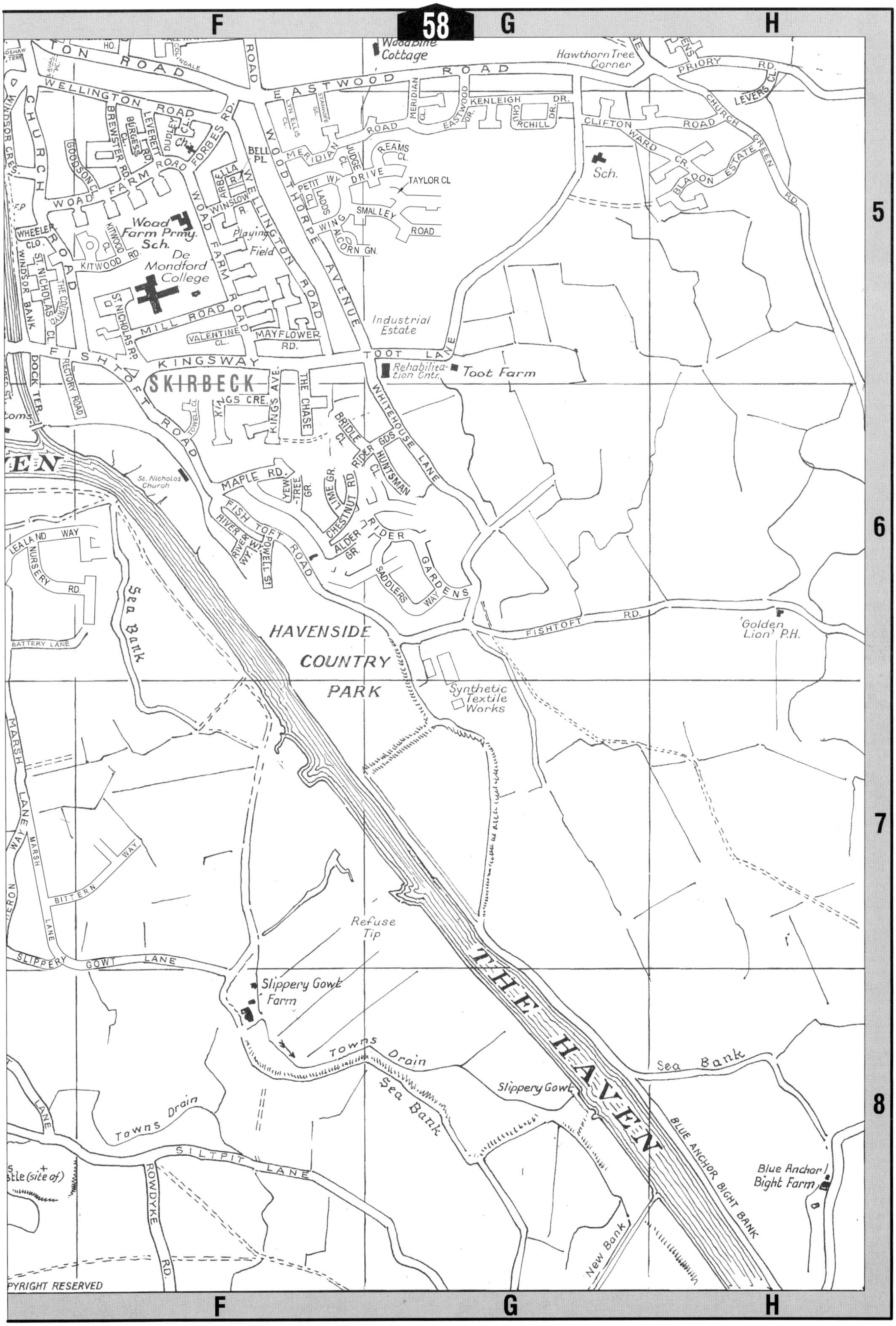
58
F
G
H
5
6
7
8
Woodbine Cottage
Hawthorn Tree Corner
EASTWOOD ROAD
PRIORY RD.
LEVERS CL.
CHURCH GREEN RD.
WELLINGTON ROAD
CHURCH ROAD
WINDSOR CRES.
GOODSON CL.
BREWSTER RD.
BURGESS RD.
LEVERETT RD.
DUDLEY CL.
FORBES RD.
WOOD FARM ROAD
BELL PL.
WOODTHORPE AVENUE
MERIDIAN CL.
MERIDIAN ROAD
EASTWOOD DR.
KENLEIGH DR.
CHURCHILL DR.
CLIFTON ROAD
WARD CR.
BLADON ESTATE
Sch.
JUDGE CL.
REAMS CL.
DRIVE
TAYLOR CL
PETIT WY
LADDS CL.
WING
SMALLEY ROAD
ACORN GN.
WINSLOW R.
Wood Farm Prmy. Sch.
De Mondford College
Playing Field
WHEELER CLO.
WINDSOR BANK
ST. NICHOLAS CL.
THE COURTY.
KITWOOD CL.
KITWOOD RD.
ST. NICHOLAS RD.
MILL ROAD
VALENTINE CL.
MAYFLOWER RD.
WELLINGTON ROAD
Industrial Estate
TOOT LANE
Rehabilitation Cntr.
Toot Farm
FISHTOFT ROAD
KINGSWAY
SKIRBECK
DOCK TER.
RECTORY ROAD
KINGS CRE.
KINGS AVE.
THE CHASE
TOWELL CL.
BRIDLE CL.
RIDER GDS
HUNTSMAN CL.
WHITEHOUSE LANE
St. Nicholas Church
MAPLE RD.
YEW TREE GR.
LIME GR.
CHESTNUT RD.
ALDER GR.
RIDER GARDENS
SADDLERS WAY
RIVER WY.
POWELL ST.
LEALAND WAY
NURSERY RD.
BATTERY LANE
Sea Bank
HAVENSIDE COUNTRY PARK
FISHTOFT RD.
'Golden Lion' P.H.
Synthetic Textile Works
MARSH LANE
MARSH LANE
BITTERN WAY
Refuse Tip
SLIPPERY GOWT LANE
Slippery Gowt Farm
Towns Drain
Sea Bank
Slippery Gowt
THE HAVEN
Sea Bank
BLUE ANCHOR BIGHT BANK
Blue Anchor Bight Farm
Towns Drain
SILTPIT LANE
ROWDYKE RD.
New Bank
LANE
COPYRIGHT RESERVED

BOSTON INDEX TO STREETS

Acacia Way C.5
Albert Court D.4
Albert Street C.4
Albert Terrace D.5
Alcorn Green F.5
Alder Grove F.6
Alfred Street E.5
Allington Garden E.3
Almond Close C.5
Almond Walk C.4
Amberley Crescent B.5
Ancaster Court D.5
Arbella Road F.5
Archer Lane D.4
Arcott Drive B.4
Argyle Street C.4
Artillery Row E.4
Arundel Crescent B.5
Ashlawn Drive F.4
Ashton Hall Drive A.5

Bain Road B.5
Bank Side C.7
Bank Street D.4
Bargate End E.4
Barge Court D.4
Bartol Crescent C.4
Bath Gardens E.5
Battery Lane E.6
Bayswood Avenue E.6
Bayswood Avenue D.6
Bell Court E.7
Bell Place F.5
Belton Close F.4
Birch Close D.8
Bittern Way E.7
Blackthorn Lane F.4
Bladon Estate H.5
Blue Anchor Bight Bank H.8
Blue Street D.5
Boardsides A.5
Bond Street D.5
Boston Long Hedges G.1
Botolph Street E.4
Bowman Close C.4
Brackenbury Way D.3
Bradford Road C.5
Bradshaw Terrace E.4
Brady Street D.4
Brewster Road F.5
Bridge Street D.5
Bridle Close F.6
Broadfield House D.5
Broadfield Lane C.5
Broadfield Street D.5
Brothertoft Road C.4
Brown's Road E.3
Buckingham Close F.4
Bunker Hill Lane E.8
Burgess Close F.5
Burleigh Gardens E.3
Burrows Close D.3
Burton Close F.3

Camelot Gardens G.4
Carlton Road C.3
Carmel Green D.6
Caroline Court E.4
Carver Road C.5
Castle Street C.4
Cater Way C.6
Cavendish Drive C.8
Chain Bridge Road B.6
Chapel Passage D.5
Chapel Street D.4
Charles Street E.5
Charter Close D.3
Cherry Walk C.5
Chester Way B.5
Chestnut Road F.6
Church Close D.4
Church Green Road H.5
Church Lane D.8
Church Road E.5
Church Street D.4
Churchill Drive G.5
Clarke Court C.8
Clifton Road G.5
Closshill Lane E.8
Colindale F.4
Colley Street D.4
Collingwood Crescent C.7
Comer Close E.4
Coningsby Close C.4
Cooks Lock C.5
Cork Tree Crescent D.6
Cornhill Lane E.4
Cotton Road C.3
COWBRIDGE E.1
Cowbridge Drain F.1
Craythorne Lane E.4

Cromwell Close C.3

Daisy Dale E.5
Davey Close D.3
Deldale Road C.7
Delfield Road C.8
Dock Terrace E.5
Dolphin Lane E.4
Drakards Lane E.5
Dudley Close F.5
Duke Street D.5

Eastwood Drive G.5
Eastwood Road F.4
Eaton Road D.5
Edwin Street D.5
Elan Close D.4
Elizabeth Road F.4
Elmwood Avenue D.6
Emery Lane D.5

Fairfax Close C.3
Fen Road A.7
Fenside Road C.3
Fernleigh Way F.4
Field Street E.4
Fieldfare Croft B.4
Fishtoft Road E.5
Five House Lane B.7
Fleming Court D.7
Forbes Road F.5
Forest Dale D.3
Foster Street E.4
Fountain Lane D.4
Fountain Place D.4
Fox Close B.3
Frampton Place C.5
FRAMPTON WEST END A.8
Francis Bernards Close C.3
Frankin Close C.3
Freiston Road E.4
Freshney Way B.5
Friar Way D.3
Frith Bank B.1
Frith Bank Drain C.1
Fydell Crescent D.5
Fydell Street C.4

Gardeners Walk C.6
Garfits Lane C.6
George Street D.5
Gilbert Drive A.5
Gilder Way H.6
Glen Drive B.5
Goodson Close E.5
Grand Sluice Lane E.3
Grants Lane E.4
Granville Avenue C.8
Granville Street C.4
Green Lane E.8
Greenacres Drive C.6
Greenback Close C.6
Greenwood Drive D.3
Greyfriars Lane E.5
Grove Street East E.4
Grove Street West E.4

Hardiway F.4
Harewood Close F.4
Hartley Street E.4
Haven Bank D.4
Haven Bridge D.5
Haven Bridge Road D.5
Haworth Way C.3
Heather Close C.5
Heron Way E.7
Hessle Avenue C.5
Hessle Court C.5
Hessle Drive C.5
High Street D.5
Highgrove Crescent F.4
Hilda Street E.3
Hob Lane C.1
Hope Gardens E.3
Horace Street D.4
Horncastle Road E.2
Hospital Lane E.3
Huntsman Close G.6
Hurle Crescent C.3

Ingelow Avenue C.3
Ingram Road C.3
Irby Place D.4
Irby Street D.4
Ivy Crescent C.5

James Street D.5
John Adams Way E.4
Joy Paine Close C.3
Jubilee Avenue D.3
Judge Close F.5

Kenleigh Drive G.5
King Street D.5
King's Avenue F.6
King's Crescent F.6
Kingsway F.5
Kitwood Close F.5
Kitwood Road F.5
Kyme Road C.3
Ladds Close F.5
Lambs Row D.4
Langrick Road C.4
Larkspur Croft B.4
Laughton Road C.4
Laval Place E.4
Lealand Way E.6
Leverett Road F.5
Levers Close H.5
Lime Grove F.6
Lincoln Lane D.4
Linden Way E.3
Lindis Road F.4
Linley Drive D.6
Liquorpond Street D.5
Locksley Close D.3
Locomotive Street D.5
London Road C.8
London Road D.5
Longhurst Gardens C.3
Low Road D.8
Lyn Ellis Close F.5

Main Ridge East E.4
Main Ridge West E.4
Manor Gardens E.4
Maple Road F.6
Margaret Drive F.4
Marian Road D.3
Market Place D.4
Marsh Avenue E.6
Marsh Lane E.6
Mastins Court E.4
Matthew Finders Way C.5
Maud Foster Drain E.1
Maud Street E.4
Mayfair Gardens F.3
Mayflower Road F.5
Medforth Lane D.3
Medlam Road C.5
Meridian Close G.5
Meridian Road F.5
Middle Drove A.3
Middlecott Close D.6
Mill Lane D.5
Mill Road F.5
Mitre Lane E.4
Monteith Crescent F.4
Mount Bridge E.5
Muster Roll Lane E.5

National Terrace E.4
Nelson Way D.5
New Bank G.8
New Hammond Beck Road A.6
New Street D.4
Norfolk Place D.4
Norfolk Street D.4
Norman Avenue D.4
North Forty Foot Bank A.4
North Forty Foot Drain A.4
North Street E.3
Nursery Road E.6

Oak Crescent D.3
Old Hammond Beck A.6
Old Hammond Beck Bank Road A.7
Orchard Grove E.4
Orchard Street C.4
Oxford Street D.5

Paddock Grove D.5
Park Lane D.4
Park Road D.6
Parkgate E.4
Parsons Drive D.3
Parthian Avenue C.8
Peck Avenue C.5
Pen Street E.4
Petticoat Lane E.4
Pettit Way F.5
Pilgrim Road E.5
Pilley's Lane E.1
Poplar Close C.6
Porcher Way C.3
Portland Street D.4
Post Office Lane D.5
Powell Street F.6
Princess Ann Road F.4
Princess Street C.4
Priory Road H.4

Pulvertoft Lane D.5
Pump Square E.4
Punchbowl Lane B.3
Puritan Way C.3

Queen Street D.5
Queen's Road E.4

Ralph's Lane B.8
Ransom's Lane D.6
Rason's Court E.4
Rawson's Lane D.1
Raybank Close D.3
Reams Close G.5
Rectory Road E.5
Red Lion Street D.4
Redcap Lane D.2
REDSTONE INDUSTRIAL SITE D.5
Revesby Avenue C.5
Revesby Close C.5
Richmond Close E.4
Rider Gardens G.6
River Way F.6
Rochford Crescent E.4
Rochford Tower Lane G.3
Rose Garth Street D.5
Rose Place E.5
Rosebery Avenue B.5
Rowan Way E.3
Rowdyke Road F.8
Rowley Road E.5
Ryton Road B.5

St. Ann's Lane D.5
St. Georges Street D.4
St. John's Road E.5
St. Leodegars Close C.8
St. Leonard Close E.3
St. Marks Terrace D.4
St. Nicholas Close E.5
St. Nicholas Road F.5
St. Thomas Drive D.6
Saddlers Way G.6
Sandringham Gardens F.4
Saundergate Lane C.8
Saundergate Lane (East) D.8
Saundergate Park C.8
Shaw Road C.3
Sheriff Way D.3
Sherwood Avenue D.3
Shodfriars Lane E.4
Shortfield Lane H.2
Sibsey Lane E.4
Sibsey Road F.2
Siltpit Lane F.8
Silver Street E.4
Silvercroft Lane A.8
Sinclair Close D.3
Sir Isaac Newton Drive E.7
SKIRBECK F.6
Skirbeck Court E.4
Skirbeck Road E.5
Sleaford Road B.5
Slippery Gowt Lane E.7
Sluice Bridge D.4
Smalley Road G.5
Solhem Avenue C.8
Solway Avenue D.7
Somersby Green F.3
Somersby Way F.3
South End E.5
South Forty Foot Drain C.6
South Parade B.5
South Parade C.5
South Square E.5
South Street E.4
South Terrace E.5
Spain Court E.5
Spain Lane E.5
Spain Place E.5
Spalding Road D.5
Spayne Road E.5
Spice Avenue C.7
Spilsby Road E.4
Spotfield Lane A.8
Stafford Street D.4
Stanbow Lane D.4
Standish Grove E.3
Stanhope Gardens F.5
Staniland Road C.5
Station Approach D.5
Station Street D.4
Stells Lane D.5
Stephenson Close E.7
Still Lane E.4
Strait Bargate D.4
Sunningdale Drive C.4
Sussex Avenue B.4
Swineshead Road A.6
Sydney Road C.4

Tattershall Road C.1
Tavener Road C.3
Tawney Street E.4
Taylor Close G.5
Tennyson Close D.5
The Bramleys D.5
The Causeway C.8
The Chase F.6
The Courtyard E.5
The Graylings b.3
The Moorings E.2
The Vineyards C.4
Thornton Avenue C.5
Thorold Street D.4
Threadneedle Street E.4
Tilney Avenue C.4
Tollfield Road F.3
Tooley Street E.5
Toot Lane G.5
Towell Close F.6
Tower Road E.4
Tower Street D.4
Town Bridge D.4
Trafalgar Place D.5
Trinity Street D.5
Tudor Drive C.3
Tunnard Street D.4
Tytton Close C.7
Tytton Lane East C.7
Tytton Lane West C.7

Union Place D.4
Union Street D.4

Valentine Close F.5
Vauxhall Road E.4
Victoria Place D.5
Vine Crescent C.7

Wainfleet Road F.3
Walden Gardens C.5
Ward Crescent G.5
Washdyke Lane B.3
Washdyke Lane C.3
Welland Road B.5
Wellington Road F.5
Westbridge Road A.5
West End Road B.6
West Row D.5
West Street D.5
Westfield Avenue C.5
Wheeler Close E.5
White Horse Lane D.5
Whitehouse Lane G.6
Whitham Court D.4
Whiting Square D.3
Whittle Close E.7
Wide Bargate E.4
Willoughby Road E.3
Windsor Bank E.4
Windsor Crescent E.5
Windsor Terrace E.4
Wing Drive G.5
Winslow Road F.5
Winston Gardens E.3
Winter Way C.8
Witham Bank East D.4
Witham Bank West C.3
Witham Gardens D.4
Witham Green D.4
Witham Place D.4
Witham Street D.4
Witham Town D.3
Woad Farm Road F.5
Woodall Close C.4
Woodside D.7
Woodthorpe Avenue F.5
Woodville Gardens East C.5
Woodville Gardens West C.5
Woodville Road C.5
Wormgate D.4
Wortleys Lane A.6
Wybert Crescent C.7
Wybert lane E.8
WYBERTON C.8
Wyberton Low Road D.6
WYBERTON WEST END B.6
Wyberton West Road C.6

Yarborough Road D.7
Yewtree Grove F.6
York Street E.4

Zara Close F.4

KIRTON

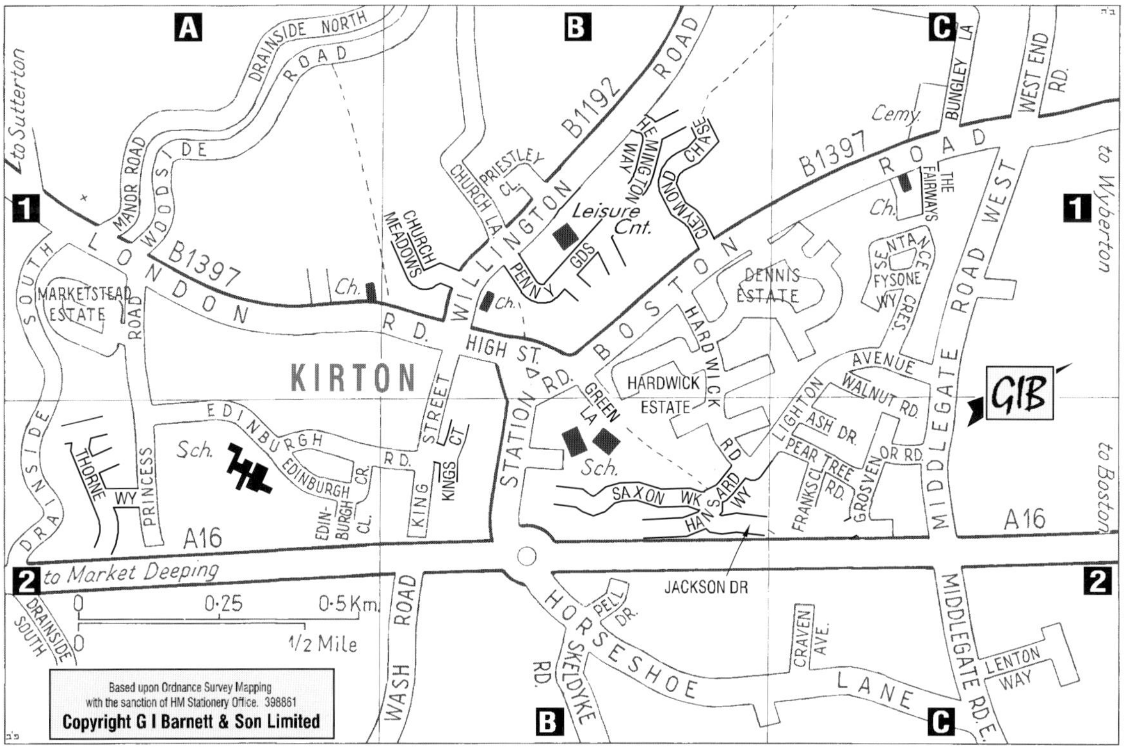

KIRTON INDEX TO STREETS

Ash Drive C.2

Boston Road B.1
Bungley Lane C.1

Church Lane B.1
Church Meadows B.1
Cleymond Chase B.1
Craven Avenue C.3

Dennis Estate B.1
Drainside North A.1
Drainside South A.2

Edinburgh Close A.2
Edinburgh Crescent A.2
Edinburgh Road A.2

Franks Close C.2
Fysone Way C.1

Green Lane B.1

Hansard Way B.2
Hardwick Estate B.1
Hardwick Road B.1
Hemington Way B.1
High Street B.1
Horseshoe Lane B.2

Jackson Drive B.2

King Street B.2
Kings Court B.2

Lenton Way C.2
Lighton Avenue C.2
London Road A.1

Manor Road A.1
Marketstead Estate A.1
Middlegate Road West C.2
Middlegate Road East C.2

Pear Tree Road CX.2
Pell Drive B.2
Penny Gardens B.1
Priestley Close B.1
Princess Road A.2

Saxon Walk B.2
Sentence Crescent C.1
Skeldyke Road B.2
Station Road B.2

The Fairways.............................C.1
Thorne Way A.2

Walnut Road C.1
Wash Road B.2
West End Road C.1
Willington Road B.1
Woodside Road A.1

DONINGTON INDEX TO STREETS

Ash Court A.2

Badgate Road B.1
Barnes Road A.2
Beech Grove A.2
Browntoft Lane B.1

Caythorpe Road B.1
Chestnut Avenue A.2
Church Lane B.1
Church Street A.1
Church View Close A.1
Cowley's Road A.2
Cross Lands B.2

Flinders Road A.2

Gleed Avenue A.1
Goxhill Avenue A.2

Herons Walk B.2
High Street A.1
Highfield Road B.2

Laurel Close A.2
Lindum Way B.2

Mallards Reach B.2
Malting Lane A.2
Manchester Way B.1
Maple Way A.2
Mill Lane B.2
Millfield Road A.2

Orchard Close B.2

Park Lane A.1

Quadring Road B.2

Salters Way A.2
Saxony Way B.2
School Lane B.2
Station Street A.2

Town Dam Lane A.2

Wykes Lane B.1

DONINGTON

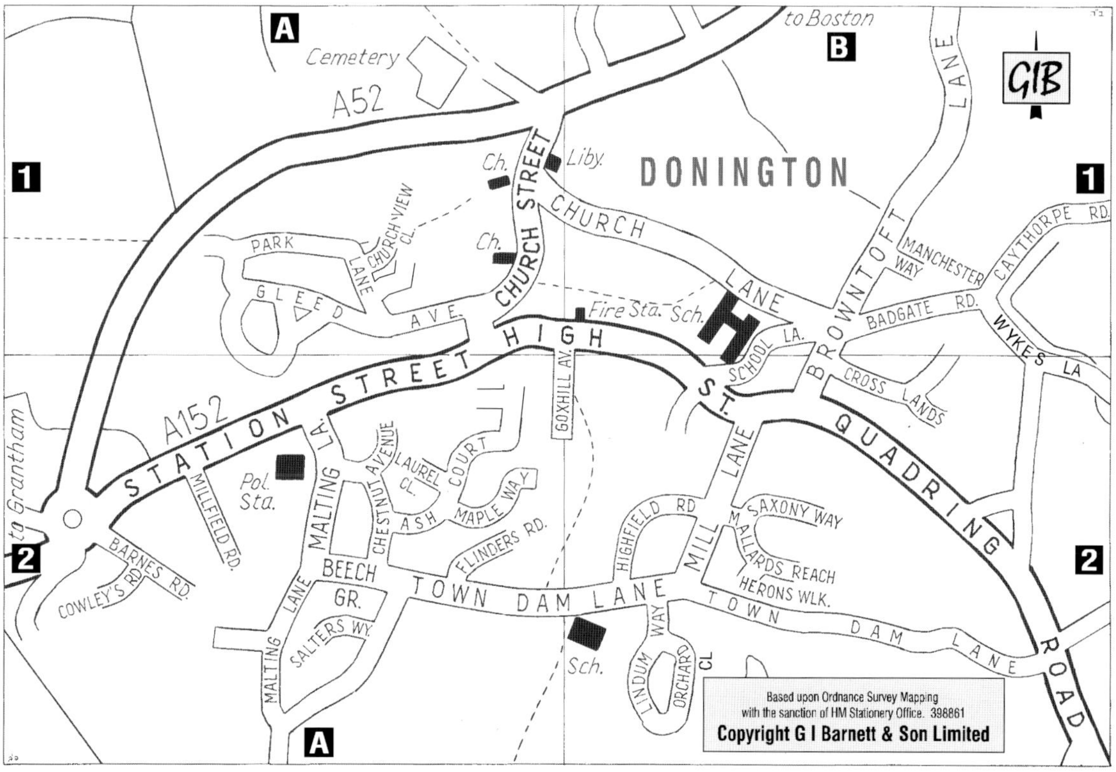

RUSKINGTON

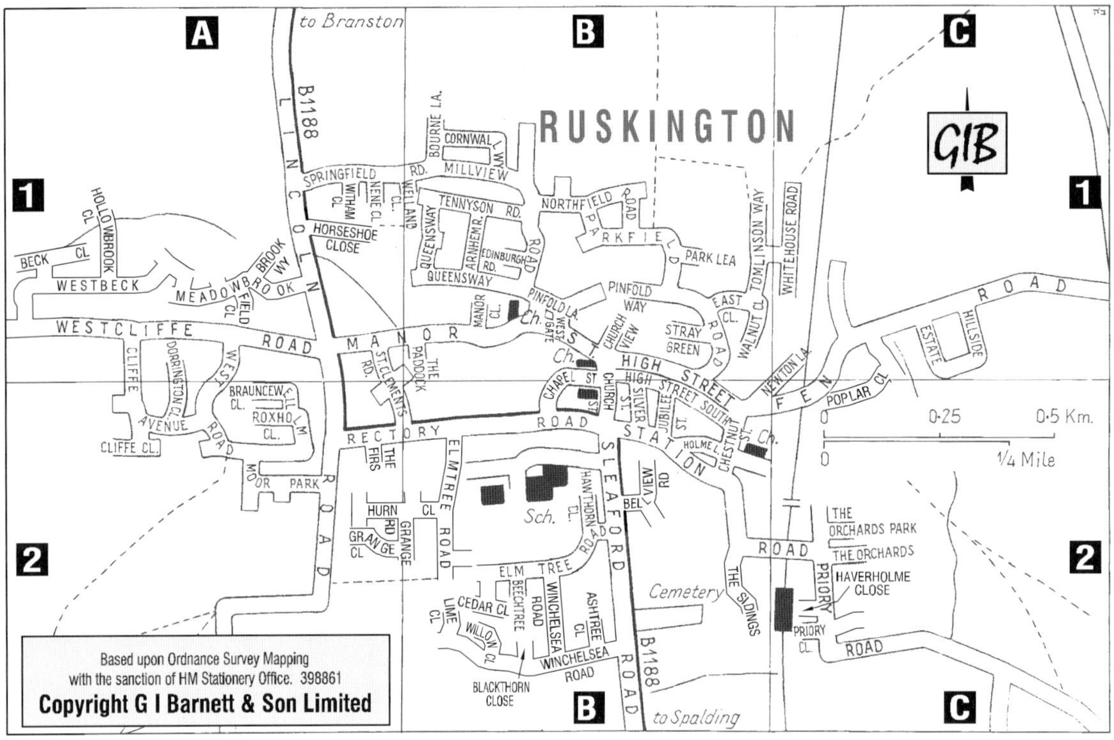

RUSKINGTON INDEX TO STREETS

Arnham Road B.1
Ashtree Close......B.2

Beachtree Close................B.2
Beck Close A.1
Bellview Road......B.2
Blackthorn Close................B.2
Bourne Lane........B.1
Brauncewell Close................A.2
Brook Way A.1

Cedar Close B.2
Chapel Street B.2
Chestnut Street ..B.2
Church Street......B.2
Church View........B.1
Cliffe Avenue A.1
Cliffe Close...........A.2
Cornway Way B.1

Dorrington Close A.1

East Close B.1
Edinburgh Road .B.1
Elm Tree Road ...B.2

Fen Road C.2
Field Close A.1

Grange Close A.2
Grange Road B.2

Haverholme Close C.2
Hawthorn Close B.2
High Street B.1
High Street South B.2
Hillside Estate C.1
Hollowbrook Close A.1
Holme Lane B.2
Horseshoe Close A.1
Hurn Close A.2

Jubilee Street B.2

Lime Close B.2
Lincoln Road A.1

Manor Close........B.1
Manor Street........A.1
Meadowbrook A.1
Millview Road B.1
Moor Park A.2

Nene Close A.1
Newton Lane B.2
Northfield road B.1

Park Lea B.1
Parkfield Road B.1
Pinfold Lane B.1
Pinfold Way B.1
Poplar Close........C.2
Priory Close C.2
Priory Road C.2

Queensway B.1

Rectory Road A.2
Roxholm Close ...A.2

St. Clements Road A.1
Silver Street B.2
Sleaford Road B.2
Springfield Road A.1
Station Road B.2
Stray Green B.1
Sycamore Road...B.2

Tennyson Road ..B.1
The Firs A.2
The Orchards C.2
The Orchards Park C.2
The Paddock B.1
The Sidings B.2
Tomlinson Way ...B.1

Walnut Close B.1
Welland Close B.1
Westbeck A.1
Westcliffe Road A.1
Westgate B.1
West Road A.1
Whitehouse Road C.1
Willow Close........B.2
Winchelsea Road B.2
Witham Close A.1

SLEAFORD INDEX TO STREETS

Abbey Road A.5
Acacia Close D.5
Aidan Road B.5
Albion Terrace B.3
Alder Road C.3
Alexandra Road C.3
Alfred Close B.5
All Saints Grove B.2
Almond Walk C.1
Althelstan Close B.5
Ambleside Close B.5
Amethyst Close A.4
Ancaster Drive B.5
Anglia Close B.5
Ark Royal Court A.4
Ashbourne Close B.5
Ashby Court D.1
Ashfield Road D.3
Aspen Drive D.4

Barley Way E.4
Barnes Close B.1
Bede Close B.5
Beech Rise D.2
Berkeley Court D.3
Bernicia Close B.5
Berry Close C.5
Birchwood Road C.1
Bishops Court C.2
Blackthorns D.4
Bonemill Lane F.1
Boston Road D.3
Boundary Pastures D.4
Brecon Way B.4
Briar Close D.4
Bridle Close C.5
Bristol Way B.3
Burns Crescent E.3
Buttler Way C.4
Byron Close E.3

Canterbury Way C.1
Caroline Close E.3
Carre Street E.3
Castle Causeway C.3
Castle Street C.3
Castle Terrace C.3
Cedar Avenue C.2
Chapel Hill Court D.4
Chapman Road B.1
Charles Street C.3
Chaucer Gardens E.3
Cherry Grove C.2
Chestnut Close D.4
Cheviot Close B.4
Christopher Crescent E.4
Church Close B.5
Church Lane D.3
Claybergh Drive C.2
Clay Hill Road B.4
Clinton Drive C.5
Cobblers Way D.4
Coleridge Gardens ..E.4
Copeland Court C.4
Cornfield View C.5
Covel Road B.1
Creamery Yard C.4
Cromwell Crescent ..E.3
Cross Keys yard D.3
Curlew Way B.4
Cygnet Close B.4
Cypress Close D.5

Dawson Road D.1
Deira Close B.5
Discovery Close A.4
Dove Close B.4
Durham Avenue C.1
Duke Street D.3

Eagle Drive B.4
East Road D.3
Eastgate D.3
Edwin Close B.5
Electric Station Road C.3
Eliot Close E.3
Elmgarth E.4
Elmore Close C.3
Ely Street C.1
Eslaford Gardens E.3
Exeter Drive C.1

Falcon Way B.4
Finch Drive B.4
Forum Way E.4
Franklin Crescent D.2
George Street C.4
Gibson Close B.1
Glebe Close B.5
Gloucester Close C.1
Grace Close D.4
Grampian Close B.4
Grantham Road B.4
Greenfield Close D.1

Hadley Road D.2
Handley Street D.3
Harvest Way C.5
Hauser Close B.5
Hawks Way B.4
Hawthorn Drive D.4
Hazelgrove C.2
Hengist Close B.5
Hereford Close C.1
Hermes Way A.4
Hervey Road C.4
Hilda Close B.5
Hill's Court D.4
Holly Close C.4
Hood Close A.4
Hussey Close D.3

Ickworth Road C.4

Jermyn Street D.3
Jonathan Gardens ..E.4
Jubilee Grove C.2
Juniper Way D.4

Keats Drive F.4
Keepers Way D.4
Kesteven Street D.3
Kestrel Close B.4
King Edward Street C.4
King John Street C.3
Kipling Close E.3

Lafford Court B.3
Larch Way D.5
Lavender Drive D.5
Leicester Street C.3
Limetree Close D.5
Lincoln Road B.1
Linnet Way B.4
Linwood Close C.2
Lomax Drive B.2
London Road C.5
Lord Street C.4

Magnolia Road D.5
Maiden Grove D.4
Maize Court..............E.4
Malvern Close B.5
Manor Place C.2
Manor Road B.5
Mareham Lane D.4
Marigold Walk E.4
Mark Avenue E.3
Market Street D.3
Meadowfield C.2
Mercia Close B.5
Millers Close C.5
Millfield Terrace C.2
Milton Way E.3
Moneys Yard D.3
Mulberry Close D.5

New Street D.3
Newcomb Court B.1
Newfield road C.2
Newton Way D.2
North Parade B.2
Northfield Road A.5
Northgate D.3
Northumbria Road ..B.5
Northwood Drive C.2
Norwich Close C.1
Nursery Court C.4

Oak Road C.5
Oat Drive..................E.4
Old Place E.3
Orchard Close E.3
Osprey Close B.4
Oswin Close B.5
Oxford Court C.1

Palmer Court B.2
Park Avenue E.3
Park Crescent E.3
Pavilion Gardens D.4
Peacock Court D.4
Pear Tree Close C.5
Peregrine Close C.4
Peterborough Way ..C.1
Pine Close D.4
Playhouse Yard C.3
Pride Parkway..........E.1
Priory Way................A.5

Quantock Court B.4
Queen Street C.4

Redwood Avenue C.5
Reform Place C.3
Rhodes Avenue C.4
Richmond Close B.4
Ripon Drive C.1
Riverside Close C.3
Robertson Drive C.2
Robin Close B.4
Romney Court D.3
Rookery Avenue B.4
Rosewood Avenue ..C.5
Rowan Close............D.5
Rudkin Drive D.1
Russell Crescent E.3
Rye Close E.4

St. Anne's Close C.1
St. Botolph's Drive ..B.1
St. Denys Avenue ..B.2
St. Edmund's Road C.4
St. Giles Avenue D.3
St. Mary's Drive C.1
St. Michael's Walk ..B.2
Sandhurst Close B.5
Sheldrake Road A.4
Shelley Drive E.3
Slea Cottages C.3
Sleaford By-Pass C.1
Southfields Road C.4
Southgate D.3
Spinners Close D.4
Spriggs Close C.4
Spring Gardens B.2
Station Road D.4
Stephens Way E.4
Stokes Drive B.1
Stone Way................B.1
Summerfield Court ..D.1
Summerfield Drive ..D.1
Swallow Close B.4
Sycamore Drive C.2

Tame Court D.3
Tamson Way D.3
Taunton Close C.1
Tennyson Avenue ..C.2
The Drove B.2
The Hoplands E.3
The Innings D.4
The Paddock E.3
The Reservation E.1
Thomas Street C.3
Thrush Close B.4
Tower View B.4
Town Road A.5
Trevitt Close B.1
Truro Close C.1

Vanguard Way A.4
Vicarage Court D.3
Victoria Avenue C.4
Victory Way A.4

Walnutgarth E.4
Water Gate C.3
Welby Close B.3
Wesley Close C.4
Wessex Close B.5
West Banks C.3
Westgate C.3
Westgate Park C.3
Wharfside Mews D.3
Wheat Grove............E.4
Willow Court D.4
Winchester Way C.1
Windsor Close B.5
Woodbridge Road ..E.2
Woodside Avenue ..D.1
Woodside Court D.1
Woodside View D.1
Wordsworth Court ..E.3
Wren Close B.4

York Road C.1

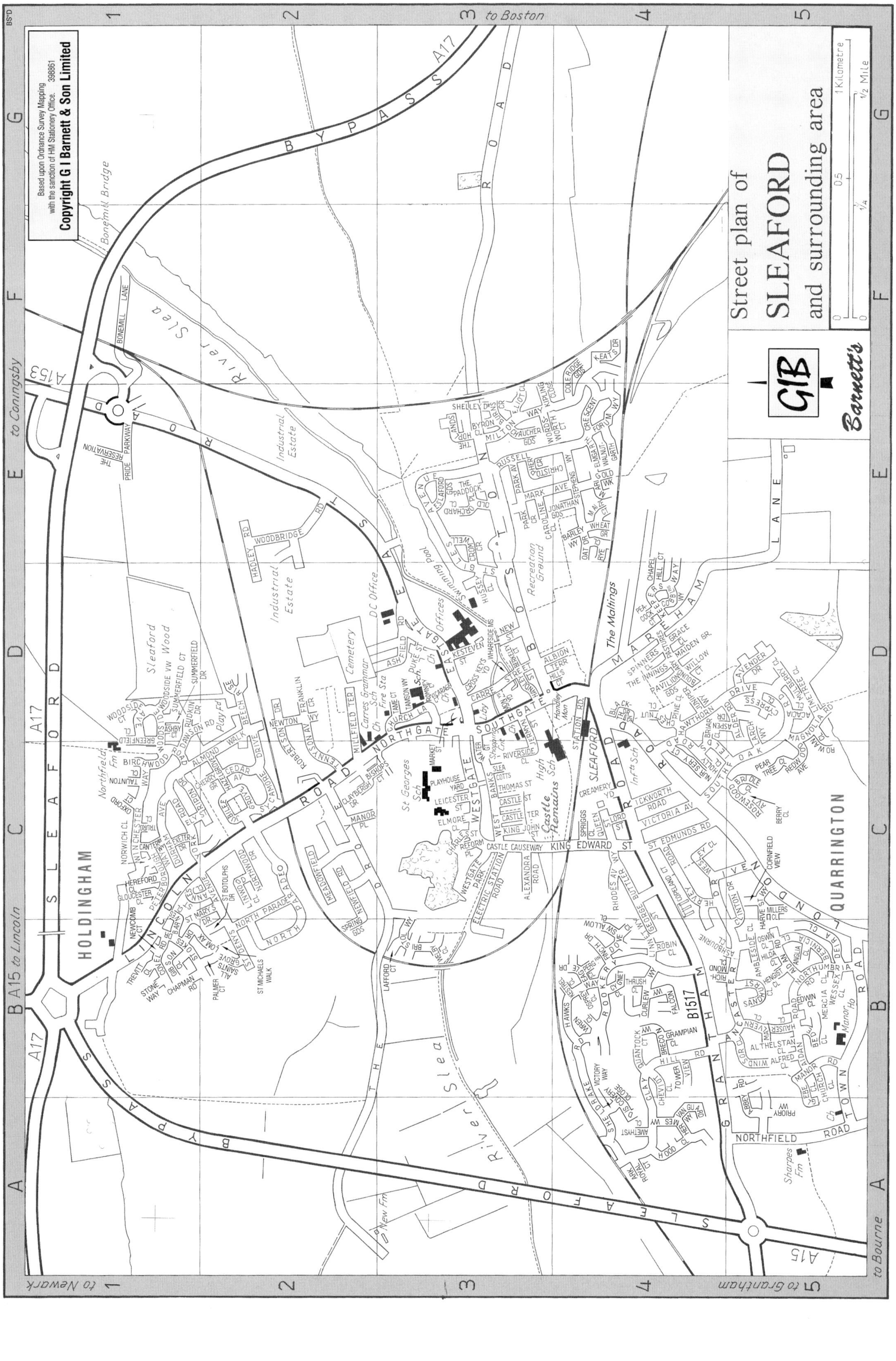
Street plan of
SLEAFORD
and surrounding area
Barnett's
Based upon Ordnance Survey Mapping with the sanction of HM Stationery Office. 398861
Copyright G I Barnett & Son Limited
1 Kilometre
1/2 Mile
to Boston
to Coningsby
A15 to Lincoln
to Newark
to Grantham
to Bourne
HOLDINGHAM
QUARRINGTON
BYPASS
SLEAFORD ROAD
LINCOLN ROAD
NORTHGATE
SOUTHGATE
EASTGATE
WESTGATE
BOSTON ROAD
MAREHAM LANE
GRANTHAM ROAD
LONDON ROAD
DRIVE
KING EDWARD ST
CASTLE CAUSEWAY
River Slea
The Maltings
Recreation Ground
Industrial Estate
Cemetery
Sleaford Wood
Castle Remains
St Georges Sch
High Sch
Carres Grammar Sch
DC Office
Northfield Fm
Sharpes Fm
Bonemill Bridge
B1517
A17
A153
A15

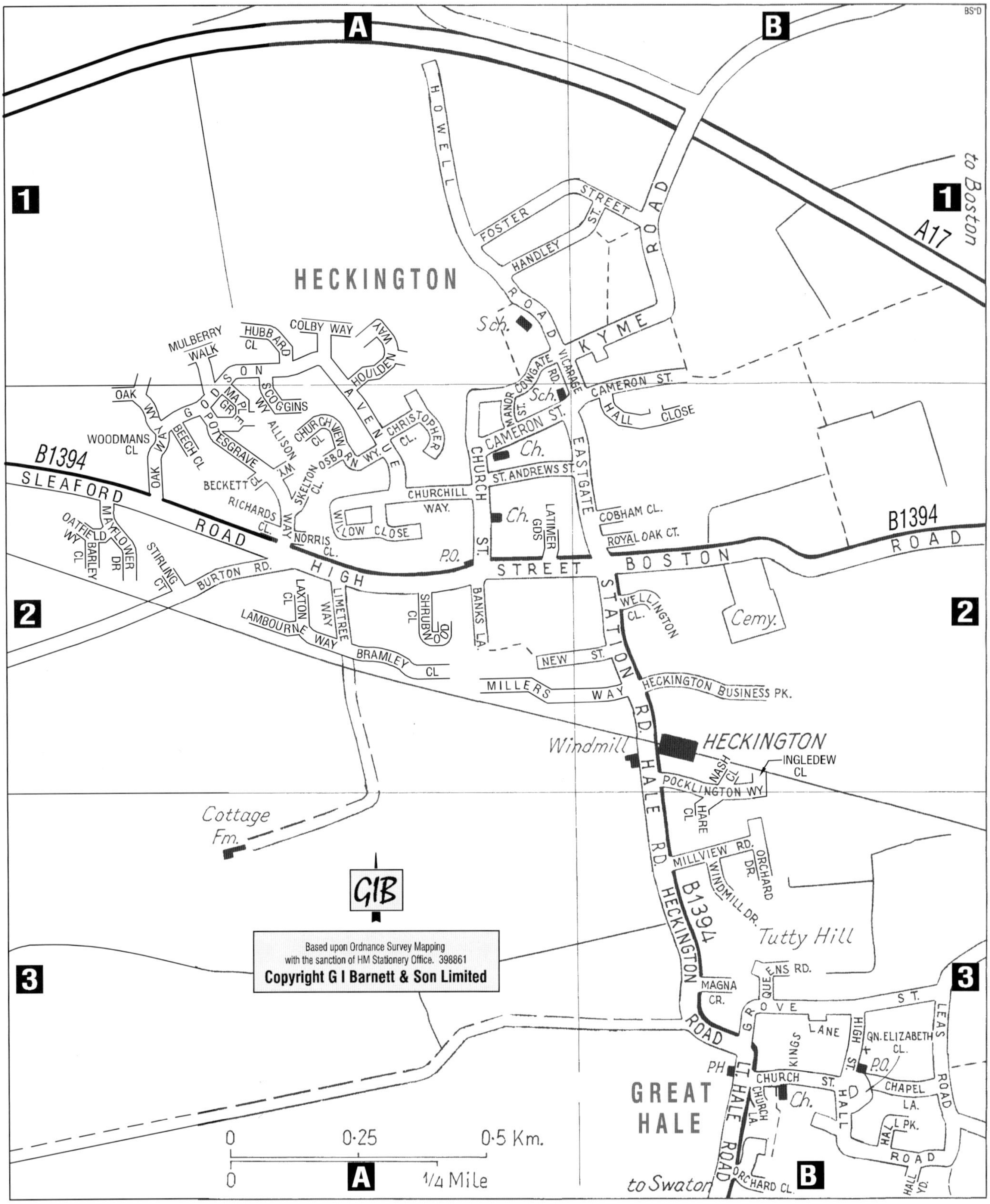

HECKINGTON/GREAT HALE INDEX TO STREETS

Allison Way A.2

Banks Lane A.2
Barley Close A.2
Beckett Close A.2
Beech Close A.2
Boston Road B.2
Bramley Close A.2
Burton Road A.2

Cameron Street A.2
Chapel Lane B.3
Church Lane B.3
Church Street, Great Hale B.3
Church Street, Heckington A.2
Churchill Way A.2
Churchview Close A.2
Christopher Close A.2
Cobham close B.2
Colby Way A.1

Cowgate A.1

Eastgate B.2

Foster Street A.1

Godson Avenue A.2
GREAT HALE B.3
Grove Street B.3

Hale Road B.2
Hall Close B.2
Hall Park B.3
Hall Road B.3
Hall Yard B.3
Handley Street A.1
Handley Street A.1
Hare Close B.3
HECKINGTON A.1
Heckington Road B.3

Heckington Business Park B.2
High Street, Gt. Hale B.3
High Street, Heckington A.2
Houlden Way A.1
Howell Road A.1
Hubbard Close A.1

Kings Lane B.3
Kyme Road B.1

Lambourne Way A.2
Latimer Gardens A.2
Laxton Close A.2
Lea Road B.3
Lime Tree Way A.2
Little Hale Road B.3

Mana Crescent B.3
Manor Street A.2
Maple Grove A.2

Mayflower Drive A.2
Millers Way A.2
Millview Road B.3
Mulberry Walk A.1

Nash Close B.2
New Street A.2
Norris Close A.2

Oak Way A.2
Oatfield Way A.2
Orchard Close B.3
Orchard Drive B.3
Osborn Way A.2

Pockington Way B.2
Pottesgrave Way A.2

Queen Elizabeth Close B.3
Queens Road B.3

Richards Close A.2
Royal Oak Court B.2

St. Andrews Street A.2
Scoggins Way A.2
Shurbwood Close A.2
Skelton Close A.2
Sleaford Road A.2
Station Road B.2
Stirling Court A.2

Vicarage Road A.1

Wellington Close A.2
Willow Close A.2
Windmill Drive B.3
Woodmans Close
(Private Road) A.2

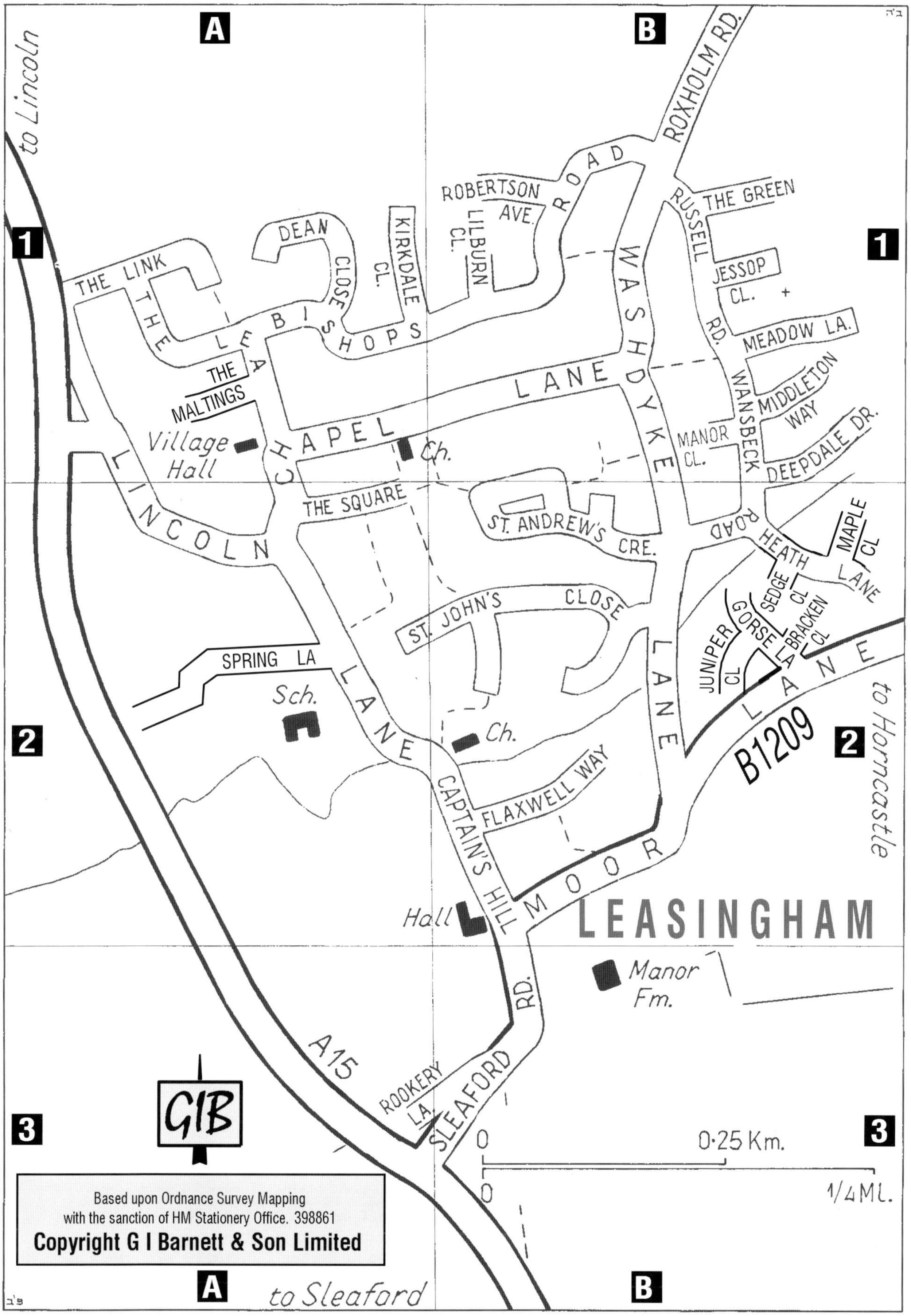

LEASINGHAM INDEX TO STREETS

Bishops Road A.1
Bracken Close B.2

Captain's Hill B.2
Chapel Lane A.1

Dean Close A.1
Deepdale Drive B.1

Flaxwell Way B.2

Gorse Lane B.2

Heath Lane B.2

Jessop Close B.1
Juniper Close B.2

Kirkdale Close A.1

Liburn Close B.1

Manor Close B.1
Maple Close B.2
Meadow Lane B.1
Middleton Way B.1
Moor Lane B.2

Robertson Avenue B.1
Rookery Lane A.3
Roxholm Road B.1
Russell Road B.1

St. Andrew's Crescent B.2
St. John's Close B.2
Sedge Close B.2
Sleaford Road B.3
Spring Lane A.2

The Green B.1
The Lea A.1
The Link A.1
The Maltings A.1

The Square A.1

Wansbeck Road B.1
Washdyke Lane B.1

METHERINGHAM

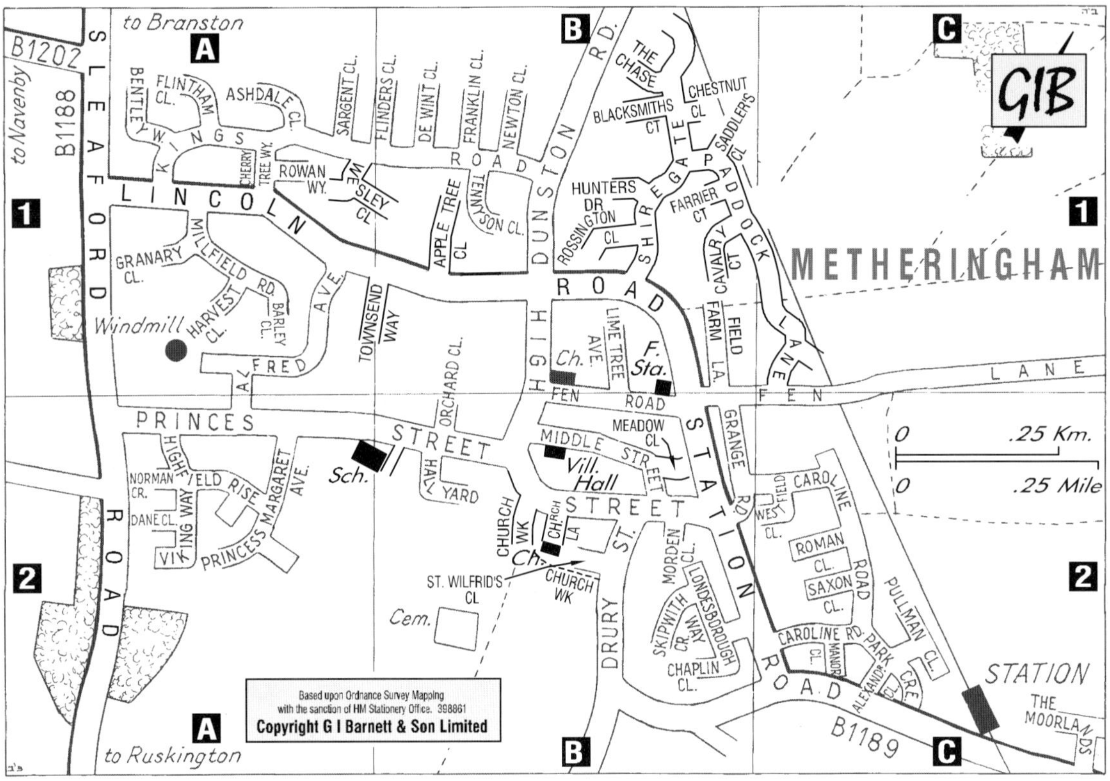

WOODHALL SPA INDEX TO STREETS

ABBEY LA. B.2
ALBANY RD. B.2
ALEXANDRA RD. B.1
ALVERSTON AVE. C.2
ARNHEM WAY B.2

BIRKDALE CL. A.1

CAME CT. B.1
CANTERBURY CL. A.1
CARNOUSTIE CL. A.1
CLARENCE RD. B.1
CORONATION RD. B.1
CROMWELL AVE. B.2

EBRINGTON CL. D.2

FOREST PINES LA. A.1

GLENEAGLES DR. A.1
GORSE CL. D.2
GREEN LA. A.1
GROVE CT. C.2
GROVE DR. C.2

HEATHER CL. C.2
HORNCASTLE RD. D.2
HOYLAKE DR. A.1
HUNSTON RD. A.1

IDDESLEIGH RD. C.2

KING EDWARD AVE. B.1
KING EDWARD CR. B.1
KING EDWARD RD. B.1
KING GEORGE AVE. C.1
KINGS WALK D.1
KIRBY LA. D.2
KIRKSTEAD CT. C.2

LONG AVE. B.2

MAPLE AVE. B.1
MOOR PARK DR. A.1

OAK CL. D.2
OAKLANDS AVE. B.2

PARK CL. B.1

ROYAL SQUARE B.1

SPA RD. C.1
ST ANDREWS WALK A.1
ST GEORGES DR. A.1
ST LEONARDS AVE. B.2
ST LEONARDS CL. B.2
ST PETERS DR. B.2
STANHOPE AVE. C.2
STATION RD. B.1
STIXWOULD RD. B.1
SUNNINGDALE CL. A.1
SYLVAN AVE. C.2

TARLESTON AVE. D.2
TATTERSHALL RD. B.2
THE BROADWAY C.1
THE CLOSE. B.1
TOR O MOOR GDS. C.2
TOR O MOOR RD. C.2
TURNBERRY DR. A.1

VICTORIA AVE. B.2

WENTWORTH WAY A.1
WITHAM RD. B.1
WITHAM RD. A.1
WOBURN GR. A.1
WOODLAND DR. D.2

WOODHALL SPA

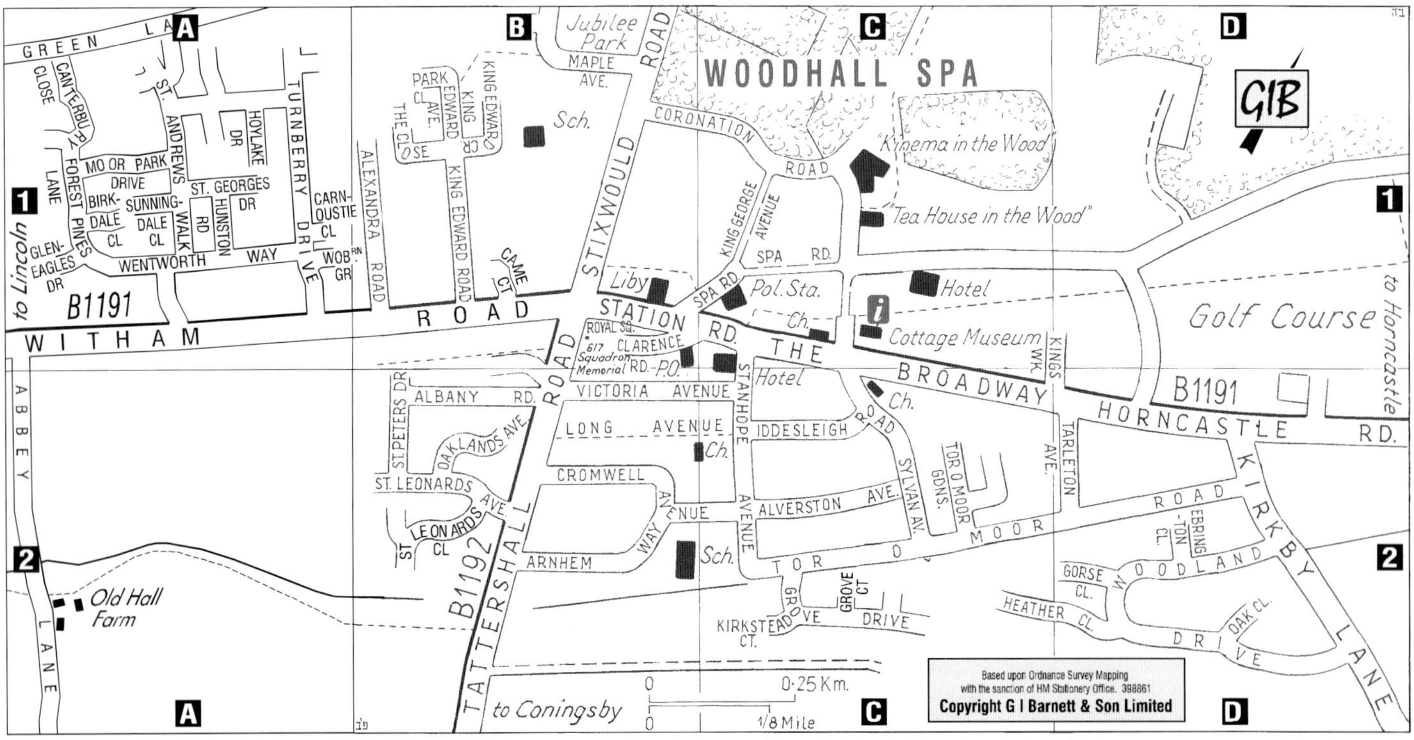

METHERINGHAM INDEX TO STREETS

Alexander Close C.2
Alfred Avenue A.1
Apple Tree Close A.1

Barley Close A.1
Bentley Way A.1
Blacksmiths Court B.1

Carbine Road C.2
Cavalry Court B.1
Chaplin Close B.2
Cherry Tree Way A.1
Chestnut Close B.1
Church Lane B.2
Church Walk B.2

Dane Close A.2
De Wint Close B.1
Drury Street B.2
Dunston Road B.1

Farrier Court B.1
Fen Lane C.1
Fen Road B.2
Field Farm Lane B.1
Finders Close B.1
Flinthorn Close A.1
Franklin Close B.1

Granary Close A.1
Grange Road B.2

Hall Yard B.2
Harvest Close A.1
High Street B.1
Highfield Rise A.2
Hunters Drive B.1

Kings Road A.1

Lime Tree Avenue B.1
Lincoln Road A.1
Londesborough Way B.2

Manor Close C.2
Meadow Close B.2
Middle Street B.2
Millfield Road A.1
Morden Close B.2

Newton Close B.1
Norman Crescent A.2

Orchard Close B.2

Paddock Lane B.1
Park Crescent C.2
Princes Street A.2
Princess Margaret Avenue A.2
Pullman Close C.2

Roman Close C.2
Rossington Close B.1
Rowan Way A.1

Saddler's Close B.1
St. Wilfrid's Close B.2
Sargent Close A.1
Saxon Close C.2
Skipwith Crescent B.2
Sleaford Road A.1
Station Road B.1

Tennyson Close B.1
The Chase B.1
The Moorlands C.2
Townsend Way A.1

Viking Way A.2

Wesley Close A.1
Westfield Close C.2

Abbey Road D.3
Abbotts Way D.3
Ada Way D.2
Adrian Close C.4
Albany Place D.5
Albany Road C.5
Albion Road C.3
Alder Close D.5
Alexander Drive D.4
Alexandra Road C.3
Almond Crescent D.3
Alvingham Road D.3
Amanda Drive C.2
Andrew Close C.2
Anthony Crescent C.2
Arundel Drive B.2
Ash Close C.2
Ashley Road C.4
Aswell Street C.4

Badminton Way B.3
Barton Court C.5
Beck Way D.5
Beech Grove C.2
Belton Walk B.2
Belvoir Court C.2
Belvoir Way B.1
Birch Road D.4
Bishops Close D.3
Blenheim Close B.2
Blue Stone Rise B.4
Bolingbroke Road B.1
Bowers Avenue D.2
Bracken Way C.2
Brackenborough Road C.1
Bradley Close D.5
Bramley Close C.4
Breakneck Lane B.4
Bridge Close C.3
Bridge Street B.3
Broadbank B.3
Broadley Crescent D.3
Brocklesby Walk B.3
Brookside Close D.5
Buckingham Road B.2
Burghley Crescent B.2
Burnt Hill Lane C.4
Burton Court D.4
Bus Street C.4
Butcher Lane C.4

Cannon Street C.3
Castle Way B.2
Cedar Close C.3
Charles Avenue D.3
Charles Street C.3
Chatsworth Drive B.3
Chequergate B.4
Chestnut Drive D.3
Christopher Close D.2
Church Close B.4
Church Lane
(Keddington) E.2
Church Street C.4
Cinder Lane C.4
Cisterngate B.3
Commercial Road D.3
Cordeaux Way C.3
Cornmarket C.4
Coronation Close C.2
Cowslip Lane E.2
Crown Walk D.4
Crow Tree Lane B.4
Cuppleditch Way C.2

David Avenue D.2
Dove Close D.2

Eastfield Court D.3
Eastfield Rise D.3
Eastfield Road D.3
Eastgate C.4
Edward Street B.4
Elkington Road A.4
Elm Drive D.2
Eresbie Roiad D.5
Eve Street C.3

Fanthorpe Lane A.2
Florence Wright Avenue ..D.5
Fowler Close......................D.4
Freer Gardens D.3
Fulmar Drive C.2

George Street B.4
Glamis Place B.3
Goodwood Close B.3
Gospelgate B.4
Grange Lane E.2
Gresledy Road D.4
Greys Court B.3
Greys Road B.3
Grimsby Road B.2
Grosvenor Crescent D.2
Grosvenor Road D.2

Halfpenny Lane A.5
Hardwick Close B.2
Harewood Crescent B.3
Havelock Close D.4
Hawker Drive D.4
Hawksmede Way D.2
Hawthorne Avenue C.3
Hazel Close D.4
High Holme Crescent C.3
High Holme Road B.3
Hill Rise Close B.3
Hill Terrace C.4
Holmes Close C.3
Horncastle Road B.5
Hubbard's Hill A.5
Hunter Place B.4

Irish Hill B.4

James Street C.3
Jenkins Close C.2
Jubilee Crescent C.2
Julian Bower C.5

KEDDINGTON D.2
Keddington Crescent C.2
Keddington Road C.2
Kenwick Close D.5
Kenwick Gardens D.5
Kenwick Pastures D.5
Kenwick Road D.5
Kestrel Drive D.2
Kidgate C.4
Kiln Lane C.3
Kiln Yard C.4
Kings Court D.3

Laburnham Crescent D.4
Lacey Gardens D.3
Langley Close D.5
Lee Street C.4
Leeks Row C.3
Legbourne Road D.5
Library Close C.3
Lime Grove C.2
Lincoln Way B.1
Linda Crescent B.4
Linden Walk C.4
Lindsey Way D.4
Little Crowtree Lane A.4
Little Eastgate Close B.4
Little Lane C.4
Little South Street B.4
London Road C.5
Longleat Drive B.3
Love Lane B.4
Lucern Close D.3
Ludater Terrace D.3
Lyndon Way D.2

Maple Close C.3
Market Place C.4
Martin Close D.2
Mayfield Crescent D.5
Meadow Close C.5
Mercer Row C.4
Meridian View B.4
Mill Lane C.3
Mill Lane
Julian Bower B.5
Millers Court C.3
Millgood Close D.4
Minster Drive D.4
Monks Avenue C.3
Monk's Dike E.3
Monk's Dyke Road C.4
Mount Olivet B.3
Mount Pleasant C.4
Mount Pleasant
Avenue D.4

New Street C.4
Newbridge Hill C.3
Newmarket C.4
Nichol Hill C.3
North Holme Road C.2
Northgate C.3
Nottingham Road B.1

Oak Close D.4
Oak Court D.4
Old Mill Park C.3
Orchard Close C.3
Orme Lane C.3

Park Avenue D.3
Park Row E.3
Parsons Halt C.3
Pasture Drive D.5
Pawnshop Passage C.4
Pippin close C.4
Pleasant Place C.3
Priory Close C.3
Priory Road C.3

Quarry Road C.4
Quarry Side B.4
Queen Street C.4
Queens Court D.4
Queensway D.4
Quorn Gardens D.4

Ramsgate C.3
Ramsgate Road C.3
Richmond Road B.1
River Lane E.2
Riverhead D.3
Riverhead Road D.3
Riverhead Court D.3
Robinson Lane C.4
Rookery Close D.2
Royal Oak Court B.4
Russet Drive C.4

St. Bernard's Avenue D.3
St. Bernard's Close D.3
St. James View C.4
St. Mary's Lane B.4
St. Mary's Park B.3
St. Michael's Road C.4
Sandringham Drive B.3
Scarborough Road B.1
Schoolhouse Lane B.4
Sea View Cottages B.3
Seymour Avenue C.4
Shaws Court B.4
Shearwater Close D.2
Sherwood Close C.4
Simons Close D.5
Somersby Court B.4
Southfield Drive C.5
South Terrace C.4
Southlands Avenue D.5
Spire View Road D.4
Spital Hill C.4
Spout Yard C.3
Spring Gardens C.4
Staines Way D.2
Station Approach C.3
Stewton Gardens D.4
Stewton Lane D.4
Stutte Close D.5
Sudbury Place B.4
Swallow Drive C.2
Sycamore Avenue D.4

Tattershall Way B.2
Temple Terrace B.3
Tennyson Road C.4
Thames Street D.3
The Link D.3
The Moorings D.3
The Mount B.3
The Paddocks B.4
The Sidings C.3
Trinity Lane D.3
Tudor Drive C.5

Union Street B.3
Upgate C.4

Vanessa Road B.4
Vicars Lane C.3
Victoria Road C.3
Virginia Drive D.3

Walkergate C.4
Wallis Road D.4
Warwick Road B.2
Watts Lane C.4
Welbeck Way B.3
Wellington Street C.3
Westgate Place B.4
Willow Drive C.2
Windsor Mews C.4
Windsor Road B.2
Woburn Close B.2
Wood Lane D.4
Wood Way D.4
Woodland Rise B.3
Woodlands C.3
Worcester Close C.4

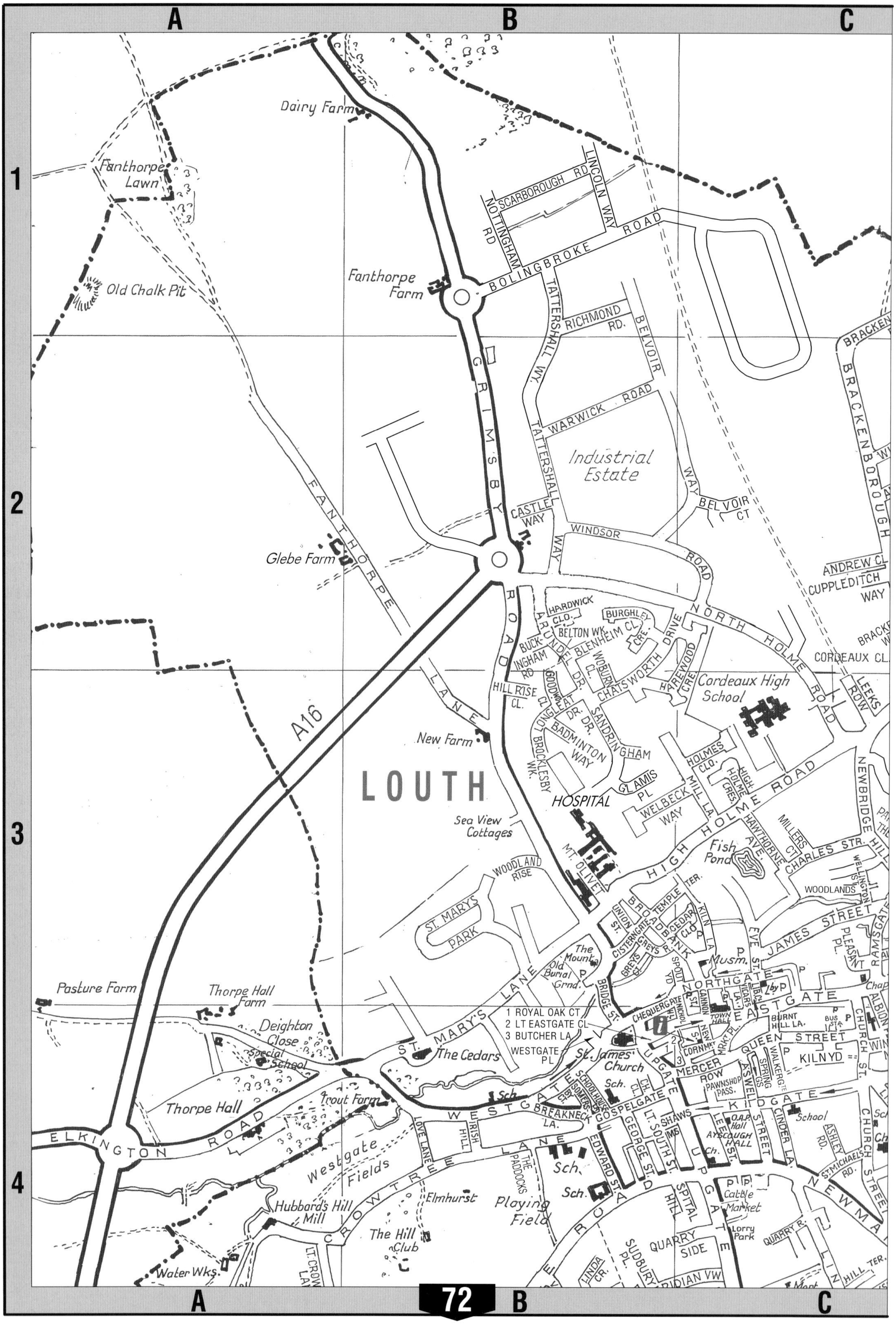
A
B
C
1
2
3
4
LOUTH
Dairy Farm
Fanthorpe Lawn
Old Chalk Pit
Fanthorpe Farm
Glebe Farm
New Farm
Sea View Cottages
Pasture Farm
Thorpe Hall Farm
Deighton Close
Special School
Thorpe Hall
Trout Farm
Westgate Fields
Hubbard's Hill Mill
Water Wks.
Elmhurst
The Hill Club
Playing Field
The Cedars
The Mount
Old Burial Grnd.
St. James' Church
Musm.
Industrial Estate
Cordeaux High School
HOSPITAL
Fish Pond
Cattle Market
Lorry Park
O.A.P. Hall
AYSCOUGH HALL
Town Hall
Sch.
School
A16
GRIMSBY ROAD
BOLINGBROKE ROAD
NOTTINGHAM RD
SCARBOROUGH RD
LINCOLN WAY
TATTERSHALL WY.
TATTERSHALL WAY
RICHMOND RD.
BELVOIR WAY
BELVOIR CT
WARWICK ROAD
WINDSOR ROAD
CASTLE WAY
FANTHORPE LANE
NORTH HOLME ROAD
HIGH HOLME ROAD
HARDWICK CLO.
BURGHLEY CRE.
BELTON WK.
BLENHEIM CL.
BUCKINGHAM RD
ARUNDEL DR.
WOBURN CL.
CHATSWORTH DRIVE
HAREWOOD CRE.
HILL RISE CL.
GOODWOOD CL
LONGLEAT DR.
SANDRINGHAM DR.
BADMINTON WAY
BROCKLESBY WK.
GLAMIS PL
WELBECK WAY
HOLMES CLO.
MILL LA.
HIGH HOLME CRES.
HAWTHORNE AVE.
MILLERS CT
CHARLES STR.
WOODLANDS
JAMES STREET
PLEASANT PL.
BRACKENBOROUGH
ANDREW CL
CUPPLEDITCH WAY
CORDEAUX CL.
LEEKS ROW
NEWBRIDGE HILL
WOODLAND RISE
ST. MARY'S PARK
ST. MARY'S LANE
MT. OLIVET
UNION ST.
BROADBANK
TEMPLE TER.
CEDAR CLO.
KILN LA.
CISTERNGATE
GREYS RD.
GREYS CT.
SPOUT YD
BRIDGE ST.
NORTHGATE
EASTGATE
CHEQUERGATE
CANNON ST.
VICARS LA.
TOWN HALL
BURNT HILL LA.
BUS STA.
QUEEN STREET
KILNYD
CHURCH ST.
1 ROYAL OAK CT.
2 LT EASTGATE CL
3 BUTCHER LA
WESTGATE PL
WESTGATE
UPGATE
MERCER ROW
CORNMKT
MRKT PL
PAWNSHOP PASS.
SPRING GDNS
WALKERGATE
KIDGATE
ASWELL STREET
CINDER LA.
ASHLEY RD.
ST. MICHAEL'S RD.
NEWMARKET
GOSPELGATE
SCHOOLHOUSE LA.
BREAKNECK LA.
SHAWS MS
LT. SOUTH ST.
GEORGE ST.
EDWARD ST.
LEE ST.
SPITAL HILL
QUARRY SIDE
QUARRY R.
SUDBURY PL.
LINDA CR.
HILL TER.
ELKINGTON ROAD
CROWTREE LANE
LOVE LANE
IRISH HILL
THE PADDOCKS
LT. CROWTREE LA.
72

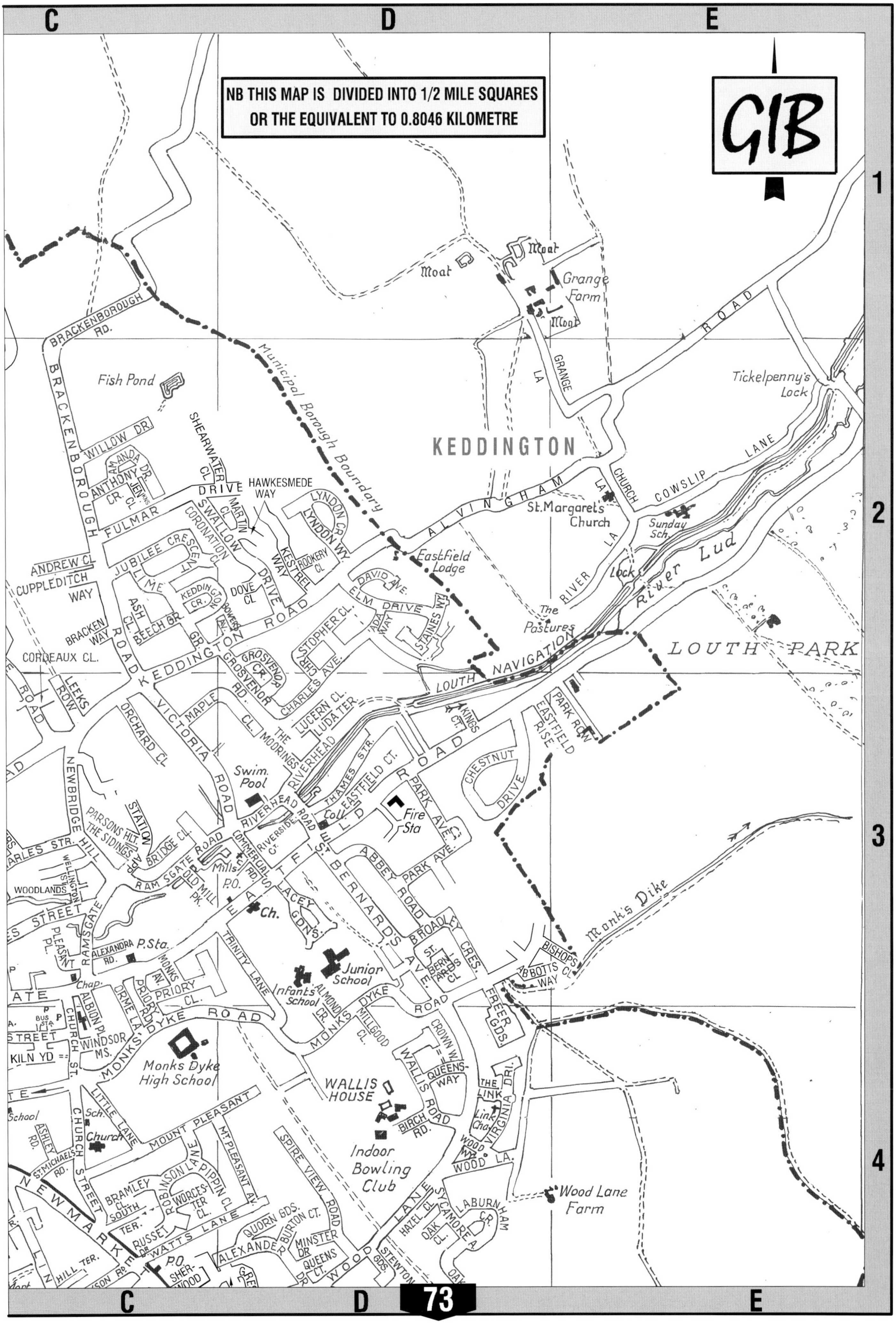
C
D
E
1
2
3
4
NB THIS MAP IS DIVIDED INTO 1/2 MILE SQUARES OR THE EQUIVALENT TO 0.8046 KILOMETRE
GIB
Moat
Grange Farm
KEDDINGTON
Municipal Borough Boundary
Fish Pond
BRACKENBOROUGH RD.
ALVINGHAM ROAD
GRANGE LA
CHURCH LA
COWSLIP LANE
Tickelpenny's Lock
St.Margaret's Church
Sunday Sch.
River Lud
RIVER LA
Lock
Eastfield Lodge
The Pastures
LOUTH PARK
LOUTH NAVIGATION
WILLOW DR.
AMANDA DR.
ANTHONY CR.
SHEARWATER CL
FULMAR DRIVE
HAWKESMEDE WAY
MARTIN CL
SWALLOW DRIVE
CORONATION CL
LYNDON CR.
LYNDON WY.
KESTREL WAY
ROOKERY CL
ANDREW CL
CUPPLEDITCH WAY
JUBILEE CRESCENT
LIME
KEDDINGTON CR.
DOVE CL
KEDDINGTON ROAD
DAVID AVE.
ELM DRIVE
STAINES WY.
ADA WAY
CHRISTOPHER CL.
ASH CL.
BEECH GR.
BRACKEN WAY
CORDEAUX CL.
LEEKS ROW
GROSVENOR CR.
GROSVENOR RD.
CHARLES AVE.
LUCERN CL.
LUDATER.
MAPLE CL.
VICTORIA ROAD
ORCHARD CL
THE MOORINGS
RIVERHEAD
KINGS CT.
EASTFIELD RISE
PARK ROW
CHESTNUT DRIVE
Swim. Pool
THAMES STR.
EASTFIELD CT.
EASTFIELD ROAD
PARK AVE.
Fire Sta
NEWBRIDGE HILL
STATION APP
PARSONS HLT.
THE SIDINGS
BRIDGE CL.
RAMSGATE ROAD
RIVERHEAD ROAD
COMMERCIAL RD
RIVERSIDE CT.
Coll.
ABBEY PARK AVE.
ABBEY ROAD
WELLINGTON ST.
WOODLANDS
Mills
OLD MILL PK.
P.O.
CHARLES STR.
EASTGATE
ST. BERNARDS AVE.
LACEY GDNS.
BROADLEY CRES.
ST. BERNARDS CL
Monk's Dike
BISHOPS CL
ABBOTTS WAY
STREET
PLEASANT PL.
RAMSGATE
ALEXANDRA RD.
P.Sta.
Ch.
MONKS AV.
TRINITY LANE
Junior School
Infants School
ALMOND CR.
PRIORY CL.
PRIORY RD.
ORME LA
ALBION PL.
Chap.
BUS STA.
CHURCH ST.
WINDSOR MS.
KILN YD
MONKS DYKE ROAD
MILLGOOD CL.
CROWN W.
FREER GDS
Monks Dyke High School
WALLIS HOUSE
WALLIS ROAD
QUEENS-WAY
THE LINK
VIRGINIA DRI.
Link Cha.
LITTLE LANE
Sch.
School
Church
ASHLEY RD.
CHURCH STREET
MOUNT PLEASANT
MT PLEASANT AV.
BIRCH RD.
WOOD WY.
WOOD LA.
Wood Lane Farm
Indoor Bowling Club
SPIRE VIEW ROAD
ST. MICHAELS RD.
NEWMARKET
ROBINSON LANE
PIPPIN CL.
WORCESTER CL.
BRAMLEY CL. SOUTH
RUSSET DR.
TER.
WATTS LANE
QUORN GDS.
BURTON CT.
MINSTER DR
QUEENS CT.
ALEXANDER DR
HAZEL CL.
OAK CL.
SYCAMORE
LABURNHAM CR.
STEWTON
WOOD GDS
HILL TER.
P.O.
SHERWOOD
73

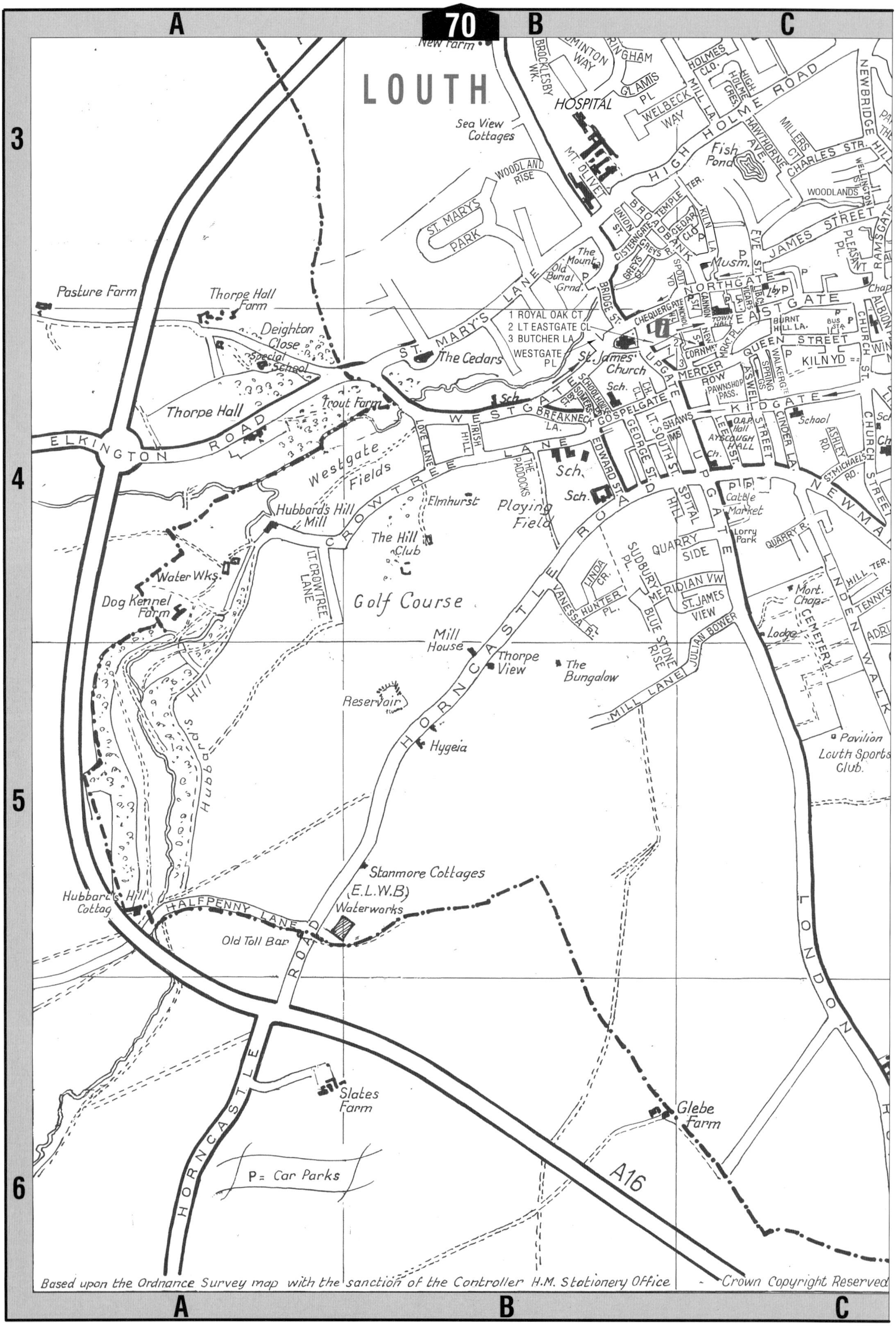
A
70
B
C
3
4
5
6
LOUTH
New Farm
BROCKLESBY WK.
HOSPITAL
GLAMIS PL
WELBECK WAY
MILL LA.
HOLMES CLO.
HIGH HOLME CRES.
HIGH HOLME ROAD
HAWTHORNE AVE.
NEWBRIDGE HILL
MILLERS CT.
CHARLES STR.
WOODLANDS
Fish Pond
MT. OLIVET
Sea View Cottages
WOODLAND RISE
ST. MARYS PARK
UNION ST.
BROADBANK
TEMPLE TER.
CEDAR CLO.
KILN LA.
EVE ST.
JAMES STREET
PLEASANT PL.
RAMSGATE
CISTERNGATE
GREYS RD.
GREYS CT.
The Mount
Old Burial Grnd.
Musm.
NORTHGATE
Lby
Chap.
ALBION PL.
BRIDGE ST.
CHEQUERGATE
NICHOL ST.
CANNON ST.
VICARS LA.
LIBY CL.
EASTGATE
BURNT HILL LA.
BUS STA.
CHURCH ST.
TOWN HALL
NEW ST.
MRKT. PL.
QUEEN STREET
CORNMKT.
WALKERGATE
SPRING GS.
KILNYD
1 ROYAL OAK CT.
2 LT EASTGATE CL.
3 BUTCHER LA.
WESTGATE PL.
Pasture Farm
Thorpe Hall Farm
Deighton Close
Special School
ST. MARY'S LANE
The Cedars
St. James' Church
UPGATE
MERCER ROW
PAWNSHOP PASS.
ASWELL STREET
KIDGATE
School
Sch.
CH. CL.
GOSPELGATE
SCHOOLHOUSE LA.
SOMERS CT.
ST. MARY'S CT.
BREAKNECK LA.
WESTGATE
Trout Farm
Thorpe Hall
ELKINGTON ROAD
Westgate Fields
LOVE LANE
IRISH HILL
LANE
THE PADDOCKS
EDWARD ST.
GEORGE ST.
LT. SOUTH ST.
SHAWS
MS
LEE ST.
O.A.P. Hall
AYSCOUGH HALL
CINDER LA.
ASHLEY RD.
ST. MICHAELS RD.
CHURCH STREET
NEWMARKET
CROWTREE LANE
Elmhurst
Playing Field
Sch.
ROAD
SPITTAL HILL
Cattle Market
Lorry Park
QUARRY R.
Hubbard's Hill Mill
The Hill Club
LT. CROWTREE LANE
QUARRY SIDE
LINDA CR.
SUDBURY PL.
MERIDIAN VW
ST. JAMES VIEW
HUNTER PL.
VANESSA R.
Water Wks.
Dog Kennel Farm
Golf Course
BLUE STONE RISE
JULIAN BOWER
Mort. Chap.
HILL TER.
TENNYSON
ADRIAN
Lodge
CEMETERY
LINDEN WALK
Mill House
Thorpe View
The Bungalow
MILL LANE
Hubbard's Hill
Reservoir
HORNCASTLE ROAD
Hygeia
Pavilion
Louth Sports Club
Stanmore Cottages
(E.L.W.B) Waterworks
Hubbard's Hill Cottag
HALFPENNY LANE
Old Toll Bar
LONDON ROAD
Slates Farm
Glebe Farm
HORNCASTLE
P= Car Parks
A16
Based upon the Ordnance Survey map with the sanction of the Controller H.M. Stationery Office
Crown Copyright Reserved

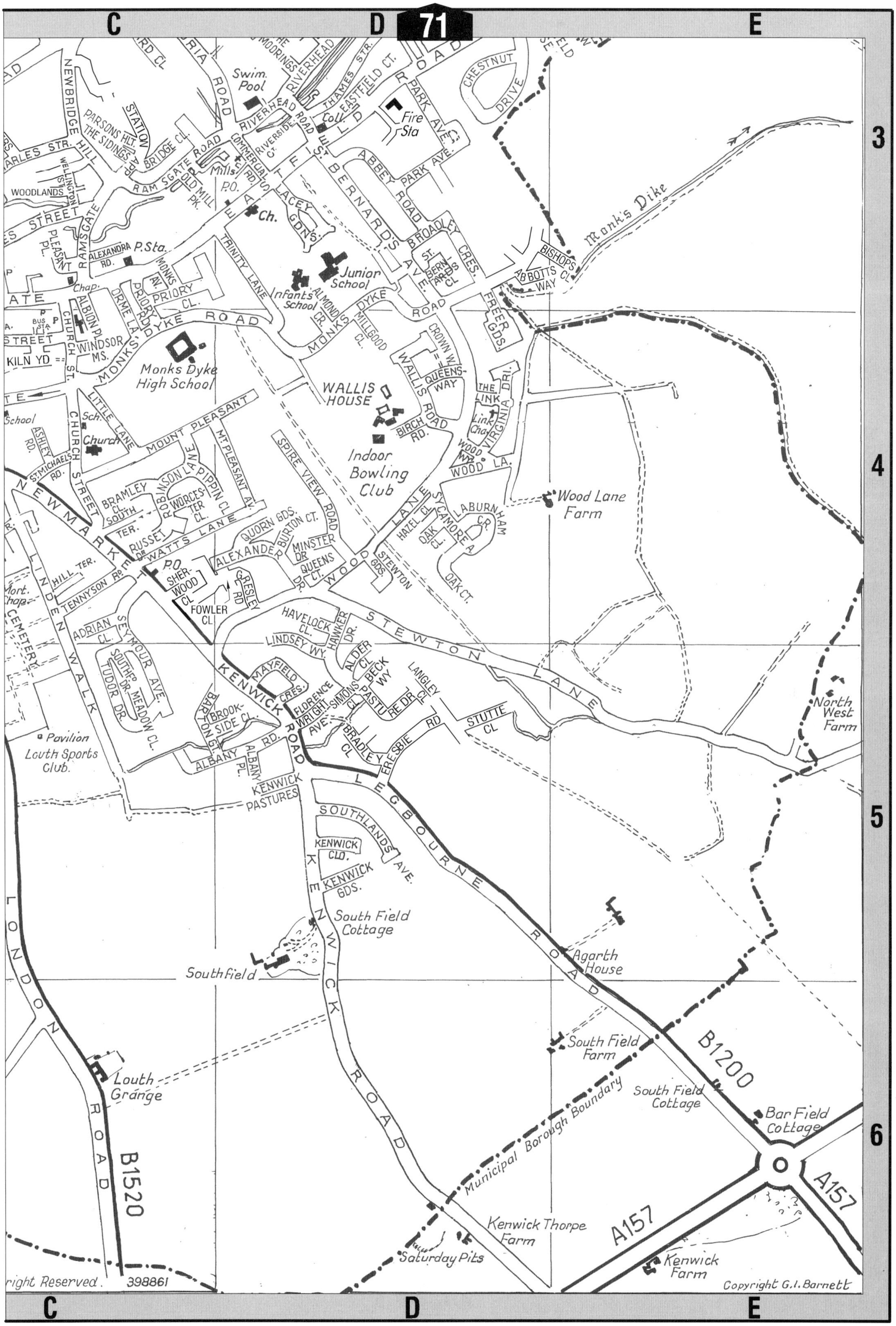
C
D
71
E
3
4
5
6
Swim. Pool
Fire Sta
CHESTNUT DRIVE
PARK AVE.
NEWBRIDGE HILL
PARSONS HLT.
THE SIDINGS
STATION APP.
BRIDGE CL.
RAMSGATE ROAD
RIVERHEAD
RIVERHEAD ROAD
RIVERSIDE CT.
THAMES STR.
EASTFIELD CT.
Coll.
COMMERCIAL RD.
Mills
OLD MILL PK.
P.O.
EASTFIELD ROAD
ST. BERNARD'S AVE.
ABBEY ROAD
LACEY GDNS.
Ch.
BROADLEY CRES.
ST. BERNARDS CL.
Monk's Dike
BISHOPS CL.
ABBOTTS WAY
WOODLANDS
WELLINGTON ST.
RAMSGATE
PLEASANT PL.
ALEXANDRA RD.
P.Sta.
MONKS AV.
PRIORY RD.
PRIORY CL.
TRINITY LANE
Junior School
Infants School
ALMOND CR.
MONKS' DYKE ROAD
MILLGOOD CL.
FREER GDS.
Chap.
ALBION PL.
BUS STA.
CHURCH ST.
EASTGATE
KILN YD
WINDSOR MS.
ORME LA.
Monks Dyke High School
WALLIS HOUSE
CROWN W.
WALLIS ROAD
QUEENSWAY
THE LINK
VIRGINIA DRI.
Link Cha.
BIRCH RD.
Indoor Bowling Club
WOOD WY.
WOOD LA.
School
Sch.
LITTLE LANE
Church
ASHLEY RD.
ST. MICHAELS RD.
CHURCH STREET
MOUNT PLEASANT
MT. PLEASANT AV.
ROBINSON LA.
PIPPIN CL.
BRAMLEY CL.
SOUTH TER.
WORCESTER CL.
RUSSET DR.
WATTS LANE
SPIRE VIEW ROAD
QUORN GDS.
BURTON CT.
MINSTER DR.
QUEENS CT.
ALEXANDER DR.
WOOD LANE
STEWTON GDS.
HAZEL CL.
SYCAMORE A.
LABURNHAM CR.
OAK CL.
OAK CT.
Wood Lane Farm
NEWMARKET
HILL TER.
TENNYSON RD.
P.O.
SHERWOOD CL.
FOWLER CL.
GRESLEY RD.
LINDEN WALK
Mort. Chap.
CEMETERY
ADRIAN CL.
SEYMOUR AVE.
SOUTHFOLD DR.
TUDOR DR.
MEADOW CL.
HAVELOCK CL.
HAWKER DR.
LINDSEY WY.
STEWTON LANE
ALDER CL.
BECK WY
LANGLEY CL.
MAYFIELD CRES.
KENWICK ROAD
FLORENCE WRIGHT AVE.
SIMONS CL.
PASTURE DR.
STUTTE CL.
BRADLEY CL.
ERESBIE RD
BROOKSIDE CL.
BARTON ST.
ALBANY RD.
ALBANY PL.
KENWICK PASTURES
Pavilion
Louth Sports Club.
North West Farm
LEGBOURNE ROAD
SOUTHLANDS AVE.
KENWICK CLO.
KENWICK GDS.
South Field Cottage
Southfield
Agarth House
LONDON ROAD
KENWICK ROAD
South Field Farm
B1200
South Field Cottage
Bar Field Cottage
Louth Grange
B1520
Municipal Borough Boundary
A157
A157
Kenwick Thorpe Farm
Saturday Pits
Kenwick Farm
right Reserved. 398861
Copyright G.I. Barnett

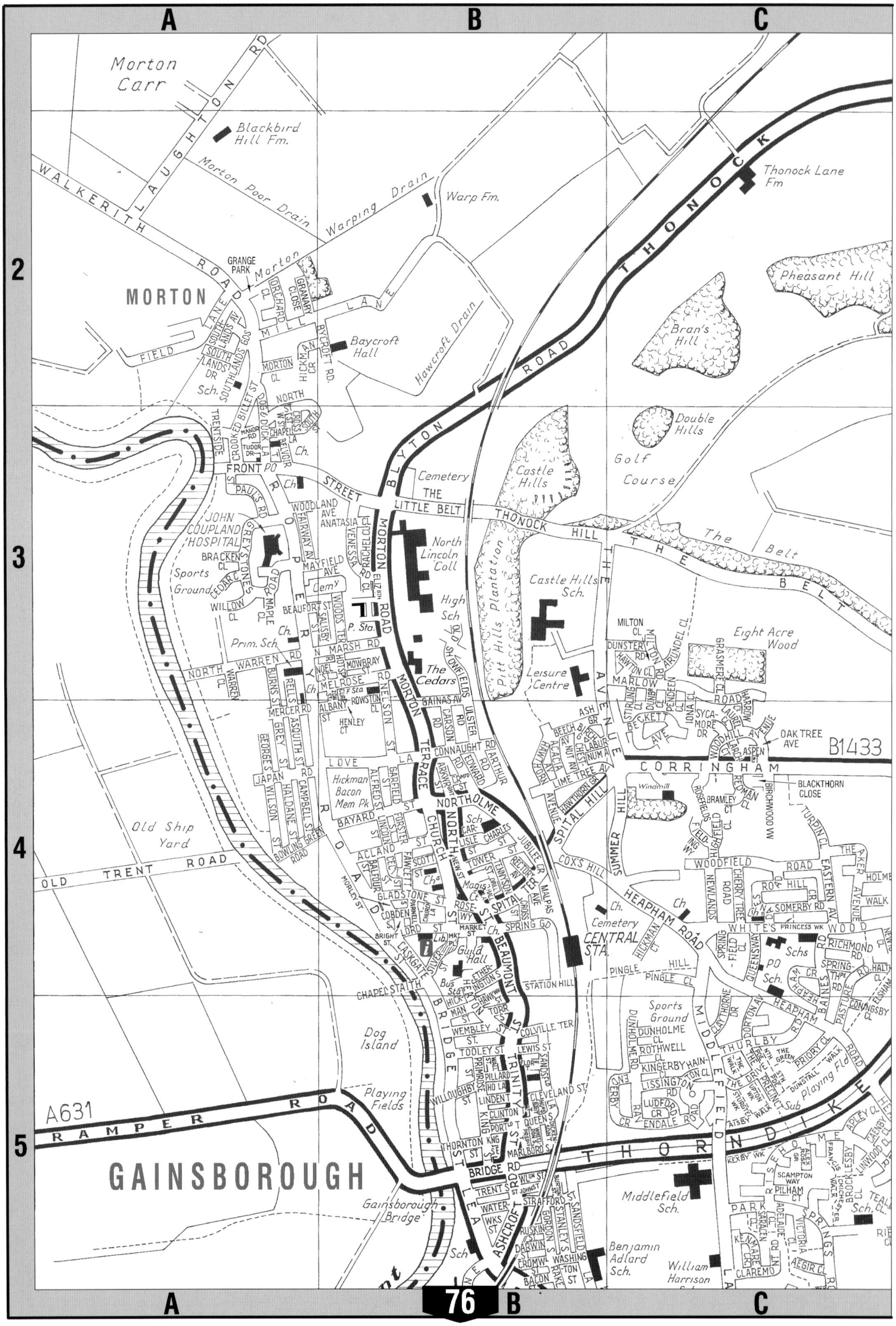
A
B
C
2
3
4
5
76
Morton Carr
Blackbird Hill Fm.
Morton Poor Drain
Morton Warping Drain
Warp Fm.
Thonock Lane Fm
WALKERITH ROAD
LAUGHTON RD
THONOCK ROAD
GRANGE PARK
MORTON
Morton Mill Lane
ORCHARD CL
GRANARY CLOSE
Baycroft Hall
Hawcroft Drain
BYCROFT RD.
HICKMAN CR
MORTON CL
FIELD LANE
SOUTHLANDS AV
SOUTHLANDS DR
SOUTHLANDS GDS
Sch.
Pheasant Hill
Bran's Hill
Double Hills
Golf Course
Castle Hills
Cemetery
BLYTON ROAD
TRENTSIDE
CROOKED BILLET ST
MANOR RD
TUDOR DR
NORTH ST
WEST ST
CROSS ST
SOUTH ST
CHAPEL LA
Ch.
FRONT ST
PO
STREET
THE LITTLE BELT
THONOCK HILL
THE BELT
The Belt
ST PAULS RD
JOHN COUPLAND HOSPITAL
GREYSTONES
BRACKEN CL
Sports Ground
CEDAR CL
WILLOW CL
MAPLE CL
WOODLAND AVE
FAIRWAY AV
ANATASIA CL
VENESSA
RACHEL CT
MAYFIELD AVE
Cem'y
MORTON ROAD
North Lincoln Coll
High Sch
Pitt Hills Plantation
Castle Hills Sch.
Eight Acre Wood
MILTON CL
MILTON RD
ARUNDEL CL
DUNSTER RD
HAWTON CL
MARLOW ROAD
GRASMERE CL
HARROW
BEAUFORT ST
SALISBURY ST
P. Sta.
Prim. Sch
N MARSH RD
MOWBRAY ST
OLD SHOWFIELDS
The Cedars
Leisure Centre
THE AVENUE
NORTH WARREN RD
WARREN CL
BURNS ST
NOEL ST
MELROSE ST
ROWSTON ST
NELSON ST
ALBANY ST
HENLEY CT
MERCER RD
RELLS ST
ASQUITH ST
GREY ST
GEORGES ST
JAPAN RD
WILSON ST
HALDANE ST
CAMPBELL ST
BOWLING GREEN ROAD
MORTON TERRACE
GAINAS AV
CARSON RD
ULSTER RD
CONNAUGHT RD
EDWARD ST
ARTHUR ST
ASH GR
BEECH AV
BIRCH AV
ACACIA AV
NUT AV
CHESTNUT AV
LABURNUM AV
HAWTHORN AV
LIME TREE AV
HAWTHORN GR
AVENUE
SPITAL HILL
SUMMER HILL
Windmill
STIRLING CL
DUNBAR CL
PENDEEN CL
IONA CL
BECKETT AVE
SYCAMORE DR
WOODHILL AVENUE
ASPEN CT
OAK TREE AVE
B1433
CORRINGHAM ROAD
BLACKTHORN CLOSE
BIRCHWOOD AV
ROSEFIELDS
BRAMLEY CT
REDMAN CL
HIGHFIELD CL
TURPIN CL
LOVE LANE
Hickman Bacon Mem Pk
ALFRED ST
GARFIELD ST
BAYARD ST
LINDUM ST
FORSTER ST
NORTHOLME
NORTH ST
CHURCH ST
Sch
CARLISLE ST
CHARLES ST
JUBILEE CR
RECTORY ST
MALPAS AVE
ACLAND ST
FAWCETT ST
SCOTT ST
BALFOUR ST
TOWER ST
TENNYSON ST
COX'S HILL
HEAPHAM ROAD
Old Ship Yard
OLD TRENT ROAD
Magistrates Ct
MORLEY ST
GLADSTONE ST
COBDEN ST
ROSE WY
SPITAL TER
SPRING GD
Cemetery
CENTRAL STA
WOODFIELD ROAD
CHERRY TREE ROAD
NEWLANDS
ROSE HILL CR
SOMERBY RD
WHITE'S WOOD
PRINCESS WK
EASTERN AV
THE AKER AVENUE
HOLME WALK
RICHMOND RD
SPRINGTHORPE RD
HALTHAM
Schs
PO
Sch.
BRIGHT ST
LORD ST
Lib
MARKET ST
Ch.
CASKGATE
Guild Hall
BEAUMONT ST
STATION HILL
PINGLE HILL
PINGLE CL
HICKMAN CT
SPRINGFIELD CL
QUEENSWAY
HEAPHAM RD
BAINES RD
PASTURE RD
CONINGSBY CL
CHAPEL STAITH
BRIDGE ST
Bus Sta
HICKMAN ST
ETHERINGTON ST
Dog Island
WEMBLEY ST
COLVILLE TER
Sports Ground
DUNHOLME CL
DUNHOLME RD
ROTHWELL CL
CLAYTHORNE DR
DORTON AV
THURLBY
THE GREEN
PRIORY CL
TOOLEY ST
LEWIS ST
TRINITY ST
SANDSFIELD LA
PRIMROSE ST
PILLARD
KINGERBY CL
HAINTON CL
MIDDLEFIELD LANE
WILLOUGHBY RD
LINDEN T
CLEVELAND ST
LISSINGTON RD
LUDFORD CR
RAVENDALE ROAD
DUNSTALL WALK
Playing Fld
A631
RAMPER ROAD
Playing Fields
CLINTON T
QUEENS
KING ST
THORNTON ST
MARLBORO S
THORNDIKE WAY
GAINSBOROUGH
BRIDGE RD
TRENT ST
WATER ST
STRAFFORD ST
LEA RD
ASHCROFT RD
Gainsborough Bridge
KEXBY WK
RISEHOLME RD
SCAMPTON WAY
PILHAM CT
BROCKLESBY CL
APLEY CL
Sch.
Middlefield Sch.
RUSKIN
GORDON ST
STANLEY ST
SANDSFIELD LA
DARWIN
WASHINGTON ST
CROMWELL ST
BACON
Benjamin Adlard Sch.
William Harrison Sch.
PARK
SARACEN CL
KENMARE CR
ADELAIDE CL
VICTORIA
CLAREMONT RD
AEGIR CL
SPRINGS

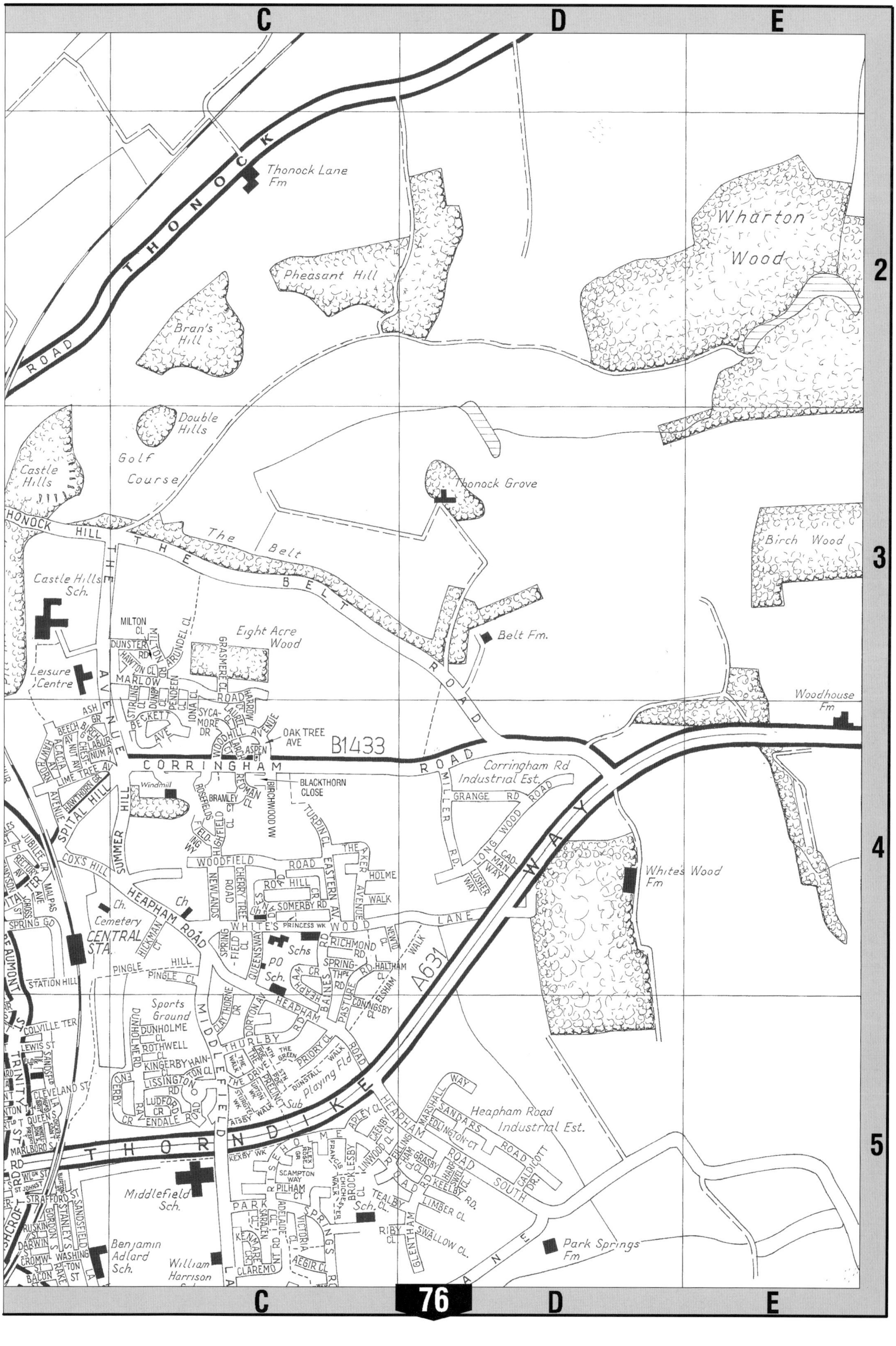
C
D
E
2
3
4
5
THONOCK ROAD
Thonock Lane Fm
Wharton Wood
Pheasant Hill
Bran's Hill
Double Hills
Golf Course
Castle Hills
Thonock Grove
THONOCK HILL
The Belt
THE BELT ROAD
Birch Wood
Castle Hills Sch.
Belt Fm.
Eight Acre Wood
Leisure Centre
MILTON CL
DUNSTER RD
MILTON RD
ARUNDEL CL
HAWTON CL
MARLOW
GRASMERE CL
ROAD
HARROW
STIRLING CL
DUNBAR CL
PENDEEN CL
IONA CL
SYCAMORE DR
LAUREL
BECKETT AVE
WOODHILL AVENUE
OAK TREE AVE
ASPEN CT
B1433
Woodhouse Fm
ASH GR
BEECH
BIRCH
LABURNUM AV
ACACIA AV
WALNUT AV
CHESTNUT AV
HAWTHORN AV
LIME TREE AV
HAWTHORN GR
AVENUE
SPITAL HILL
CORRINGHAM ROAD
Windmill
SUMMER HILL
ROSEFIELDS
BRAMLEY CT
REDMAN CL
BLACKTHORN CLOSE
BIRCHWOOD WY
TURPIN CL
Corringham Rd Industrial Est.
GRANGE RD
MILLER RD
LONG WOOD ROAD
CADMAN WAY
LUSHER WAY
WAY
White's Wood Fm
FIELDING WY
HIGHFIELD
WOODFIELD ROAD
ROAD
THE AKER
HOLME
COX'S HILL
NEWLANDS
CHERRY TREE ROAD
HILL CR
EASTERN AV
AVENUE
WALK
SOMERBY RD
HEAPHAM ROAD
Ch.
Ch
WHITE'S WOOD LANE
PRINCESS WK
Cemetery
CENTRAL STA.
HICKMAN CT
SPRINGFIELD CL
QUEENSWAY
Schs
RICHMOND RD
SPRINGTHORPE RD
HALTHAM CL
ELSHAM CL
A631
PO
Sch.
BANES RD
PASTURE
CONINGSBY CL
PINGLE HILL
PINGLE CL
STATION HILL
SPRING GD
MALPAS AVE
JUBILEE CR
RECTORY AV
CROSS
Sports Ground
DUNHOLME CL
DUNHOLME RD
ROTHWELL CL
KINGERBY CL
LISSINGTON RD
LUDFORD CR
RAVENDALE CR
HAINTON CL
CLAYTHORNE DR
DORTON AV
MIDDLEFIELD LANE
THURLBY
THE WALK
THE DRIVE
THE GREEN
PRIORY CL
DUNSTALL WALK
Playing Fld
Sub
ASTBY WALK
COLVILLE TER
LEWIS ST
SANDSFIELD
CLEVELAND ST
TRINITY ST
QUEENS
MARLBORO S
BEAUMONT
THORNDIKE WAY
Heapham Road Industrial Est.
MARSHALL WAY
SANDARS ROAD
EDLINGTON CT
CALDICOTT DR
ROAD SOUTH
HEAPHAM ROAD
APLEY CL
CAENBY CL
LINWOOD CL
GRASBY CL
HARPSWELL CL
KEELBY RD
LIMBER CL
SWALLOW CL
GLENTHAM CL
RIBY CL
TEALBY CL
RISEHOLME
KEXBY WK
SCAMPTON WAY
PILHAM CT
FRANCIS WALK
CHICHESTER WALK
BROCKLESBY CL
Sch.
PARK SPRINGS
SARACEN CL
ADELAIDE CL
VICTORIA
KENMARE CR
CLAREMONT
AEGIR CL
Middlefield Sch.
Benjamin Adlard Sch.
William Harrison Sch.
LANE
Park Springs Fm
ST JOHNST
STRAFFORD ST
GORDON ST
STANLEY ST
SANDSFIELD LA
RUSKIN ST
DARWIN ST
CROMWELL ST
BACON ST
WASHINGTON ST
RAKE
76

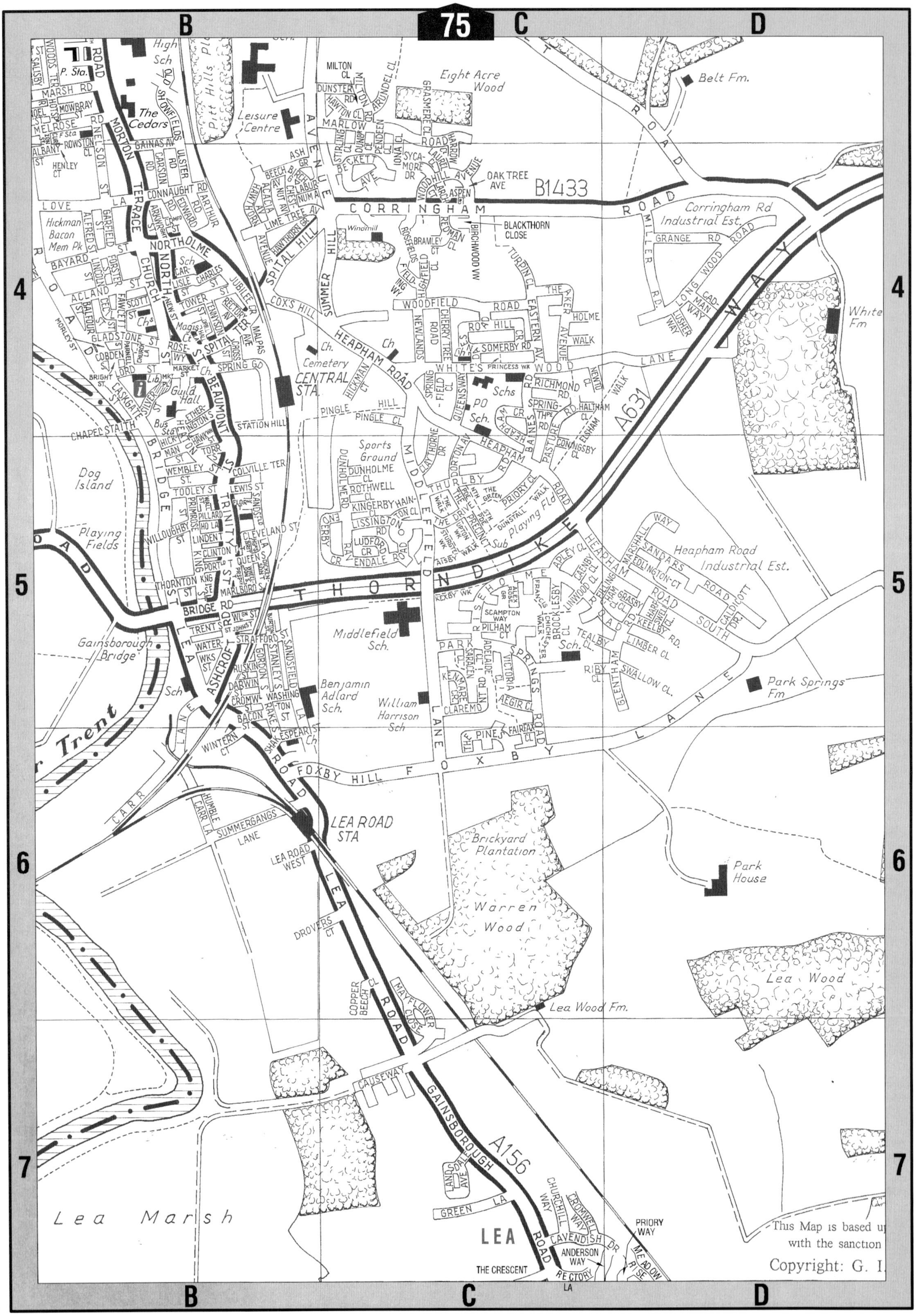
75
B
C
D
4
5
6
7
High Sch
The Cedars
Leisure Centre
Pitt Hills Pl
MILTON CL
Eight Acre Wood
Belt Fm.
B1433
CORRINGHAM ROAD
Corringham Rd Industrial Est.
BLACKTHORN CLOSE
OAK TREE AVE
Windmill
MORTON TERRACE
NORTHOLME
SPITAL HILL
HEAPHAM ROAD
WOODFIELD ROAD
WHITE'S WOOD LANE
Cemetery
CENTRAL STA
White Fm
A631
Hickman Bacon Mem Pk
Dog Island
Playing Fields
CHAPEL STAITH
STATION HILL
Sports Ground
MIDDLEFIELD
THORNDIKE WAY
Heapham Road Industrial Est.
Playing Fld
BRIDGE RD
Gainsborough Bridge
R. Trent
Middlefield Sch.
Benjamin Adlard Sch.
William Harrison Sch
Park Springs Fm
FOXBY HILL
FOXBY LANE
LEA ROAD STA
Brickyard Plantation
Warren Wood
Park House
Lea Wood
Lea Wood Fm.
SUMMERGANGS LANE
LEA ROAD WEST
DROVERS CT
CAUSEWAY
GAINSBOROUGH ROAD
A156
GREEN LA
LEA
THE CRESCENT
CAVENDISH DR
ANDERSON WAY
RECTORY LA
PRIORY WAY
MEADOW RISE
Lea Marsh
This Map is based u
with the sanction
Copyright: G. I.

Acacia Avenue B.4
Acland Street B.4
Adelaide Close C.5
Aegir Close C.5
Aisby Walk C.5
Alex Rose Grove C.5
Alfred Street B.4
Anatasia Close B.3
Anderson Way C.7
Apley Close C.5
Arkwright Street B.4
Arthur Road B.4
Arundel Close C.3
Ash Green B.4
Ashcroft Road B.5
Aspen Court C.4
Asquith Street A.4

Bacon Street B.5
Baines Road C.5
Balfour Street B.4
Bayard Street B.4
Beaufort Street A.3
Beaumont Street B.4
Beckett Avenue C.4
Beech Avenue B.4
Belvoir Terrace A.3
Birch Grove B.4
Birchwood View......................C.4
Blackthorn Close....................C.4
Blyton Road A.3
Bowling Green Road A.4
Bracken Close A.3
Bramley Court C.4
Bridge Road B.5
Bridge Street B.5
Britannia Terrace B.5
Brocklesby Close C.5
Burns Street A.3
Burton Street B.5
Bycroft Road B.2

Cadman Way D.4
Caenby Close C.5
Caldicott Drive D.5
Campbell Street A.4
Carlisle Street B.4
Carr Lane B.6
Carson Road B.4
Caskgate Street B.4
Causeway C.7
Cavendish Drive C.7
Cecil Street B.4
Cedar Court A.3
Chapel Lane A.3
Chapel Staith B.4
Charles Street B.4
Cherry Tree Road C.4
Chestnut Avenue B.4
Church Lane B.4
Church Street B.4
Churchill Way C.7
Claremont Road C.5
Copper Beech Close C.6
Corringham Road C.4
Cox's Hill B.4
Cromford Street B.4
Cromwell Street B.5
Cromwell Way C.7
Crooked Billet Street A.3
Curzon Street B.3
Cross Street A.3
Cross Street B.4

Danes Road C.4
Darwin Street B.5
Dickenson Terrace B.5
Dog and Duck Lane A.2
Dorton Avenue C.5
Drill Hall Lane B.4
Drovers Court B.6
Dunbar Close C.4
Dunholme Close C.5
Dunholme Road C.5

Dunstall Walk C.5
Dunster Road C.3
Eastern Avenue C.4
Edlington Court D.5
Edward Road B.4
Elizabeth Close B.3
Elsham Walk C.5
Enderby Crescent C.5
Etherington Street B.4

Fairfax Close C.6
Fairway Avenue A.3
Fawcett Street B.4
Field Lane A.2
Fielding Way C.4
Fillingham Close C.5
Florence Terrace B.5
Forster Street B.4
Foxby Hill B.6
Foxby Lane C.6
Francis Chichester
Walk C.5
Front Street A.3

Gainas Avenue B.3
Gainsborough Road C.7
Garfield Street B.4
George Street A.4
Gladstone Street B.4
Glentham Road D.5
Gordon Street B.5
Granary Close A.2
Grange Park A.2
Grange Road D.4
Grasby Close D.5
Grasmere Close C.3
Green lane C.7
Grey Street A.4
Greystones Road A.3

Hainton Close C.5
Haldane Street A.4
Harpswell Close D.5
Harrow Close C.3
Hawksworth Street B.5
Hawthorn Grove B.4
Hawthorne Avenue B.4
Hawton Close C.3
Heapham Crescent C.4
Heapham Road C.4
Heapham Road South C.5
Heaton Street B.4
Henley Court B.4
Hickman Court C.4
Hickman Crescent A.2
Hickman Street B.5
High Street B.5
Highfield Close C.4
Hotspur Road B.3
Humble Carr Lane B.6

Iona Close C.4

Japan Road A.4
Jubilee Crescent B.4

Keelby Road D.5
Kenmare Crescent C.5
Kexby Walk C.5
Kingerby Close C.5
King Street B.5
King Street East B.5

Laburnum Avenue B.4
Landsdale Avenue C.7
Larch Court C.4
Laughton Road A.2
Laurel Close C.4
Lea Road B.5
Lea Road West B.6
Lewis Street B.5
Limber Close D.5
Lime Tree Avenue B.4
Lincoln Street B.4

Linden Terrace B.5
Linwood Close C.5
Lissington Road C.5
Long Wood Road D.4
Lord Street B.4
Love Lane B.4
Ludford Crescent C.5
Lusher Way D.4

Malpass Avenue B.4
Manor Road A.3
Maple Close A.3
Market Street B.4
Marlborough Street B.5
Marlow Road C.3
Marshall Way D.5
Mayfield Avenue A.3
Mayflower Close C.6
Meadow Rise D.7
Melrose Road B.3
Mercer Road A.4
Middlefields Lane C.5
Miller Lane A.2
Mill Lane A.2
Milton Close C.3
Milton Road C.3
Morton Close A.2
Morton Terrace B.3
Mowbray Street B.3

Nelson Street B.3
New Street B.4
Newlands C.4
Newton Close C.4
Noel Street B.3
North Marsh Road B.3
North Parade C.5
North Street A.2
North Street B.4
North Warren Road A.3
Northolme B.4

Oak Tree Avenue C.4
Old Showfields B.3
Old Trent Road A.4
Orchard Close A.2

Park Springs Road C.5
Parnell Street B.4
Pasture Road C.5
Pendeen Close C.4
Pilham Court C.5
Pillared House Lane B.5
Pingle Close C.4
Pingle Hill C.4
Portland Terrace B.5
Primrose Street B.5
Princess Walk C.4
Priory Close C.5
Priory Way D.7
Prospect Terrace B.5

Queen Street B.5
Queensway C.4

Rachel Close B.3
Rake Street B.5
Ramper Road A.5
Ravendale Road C.5
Rectory Avenue B.4
Rectory Lane C.7
Redman Close C.4
Rell Street A.3
Riby Close C.5
Richmond Road C.4
Riseholme Road C.5
Ropery Road A.3
Rosefields C.4
Roseway B.4
Rothwell Close C.5
Rowston Close B.3
Ruskin Street B.5
St. John's Terrace B.5
St. Paul's Road A.3

Salisbury Street B.3
Sandars Road D.5
Sandsfield Lane B.5
Saracen Close C.5
Scampton Way C.5
Scott Street B.4
Shakespeare Street B.6
Silver Street B.4
Somerby Road C.4
South Parade C.5
South Street A.3
Southlands Avenue A.2
Southlands Drive A.2
Southlands Gardens A.2
Spital Hill B.4
Spital Terrace B.4
Spring Gardens B.4
Springfield Close C.4
Springthorpe Road C.4
Stanley Street b.5
Station Hill B.4
Stirling Close C.4
Strafford Street B.5
Sturgate Walk C.5
Summer Hill C.4
Summergangs Lane B.6
Swallow Close D.5
Sycamore Drive C.4

Tealby Close C.5
Tennyson Street B.4
The Avenue B.3
The Belt Road C.3
The Crescent C.7
The Drive C.5
The Green C.5
The Little Belt B.3
The Pines C.6
The Precinct C.5
The Walk C.5
Theaker Avenue C.4
Thonock Hill B.3
Thonock Road C.2
Thorndike Way B.5
Thornton Street B.5
Thurlby Road C.5
Tooley Street B.5
Torr Street B.5
Tower Street B.4
Trent Street B.5
Trentside A.3
Trinity Street B.5
Tudor Drive A.3
Turpin Close C.4

Ulster Road B.3
Upton Walk C.5

Venessa Road B.3
Victoria Close C.5

Walkerith Road A.2
Wall Street B.5
Warren Close A.3
Washington Street B.5
Waterworks Street B.5
Wellington Street B.5
Wembley Street B.5
West Street A.3
Wheeldon Street B.5
White's Wood Lane C.4
Willoughby Street B.5
Willow Close A.3
Wilson Street A.4
Wintern Court B.6
Woodfield Road C.4
Woodhill Avenue C.4
Woodland Avenue A.3
Woods Terrace B.3

MARKET RASEN

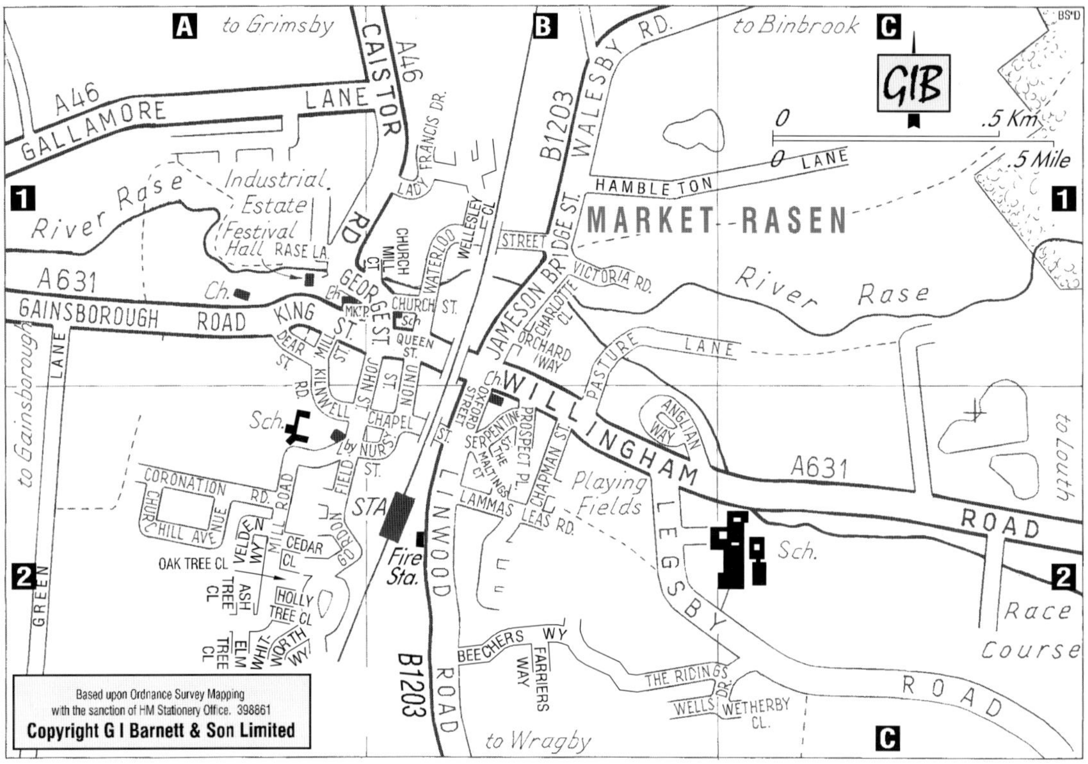

MARKET RASEN INDEX TO STREETS

Anglian Way B.2
Ash Tree Close A.2

Beechers Way B.2

Caistor Road B.1
Cedar Close A.2
Chapel Street B.2
Chapman Street B.2
Charlotte Close B.1
Church Mill Court B.1
Church Street B.1
Churchill Avenue A.2
Coronation Road A.2

Dear Street A.1

Elm Tree Close A.2

Farriers Way...B.2

Gainsborough Road A.1
Gallamore Lane A.1
George Street A.1
Gordon Field A.2
Green Lane A.2

Hambelton Lane B.1
Holly Tree Close A.2

Jameson Bridge Street B.1
John Street B.1

Kilnwell Road A.1
King Street A.1

Lady Francis Drive B.1
Lammas Leas Road B.2
Legsby Road B.2
Linwood Road B.2

Market Place A.1
Mill Road A.2
Mill Street A.1

Oak Street Close A.2
Orchard Way B.1
Oxford Street B.2

Pasture Lane B.1
Prospect Place B.2

Queen Street B.1

Serpentine Street B.2

The Maltings Court B.2
The Ridings B.2

Union Street B.1

Velden Way A.2
Victoria Road B.1

Walesby Road B.1
Waterloo Street B.1
Wellesley Close B.1
Wells Drive B.2
Wetherby Close C.2
Willingham Road B.2
Whitworth Way A.2

SCOTTER INDEX TO STREETS

Ash Grove A.2
Astley Crescent B.2

Barlings Close B.1
Barnes Green B.1
Becks Lane A.2
Beechwood Drive A.2
Beltbutts View A.2
Bramley Grove A.2

Cecil Close B.2
Cedar Close A.2
Charles Avenue B.2
Chestnut Close A.2
Church Lane B.2
Clay Lane B.2
Colin's Walk B.2

Dar Brook Road B.1

Elizabeth Close B.1
Eminson Close.......................................B.1

Franklin Road B.1

Gainsborough Road A.2
Gravel Pit Road B.1

Hawthorn Avenue A.2
High Street B.2
High Street West A.1
Hobbs Lane B.2

Jubilee Close A.2

Kirton Road B.1

Lark Rise A.2
Lindholme Bridge B.2

Messingham Road B.1
Mill Crescent B.2

North Moor Road B.1

Orchard Avenue B.2

Pinetree Avenue B.2
Poplar Grove B.2

Revill Close B.2
Riverside B.1
Rooklands A.2

St. Peters Grove B.2
St. Peters Road B.2
Sands Lane A.2
Scotterthorpe Road A.1
Sotuhcliffe Road A.2

The Green B.2

Wakefield Avenue C.1
Wakerley Road A.2
Westfield Road B.2

SCOTTER

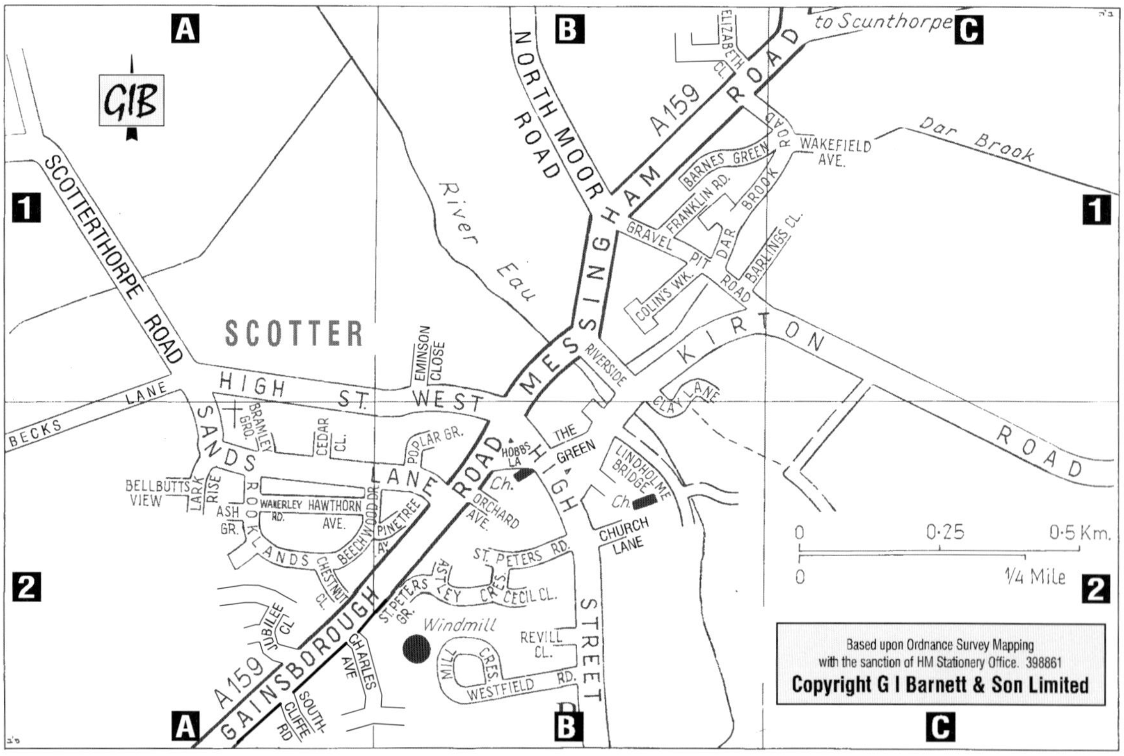

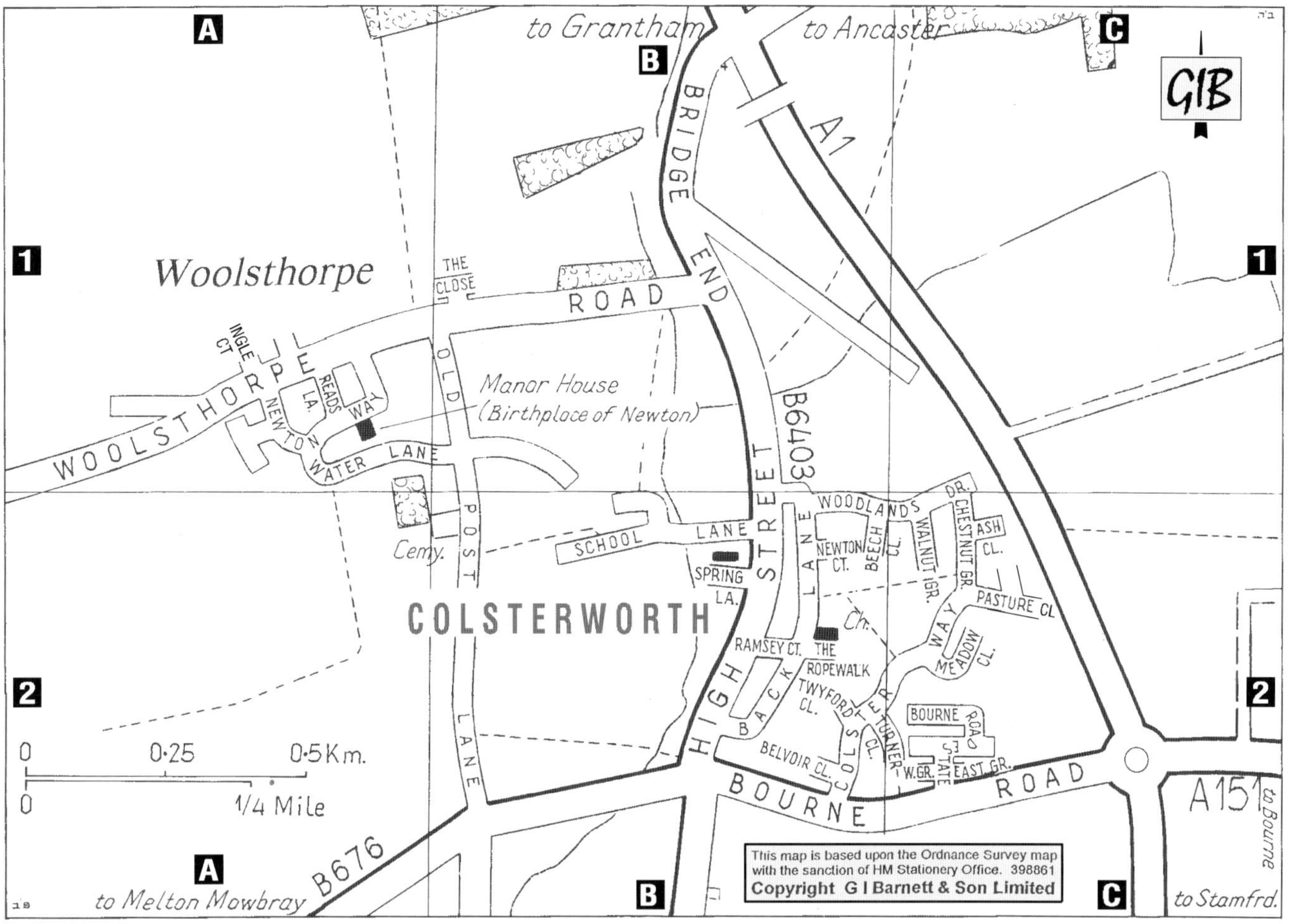

COLSTERWORTH INDEX TO STREETS

Ash Close C.2

Back Lane B.2
Beech Close B.2
Belvior Close B.2
Bourne Road B.2
Bourne Road Estate C.2
Bridge End B.1

Chestnut Grove C.2
Colster Way B.2

East Grove C.2

High Street B.2

Ingle Court A.1

Lincoln Lane A.2

Meadow Close C.2

Newton Court B.2
Newton Way B.1

Old Post Lane B.1

Pasture Close C.2

Ramsey Court B.2
Reads Lane A.1

School Lane B.2
Spring Lane B.2

The Close B.1
The Ropewalk B.2
Turner Close B.2
Twyfrod Close B.2

Walnut Grove C.2
Water Lane A.1
West Grove C.2
Woodlands Drive B.2
WOOLSTHORPE A.1
Woolsthorpe Road A.1

BILLINGHAY

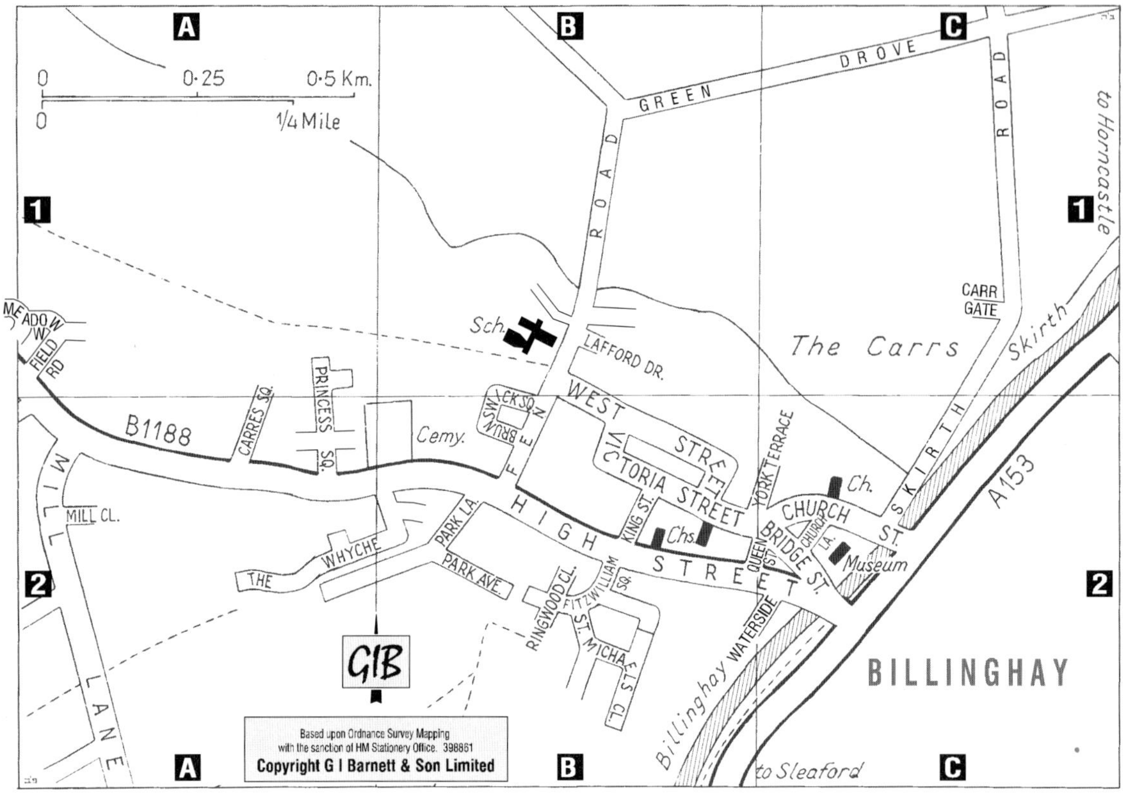

BILLINGHAY INDEX TO STREETS

Bridge Street C.2
Brunswick Square B.2

Carr Gate C.1
Carres Square A.2
Church Lane C.2
Church Street C.2

Fen Road B.2
Field Road A.1
Fitzwilliam Square B.2

Green Drove B.1

High Street B.2

King Street B.2

Lafford Drive B.1

Meadow Way A.1
Mill Close A.2
Mill Lane A.2

Park Avenue B.2
Park Lane B.2
Princess Square A.1

Queen Street B.2

Ringwood Close B.2

St. Michaels Close B.2
Skirth Road C.2

The Whyche A.2

Victoria Street B.2

Waterside B.2
West Street B.2

York Terrace C.2

HOLTON LE CLAY INDEX TO STREETS

Ashby Close B.2

Beaumonde A.2
Beech Grove B.2
Belmont A.2
Beverley Close B.2

Cambrian Way A.1
Campions Close B.2
Carmen Crescent A.1
Church Lane B.1
Church Walk B.1

Eastfield Rise B.1
Edinborough Drive A.1
Evendine Court C.2

Fenwick Court B.2
Forge Way A.1
Freeman Court B.2

Garth Way B.2
Glebe Close A.1
Grainsby Avenue B.2

Hays Close A.1
Heron Way A.1
Holton Court A.2
Holton Mount A.1

Lancaster Gate A.2
Langton Road B.2
Lime Grove B.2
Lindsey Drive A.1
Louth Road A.1

Magnolia Drive B.2
Mount Pleasant A.2

Newstead Avenue B.2
Nursery Gardens B.2

Osbourne Drive B.2

Pelham Road A.1
Peppercorn Walk B.2
Picksley Crescent B.2
Pinfold Gardens B.2
Pinfold Lane B.2

Ravendale Close B.2
Riby Court B.2

St. Peter's Close B.1
Sarge Close B.2
Silver Street B.2
South View B.2
Southfield B.2

Tetney Lane B.1
The Crescent A.1
The Smoothing B.1

Wayside Close B.2
Whisby Court C.2
Wold View A.2
Worsley Close A.1

Yarborough Close A.1

HOLTON LE CLAY

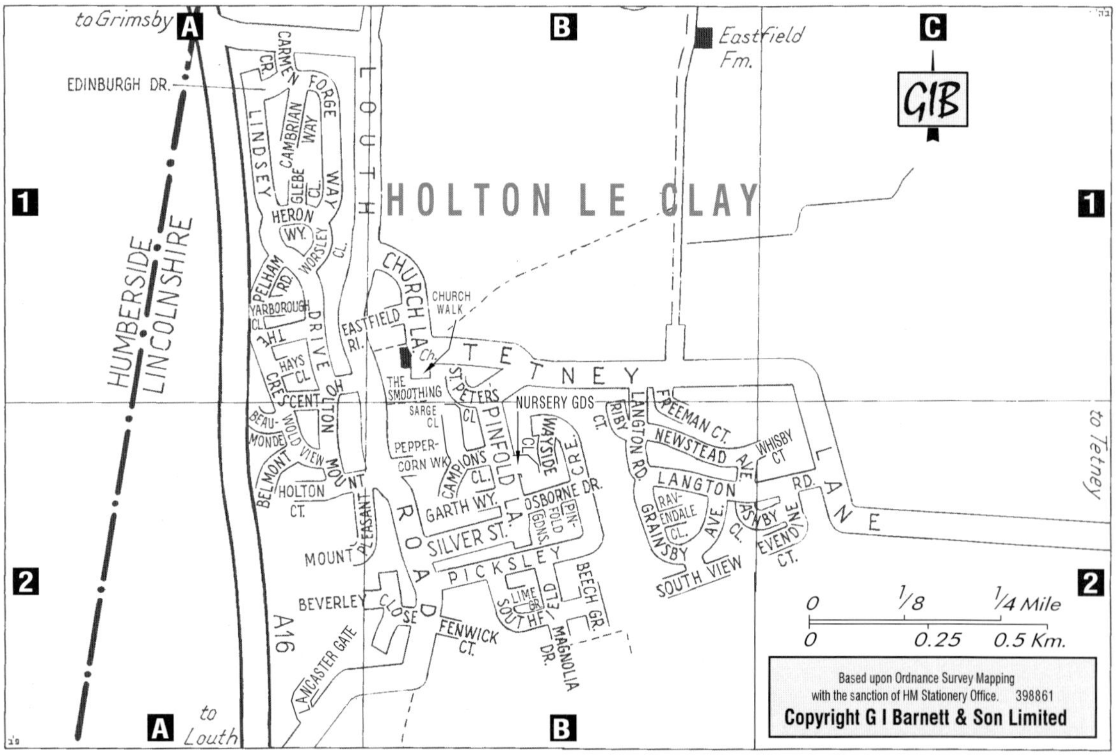

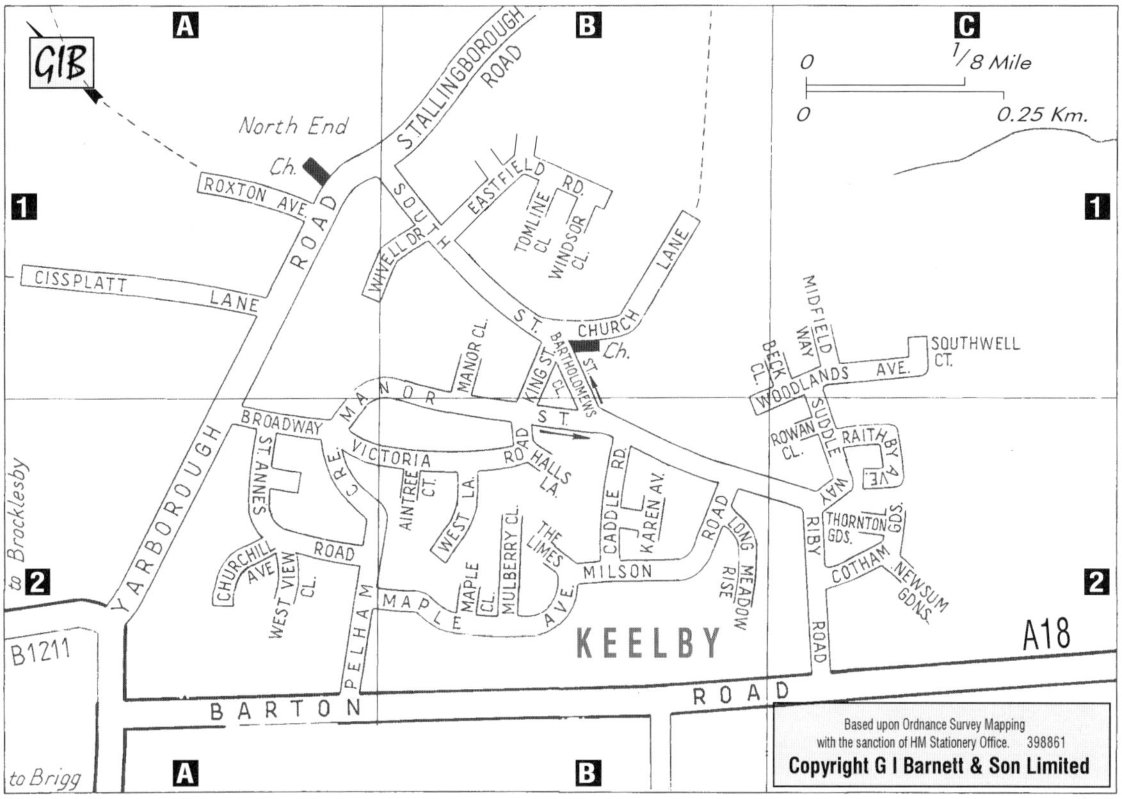

KEELBY INDEX TO STREETS

Aintree Court B.2

Barton Road A.2
Beck Close C.1
Broadway A.2

Caddle Road B.2
Church Lane B.1
Churchill Lane A.2
Cissplatt Lane A.1
Cotham Gardens C.2

Eastfield Road B.1

Halls Lane B.2

Karen Avenue B.2
King Street B.1

Long Meadow Rise B.2

Manor Close B.1
Manor Street A.2
Maple Avenue B.2
Maple Close B.2
Midfield Way C.1
Milson Road B.2
Mulberry Close B.2

Newsum Gardens C.2

Pelham Crescent A.2

Raithby Avenue C.2
Riby Road C.2
Rowan Close C.2
Roxtan Avenue A.1

St. Annes Road A.2
St. Bartholomews Close B.1
South Street B.1
Southwell Court C.1
Stallingborough Road B.1
Suddell Way C.2

The Limes B.2
Thornton Gardens C.2
Tomline Close B.1

Victoria Road A.2

West Lane B.2
West View Close A.2
Windsor Close B.1
Wivell Drive B.1
Woodlands Avenue C.1

Yarborough Road A.2

CONINGSBY/ TATTERSHALL INDEX TO STREETS

Abbey Close B.1
Allen Road C.1
Ash Drive B.2
Auden Court B.1

Baxter Close B.2
Beech Close B.2
Birch Close B.2
Blenheim Road B.2
Brent Road A.1
Browning Court B.1
Butts Lane B.1

Canberra Close B.2
Carrington Close C.1
Castlefields C.1
Castleview A.1
Cherry Tree Way B.2
Chestnut Drive B.2
Coldham Road C.1
Coleridge Court ..B.1
CONNINGSBY A.1
Cooke Crescent ..B.2
Cromwell Place B.1
Cross Keys Lane C.2
Curzon Estate A.1

Dogdyke Road A.2
Dryden Court B.1

East Drive A.1
Eusden Court B.1

Fairfield B.1
Farriers Way A.1
Finney Close C.1
Fitzgerald Court B.1
Fortescue Close A.1

Gayle Road A.1
Goldsmith Court B.1
Granary Lane A.1
Greenfield Road C.1

Heatcote Road B.1
High Street, Coningsby B.1
High Street, Tattershall A.1
Hoplands Road B.1
Hudson Drive C.1
Hunters Lane B.1

Ingham Court C.1
Ingham Road C.1

Johnson Court B.1

Keble Court B.1
Kerrick Court B.1
Kirby Lane B.1

Lancaster Drive ..B.2
Laythorpe Gardens B.1
Lewis Road B.2
Lodge Road A.1

Manor Road A.1
Market Place A.1
Marmion Road C.1
Marsh Lane A.1
Mill Farm Estate B.1
Milson Close B.2
Mitchell Road C.1

North Lane A.1

Old Boston Road B.2
Old Smithy Court B.1
Orchard Way B.2
Overton Road B.2

Park Lane B.1
Pingle Close C.1
Providence Place B.1

Reed Way C.1

School Lane B.1
Sherwood Road C.2
Silver Street B.1
Sleafodr Road A.1
Stenner Road C.1

TATTERSHALL ..A.1
Teal Road A.1
Tomlinson Close A.1
The Park B.1
Thorpe Place B.1
Thorpe Road B.1
Tumby Road C.1

Washington Close B.2
Wesselow Road C.1
West Drive A.1
Wharfe Lane B.1
Willow Drive B.2
Willows Court A.1

CONINGSBY/TATTERSHALL

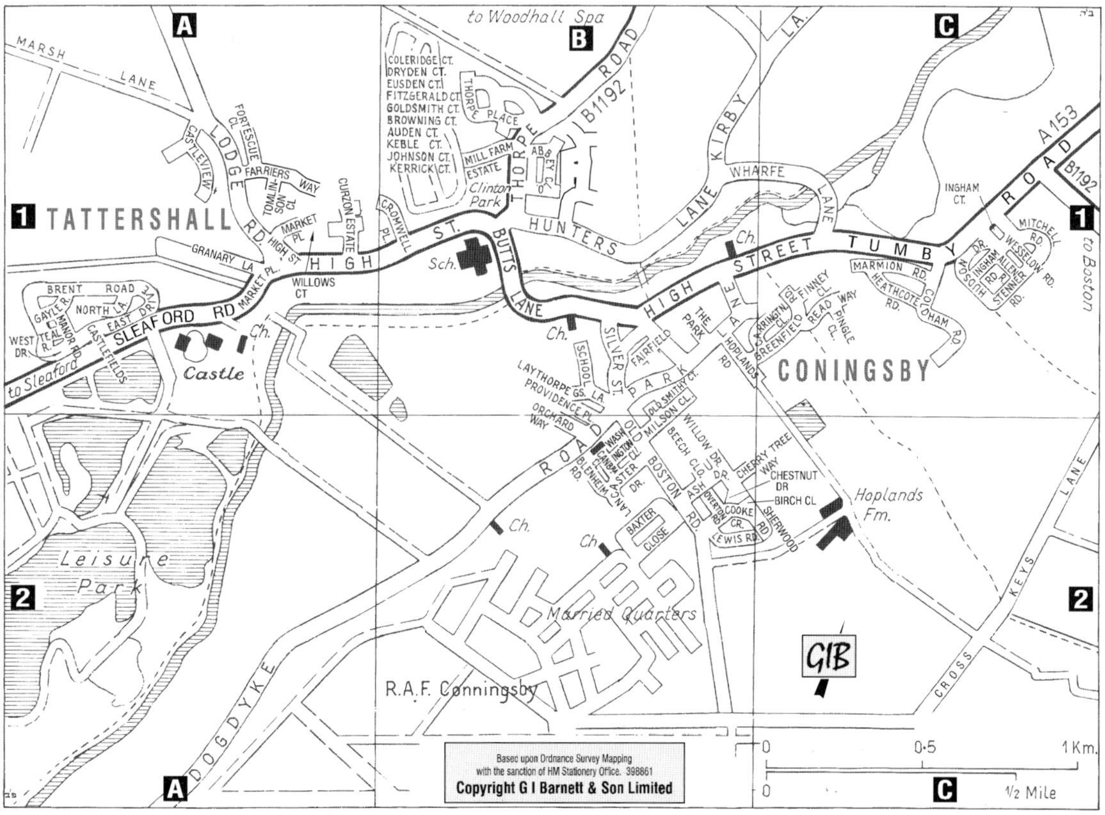

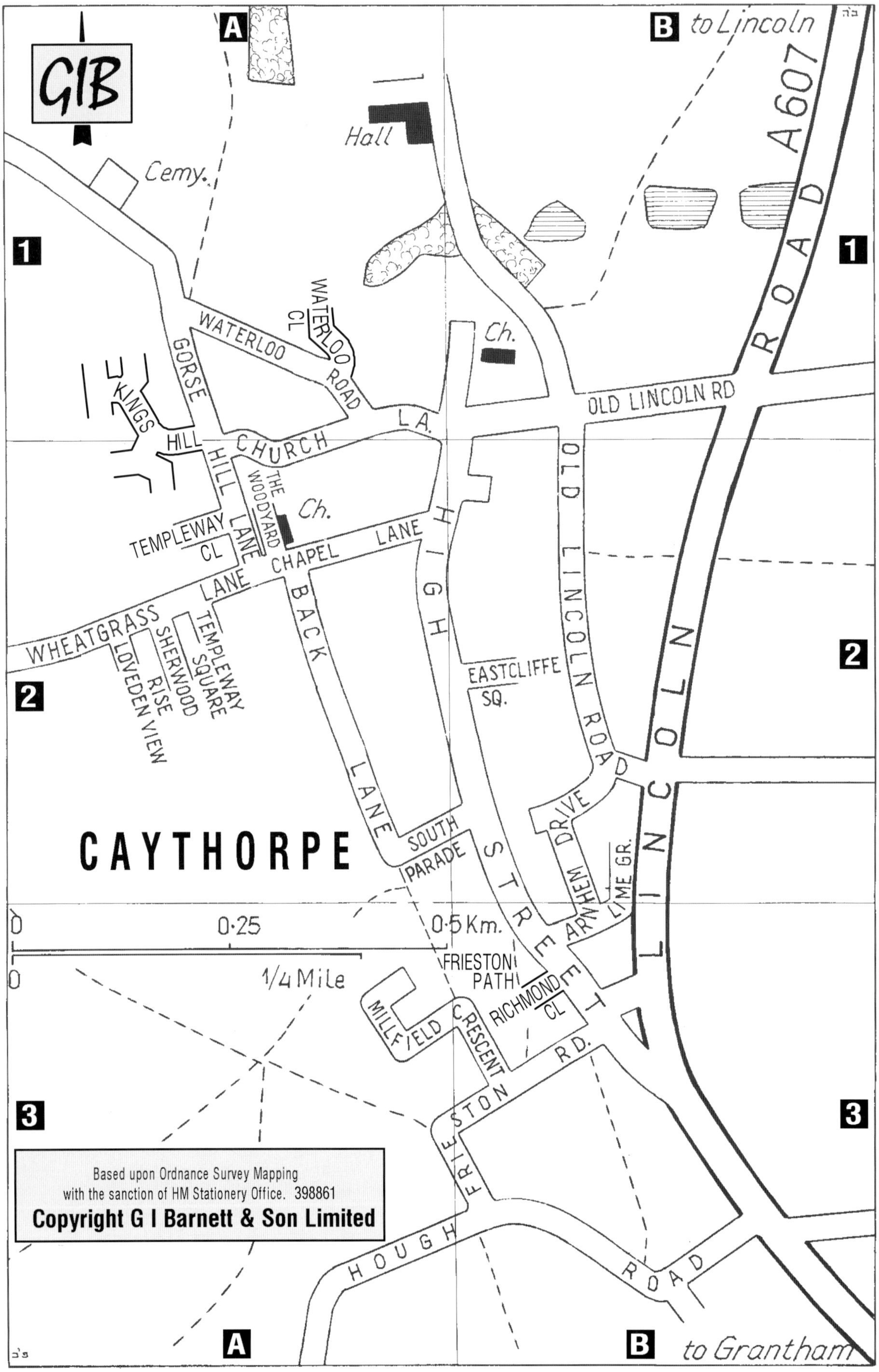

CAYTHORPE INDEX TO STREETS

Arnhem Drive B.3
Back Lane A.2
Chapel Lane A.2
Church Lane A.2
Eastcliffe Square B.2
Frieston Road B.3
Gorse Hill Lane A.1
High Street A.2
Hough Road A.3
Kings Hill A.1
Lime Grove B.3
Lincoln Road A.3
Loveden View A.2
Millfield Crescent A.3
Richmond Close B.3
Sherwood Rise A.2
South Parade A.2
The Woodyard A.2
Templeway Close A.2
Templeway Square A.2
Waterloo Close A.1
Waterloo Road A.1
Wheatgrass Lane A.2

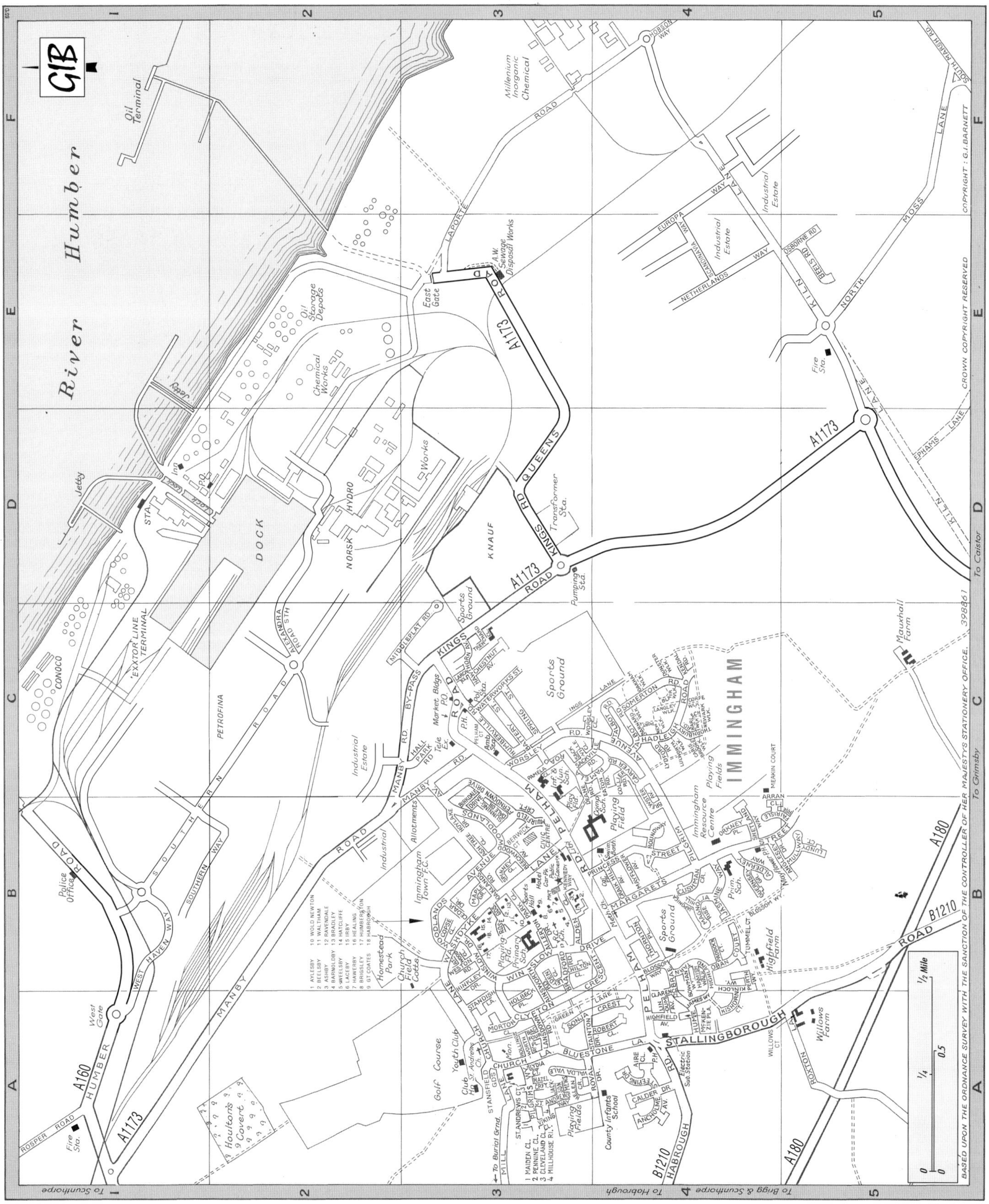

IMMINGHAM INDEX TO STREETS

Ainsworth Road A.3
Aire Close A.4
Alden Close B.3
Aldernery Way B.4
Allerton Drive B.3
Ancholme Avenue . . .A.4
Arran Close B.4
Ash Tree Close B.3
Atwood Close B.3

Balfour Place A.3
Barnard Walk C.4
Battery Street C.3
Beechwood Avenue . .B.3
Beels Road E.5
Birkdale Drive B.3
Blair Walk C.4
Blossom Way B.4
Bluestone Way A.3
Bowman Way B.4
Bradford Road B.3
Brewster Avenue B.4

Calder Drive A.4
Carisbrooke Walk . . .C.4
Carver Road C.4
Cedar Drive B.3
Chestnut Avenue C.3
Chilton Close B.3
Church Lane A.3
Clarence Close A.4
Cleveland Close A.3
Clyfton Crescent A.3
Collier Road C.4
Copse Close B.3
Corfe Walk C.4
Craik Hill Avenue B.4
Cushman Crescent . .B.4

Deane Road B.3
Dunster Walk C.4

Eaton Road C.4
Ephams Lane D.5
Europa Way F.4

Green Lane F.P A.3
Guernsey Grove B.4

Haborough Road A.4
Hadleigh Road C.4
Hall Park Road C.3
Hamish Walk B.4
Harlech Walk C.4
Hawthorne Avenue . .C.3
Hazel Croft A.3
Helen Crescent A.3
Highfield Avenue A.4
Highfield Tarn B.4
Hinkley Drive B.3
Hobson Way F.4
Holbeck Place A.3
Holylake Drive B.3
Humber Road A.1
Humberville Road . . .C.3
Hume Brae A.4

Ings Lane C.3

Jackson Mews A.3
James Way A.4
Japonica Hill B.4
Jasmine Way B.4

Kendal Road C.4
Kennedy Way B.3
Kiln Lane D.5
Kings Road C.3
Kinloch Way B.4
Kishorn Court A.4

Langley Walk C.4
Lansdown Road A.3
Laporte Road E.3
Larch Close C.3
Leyden Close B.3
Lindum Avenue A.4
Lulworth Walk C.4
Lundy Court B.5
Lydia Court A.3
Lyndford Road C.4

Magnolia Rise B.4
Maiden Close A.3
Manby Road A.2
Manby Road By-Pass C.3
Maple Grove B.3
Margarets Streets . . .B.4
Mayflower Avenue . . .B.4
McKenzie Place A.4
Meakin Court C.4
Middleplat Road C.3
Mill Lane A.3
Millhouse Rise A.3
Morton Close A.3
Mullway B.5

Netherlands Way E.4
Newark Walk C.4
Newport Walk C.4
North Moss Lane E.5

Oakham Walk C.4
Oaklands Road B.3
Oban Court B.4
Orkney Place B.4
Osbourne Road E.5

Paddock Court B.4
Pamela Close C.3
Pamela Road C.4
Park lane B.3
Pelham Road A.4
Pehine Close A.3
Perth Way B.4
Pilgrim Avenue B.4
Pilgrims Way A.3
Princess Street B.4

Queens Road D.3

Robert Close A.4
Rosper Road A.1
Roundway B.4
Roval Drive A.3
Roxton Lane A.5

Sackvill Close C.3
Sackville Road C.3
Scandinavia Way E.4
Shetland Way B.4
Somerton Road C.4
Sonia Crest A.3
South Marsh Road . .A.3
Spinney Close B.3
Spring Street C.3
Stainton Drive A.3
Stallingborough Road A.4
Standish Lane A.3
Stansfield Gardens . . .A.3
Steeping Drive A.4
Sunningdale Drive . . .B.3
Salbot Road C.4

Thornebury Road . . .C.4
Thornton Place B.4
Tor Line Terminal C.1
Trenchard Close C.3
Tummel Court B.4
Vaida Vale A.3
Viking Close A.3

Washdyke Lane B.3
Waterworks Street . . .C.3
Weston Road B.3
Willows Court A.5
Winslow Drive B.3
Woodlands Avenue . .B.3
Worsley Close C.3
Worsley Road C.3

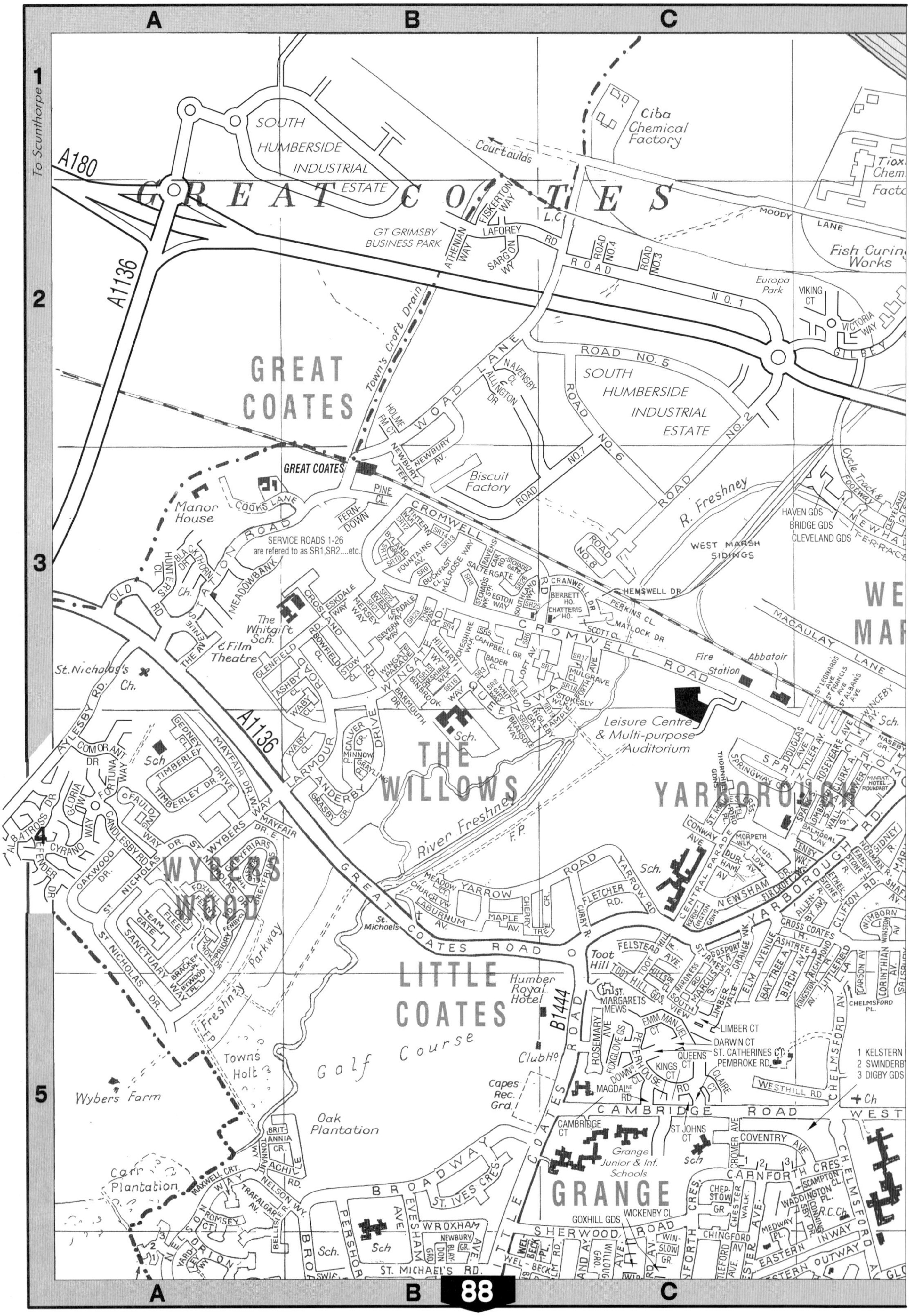
A
B
C
1
2
3
4
5
To Scunthorpe
A180
A1136
GREAT COATES
SOUTH HUMBERSIDE INDUSTRIAL ESTATE
Ciba Chemical Factory
Courtaulds
Tioxide Chemical Factory
MOODY LANE
Fish Curing Works
GT GRIMSBY BUSINESS PARK
ATHENIAN WAY
FISKERTON WAY
LAFOREY RD
SARGON WAY
L.C.
ROAD NO.4
ROAD NO.3
ROAD NO.1
Europa Park
VIKING CT
VICTORIA WAY
GILBEY
ROAD NO.5
ROAD NO.6
ROAD NO.2
ROAD NO.7
ROAD NO.8
Town's Croft Drain
WOAD LANE
NAVENSBY CL.
ALLINGTON DR
HOLME FM CT.
NEWBURY AV.
NEWBURY TER.
Biscuit Factory
GREAT COATES
PINE CL.
FERNDOWN
R. Freshney
WEST MARSH SIDINGS
Cycle Track & Footway
HAVEN GDS
BRIDGE GDS
CLEVELAND GDS
NEWHAVEN TERRACE
Manor House
COOKS LANE
STATION ROAD
SERVICE ROADS 1-26 are refered to as SR1,SR2....etc.
CROMWELL
HUNTERS CL.
BLACKTHORN DR
MEADOWBANK
OLD RD
THE AVENUE
Ch.
The Whitgift Sch.
& Film Theatre
CROSLAND RD.
ESKDALE WAY
MERSEY WAY
WARDALE
SEVERN WAY
FOUNTAINS AV.
BUCKFAST CL.
MELROSE WAY
SALTERGATE
ST CHADS WK
EGTON WAY
SOUTHLAND WAY
CRANWELL DR
HEMSWELL DR
BERRETT HO.
CHATTERIS HO.
PERKINS CL.
MATLOCK DR
SCOTT CL.
CROMWELL ROAD
Fire Station
Abbatoir
MACAULAY LANE
WEST MARSH
St.Nicholas's Ch.
GLENFIELD RD
ASHBY CL.
WABY CL.
BOWFIELD CL.
STOW CL.
WINGATE PARADE
WINGATE RD.
HILLARY WY
CHESHIRE WLK
SINBROOK WAY
BARMOUTH DR.
CHESHIRE WK
CAMPBELLS GR
BADER CL.
LOFT AV.
MULGRAVE
STOKESLY WLK
INGLEBY GR.
BRANSDALE WAY
QUEENSWAY
Sch.
Leisure Centre & Multi-purpose Auditorium
ST LEONARDS AVE
ST FRANCIS AVE
ST ALBANS AVE
WINCEBY AV.
Sch.
AYLESBY RD.
COMORANT DR
FORTUNA WAY
GLORIA WY
ALBATROSS DR
CYRANO WAY
DEFENDER DR
CANDLESBY RD
OAKWOOD DR.
FAULDING WAY
Sch
GEDNEY CL.
TIMBERLEY
TIMBERLEY DR.
MAYFAIR DRIVE
MAYFAIR DR.W.
MAYFAIR DR. E.
WYBERS WAY
GREYFRIARS
ST. NICHOLAS DR.
FOXHILL
FLEET
TEAM GATE
SANCTUARY WAY
BRACKEN
PRIORY
WYBERS WOOD
LARMOUR RD
ANDERBY DRIVE
CALVER CR.
MINNOW CL.
GRAYLING CL.
GRASBY CR.
THE WILLOWS
River Freshney
F.P.
YARBOROUGH
DOUGLAS AVE
TYLER AV.
ROSEVEARE AVE
CLARK AV.
SPRINGWAY CR.
CONWAY AVE
CENTRAL PARADE
MORPETH WLK
DURHAM AV.
NEWSHAM DR
FIRCROFT RD
YARBOROUGH RD
ENBY WK
CLIFTON RD.
ALLEN R.
WIMBORN
MEADOW CT
YARROW RD.
CHURCH VW
LABURNUM AV.
MAPLE AV.
CHERRY TRE
FLETCHER RD.
YARROW RD
CURRY R.
St. Michaels
GREAT COATES ROAD
LITTLE COATES
Humber Royal Hotel
Toot Hill
FELSTEAD AVE
TOOT HILL GDS
ST. MARGARETS MEWS
B1444
ROSEMARY AVE
FOXGLOVE GS
EMMANUEL CT
PETERHOUSE
DOWNING CL
KINGS CT
QUEENS CT
CLAIRE CT
MAGDALENE RD
LIMBER CT
DARWIN CT
ST. CATHERINES CT
PEMBROKE RD
WESTHILL RD
GOSPORT
ST JAMES
MARCUS ST.
GRANGE WK
ELM AVENUE
BAY TREE AV.
BIRCH AV.
ASHTREE AV.
CROSS COATES RD.
KINGSTON
RICHMOND
LITTLEFIELD
CARSON AV.
CORINTHIAN AV.
CHELMSFORD PL.
CHELMSFORD AV.
1 KELSTERN
2 SWINDERBY
3 DIGBY GDS
Ch
Freshney Parkway
F.P.
Towns Holt
Golf Course
Club Ho.
Capes Rec. Grd.
Wybers Farm
Oak Plantation
Carr Plantation
BRITANNIA CR.
ACHILLE RD.
NELSON WY.
TRAFALGAR AV.
MAXWELL CRT.
ROMSEY CT
BROADWAY
ST. IVES CRES.
LITTLE COATES ROAD
CAMBRIDGE ROAD
CAMBRIDGE CT
ST JOHNS CT
Grange Junior & Inf. Schools
Sch
COVENTRY AVE
CROMER AVE
CARNFORTH CRES.
SCAMPTON CL.
WADDINGTON PL.
R.C.Ch.
GRANGE
CHEPSTOW GR
CHESTER AVE
GOXHILL GDS
WICKENBY CL
SHERWOOD RD
PERSHORE AVE
EVESHAM AVE
WROXHAM AVE
NEWBURY GR.
Sch
Sch.
ST. MICHAEL'S RD.
CHINGFORD AV
EASTERN INWAY
EASTERN OUTWAY
MEDWAY PL.
WELBECK PL.
88

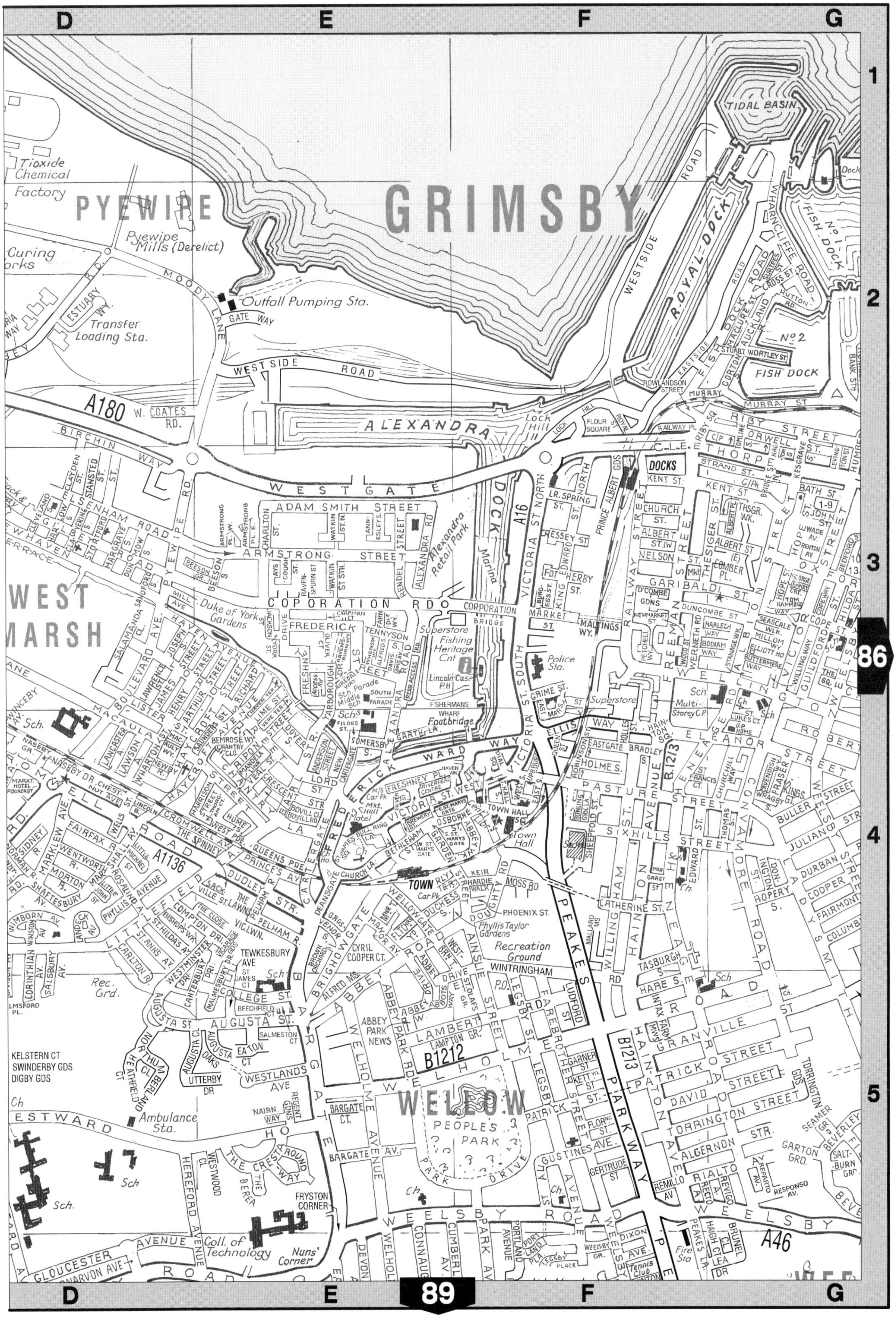
D
E
F
G
1
2
3
4
5
86
89
GRIMSBY
PYEWIPE
WEST MARSH
WELLOW
TIDAL BASIN
ROYAL DOCK
No 1 FISH DOCK
No 2 FISH DOCK
ALEXANDRA
DOCK
Tioxide Chemical Factory
Pyewipe Mills (Derelict)
Outfall Pumping Sta.
Transfer Loading Sta.
MOODY LANE
GATE WAY
WESTSIDE ROAD
WEST SIDE ROAD
A180
W. COATES RD.
BIRCHIN WAY
WESTGATE
ADAM SMITH STREET
ARMSTRONG STREET
CORPORATION RD
FREDERICK ST
Alexandra Retail Park
Marina
A16
VICTORIA ST NORTH
VICTORIA ST SOUTH
PRINCE ALBERT GDS
DOCKS
RIBY STREET
CLEETHORPE RD
Lock Hill
FLOUR SQUARE
RAILWAY STREET
FREEMAN STREET
GARIBALDI ST
Duke of York Gardens
Superstore Fishing Heritage Cnt
Police Sta.
Superstore
Multi-Storey C.P.
Footbridge
FREDERICK WARD WAY
VICTORIA ST WEST
TOWN HALL SQ
Town Hall
TOWN
BETHLEHAM ST
BULL RING
DEANSGATE
CHURCH LA
A1136
CROMWELL RD
PEAKES PARKWAY
B1213
B1212
Recreation Ground
Phyllis Taylor Gardens
WINTRINGHAM RD
PASTURE STREET
SIXHILLS STREET
HAINTON AVENUE
CONVAMORE ROAD
BULLER STREET
LEDGE ROAD
GRANVILLE ST
PATRICK STREET
DAVID STREET
TORRINGTON STREET
ALGERNON STR.
PEOPLES PARK
PARK DRIVE
WELHOLME ROAD
WELHOLME AVENUE
ABBEY PARK RD
BARGATE
BARGATE AVE.
ST AUGUSTINES AVE.
WEELSBY ROAD
WEELSBY STREET
A46
Fire Sta
Coll. of Technology
Nuns' Corner
FRYSTON CORNER
Ambulance Sta.
Rec. Grd.
KELSTERN CT
SWINDERBY GDS
DIGBY GDS
GLOUCESTER AVENUE
HEREFORD AVENUE
THE CRESTA
MACAULAY ST
BOULEVARD AVE
HAVEN AVENUE
LEDBURY ST
YARBOROUGH DR
SOMERSBY ST
CARTERGATE
BRIGHOWGATE
WELLOWGATE
AUGUSTA ST
COLLEGE ST
TEWKESBURY AVE

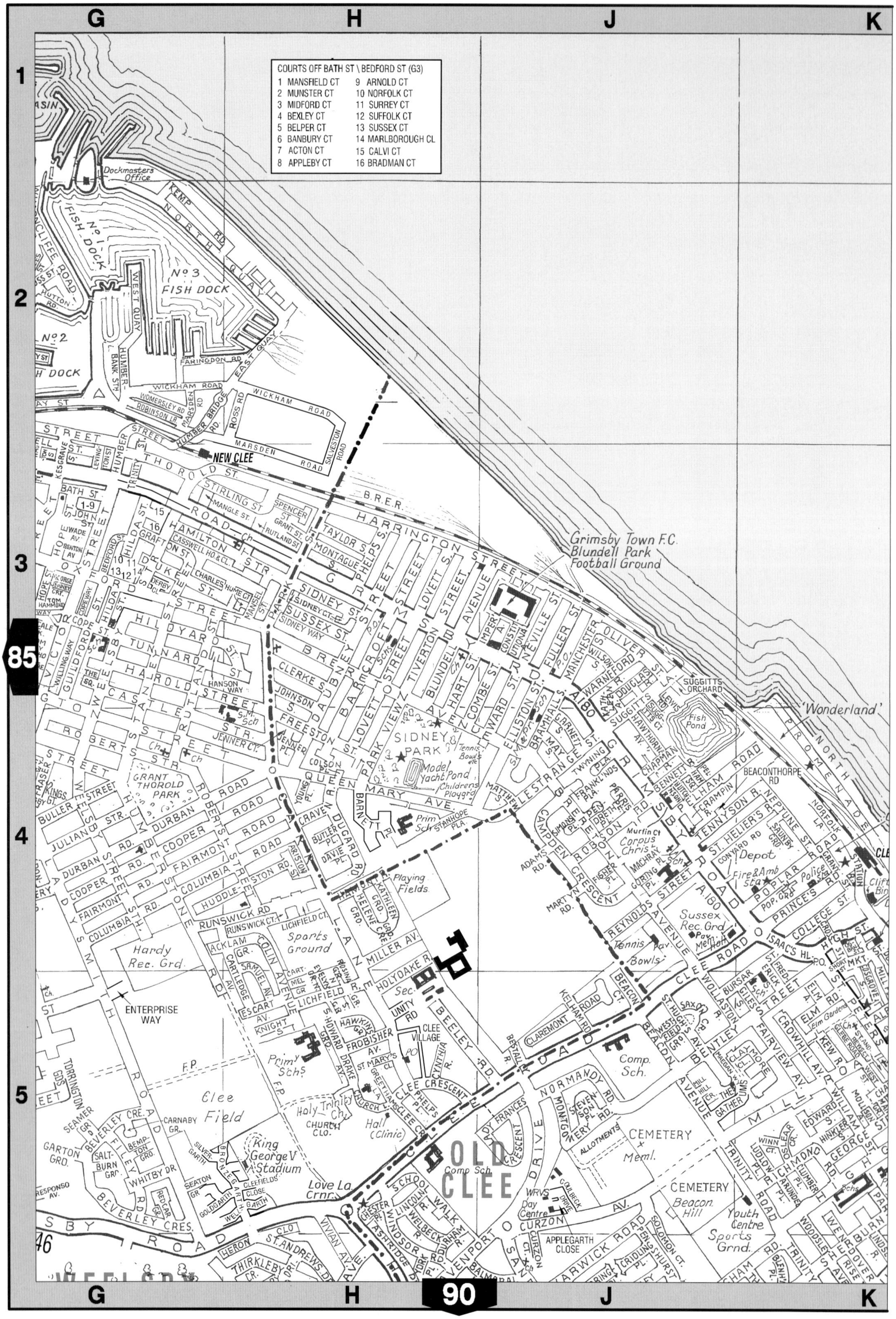
G
H
J
K
1
2
3
4
5
85
90
COURTS OFF BATH ST \ BEDFORD ST (G3)
1 MANSFIELD CT
2 MUNSTER CT
3 MIDFORD CT
4 BEXLEY CT
5 BELPER CT
6 BANBURY CT
7 ACTON CT
8 APPLEBY CT
9 ARNOLD CT
10 NORFOLK CT
11 SURREY CT
12 SUFFOLK CT
13 SUSSEX CT
14 MARLBOROUGH CL
15 CALVI CT
16 BRADMAN CT
Dockmasters Office
No 1 FISH DOCK
No 3 FISH DOCK
No 2
KEMP RD
NORTH QUAY
WEST QUAY
EAST QUAY
FARINGDON RD
WICKHAM ROAD
MARSDEN ROAD
SALVESTON ROAD
ROSS RD
HUMBER BRIDGE RD
NEW CLEE
THOROLD ST.
B.R.E.R.
HARRINGTON STREET
Grimsby Town F.C.
Blundell Park
Football Ground
SUGGITTS ORCHARD
Fish Pond
'Wonderland'
NORTH PROMENADE
BEACONTHORPE RD
SIDNEY PARK
Model Yacht Pond
Childrens Playgd
QUEEN MARY AVE
Prim Sch
Playing Fields
Sports Ground
Hardy Rec. Grd
ENTERPRISE WAY
Clee Field
Holy Trinity Ch.
King George V Stadium
Love La. Crnr.
OLD CLEE
Comp Sch.
CEMETERY
Meml.
Beacon Hill
Youth Centre
Sports Grnd.
Sussex Rec. Grd
Depot
Fire&Amb Sta
Police Sta
GRIMSBY ROAD
A180
CLEE ROAD
CLEE VILLAGE
BEELEY RD.
CLEE CRESCENT
NORMANDY RD
CURZON AV.
APPLEGARTH CLOSE
BEVERLEY CRES.
WHITBY DR.
CAMPDEN CRESCENT
REYNOLDS STREET
TENNYSON R.
HIGH ST.
ISAAC'S HL.
MILL RD

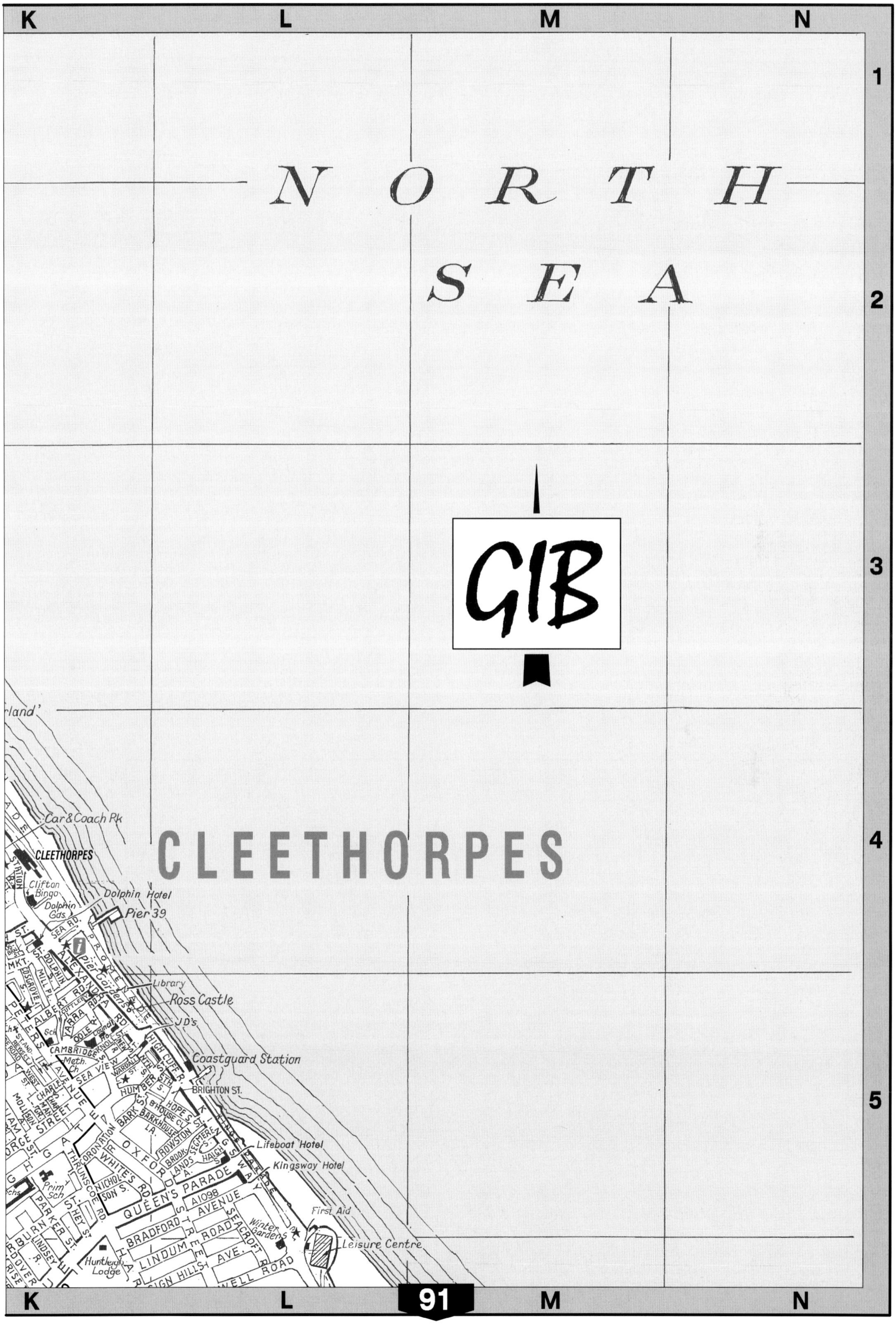
K L M N
1 2 3 4 5
NORTH SEA
GIB
CLEETHORPES
Car & Coach Pk
CLEETHORPES STATION
Clifton Bingo
Dolphin Gds.
Dolphin Hotel
Pier 39
SEA RD.
MKT. ST.
DOLPHIN ST.
ALEXANDRA RD.
Pier Gardens
ALBERT RD.
CAMBRIDGE ST.
Library
Ross Castle
JD's
Coastguard Station
BRIGHTON ST.
HIGH CLIFF R.
SEA VIEW ST.
HUMBER ST.
BARK ST.
BARKHOUSE LA.
HOPE ST.
ROWSTON ST.
HAIGH ST.
KINGS PARADE
KINGSWAY
Lifeboat Hotel
Kingsway Hotel
First Aid
Winter Gardens
Leisure Centre
STREET
CORONATION RD.
WHITE'S RD.
OXFORD STREET
QUEEN'S PARADE
A1098
AVENUE
SEACROFT RD.
BRADFORD AVE.
LINDUM ROAD
Prim Sch
PARKER ST.
HEY ST.
LINDSEY R.
Huntleigh Lodge
Meth. Ch.
Sch
91

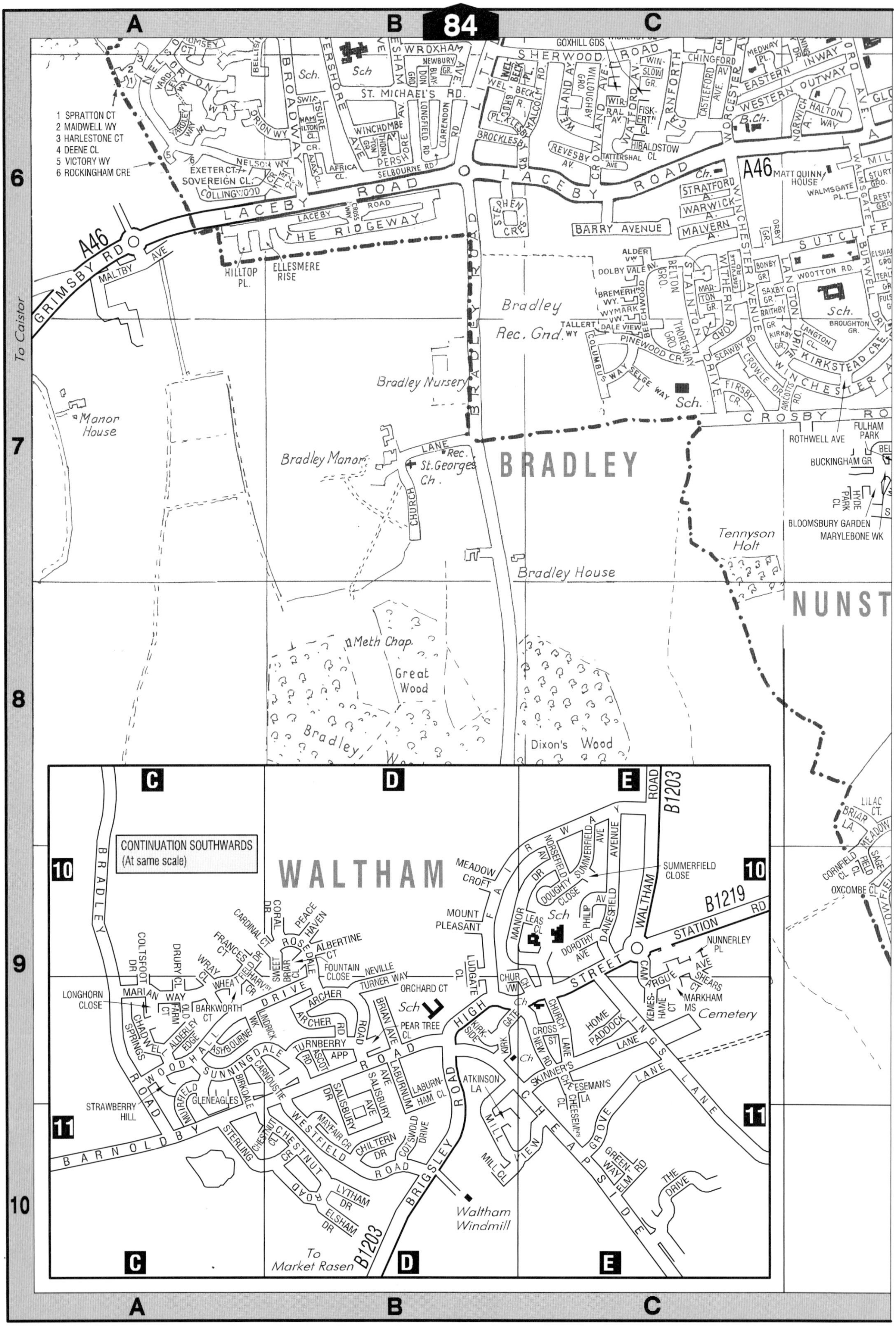
84
A
B
C
6
7
8
9
10
11
1 SPRATTON CT
2 MAIDWELL WY
3 HARLESTONE CT
4 DEENE CL
5 VICTORY WY
6 ROCKINGHAM CRE
To Caistor
A46
GRIMSBY RD
LACEBY ROAD
THE RIDGEWAY
SHERWOOD ROAD
ST. MICHAEL'S RD.
BROADWAY
BARRY AVENUE
BRADLEY ROAD
Bradley Rec. Gnd.
Bradley Nursery
Manor House
Bradley Manor
St. Georges Ch.
BRADLEY
Tennyson Holt
Bradley House
NUNST
Meth Chap.
Great Wood
Bradley Wood
Dixon's Wood
CROSBY RD
WINCHESTER AVENUE
CONTINUATION SOUTHWARDS
(At same scale)
WALTHAM
C
D
E
B1203
B1219
STATION RD
HIGH STREET
WALTHAM ROAD
BARNOLDBY ROAD
WESTFIELD ROAD
BRIGSLEY ROAD
CHEAPSIDE
Cemetery
Waltham Windmill
To Market Rasen

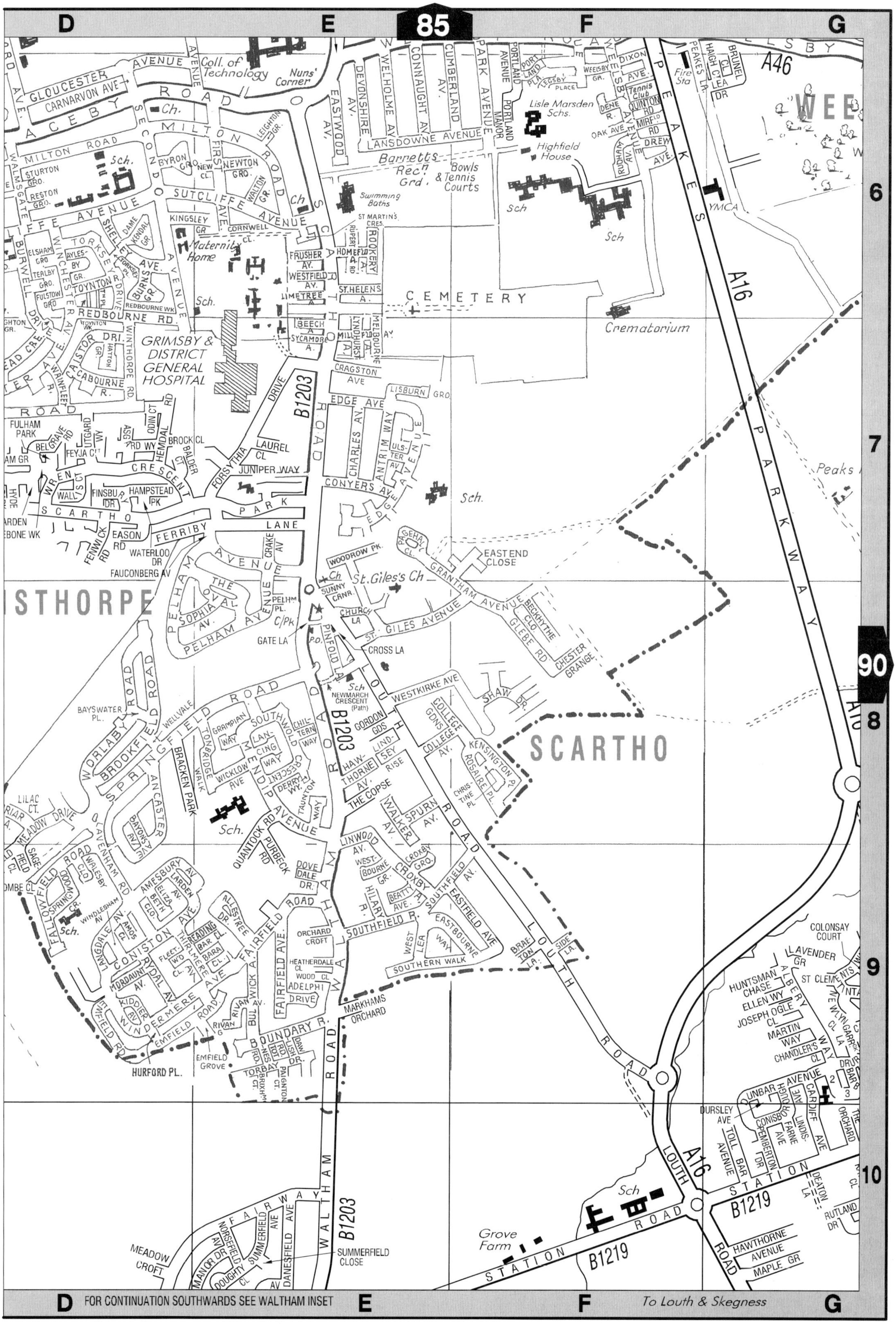
D
E
85
F
G
SCARTHO
ISTHORPE
GRIMSBY & DISTRICT GENERAL HOSPITAL
CEMETERY
Crematorium
St.Giles's Ch
Coll. of Technology
Nuns' Corner
Lisle Marsden Schs.
Highfield House
Barretts Rec'n Grd.
Bowls & Tennis Courts
Swimming Baths
Maternity Home
PEAKS PARKWAY
A16
A46
B1203
B1219
LOUTH ROAD
STATION ROAD
WALTHAM ROAD
SCARTHO ROAD
SPRINGFIELD ROAD
WINDERMERE AVE
BOUNDARY R.
FAIRWAY
SOUTHERN WALK
GRANTHAM AVENUE
ST. GILES AVENUE
LANSDOWNE AVENUE
Grove Farm
Peaks
6
7
8
9
10
90
FOR CONTINUATION SOUTHWARDS SEE WALTHAM INSET
To Louth & Skegness

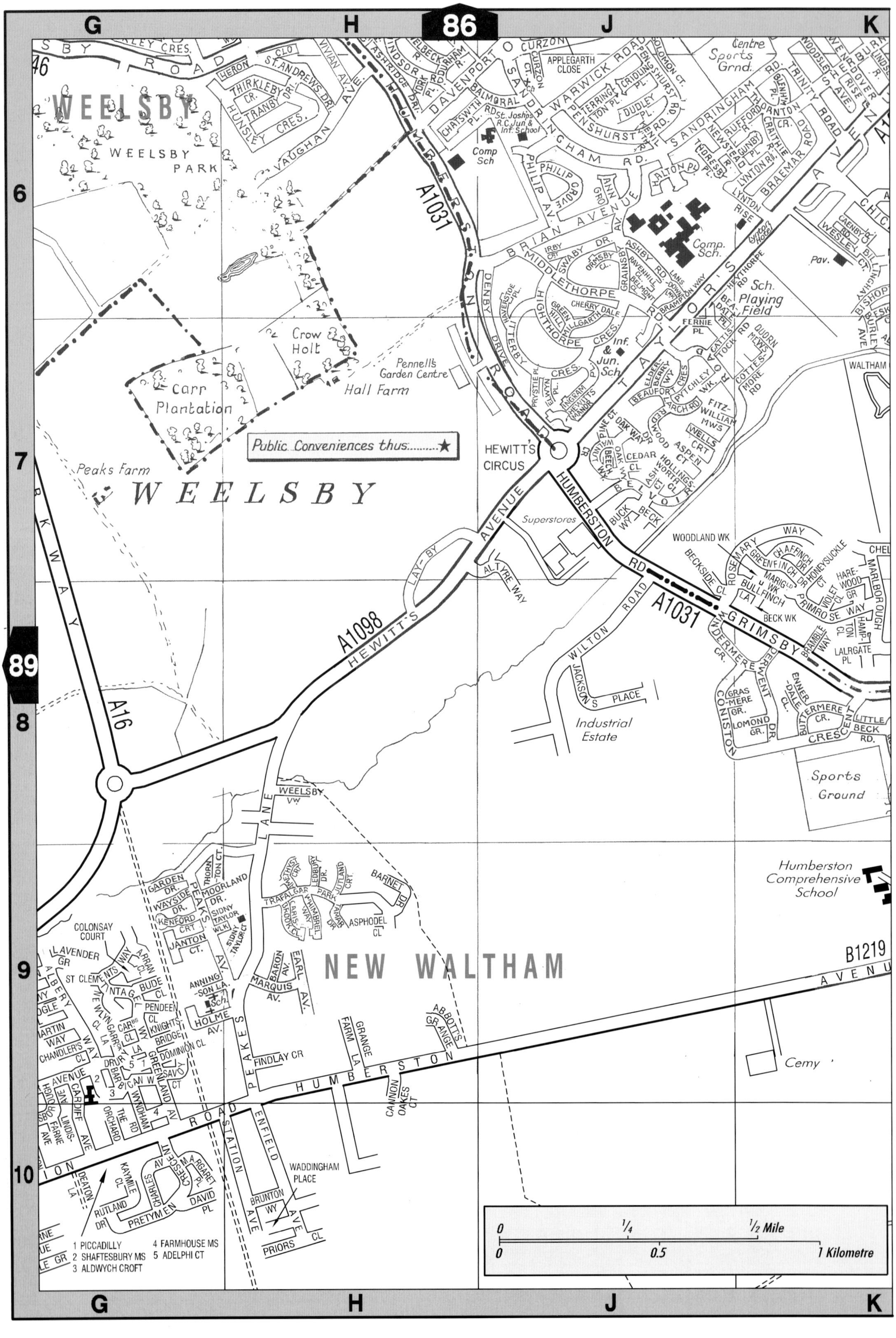
G
H
86
J
K
6
7
89
8
9
10
WEELSBY
WEELSBY PARK
WEELSBY
Carr Plantation
Crow Holt
Hall Farm
Peaks Farm
Pennell's Garden Centre
Public Conveniences thus..........★
HEWITT'S CIRCUS
Superstores
Industrial Estate
Sports Ground
Sch. Playing Field
Comp Sch
Comp. Sch.
St. Joshps R.C.Jun & Inf. School
Inf. & Jun. Sch
Humberston Comprehensive School
NEW WALTHAM
Cemy
Pav.
Centre Sports Grnd.
A1031
A1098
A16
B1219
HEWITT'S AVENUE
HUMBERSTON ROAD
HUMBERSTON AVENUE
GRIMSBY RD
TAYLORS AVENUE
SANDRINGHAM RD.
BRIAN AVENUE
MIDDLETHORPE
HIGHTHORPE CRES.
DENBY DRIVE
WARWICK ROAD
DAVENPORT
APPLEGARTH CLOSE
PENSHURST RD.
TRINITY ROAD
BRAEMAR ROAD
WILTON ROAD
JACKSON'S PLACE
PEAKS LANE
PEAKES AV.
STATION AVE
ENFIELD AVE
WEELSBY VW
WADDINGHAM PLACE
COLONSAY COURT
LAVENDER GR
ST CLEMENTS
MOORLAND DR.
BARNET DR
ASPHODEL CL
MARQUIS AV.
EARL AV.
BARON AV.
ABBOTTS GRANGE
GRANGE FARM LA
FINDLAY CR
CANNON OAKES CT
BRUNTON WY
PRIORS CL
PRETYMEN CRES
DAVID PL
MARGARET PL
RUTLAND DR
KAYMILE CL
DEATON LA
CONISTON CR.
DERWENT DR
BUTTERMERE CR.
LITTLE BECK RD.
WOODLAND WK
BECK WK
LALRGATE PL
1 PICCADILLY
2 SHAFTESBURY MS
3 ALDWYCH CROFT
4 FARMHOUSE MS
5 ADELPHI CT
0
1/4
1/2 Mile
0
0.5
1 Kilometre

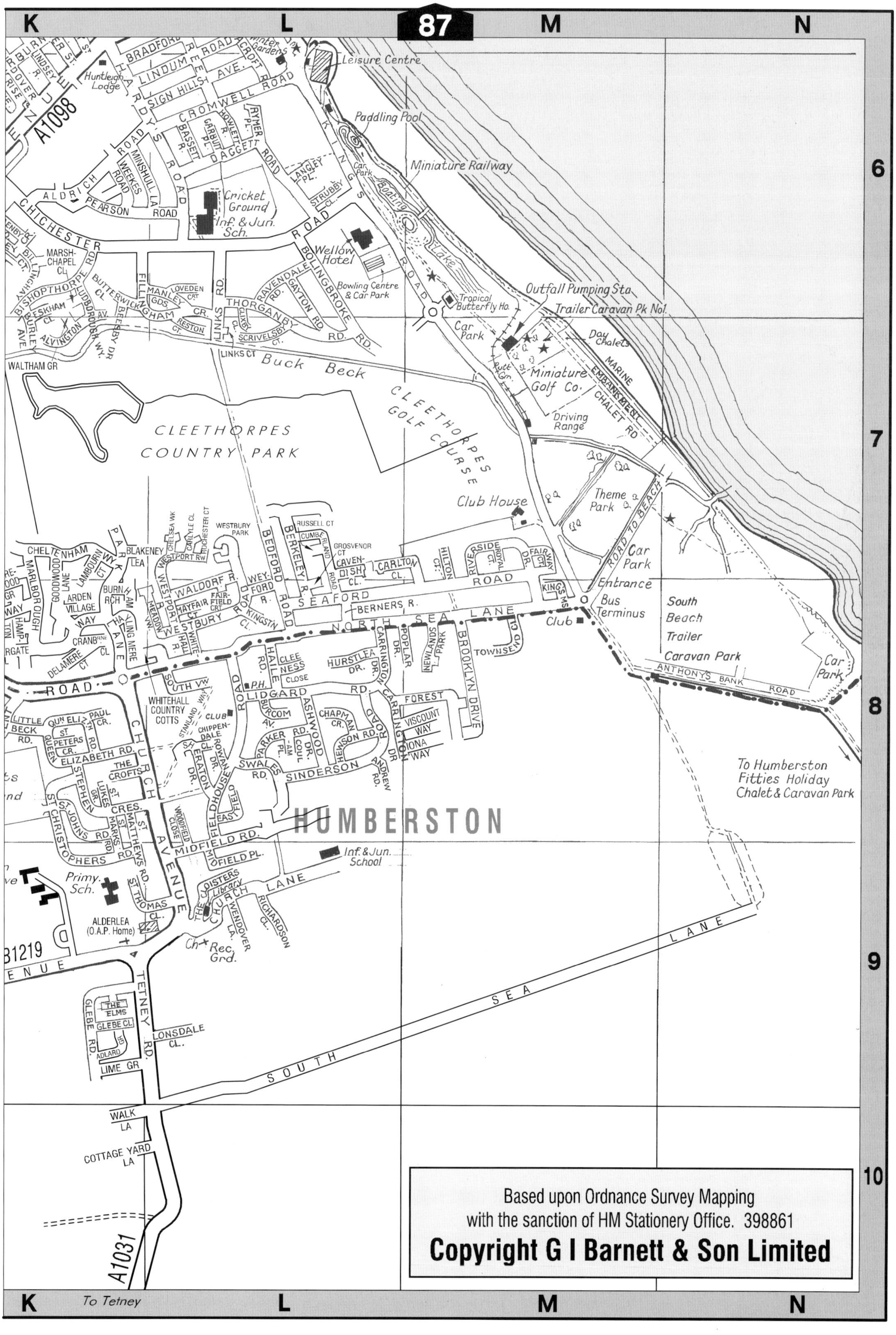

Based upon Ordnance Survey Mapping
with the sanction of HM Stationery Office. 398861

Abbey Drive East E.4
Abbey Drive West E.5
Abbey Park Mews E.5
Abbey Park Road E.5
Abbey Road E.5
Abbey Walk F.4
Abbott's Grange H.9
Abbotts Way F.5
Achille Road G.4
Acklam Grove G.4
Acton Court G.3 (H.2)
Adam Smith Street E.3
Adams Road J.4
Adelphi Court G.8
Adelphi Drive E.9
Adlard Grove K.9
Afica Close B.6
Ainslie Street F.4
Airedale Way E.3
Ajax Close B.6
Albatross Drive A.4
Albert Place G.3
Albert Road K.5
Albert Street F.3
Albertine Court D.10 (Waltham Inset)
Albery Way G.9
Albion Street G.4
Alder View C.6
Alderlea K.9
Alderley Edge C.11 (Waltham Inset)
Aldrich Road K.6
Aldwych Crot G.9
Alexandra Road (Cleethorpes) K.4
Alexandra Road (Grimsby) E.4
Alfred Mews E.5
Alfred Street E.3
Algernon Street F.5
Allenby Avenue D.4
Allestree Drive E.9
Allington Drive B.2
Altyre Way J.7
Alvington Avenue K.7
Amcotts Road D.7
Amesbury Avenue D.9
Amethyst Court H.9
Amos Close D.9
Ampleforth Avenue C.4
Ancaster Avenue D.8
Anderby Drive B.4
Anderson Street E.4
Andrew Road L.8
Ann Grove J.6
Annesley Street E.3
Anningson Lane G.9
Antony's Bank Road N.8
Antrim Way E.7
Appleby Court G.3 (H.2)
Applegarth Close J.5
Archer Road D.11 (Waltham Inset)
Arden Village K.8
Ariston Street H.4
Armstrong Place East E.3
Armstrong Place West E.3
Armstrong Street E.3
Arnold Court G.3 (H.2)
Arran Close G.9
Arthur Street D.4
Arundel Place K.5
Ascot Road D.11 (Waltham Inset)
Asgard Way D.7
Ash Court J.7
Ashbourne C.11 (Waltham Inset)
Ashby Road J.6
Ashley Close B.3
Ashridge Drive H.5
Ashtree Avenue C.4
Ashwood Drive L.8
Aspen Court K.7
Asphodel Close H.9
Athenian Way B.2
Atkinson Lane D.11 (Waltham Inset)
Auckland Road G.2
Augusta Close D.5
Augusta Oaks E.5
Augusta St. Extension D.5
Aygusta Street E.5
Aylesby Grove D.6
Aylesby Park A.4
Aylesby Road A.4
Ayscough Street E.3

Balder Court D.7
Balmoral Avenue D.4
Balmoral Road J.6
Banbury Court G.3 (H.2)
Barbara Close E.9
Barbican Way G.9
Barcroft Street H.3
Bargate E.5
Bargate Avenue E.5
Bargate Court E.5
Bark Street K.5
Barkhouse Close L.5
Barkhouse Lane L.5
Barkworth Court C.11 (Waltham Inset)
Barmouth Drive B.3
Barnet Drive H.9
Barnett Place H.4
Barnoldby Road C.11 (Waltham Inset)
Baron Avenue H.9
Baroness Road C.5
Barry Avenue C.6
Bassett Road L.6
Bath Street G.3
Bay Tree Avenue C.5
Bayons Avenue D.8
Bayswater Place D.8
Beacon Avenue J.5
Beacon Court J.5
Beaconthorpe Road J.4
Beadale Place J.6
Beatty Avenue E.9
Beaufort Crescent J.7
Beck Walk K.8
Beckhythe Close F.8
Beckside Close K.8
Bedford Road L.7
Bedford Street G.3
Beech Avenue E.7
Beech Way J.7
Beechfield Court E.5
Beechwood Avenue C.7
Beeley Road H.5
Beesby Drive K.7
Beeson Grove E.3
Beeson Street E.3
Belgrave Road D.7
Bellfinch Close K.8
Bellisle Road A.5
Belmont Close J.6
Belper Court G.3 (H.2)
Belton Grove C.6
Belvoir Road J.7
Bempton Grove G.5
Bemrose Way E.4
Bennett Road J.4
Bentley Street J.5
Benton Avenue G.3
Berkeley Road L.7
Berners Road L.8
Berrett House C.3
Bestall Road E.5
Bethlehem Street E.4
Beverley Crescent G.5
Bexley Court G.3 (H.2)
Billinghay Court K.7
Binbrook Way B.3
Birch Avenue C.5
Birchin Way D.2
Birkdale C.11 (Waltham Inset)
Bishops Walk D.4
Bishopthorpe Road K.7
Blackthorne Drive A.3
Blackeney Lea K.7
Blaydon Grove B.6
Blenheim Place K.8
Bloomsbury Garden D.7
Blundel Avenue H.3
Bodiam Way G.3
Bolingbroke Road L.6
Bonby Grove C.6
Boulevard Avenue D.3
Boundary Road E.9
Bovill Close E.4
Bovill House E.4
Bower Avenue D.4
Bowfield Close B.3
Bowing Green Lane F.4
Bracken Park D.8
Bracken Place A.5
Bradford Avenue K.5
BRADLEY A.8
BRADLEY B.7
Bradley Road B.7
Bradley Road (Waltham) C.10 (Waltham Inset)
Bradley Street F.4
Bradman Court G.3
Braemar Road K.6
Braeton Lane 9
Bramble Way K.8
Bramhall Street J.4
Brampton Way J.6
Bransdale Way B.4
Bremerhaven Way C.6
Brereton Avenue H.3
Brewery Street E.4
Brian Avenue D.11 (Waltham Inset)
Brian Avenue J.6
Brair Lane D.8
Bridge Gardens D.3
Bridge Street North G.3
Brighowgate E.5
Brighton Street L.5
Brigsley Road D.11 (Waltham Inset)
Britannia Crescent A.5
Brixham Court E.9
Broadway B.5
Brock Close D.7
Brocklesby Place B.6
Brocklesby Road B.6
Bronzegarth H.5
Brookfield Road D.8
Brooklands Avenue L.5
Brooklyn Drive M.8
Broughton Grove D.7
Brown Orchard E.4
Brunel Close G.6
Brunton Way H.10
Buck Beck Way J.7
Buckfast Close B.3
Buckfast Way B.3
Buckingham Grove D.7
Bude Close G.9
Bull Ring Lane E.4
Buller Street G.4
Bulwick Avenue E.9
Burcom Avenue L.8
Burgess Street F.4
Burham Reach K.8
Burley Avenue K.7
Burns Grove D.6
Bursar Street J.5
Burwell Drive D.6
Butler Place H.4
Buttermere Way G.3
Buttermore Crescent K.8
Butterwick Close K.7
Byewood Place A.5
Byland Grove B.3
Byron Grove D.6

Cabourne Road D.7
Caenby Road K.6
Caistor Road D.7
Calver Crescent B.4
Calvi Court G.3
Camargue Avenue E.10 (Waltham Inset)
Cambridge Court C.5
Cambridge Road C.5
Cambridge Street K.5
Campden Crescent J.4
Candlesbury Road A.4
Cannon Oaks Court H.9
Canterbury Drive D.5
Carbis Close G.9
Cardiff Avenue G.9
Cardinal Court D.10 (Waltham Inset)
Carisbrook Close H.9
Carlton Close L.7
Carlton Road D.4
Carlyle Close L.7
Carnaby Road G.5
Carnavon Avenue D.6
Carnforth Crescent C.6
Carnoustie C.11 (Waltham Inset)
Carr Lane H.4
Carrington Drive L.8
Carson Avenue D.5
Cartergate E.4
Cartledge Avenue H.4
Cartmel Grove H.5
Casswell Close G.3
Casswell House G.3
Castle Street G.3
Castleford Avenue C.6
Catherine Street F.4
Cattistock Road K.7
Cavendish Close L.7
Cavendish Street G.4
Cavendish Way G.4
Cedar Close J.7
Central Parade C.4
Chadwell Springs C.11 (Waltham Inset)
Chaffinch Drive K.8
Chalet Road M.7
Chandler's Close G.9
Chantry Close E.4
Chantry Lane E.4
Chapman Crescent L.8
Chapman Grove K.5
Chapman Road J.4
Charles Avenue E.7
Charles Avenue G.10
Charles Hume Court H.3
Charles Street K.5
Charlton Street E.3
Chatsworth Place H.6
Chatteris House C.3
Cheapside E.11 (Waltham Inset)
Cheesman's Lane E.11 (Waltham Inset)
Chelmsford Avenue D.5
Chelmsford Place D.5
Chelsea Walk L.7
Cheltenham Way K.7
Chepstow Grove C.5
Cherry Dale J.6
Cherry Tree Crescent B.4
Chester Grange F.8
Chester Place H.5
Chester Walk C.5
Chestnut Close D.11 (Waltham Inset)
Chestnut Road D.11 (Waltham Inset)
Chestnut Walk D.4
Chichester Road L.6
Chiltern Drive D.11 (Waltham Inset)
Chiltern Way E.8
Chingford Avenue C.6
Chipendale Close L.8
Christine Place F.8
Church Avenue K.8
Church Close H.5
Church Lane B.7
Church Lane L.9
Church Lane (West Marsh) E.4
Church Lane, Humberston K.8
Church Lane, Old Clee H.5
Church Lane, Scartho E.8
Church Road L.9
Church Street F.3
Church View B.4
Churchill Way G.4
Claire Court C.5
Claremont Road J.5
Clarendon Road B.6
Clark Avenue D.4
Clavering Street D.3
Clayden Street D.3
Claymore Close K.5
Clee Crescent H.5
Clee Fields Close G.5
Clee Road H.5
Clee Village H.5
Cleeness Close L.8
Cleethorpe Road F.3
CLEETHORPES L.4
Clerke Street H.3
Cleveland Gardens D.3
Cleveland Street D.3
Clifton Road D.4
Clixby Close L.6
Clumber Place K.5
Colin Avenue H.4
College Avenue E.8
College Gardens E.8
College Street (Cleethorpes) K.4
College Street (Grimsby) E.5
Collingwood Crescent A.6
Colonsay Court G.9
Colson Place H.4
Coltsfoot Drive C.11 (Waltham Inset)
Columbia Road G.4
Columbus Way C.7
Combe Street H.4
Comber Place G.3
Comorant Drive A.4
Compton Drive D.4
Conisborough Avenue G.10
Coniston Avenue D.9
Coniston Crescent J.8
Connaught Avenue E.6
Conningsby Drive D.5
Constitutional Avenue J.3
Convamore Road G.4
Conway Avenue C.4
Conyard Road J.4
Conyers Avenue E.7
Cook Lane A.3
Cooper Road G.4
Cope Street G.3
Cope Way G.3
Coral Drive D.10 (Waltham Inset)
Corinthain Avenue D.5
Cornfield Close D.9
Cornwell Close E.6
Coronation Road K.5
Corporation Bridge F.3
Corporation Road E.3
Cosgrove Street K.4
Cotswold Drive D.11 (Waltham Inset)
Cottage Yard Lane K.9
Cottesmore Road K.7
Coulam Place L.8
Coulbeck Drive J.5
Coventry Avenue C.5
Cragston Avenue E.7
Craithnie Road K.6
Crake Avenue E.7
Crampin Road J.4
Cranbourne Close K.8
Cranwell Drive C.3
Craven Road H.4
Crescent Street E.4
Cressey Street F.3
Cridling Place J.6
Cromer Avenue C.5
Cromwell Avenue D.4
Cromwell Road (Cleethorpe) L.6
Cromwell Road (West Marsh) D.4
Crosby Road C.7
Crosland Road B.3
Cross Coates Road C.4
Cross Lane E.8
Cross Street, Cleethorpes K.4
Cross Street, Grimsby G.2
Cross Way B.6
Crowhill Avenue K.5
Crowland Avenue C.6
Crowle Drive C.7
Croxby Avenue E.9
Croxby Close E.9
Cumberland Road B.5
Curry Road C.4
Curzon Avenue J.5
Curzon Court J.6
Cuttleby K.5
Cynthia Road H.5
Cyrano Way A.4
Cyril Cooper Court E.4

Daggett Road L.6
Dale View C.7
Dame Kendal Road D.6
Danesfield Avenue D.10 (Waltham Inset)
Darwin Court C.5
Daubney Street H.3
Davenport Drive H.6
Dave Place D.10
Dave Street F.5
Davie Place H.4
Davisons Avenue E.3
Dawlish Road E.9
Deangate E.4
Deaton Lane G.10
Deene Close A.6
Derby Close G.3
Derry Way E.8
Derwent Drive K.8
Devonshire Avenue E.6
Dial Square F.4
Digby Gardens C.5
Dixon Avenue F.6
Dolby Vale C.6
Dolphin Street K.4
Dominion Close G.9
Donington Street G.4
Dorothy Avenue E.10 (Waltham Inset)
Doughty Road F.4
Douglas Avenue C.4
Douglas Road J.3
Doughty Close D.10 (Waltham Inset)
Dovedale Drive E.9
Dover Street E.4
Downing Street C.5
Drake Avenue H.5
Drew Avenue F.6
Drury Close C.11 (Waltham Inset)
Drury Lane G.9
Dudley Place J.6
Dudley Street E.4
Dugard Road H.4
Duke Street G.3
Dunbar Avenue G.9
Duncombe Gardens F.3
Duncombe Street F.3
Dunmow Street D.3
Durban Road G.4
Durchess Street E.4
Durham Avenue C.4
Durham Road H.6
Dursley Avenue G.10
Dymoke Drive A.5

Earl Avenue H.9
Earl Street E.4
Eason Road D.7
East End Close F.7
East Marsh Street F.3
East Quay H.2
East St. Marys Gate E.4
East Street F.4
Eastbourne Way E.9
Eastern Inway C.6
Eastfield L.8
Eastside Road F.2
Eatsfield Avenue F.9
Eastgate F.4
Eastville Road C.6
Eastwood Avenue E.6
Edge Avenue E.7
Edward Street (Cleethorpes) K.5
Edward Street, Grimsby F.4
Egton Way B.3
Elderberry Way J.7
Elanor Street F.4
Eliston Street J.4
Elizabeth Close D.9
Ellen Way G.9
Ellesmere Rise B.6
Elliot House G.3
Ellis Way F.4
Elm Avenue (Cleethorpes) K.5
Elm Avenue (Little Coates) C.5
Elm Road E.11 (Waltham Inset)
Elm Road K.5
Elsham Road D.3
Elsham Drive D.11 (Waltham Inset)
Elsham Grove D.6
Elwyn Place J.7
Emfield Grove E.9
Emfield Road D.9
Emmanuel Court C.5
Enfield Avenue H.10
Ennerdale Close K.8
Enterprise Way G.5
Escart Avenue H.5
Eskdale Way B.3
Eskham Close K.7
Estury Way D.2
Ethelstone Road D.4
Evelyn Grove North H.5
Evelyn Grove South H.5
Evesham Avenue B.5
Exeter Court A.6

Fairfax Road D.4
Fairfield Avenue E.9
Fairfield Court L.8
Fairfield Road E.9
Fairmont Road G.4
Fairview Avenue K.5
Fairway D.10
Fairway Court M.7
Fallowfield Road D.9
Fannystone Road D.4
Farebrother Street F.5
Faringdon Road G.2
Farmhouse Mews G.10
Farndale Way E.3
Fauconberg Avenue E.7
Faulding Way A.4
Ferndown B.3
Felstead Avenue C.4
Fenby Close A.4
Fenwick Road D.7
Fern Hill A.4

Fernie Place J.7
Ferriby Lane E.7
Feyja Croft D.7
Fieldhouse Road L.8
Fildes Street E.4
Filey Road G.5
Fillingham Crescent K.6
Findlay Crescent H.9
Finsbury Drive D.7
Firsby Crescent C.7
First Avenue E.6
Fish Dock Drive G.2
Fisher Place J.4
Fishermans Wharf E.3
Fiskerton Close C.6
Fiskerton Way B.2
Fitzwilliam Mews K.7
Fleetwood Close D.9
Fletcher Road C.4
Fletchers Yard E.4
Florence Street F.5
Flottergate E.4
Flour Square F.2
Forest Way M.8
Forsythia Drive E.7
Fortuna Way A.4
Fotherby Street F.3
Fountain Close D.10 (Waltham Inset)
Fountains Avenue B.3
Foxglove Gardens C.5
Foxhill A.4
Frances Court C.10 (Waltham Inset)
Franklands Place J.4
Fraser Street G.4
Frederic Street E.3
Frederick Street K.5
Frederwick Ward Way E.4
Freeman Street F.3
Freeston Street H.4
Frechney Drive E.3
Freshney Place E.4
Frobishner Avenue H.5
Frusher Avenue E.6
Fulham Place D.7
Fuller Street J.3
Fulstow Grove D.6

Garbutt Place L.6
Garden drive G.9
Garden Street E.4
Garibaldi Street F.3
Garner Street F.5
Garnett Street J.4
Garrick Lane G.9
Garth Lane E.4
Garton Grove G.5
Gate Lane E.8
Gate Way E.2
Gayton Road L.6
Gedney Close A.4
George Jenney Court G.3
George Street K.5
Gertrude Street F.5
Gilbey Road D.2
Gilbey Road D.3
Giles Street K.5
Glebe Close K.9
Glebe Road K.9
Glebe Road, Cleethorpes K.5
Glebe Road, Scartho F.8
Gleneagles C.11 (Waltham Inset)
Glenfield Road A.3
Gloria Way A.4
Gloucester Avenue D.6
Goldgarth G.5
Goodwood Lane K.7
Gordon Gardens E.7
Goring Place J.4
Gorton Street G.2
Gosport Road C.4
Goxhill Gardens C.6
Grafton Street G.3
Grainsby Avenue J.6
Grampian Way E.8
GRANGE C.5
Grange Farm Lane H.9
Grange Walk C.4
Grant Street H.3
Grant Street K.4
Grantham Avenue E.7
Granvile Street F.5
Grasby Crescent B.4
Garsmere Grove K.8
Graylings Close B.4
GREAT COATES A.2
GREAT COATES B.3
Great Coates Road B.4
Green Finch Drive K.8
Green Hill J.6
Greenfinch Drive K.7
Greenland Avenue G.9
Greenway E.11 (Waltham Inset)
Greethams Lane H.5
Grey Friars A.4
Grime Street F.3
GRIMSBY E.3
Grimsby Road (Humberston) J.7
Grimsby Road (Little Coates) A.6
Grimsby Road, Grimsby H.3
Grosvenor Court L.7
Grosvenor Street E.4
Grove Crescent H.4
Grove Lane E.11

(Waltham Inset)
Guildford Street G.3
Gunby Place K.6

Haigh Court G.6
Haigh Street L.5
Haile Road L.8
Hainton Avenue F.4
Hainton Square F.4
Halton Place J.6
Halton Way D.6
Hamilton Close B.6
Hamilton Street G.3
Hamont Road H.4
Hampstead Park D.7
Hampton Close K.8
Hampton Court J.6
Hanson Way G.3
Hardy's Road K.6
Hare Street F.5
Harewood Grove K.8
Hargrave Road D.3
Harlech Way G.3
Harlestone Court A.6
Harlow Street D.3
Harold Street G.3
Harrington Street H.3
Harrison Street E.4
Hart Street H.3
Harvest Crescent C.11 (Waltham Inset)
Hatton Grove D.7
Haven Avenue D.3
Haven Gardens D.3
Haven Terrace E.4
Haven Walk F.4
Haverstow Place J.6
Hawkins Grove H.5
Hawthorne Avenue (Cleethorpes) J.4
Hawthorne Avenue E.8
Hawthorne Avenue G.10
Hawthorne Avenue (Scartho) E.8
Haycroft Avenue D.4
Haycroft Street D.4
Hayling Mere K.8
Heatherdale Close E.9
Heathfield Court D.5
Heimdal Road D.7
Helene Grove H.4
Hemswell Drive C.3
Heneage Road F.4
Henry Street D.3
Hereford Avenue D.5
Heron Close H.6
Hewitt's Avenue H.8
Hewitts Manor J.7
Hey Street K.5
Heythorpe Road J.6
Hibaldstow Close C.6
High Cliff Road L.5
High Street K.4
High Street (Waltham) D.11 (Waltham Inset)
Highgate K.5
Highthorpe Crescent J.6
Hilary Road E.9
Hilda Street G.3
Hildyard Street G.3
Hilltop Place A.6
Hilton Court M.7
Hinkler Street K.5
Holles Street F.4
Hollingsworth Close K.7
Holme Avenue G.9
Holme Farm Court B.2
Holme Street F.4
Holyoake Road H.5
Home Paddocks E.11 (Waltham Inset)
Homefiled Avenue E.6
Honeysuckle Court K.8
Hope Street G.3
Hope Street, Cleethorpes L.5
Howard Grove H.5
Howlett Road L.6
Huddleston Road G.4
Humber Bank South G.2
Humber Bridge Road G.2
Humber Street G.3
Humber Street K.5
HUMBERSTON K.8
Humberston Avenue H.9
Humberston Road H.6
Humberstone Road G.4
Hume Street E.4
Hunsley Crescent H.6
Hunter's Close A.3
Huntsmans Chase G.9
Hurford Place D.9
Hurstlea Drive L.8
Hutchinson Road J.4
Hutton Road G.2
Hyde Park Close D.7

Imperial Avenue J.3
Industrial Estate C.2
Ingleby Grove C.4
Ingram Place J.7
Ings Lane E.11 (Waltham Inset)
Intax Farm Mews F.5
Iona Way M.8
Irby Court J.6
Isaac's Hill K.4
Itterby Crescent J.7

Jacksons Place J.8
Jackson Street E.3
James Street D.3
Janton Court G.9
Jenner Court H.4
Jenner Place H.4
John Street G.3
Johnson Street H.3
Joseph Ogle Close G.8
Joseph Street D.3
Julian Street G.4
Juniper Way E.7
Jutland Court H.9

Kathleen Avenue J.4
Kathleen Grove H.4
Kaymile Close G.10
Keir Hardie Walk F.4
Kelham Road J.5
Kelstern Court C.5
Kemeshame Court E.11 (Waltham Inset)
Kemp Road G.2
Kenford Court G.9
Kenilworth Road J.6
Kensington Place F.8
Kent Street G.3
Kesgrave Street G.3
Kettlewell Street F.5
Kew Road K.5
Kiddier Avenue D.9
King Edward Street North F.3
King Street F.2
Kings Court C.5
Kings Gate G.4
Kings Mews M.8
Kings Parade L.5
Kings Road L.6
Kingsley Grove D.6
Kingston Avenue D.5
Kingston Close L.8
Kingsway L.5
Kirby Grove D.7
Kirk Gate D.11 (Waltham Inset)
Kirkside D.11 (Waltham Inset)
Kirkstead Crescent D.7
Kirmington Gardens C.4
Knight Street H.5
Knightsbridge G.9
Knoll Street K.5

Laburnham Avenue B.4
Laburnum Avenue D.11 (Waltham Inset)
Laburnum Close D.11 (Waltham Inset)
Laceby Road A.6
Lady Frances Crescent J.5
Ladysmith Road G.4
Laforey Road B.2
Larlgate Place K.7
Lambert Road E.5
Lambourne Court K.6
Lampton Grove F.5
Lancaster Avenue D.4
Lancing Way E.8
Landeck Avenue D.4
Langdale Avenue D.9
Langley Place L.6
Langton Drive D.6
Langton Grove D.7
Lansdown Avenue E.6
Lansdown Link J.6
Larch Road J.7
Larden Avenue D.9
Larlgate Place K.7
Larmour Road B.4
Laurel Close E.7
Lavender Grove G.9
Lavenham Road D.8
Lawrence Street D.3
Lawson Avenue D.4
Lea Drive G.6
Leas Close E.10 (Waltham Inset)
Ledbury Drive H.9
Legsby Avenue F.5
Legsby Place F.6
Legsby Street F.5
Leighton Grove E.6
Lestrange Street J.4
Levington Street G.3
Lewis Road J.3
Lichfield Court H.4
Lichfield Road H.5
Lidgard Road L.8
Lilac Court D.8
Limber Court C.5
Limber Vale C.5
Lime Grove K.9
Lime Street E.4
Limetree Avenue E.6
Lincoln Boulevard D.4
Lincoln Road H.5
Lindisfarne Avenue G.10
Lindrick Walk C.11 (Waltham Inset)
Lindsey Rise E.8
Lindsey Road K.7
Lindum Road K.6
Links Court L.7
Links Road L.7
Linwood Avenue E.8
Lisburn Grove E.7
Lister Street D.3

Little Beck Road K.8
LITTLE COATES B.5
Little Coates Road B.6
Littlefield Lane D.4
Lock Hill F.2
Loft Avenue B.3
Lombard Street D.4
Lomond Grove K.8
Longfield Road B.6
Longhorn Close C.11 (Waltham Inset)
Lonsdale Close L.9
Lord Street D.3
Louth Road E.8
Louth Road, New Waltham F.9
Loveden Court L.6
Lovett Street H.4
Lower Burgess Street F.3
Lower Spring Street F.3
Ludborough Way K.7
Ludford Street F.5
Ludgate Close D.11 (Waltham Inset)
Ludlow Avenue C.4
Ludlow Place K.5
Lukes Court G.4
Lyndhurst Avenue E.7
Lynton Rise K.6
Lytham Drive D.11 (Waltham Inset)

Macaulay Lane D.3
Macaulay Street D.3
Macaulay Way D.4
Machray Place J.4
Maclure Street G.2
Maegan Way K.5
Magdalene Road C.5
Maidwell Way A.6
Malcolm Road C.7
Mallard Mews F.4
Malmesbury Drive E.5
Maltby Avenue A.6
Maltings Way F.3
Malvern Avenue C.6
Manchester Street J.3
Mandela Link E.4
Manley Gardens L.6
Manningtree Close F.5
Manor Avenue E.4
Manor Drive E.10 (Waltham Inset)
Manor Terrace E.4
Mansel Street H.3
Mansfield Court G.3 (H.2)
Manson Close B.6
Maple Avenue B.4
Maple Grove G.10
Marcus Street C.5
Margaret Place G.10
Margaret Street F.4
Margrave Street D.3
Marion Way C.11 (Waltham Inset)
Market Street (Cleethorpes) K.4
Market Street, Grimsby F.3
Markham Mews E.11 (Waltham Inset)
Markhams Orchard E.9
Marklew Avenue D.4
Marlbrough Close G.3 (H.2)
Marlborough Way K.8
Marquis Avenue H.9
Marsden Road G.2
Marshall Avenue D.4
Marshchapel Close K.7
Martin Way G.9
Marton Grove C.6
Martyn Road J.4
Marylebone Walk D.7
Matlock Drive C.3
Matt Quinn House D.6
Matthew Street J.4
Maxwell Court A.5
May Street J.4
Mayfair Court L.8
Mayfair Crescent D.11 (Waltham Inset)
Mayfair Drive East B.4
Mayfair Drive West A.4
Meadow Court B.4
Meadow Croft D.10 (Waltham Inset)
Meadow Drive D.8
Meadow View L.8
Meadowbanck A.3
Medway Place C.4
Melbourne Avenue E.7
Melrose Way B.3
Mendip Avenue E.8
Mersey Way B.3
Middle Court F.4
Middlethorpe Road J.6
Midfield Place L.9
Midfield Road L.9
Milford Court G.3 (H.2)
Mill Avenue D.3
Mill Close D.11 (Waltham Inset)
Mill Garth J.7
Mill Hill Crescent J.5
Mill Place K.4
Mill Road K.5
Mill View D.11 (Waltham Inset)
Miller Avenue H.4
Millfield Avenue E.7

Millom Way G.3
Milton Road D.6
Minnow Close B.4
Minshull Lane K.6
Mirfield Road F.6
Mollison Avenue K.5
Montague Street H.3
Montgomery Road J.5
Moody Lane C.2
Moorland Drive G.9
Mordaunt Avenue D.9
Morpeth Walk C.4
Morton Road D.4
Moss Road F.4
Mount Pleasant D.10 (Waltham Inset)
Muirfield C.11 (Waltham Inset)
Mulgrave Close C.3
Munster Court G.3 (H.2)
Murray Street F.2

Nagton Street G.3
Nairn Way E.5
Naseby Drive D.4
Naseby Grove D.4
Navensby Close B.2
Nelson Street F.3
Nelson Way A.6
Neptune Street K.4
Neville Street J.3
Neville Turner Way D.11 (Waltham Inset)
New Cartergate E.4
New Close E.6
New Dock Street F.2
New Road E.11 (Waltham Inset)
New Road K.5
NEW WALTHAM H.9
Newbury Avenue B.3
Newbury Grove B.6
Newbury Terrace B.3
Newby Road D.4
Newhaven Terrace D.3
Newlands Park M.8
Newlyn Close G.8
Newmarch Crescent E.8
Newmarket Street F.3
Newsham Drive C.4
Newstead Road J.6
Newton Grove E.6
Nicholson Street K.5
Norfolk Court G.3 (H.2)
Norfolk Lane K.4
Norman Road D.4
Normandy Road J.5
Norsefield Avenue E.10 (Waltham Inset)
North Quay G.2
North Sea Lane L.8
North Street K.5
Northumberland Close D.5
Norwich Avenue D.6
Nunnerley Place E.10 (Waltham Inset)
NUNSTHORPE E.6

Oak Avenue F.6
Oakway J.7
Oakwood Drive A.4
Odin Court D.7
OLD CLEE H.5
Old Farm Court C.11 (Waltham Inset)
Old Fleet A.4
Old Road A.3
Oole Road K.5
Orby Grove C.6
Orchard Court D.11 (Waltham Inset)
Orchard Croft E.9
Orion Way A.6
Ormsby Close J.6
Orwell Street G.2
Osbourne Street E.4
Osbourne Street K.4
Oslear Crescent K.5
Oxcombe Close D.9
Oxford Street (Cleethorpes) K.5
Oxford Street, Grimsby G.3

Pagehall Close E.7
Paignton Court E.9
Park Avenue F.6
Park Drive E.5
Park Lane K.7
Park Street H.3
Park View H.4
Parker Road L.8
Parker Street K.5
Parris Place J.4
Pasture Street F.4
Patrick Street F.5
Paul Crescent K.8
Peace Haven D.10 (Waltham Inset)
Peake's Parkway F.4-G.8
Peakes Lane F.6
Peaks Lane H.9
Pear Tree Close D.11 (Waltham Inset)
Pearson Road K.6
Pelham Avenue D.8
Pelham Place E.8
Pelham Road (Cleethorpes) J.4
Pelham Road (West March) E.4

Pelham Square ... J.4
Pemberton Drive ... G.10
Pendeen Close ... G.9
Pendreth Place ... J.4
Penhurst Road ... J.6
Perkins Close ... C.3
Pershore Avenue ... B.5
Petchel Way ... F.3
Peterhouse Road ... C.5
Phelps Place ... H.5
Phelps Street ... H.3
Philip Avenue ... E.10
(Waltham Inset)
Philip Avenue ... J.6
Philip Grove ... J.6
Phoenix Street ... F.4
Phyllis Avenue ... D.4
Piccadilly ... G.9
Pine Close ... B.3
Pine Court ... J.7
Pinewood Crescent ... C.7
Pinfold Lane ... E.8
Politt Street ... F.2
Poplar Drive ... M.8
Poplar Grove ... K.4
Poplar Road ... K.4
Portland Avenue ... F.6
Portland Manor ... F.6
Portland Place ... F.6
Prettymen Crescent ... G.9
Primrose Way ... K.8
Prince Albert Gardens ... F.3
Prince's Avenue ... E.4
Prince's Road ... K.4
Priors Close ... H.10
Priory Road ... A.5
Promendade ... K.4
Prystie Place ... J.7
Purbeck Road ... E.9
PYEWIPE ... D.2
Pyewipe Rise ... E.2
Pyewipe Road ... D.3
Pytchley Walk ... J.7

Quantock Road ... E.9
Queen Elizabeth Road ... K.8
Queen Mary Avenue ... H.4
Queen Street ... F.4
Queens Court ... C.5
Queens Parade (West Marsh) ... E.4
Quees Parade (Cleethorpes) ... K.5
Quinton Road ... F.6
Quorn Mews ... J.7

Railway Place ... F.2
Railway Street ... F.3
Railway Terrace ... E.4
Raithby Grove ... C.6
Ravendale Road ... L.6
Ravenhill Close ... J.6
Ravensburn Way ... E.3
Ravenspurn Street ... E.3
Ravenscar Road ... B.3
Reading Close ... D.9
Reading Close ... E.9
Recto Avenue ... F.5
Redbourne Road ... D.6
Redbourne Walk ... D.6
Redcar Grove ... G.5
Redwood Drive ... J.7
Regent Gardens ... E.5
Remillo Avenue ... F.5
Rendel Street ... E.3
Reparto Avenue ... G.5
Responso Avenue ... G.5
Reton Court ... L.7
Reston Grove ... D.6
Revesby Avenue ... C.6
Revigo Avenue ... G.5
Reynolds Street ... J.4
Rialto Avenue ... F.5
Riby Square ... F.2
Riby Street ... G.2
Richard Street ... E.3
Richardson Close ... L.9
Richmond Road (Cleethorpes) ... K.5
Richmond Road (West Marsh) ... D.4
Ripon Street ... E.4
Rivan Avenue ... E.9
Rivan Grove ... E.9
Riverside Drive ... M.7
Roberts Street ... G.4
Robinson Lane ... G.2
Robinson Street ... F.4
Robson Road ... J.4
Rochester Court ... L.7
Rockingham Crescent ... A.6
Romsey Court ... A.5
Rookery Avenue ... E.6
Ropery Street ... G.4
Rosaire Place ... F.8
Rosalind Avenue ... D.4
Rosedale ... D.10
(Waltham Inset)
Rosemary Avenue ... C.5
Rosemary Way ... K.8
Roseverre Avenue ... D.4
Rosina Grove North ... H.4
Rosina Grove South ... H.5
Rothwell Avenue ... D.7
Roundway ... E.5
Rowan Drive ... L.8
Rowlandson Street ... F.2
Rowston Street ... L.5
Royal Court ... M.7
Royal Street ... F.2
Rudham Avenue ... F.6
Rufford Road ... K.6
Runswick Road ... G.4
Rupert Road ... E.6
Russell Court ... L.7
Rutland Street ... G.4
Rutland Street ... H.3
Rydal Avenue ... D.9
Rymer Place ... L.6

Sackville Street ... E.4
Sagefield Close ... D.9
Salamander Close ... D.3
Salisbury Avenue ... D.11
(Waltham Inset)
Salisbury Drive ... D.11
(Waltham Inset)
Salmeston Court ... E.5
Salsbury Avenue ... D.5
Saltburn Grove ... G.5
Saltergate ... B.3
Salveston Road ... H.3
Samuel Avenue ... H.4
Sanctuary Way ... A.4
Sandford Street ... D.3
Sandringham Road ... J.6
Sargon Way ... B.2
Saunby Grove ... K.4
Saunders Street ... E.4
Savoy Court ... G.9
Saxby Grove ... C.6
Saxon Crescent ... J.5
Scampton Close ... D.5
SCARTHO ... F.8
Scartho Park ... D.7
Scartho Road ... E.6
Scawby Road ... C.7
School Walk ... H.5
Scott Close ... C.3
Scrivelsby Court ... L.7
Sea Road ... K.4
Sea View Street ... K.5
Seacroft Road ... L.5
Seaford Road ... L.8
Seamer Grove ... G.5
Seascale Walk ... G.3
Seaton Grove ... G.5
Second Avenue ... D.6
Segmere Street ... L.5
Selbourne Road ... B.6
Selge Way ... C.7
Service Road 1 ... B.3
Service Road 10 ... B.3
Service Road 11 ... B.3
Service Road 12 ... B.3
Service Road 13 ... B.3
Service Road 14 ... B.3
Service Road 15 ... B.3
Service Road 16 ... B.3
Service Road 17 ... C.3
Service Road 18 ... C.3
Service Road 19 ... C.3
Service Road 2 ... B.3
Service Road 20 ... B.4
Service Road 21 ... B.3
Service Road 22 ... B.3
Service Road 23 ... B.3
Service Road 25 ... B.3
Service Road 26 ... B.3
Service Road 3 ... B.3
Service Road 4 ... B.3
Service Road 5 ... B.3
Service Road 6 ... B.3
Service Road 7 ... C.3
Service Road 8 ... B.3
Service Road 9 ... B.3
Severn Way ... B.3
Shaftesbury Avenue ... D.4
Shaftesbury Mews ... G.9
Shaw Drive ... F.8
Shears Court ... E.10
(Waltham Inset)
Sheepfold Street ... F.4
Shelley Avenue ... D.6
Sheraton Drive ... L.8
Sherburn Street ... K.6
Sherwood Road ... C.5
Short Street ... E.4
Short Street ... K.4
Side Lane ... F.9
Sidney Court ... H.3
Sidney Road ... D.4
Sidney Street ... H.3
Sidney Taylor Court ... H.9
Sidney Taylor Walk ... G.9
Sidney Way ... H.3
Sign Hills Avenue ... L.6
Silver Street ... E.4
Silvergarth ... G.5
Simons Place ... J.4
Sinderson Road ... L.8
Sixhills Street ... F.4
Skinner's Lane ... E.11
(Waltham Inset)
Solomon Court ... J.5
Somersby Street ... E.4
Sophia Avenue ... D.8
South Parade ... E.3
South Sea Lane ... L.9
South St. Marys Gate ... E.4
South Street ... L.5
South View ... C.5
South View ... L.8
Southern Walk ... E.9
Southfield Avenue ... E.9
Southfield Road ... E.9
Southland Way ... B.3
Southwold Crescent ... E.8
Sovereign Close ... B.6
Spark Street ... D.4
Spencer Street ... H.3
Spratton Court ... A.6
Spring Bank ... C.4
Springfield Road ... D.8
Springway Crescent ... C.4
Springwood Crescent ... D.9
Spurn Avenue ... E.8
St. Albans Avenue ... D.4
St. Andrews Court ... K.5
St. Andrews Drive ... H.6
St. Ann's Avenue ... D.4
St. Augustine's Avenue ... F.5
St. Catherines Court ... C.5
St. Chads Gate ... B.3
St. Chads Walk South ... B.3
St. Christophers Road ... K.8
St. Clements Way ... G.8
St. Francis Avenue ... D.4
St. Francis Court ... F.4
St. Giles Avenue ... E.8
St. Helens Avenue ... E.6
St. Helier's Road ... J.4
St. Hilda's Avenue ... D.4
St. Hugh's Avenue ... J.5
St. Ives Crescent ... B.5
St. James Avenue ... C.4
St. James Court ... E.4
St. Johns Road ... K.8
St. Leonards Avenue ... D.4
St. Lukes Court ... G.4
St. Luke Grove ... K.8
St. Margaret's Mews ... C.5
St. Marks Road ... K.8
St. Martins Crescent ... E.6
St. Matthews Road ... K.8
St. Mawes Crescent ... C.4
St. Michael's Road ... B.6
St. Nicholas Drive ... A.4
St. Olafs Grove ... F.5
St. Peters Avenue ... K.5
St. Peters Crescent ... K.8
St. Thomas Close ... K.9
Stainton Drive ... C.6
Stanage Walk ... G.3
Stanhope Place ... H.4
Stanland Way ... L.8
Stanley Street ... G.4
Stanstead Street ... D.3
Station Avenue ... H.10
Station Road ... E.10
(Waltham Inset)
Station Road ... F.10-G.10
Station Road (Cleethorpes) ... K.4
Station Road (Great Coates) ... A.3
Stephen Crescent ... B.6
Stephen Crescent ... K.8
Sterling Crescent ... C.11
(Waltham Inset)
Stevenson Place ... J.5
Stirling Street ... D.3
Stokesley Walk ... C.3
Stortford Street ... D.3
Stow Close ... B.3
Strand Street ... G.3
Stratford Avenue ... C.6
Strawberry Hill ... C.11
(Waltham Inset)
Street John's Court ... C.5
Stuart Wortley Street ... G.2
Sturton Grove ... D.6
Suffolk Court ... C.3 (H.2)
Suggitts Court ... J.4
Suggitts Lane ... J.4
Suggitts Orchard ... J.3
Summerfield Avenue ... D.10
(Waltham Inset)
Sunningdale ... C.11
(Waltham Inset)
Sunny Corner ... E.8
Surrey Court ... G.3 (H.2)
Surtees Street ... G.2
Sussex Court ... G.3 (H.2)

Sussex Street ... H.3
Sutcliffe Avenue ... D.6
Swaby Drive ... J.6
Swales Road ... L.8
Sweet Brair Close ... D.10
(Waltham Inset)
Swiftsure Crescent ... B.6
Swinderby Gardens ... C.5
Sycamore Avenue ... E.7

Tallert Drive ... C.7
Tamar Drive ... H.9
Tasburgh Street ... F.4
Tattershal Avenue ... C.6
Taunton Way ... E.8
Taylor Street ... H.3
Taylor's Avenue ... J.7
Tealby Grove ... D.6
Team Gate ... A.4
Telford Place ... C.4
Telford Place ... C.5
Tennyson Road ... J.4
Tennyson Street ... E.3
Terrington Place ... J.6
Tetney Road ... K.9
Tewksbury Avenue ... E.5
The Avenue ... A.3
The Berea ... E.5
The Cloisters ... A.4
The Cloisters ... L.9
The Close ... E.4
The Copse ... E.8
The Cresta ... E.5
The Crofts ... K.8
The Elms ... K.9
The Gatherums ... J.5
The Lawns ... E.4
The Orchard ... G.10
The Oval ... E.8
The Ridgeway ... B.6
The Spinney ... E.4
The Square ... G.3
THE WILLOWS ... B.4
Thesinger Street ... G.3
Thesinger Walk ... G.3
Thirkleby Crescent ... H.6
Thirlmere Avenue ... D.9
Thomas Street ... G.4
Thores Way Grove ... C.7
Thoresby Place ... J.6
Thorganby Road ... L.6
Thorgham Court ... E.4
Thornhill gardens ... C.4
Thornton Court ... G.9
Thornton Crescent ... K.6
Thornton Crescent ... K.6
Thornton Grove ... B.6
Thornton Grove ... B.6
Thorold Street ... G.3
Thrunscoe Road ... K.5
Timberley Drive ... A.4
Tintagel Way ... G.9
Tintern Walk ... B.3
Tiverton Street ... H.3
Toll Bar Avenue ... G.10
Tom Hammond Way ... G.3
Tomlin Street ... G.2
Tonbridge Walk ... F.8
Tonnant Way ... A.5
Toothill Road ... C.4
Torbay Drive ... E.9
Torksey Drive ... D.6
Torksey Place ... D.6
Torrington Gardens ... G.5
Torrington Street ... F.5
Totnes Road ... E.9
Town Hall Square ... F.4
Townsend Close ... M.8
Toynton Place ... D.6
Toynton Road ... D.6
Toynton Walk ... D.6
Trafalgar Avenue ... A.5
Trafalgar Park ... H.9
Tranby Drive ... H.6
Trinity Road ... K.5
Trinity Street ... G.3
Tunnard Street ... G.3
Turnberry Approach ... D.11
(Waltham Inset)
Twining Place ... J.4
Tyler Avenue ... D.4
Tyne Way ... B.3

Ulster Avenue ... E.7
Unity Road ... H.5
Utgard Way ... D.7
Utterby Drive ... D.5

Vaughan Avenue ... H.6
Veal Street ... E.4
Vere Terrace ... E.4
Vicarage Gardens ... E.4
Vicarage Lawn ... E.4
Victor Street ... G.3
Victoria Street North ... F.3
Victoria Street South ... F.4
Victoria Street West ... E.4
Victoria Way ... D.2
Victory Way ... A.6
Viking Court ... D.2
Violet Close ... K.8
Viscount Way ... M.8
Vivian Avenue ... H.5

Waby Close ... B.4
Waddingham Place ... H.10
Waddington Place ... D.5
Wade Avenue ... G.3
Wainfleet Road ... D.7
Waldorf Road ... L.8
Walesby Close ... D.9
Walk Lane ... K.9
Walker Avenue ... E.8
Wall Street ... D.4
Wallis Court ... D.7
Walmsgate ... D.6
Walmsgate Place ... D.6
Walnut Crescent ... J.7
WALTHAM ... D.10
(Waltham Inset)
Waltham Grove ... K.7
Waltham Road ... D.10
(Waltham Inset)
Waltham Road ... E.9
Walton Grove ... E.6
Ward Street ... J.4
Wardall Street ... K.5
Warneford Road ... J.3
Warwick Avenue ... C.6
Warwick Road ... J.6
Waterloo Drive ... D.7
Watford Avenue ... C.6
Watkin Street North ... E.3
Watkin Street South ... E.3
Wayside Drive ... G.9
Weekes Road ... K.6
WEELSBY ... G.7
Weelsby Avenue ... F.6
Weelsby Grove ... F.6
Weelsby Road ... E.5
Weelsby Street ... G.3
Weelsby Street South ... G.4
Welbeck Place ... B.6
Welbeck Road (Little Coates) ... B.6
Welbeck Road, Old Clee ... H.5
Welholme Avenue ... E.5
Welholme Road ... E.5
Wellland Avenue ... C.6
Wellgarth ... G.5
Wellington Street ... F.3
Wellowgate ... E.4
Wells Court ... J.7
Wells Street ... D.4
Wellvale ... D.8
Welsby View ... H.8
Wendover Lane ... L.9
Wendover Rise ... K.5
Wentworth Road ... D.4
Wesley Crescent ... K.6
West Coates Road ... D.2
West Lea ... E.9
WEST MARSH ... D.3
West Parade ... E.4
West Quay ... G.2
West St. Marys Gate ... E.4
West Street, Cleethorpes ... K.5
West Street, Grimsby ... F.4
Westbourn Terrace ... E.4
Westbourne Grove ... E.9
Westbury Park ... L.7
Westbury Road ... L.8
Westerdale Way ... B.3
Western Outway ... C.6
Westfield Avenue ... E.6
Westfield Grove ... J.5
Westfield Road ... D.11
(Waltham Inset)
Westgate ... E.3
Westhill Road ... C.5
Westkirke Avenue ... E.8
Westland Avenue ... E.5
Westminster Drive ... D.5
Westport Road ... L.8
Westside Road ... E.2
Westward Ho ... D.5
Westward Road ... E.5
Weyford Road ... L.7
Wharncliffe Road ... G.2
Wharton Street ... D.4
Wheatfield Drive ... C.11
(Waltham Inset)
Whenside Way ... E.3
Whimbrel Way ... H.9
Whitby Drive ... G.5
White's Road ... K.5
Whitehall Country Cottages ... L.8
Whitehall Road ... L.8
Whitgift Way ... B.3
Wickenby Close ... C.6
Wickham Road ... G.2
Wicklow Avenue ... E.8
William Street ... K.5
Willing Way ... G.3 (H.2)
Willingham Street ... F.4
Willoughby Grove ... C.6
Wilson Street ... J.3
Wilton Road ... J.8
Wimborn Avenue ... D.4
Winceby Avenue ... D.4
Winchester Avenue ... C.6
Winchombe Avenue ... B.6
Windermere Avenue ... 9
Windermere Crescent ... J.8
Windlesham Avenue ... D.9
Windsor Road ... H.5
Wingate Parade ... B.3
Winn Court ... K.5
Winslow Grove ... C.6
Winston Avenue ... D.4
Winthorpe Road ... D.7
Wintringham Road ... F.4
Wirral Avenue ... C.6
Withern Road ... C.6
Woad Lane ... B.2
Wollaston Road ... J.5
Womesley Road ... G.2
Wood Close ... F.3
Woodfield Close ... L.8
Woodhall Drive ... C.11
(Waltham Inset)
Woodland Walk ... K.8
Woodrow Park ... E.7
Woodsley Avenue ... K.5
Wootton Road ... D.6
Worcester Avenue ... C.6
Worlaby Road ... D.8
Wragby Street ... G.4
Wray Close ... C.11
(Waltham Inset)
Wren Crescent ... D.7
Wroxham Avenue ... B.5
Wybers Way ... A.4
WYBERS WOOD ... A.4
Wymark View ... C.6
Wyndham Road ... G.9
YARBOROUGH ... C.4
Yarborough Drive ... E.3
Yarborough Road ... C.4
Yardley Way ... A.6
Yarra Road ... K.5
Yarrow Road ... B.4
York Place ... H.6
York Street ... E.3
Young Place ... H.4
... C.11 (Waltham Inset)

Abbotts Close F.3
Aberdeen Close B.2
Adelaide Street E.3
Airedale Road C.2
Albert Road E.3
Alexandra Road E.2
All Saints Place D.3
All Saints Street D.3
Ancaster Road C.2
Andrew Road D.2
Angus Close B.2
Anne Road D.2
Argyll Way C.3
Armley Grove E.1
Arran Road B.2
Ash Place B.3
Austin Friars Lane D.4
Austin Street D.3
Axiom Court F.3
Ayr Close B.2

Back Lane E.3
Bain Close E.2
Barn Hill D.3
Barnack Road E.4
Barnwell Road B.2
Bath Row D.3
Beech Grove A.2
Belton Street E.3
Belvior Close B.2
Bentley Street E.3
Berrybut Way E.1
Beverly Gardens C.2
Birch Road B.2
Blackfriars Street E.3
Blackthorn A.2
Bluebell Road A.1
Braemar Close B.3
Bramble Grove A.2
Brazenose E.3
Broad Street E.3
Brooke Avenue B.3
Brownlow Quay E.3
Brownlow Street E.3
Bugle Lane ....(7) E.3
Burghley Court E.3
Burghley House G.5
Burghley Lane E.4
Burghley Road C.2
Burns Road C.3
Buttercup Close A.2
Byron Way B.3

Caithness Road B.2
Caledonian Road C.2
Cambridge Road C.2
Campion Grove A.2
Castle Dyke D.3
Castle Street D.3
Casterton Lane A.4
Casterton Road B.2
Cecil Court E.3
Cedar Road A.2
Chapel Yard E.3
Charles Road D.2
Charlock Drive A.2
Chatsworth Road C.2
Cherryholt Road E.3
Chestnut Gardens B.3
Cheyne Lane E.3
Church Court E.4
Church Lane E.4
Church Street E.4
Churchill Road D.2
Clare Close D.3
Cliff Crescent D.3
Cliff Road D.3
Clover Gardens A.2
Conduit Road E.2
Conduit Terrace E.2
Cornflower Close A.2
Cornstall Buildings E.3
Cornwall Road D.2
Cottesmore Road B.3
Cromarty Road B.2
Cross Keys Lane ....(5) E.3

Daniel Court E.4
Darwin Close D.2
Doney Steps D.3
Doughty Street F.2
Downing Crescent D.2
Drift Avenue E.2
Drift Gardens E.2
Drift Road E.2
Duncomb's Yard ....(13) E.4
Dundee Close B.3
Dundee Drive B.3

East Street E.3
Edinburgh Road D.2
Edmonds Close F.2
Edward Road D.2
Eight Acres D.3
Elizabeth Road D.2
Elm Street E.3
Elton Close C.2
Emlyns Field E.3
Emlyns Street E.2
Emmanuel Road D.1
Empingham Road A.3
Ermine Close C.3
Ermine Way C.3
Essex Road D.2
Exeter Court ....(16) D.3
Exeter Gardens C.4
Exton Close B.3

Falkirk Close B.2
Fane Close D.2
Fife Close B.2
Fir Road A.2
First Drift D.5
Fitzwilliam Road C.2
Fontwell Gardens D.3
Foundry lane D.3
Foundry Road D.3
Fox Dale C.3
Foxglove Road A.1

Gainsborough Road C.2
Garden Close B.3
Gas Lane E.3
Gas Street E.3
Girton Way D.2
Glen Crescent E.1
Gleneagles Close B.2
Gloucester Road D.2
Goldsmiths lane E.3
Gooches Court ....(8) D.3
GREAT CASTERTON A.1
Great North Road A.2
Green Lane D.2
Guash Way F.1
Gypsy Lane F.2

Haddon Road C.2
Harcourt Terrace D.3
Hardwick Road C.2
Hazel Grove B.3
High Street E.3
High Street ....
St. Martins E.4
Highgrove Gardens B.3
Highlands Way C.3
Hilary Close E.2
Holland Road E.2
Horseshoe Lane D.3

Ironmonger Street E.3
Irnham Road E.2

Keats Grove B.3
Keble Close D.2
Keble Court D.2
Kesteven Road D.2
Kettering Road D.5
King's Mill D.4
King's Mill Lane D.3
Kings Road D.2
Kipling Close B.3

Laburnham Villas D.3
Lambert Mews E.4
Lambeth Walk C.2
Lancaster Road D.2
Launde Gardens B.3
Lavender Way A.1
Lime Tree Road A.2
Lincoln Street E.2
Lindsey Road E.2
Little Casterton Road C.1
Lonsdale Road B.3
Losecoat Close F.1
Luffenham Close B.3
Lumby's Terrace E.4
Lyndon Way B.3

Maiden Lane E.3
Mallory Lane ....(9) D.3
Malting Yard E.4
Marigold Close A.2
Masterton Close E.2
Masterton Road E.1
Melanchonly Walk D.4
Melbourne Road E.2
Melrose Close B.2
Montrose Close B.2
Moray Close B.2
Mountbatten Avenue D.2

Nairn Road B.3
New Boults Lane D.3
New Cross D.3
New Street E.2
Newgate Street E.3
Newham Road D.2
NEWSTEAD G.2
NEWTOWN F.3
Norfolk Square D.2
North Street D.3
NORTHFIELDS E.1
Northfields Court......................E.2
Northumberland Road D.3

Oak Road A.2
Oban Close B.2
Old Barn Passage ....(6) E.3
Old Great North Road E.4
Orchard Close D.3
Orchard Road D.3
Oxford Road D.2

Park Lane E.4
Pembroke Road C.2
Penfold Lane E.4
Perth Road B.3
Peter Gate ....(17) D.3
Peterhouse Close D.1
Phillips Court E.4
Pine Close B.2
Pinfold Lane E.3
Primrose Way A.2
Princes Road E.2
Priory gardens F.3
Priory Road E.3

Queen Elizabeth Avenue G.4
Queens Street E.2
Queen's Walk C.3

Radcliffe Close D.3
Radcliffe Road D.3
Recreation Ground Road E.3
Red Lion Square D.3
Red Lion Street F.3
Redcot Gardens D.3
Reform Street C.3
Rock Road D.3
Rockingham Road C.2
Roman Bank C.3
Roxburgh Road C.2
Rutland Road F.1
Rutland Terrace ....(18) D.3
Ryhall Road F.1

St. Clements C.3
St. George's Square ....(11) E.3
St. George's Street E.3
St. John's lane ....(4) E.3
St. John's Terrace D.3
St. Leonard's Street E.3
St. Martin's Close ....(12) E.4
St. Mary's Hill E.3
St. Mary's Passage ....(3) E.3
St. Mary's Place ....(2) E.3
St. Mary's Street E.3
St. Paul's Street E.3
St. Peter's Hill D.3
St. Peter's Street D.3
St. Peter's Vale ....(10) D.3
Sandringham Close D.2
Sargents Court D.2
Scotgate D.3
Second Drift D.5
Selwyn Road D.2
Sheep Market D.3
Sherwood Close C.3
Sidney Farm Lane A.2
Silver Lane E.3
Somerby Close D.2
Somerville Road C.2
Sorrel Close A.2
Stirling Road C.3
Stamford Walk ....(1) E.3
Stanley Street E.3
Stra Lane E.3
Station Road E.4
Sussex Road D.2
Sutherland Way C.3
Sweetbriar A.1

Tennyson Way C.3
Tenter Lane ....(15) E.3
The Hermitage C.3
The Paddock A.4
Tinwell Road A.4
Tinwell Road lane C.4
Tobias Grove A.2
Tolethorpe Square D.2
TOLL BAR A.1
Torkington Gardens D.3
Torkington Street C.3
Trafalgar Terrace E.3
Trinity Road D.2
Troon Close B.2
Turnpole Close E.1

Uffinhton Road F.3

Vence Close C.3
Victoria Road D.2
Vine Street E.3

Walcot Way B.2
Water Street E.4
Waterfurlong D.4
Waverley Gardens C.2
Waverley Place C.2
Welland Mews E.3
Wellington Lane E.3
West End Villas D.3
West Street D.3
West Street Gardens D.3
Wharf Road E.3
Willoughby Road E.2
Willow Road B.2
Windmill Way C.3
Windsor Close D.2
Witham Close E.2
Wooded Walk E.2
Woodhead Close E.1
Worcester Crescent D.2
Wothorpe Road E.4

York Road D.3

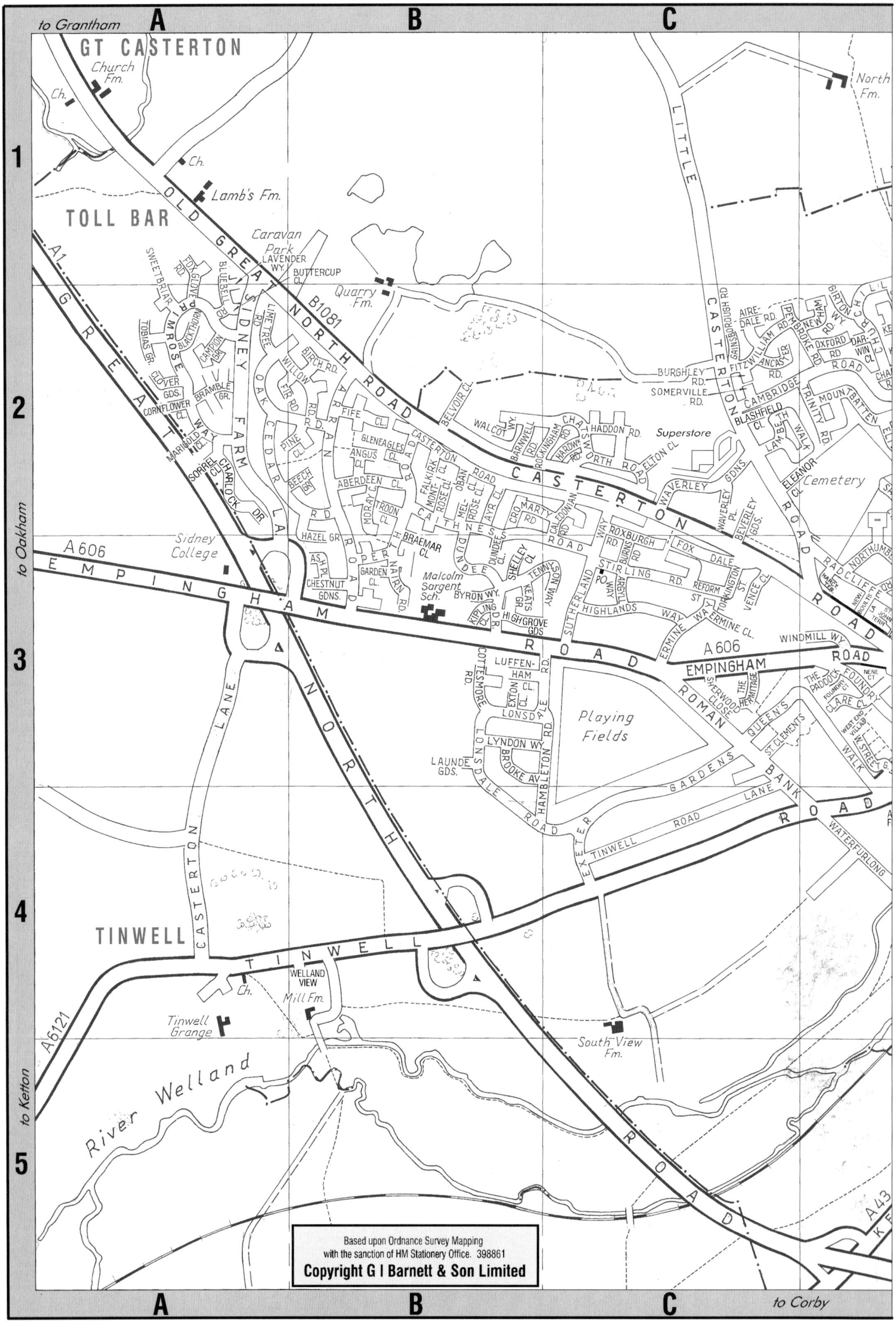
to Grantham
A
B
C
1
2
3
4
5
to Oakham
to Ketton
to Corby
GT CASTERTON
Church Fm.
Ch.
Lamb's Fm.
TOLL BAR
Caravan Park
LAVENDER WY.
BUTTERCUP CL
Quarry Fm.
B1081
OLD GREAT NORTH ROAD
A1
GREAT NORTH ROAD
SWEETBRIAR
FOXGLOVE RD.
BLUEBELL RD.
PRIMROSE
TOBIAS GR.
BLACKTHORN
CAMPION GR.
CLOVER GDS.
CORNFLOWER CL.
BRAMBLE GR.
MARIGOLD CL.
SORREL CL.
CHARLOCK DR.
SIDNEY FARM LA.
LIME TREE RD.
OAK CEDAR
WILLOW
FIR RD.
BIRCH RD.
PINE CL.
BEECH GR.
HAZEL GR.
ARRAN RD.
FIFE CL.
GLENEAGLES
ANGUS CL.
ABERDEEN CL.
MORAY CL.
TROON CL.
CAITHNESS
BRAEMAR CL
MONTROSE CL.
FALKIRK
MELROSE CL.
OBAN
AYR CL.
DUNDEE CL.
CROMARTY RD
CALEDONIAN RD
ASHPL.
CHESTNUT GDNS.
PERTH RD
GARDEN CL.
NAIRN RD.
Malcolm Sargent Sch.
BYRON WY.
KIPLING CL.
KEATS GR.
HIGHGROVE GDS
SHELLEY CL
TENNYSON WAY
SUTHERLAND WAY
Sidney College
A606
EMPINGHAM ROAD
CASTERTON ROAD
BELVOIR CL.
WALCOT WY.
BARNWELL RD.
ROCKINGHAM RD.
HARROWDEN RD.
CHATSWORTH RD
HADDON RD.
ELTON CL
Superstore
WAVERLEY GDNS.
WAVERLEY PL.
BEVERLEY GDS.
ROXBURGH RD.
BURNS RD.
STIRLING RD.
ARGYLL WAY
PO
FOX DALE
REFORM ST
TORKINGTON ST.
VENCE CL.
HIGHLANDS WAY
ERMINE WAY
ERMINE CL.
WINDMILL WY
LITTLE CASTERTON RD.
GAINSBOROUGH RD.
BURGHLEY RD.
SOMERVILLE RD.
AIREDALE RD.
FITZWILLIAM RD.
LANCASTER RD.
PEMBROKE RD.
NEWNHAM RD.
GIRTON WY.
OXFORD RD
DARWIN CL
CHURCHILL RD
CAMBRIDGE RD
BLASHFIELD CL
LAMBETH WALK
TRINITY RD.
MOUNTBATTEN
ELEANOR CL
Cemetery
RADCLIFFE ROAD
NORTHUMB
LUFFENHAM CL.
EXTON CL.
COTTESMORE RD.
LONSDALE RD.
LYNDON WY.
BROOKE AV
LAUNDE GDS.
HAMBLETON RD.
Playing Fields
ROMAN BANK
SHERWOOD CLOSE
THE HERMITAGE
QUEEN'S
ST. CLEMENTS
THE PADDOCK
FOUNDRY RD
FOUNDRY CT
NENE CT
CLARE CL
WEST END VILLAS
W. STREET
WALK
GARDENS LANE
TINWELL ROAD
EXETER
WATERFURLONG
CASTERTON LANE
TINWELL
TINWELL ROAD
Ch.
WELLAND VIEW
Mill Fm.
Tinwell Grange
A6121
South View Fm.
River Welland
North Fm.
A43
Based upon Ordnance Survey Mapping with the sanction of HM Stationery Office. 398861
Copyright G I Barnett & Son Limited

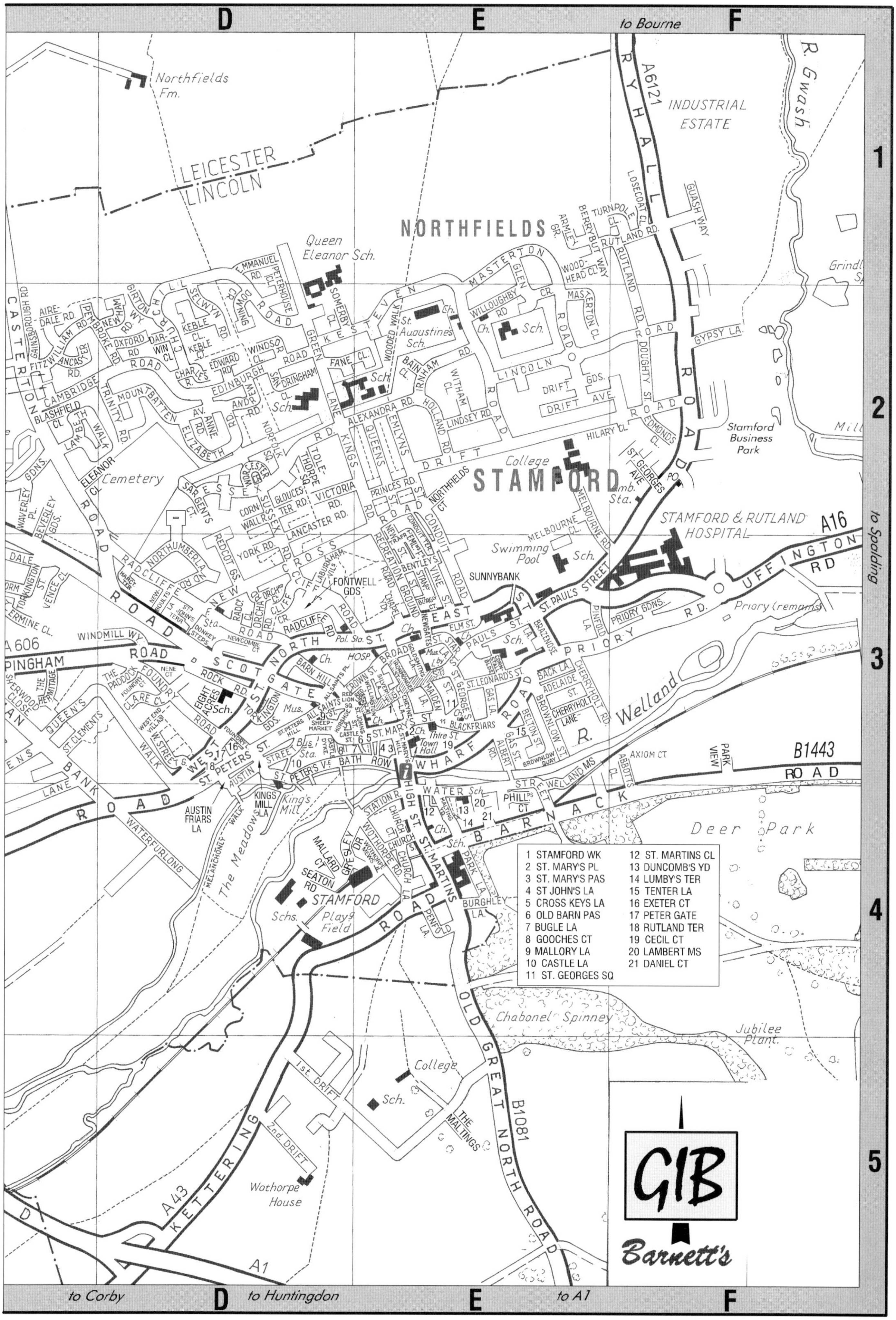
D
E
F
to Bourne
to Spalding
to Corby
to Huntingdon
to A1
1
2
3
4
5
NORTHFIELDS
STAMFORD
LEICESTER
LINCOLN
Northfields Fm.
INDUSTRIAL ESTATE
R. Gwash
Stamford Business Park
STAMFORD & RUTLAND HOSPITAL
A16
A6121
RYHALL ROAD
UFFINGTON RD
Priory (remains)
R. Welland
B1443
BARNACK ROAD
Deer Park
Chabonel Spinney
Jubilee Plant.
OLD GREAT NORTH ROAD
B1081
A43
KETTERING ROAD
A1
A 606
The Meadows
Cemetery
Queen Eleanor Sch.
St. Augustines Sch.
College
Swimming Pool
SUNNYBANK
Town Hall
King's Mill
STAMFORD Play Field
Wothorpe House
1 STAMFORD WK
2 ST. MARY'S PL
3 ST. MARY'S PAS
4 ST JOHN'S LA
5 CROSS KEYS LA
6 OLD BARN PAS
7 BUGLE LA
8 GOOCHES CT
9 MALLORY LA
10 CASTLE LA
11 ST. GEORGES SQ
12 ST. MARTINS CL
13 DUNCOMB'S YD
14 LUMBY'S TER
15 TENTER LA
16 EXETER CT
17 PETER GATE
18 RUTLAND TER
19 CECIL CT
20 LAMBERT MS
21 DANIEL CT
GIB
Barnett's

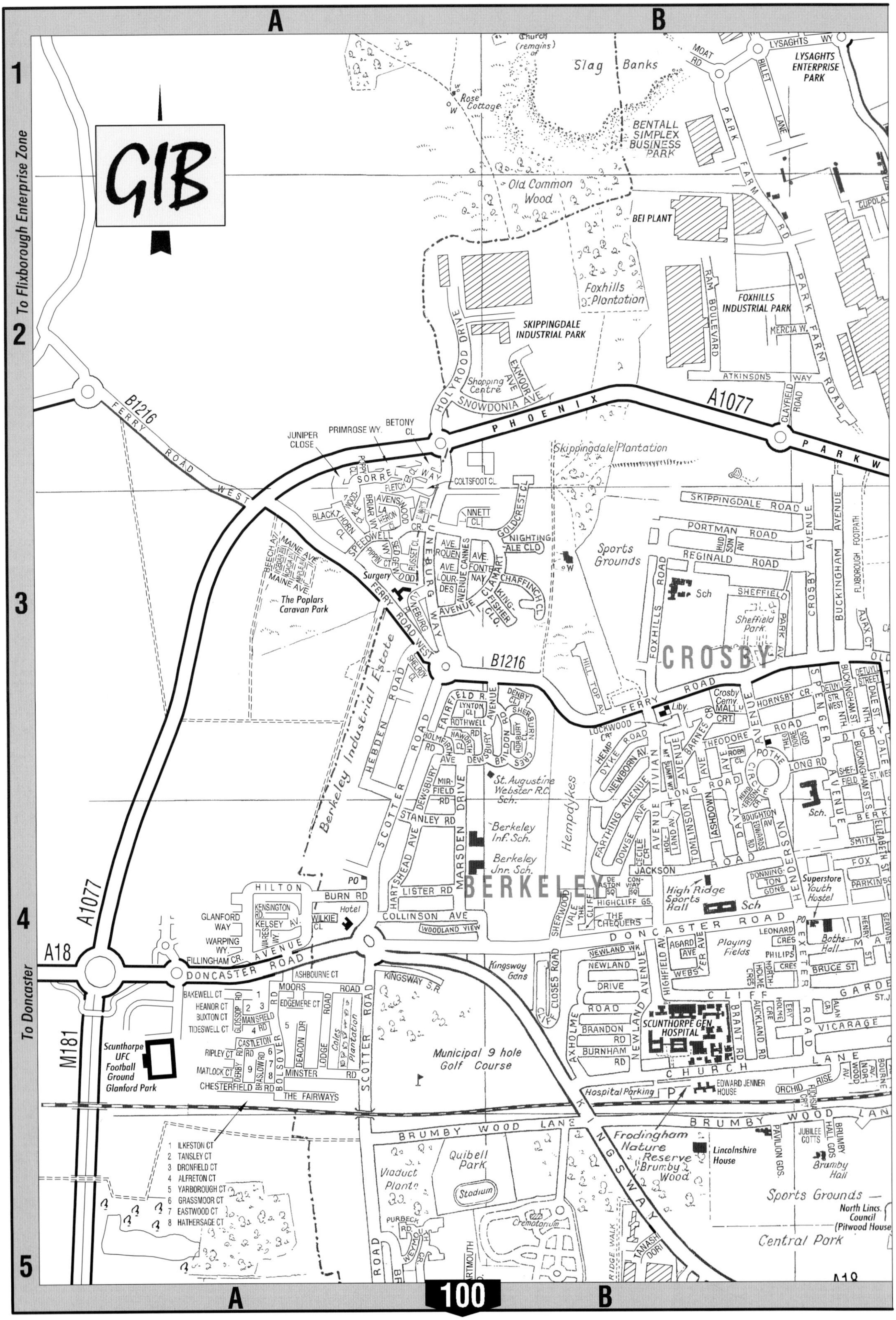
A
B
1
2
3
4
5
GIB
To Flixborough Enterprise Zone
To Doncaster
Slag Banks
Church (remains of)
Rose Cottage
MOAT RD
LYSAGHTS WY
LYSAGHTS ENTERPRISE PARK
BILLET LANE
PARK FARM ROAD
BENTALL SIMPLEX BUSINESS PARK
Old Common Wood
BEI PLANT
CUPOLA
Foxhills Plantation
FOXHILLS INDUSTRIAL PARK
RAM BOULEVARD
MERCIA W.
SKIPPINGDALE INDUSTRIAL PARK
HOLYROOD DRIVE
EXMOOR AVE
Shopping Centre
SNOWDONIA AVE
ATKINSONS WAY
CLAYFIELD ROAD
A1077
PHOENIX PARKWAY
B1216
FERRY ROAD WEST
JUNIPER CLOSE
PRIMROSE WY.
BETONY CL
SORREL WAY
COLTSFOOT CL
Skippingdale Plantation
SKIPPINGDALE ROAD
PORTMAN ROAD
REGINALD ROAD
Sports Grounds
BLACKTHORN CL
SPEEDWELL CR.
LUNEBURG WAY
GOLDCREST CL
NIGHTINGALE CLO
CHAFFINCH CL
KINGFISHER CLO.
ROUEN AVE.
CANNES AVENUE
FONTENAY
LOURDES AVE.
Surgery
MAINE AVE
The Poplars Caravan Park
Sch
SHEFFIELD PARK AV
Sheffield Park
FOXHILLS ROAD
CROSBY AVENUE
BUCKINGHAM AVENUE
FLIXBOROUGH FOOTPATH
AJAX CT
CROSBY
HILL TOP AV
FERRY ROAD
Liby.
Crosby Cemy.
HORNSBY CR.
SPENCER AVENUE
BUCKINGHAM ST. NTH.
DETUYLL STREET
DALE ST. NTH.
DIGBY
Berkeley Industrial Estate
HEBDEN ROAD
SCOTTER ROAD
FAIRFIELD R.
LYNTON CL
ROTHWELL RD
DENBY CL
SHERBURN CRES
BAILDON RD
HORBURY CL
HOLMFIRTH RD
DEWSBURY AVE
MIRFIELD RD
St. Augustine Webster R.C. Sch.
LOCKWOOD CRT
HEMP DYKE ROAD
NEWBORN AV.
FARTHING AVENUE
VIVIAN AVENUE
BARNES CR
THEODORE ROAD
LONG ROAD
POTHECARY CRT
LONG RD
Sch.
STANLEY RD
HARTSHEAD AVE
MARSDEN DRIVE
Berkeley Inf. Sch.
Berkeley Jnr. Sch.
Hempdykes
DOWSE AVE
TOMLINSON AVE
ASHDOWN AVE
DAVY ROAD
HENDERSON AVENUE
BOUGHTON AV
EDWARDS RD
JACKSON
SMITH
FOX
PARKINSON
BERKELEY
LISTER RD
COLLINSON AVE
WOODLAND VIEW
DONNINGTON GDNS
High Ridge Sports Hall
Superstore
Youth Hostel
HIGHCLIFF GS.
THE CHEQUERS
SHERWOOD VALE
DONCASTER ROAD
PO
HILTON AVENUE
BURN RD
Hotel
KENSINGTON RD.
KELSEY AV.
GLANFORD WAY
WILKIE CL
WARPING WY.
FILLINGHAM CR.
A18
DONCASTER ROAD
ASHBOURNE CT
NEWLAND WK
NEWLAND DRIVE
NEWLAND AVENUE
HIGHFIELD AV.
AGARD AVE
WEBSTER AVE
Playing Fields
LEONARD CRES
PHILIPS CRES
EXETER ROAD
Baths Hall
BRUCE ST
HENRY ST
Kingsway Gdns
CLOSES ROAD
CLIFF ROAD
KINGSWAY S.R.
MOORS ROAD
BAKEWELL CT
HEANOR CT
BUXTON CT
TIDESWELL CT
GLOSSOP RD
MANSFIELD RD
EDGEMERE CT
DEACON DR
LODGE ROAD
Coles Plantation
CASTLETON RD
RIPLEY CT
MATLOCK CT
CHESTERFIELD RD
BRASLOW RD
BOLSOVER RD
MINSTER RD
THE FAIRWAYS
Scunthorpe UFC Football Ground Glanford Park
M181
Municipal 9 hole Golf Course
AXHOLME ROAD
BRANDON RD
BURNHAM RD
SCUNTHORPE GEN. HOSPITAL
BRANT RD
AUCKLAND RD
HOLME CRES
VICARAGE
GARDENS
CHURCH LANE
Hospital Parking
EDWARD JENNER HOUSE
ORCHID RISE
BRUMBY WOOD LANE
1 ILKESTON CT
2 TANSLEY CT
3 DRONFIELD CT
4 ALFRETON CT
5 YARBOROUGH CT
6 GRASSMOOR CT
7 EASTWOOD CT
8 HATHERSAGE CT
Quibell Park
Stadium
Viaduct Plantn
PURBECK RD
Crematorium
KINGSWAY
Frodingham Nature Reserve Brumby Wood
Lincolnshire House
PAVILION GDS.
JUBILEE COTTS
BRUMBY HALL GDS
Brumby Hall
Sports Grounds
North Lincs. Council (Pitwood House)
Central Park
A18
100

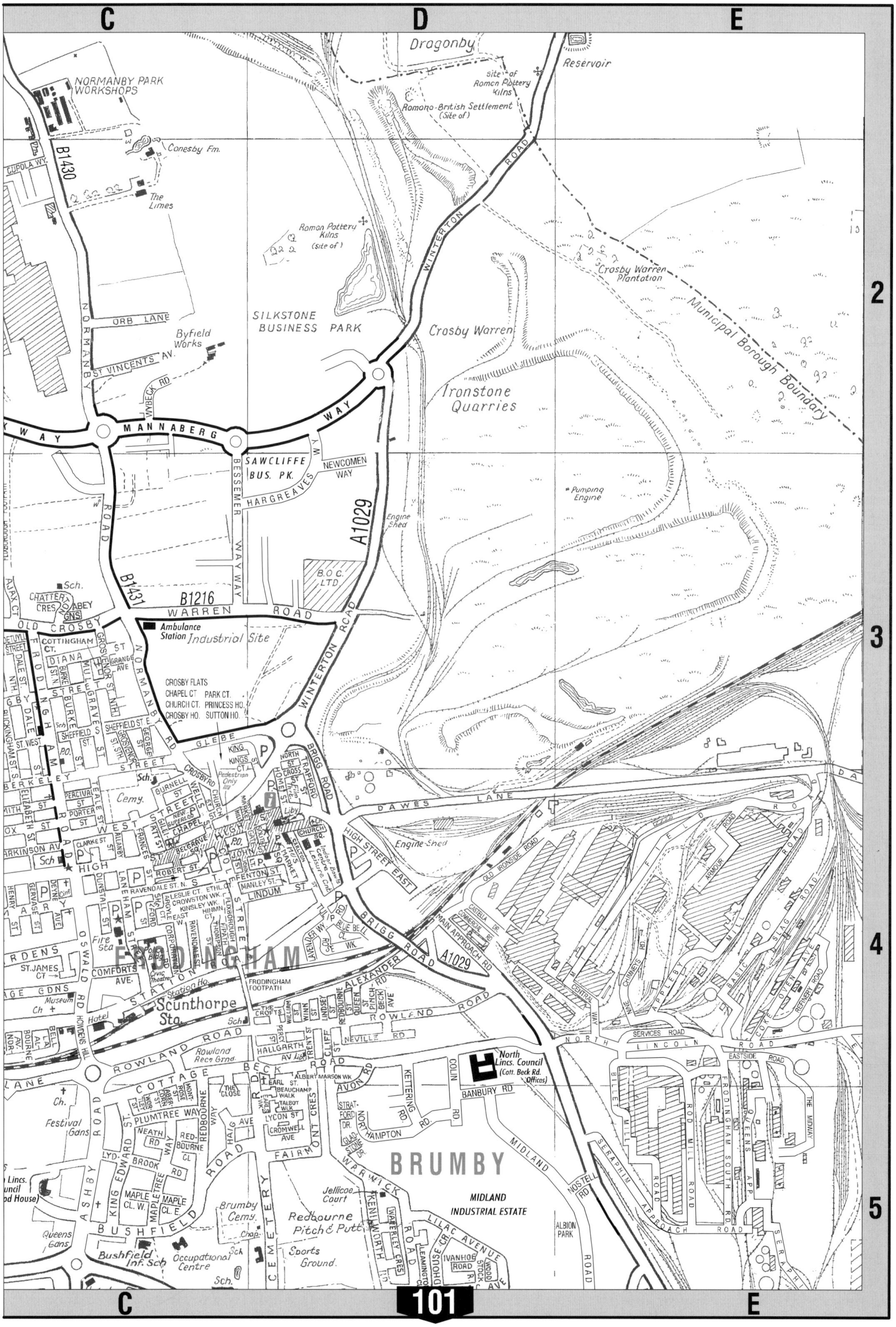
C
D
E
2
3
4
5
Dragonby
Reservoir
Site of Roman Pottery Kilns
Romano-British Settlement (Site of)
NORMANBY PARK WORKSHOPS
Conesby Fm.
CUPOLA WY.
B1430
The Limes
Roman Pottery Kilns (Site of)
Crosby Warren Plantation
Municipal Borough Boundary
WINTERTON ROAD
ORB LANE
SILKSTONE BUSINESS PARK
Crosby Warren
Byfield Works
ST VINCENTS AV.
WYBECK RD
Ironstone Quarries
NORMANBY
MANNABERG WAY
SAWCLIFFE BUS. PK.
NEWCOMEN WAY
BESSEMER WAY
HARGREAVES WAY
Pumping Engine
Engine Shed
A1029
B.O.C. LTD
B1431
B1216
WARREN ROAD
Ambulance Station
Industrial Site
CHATTERTON CRES
ABEY GNS
OLD CROSBY
COTTINGHAM CT.
DIANA ST
BURKE ST
MULGRAVE ST
GROSVENOR ST
CROSBY FLATS
CHAPEL CT
CHURCH CT.
CROSBY HO.
PARK CT.
PRINCESS HO.
SUTTON HO.
WINTERTON ROAD
GLEBE
KING KINGS CT.
SHEFFIELD ST
GEORGE ST
BRIGG ROAD
NORTH ST
CROSS ST
TRAFFORD ST
DAWES LANE
Cemy.
GURNELL ST
WELLS ST
CROSBY RD
BERKELEY ST
PERCIVAL ST
PORTER ST
WEST ST
ELIZABETH ST
BELGRAVE SQ
CHURCH SQ
Liby
HIGH STREET EAST
Engine Shed
OLD IRONSIDE ROAD
FIELD ROAD
ARMOUR ROAD
CLARKE ST
HIGH ST
ROBERT ST
FENTON ST
MANLEY ST
LINDUM ST
RAVENDALE ST
LAVENDER WY
BLUE BELL CL
BRIGG ROAD
MAIN APPROACH RD
COMMERCIAL RD
CASTELLA DR
A1029
FRODINGHAM
Fire Sta
Civic Theatre
COMFORTS AVE.
OSWALD RD
STATION RD
FRODINGHAM FOOTPATH
ALEXANDER RD
Scunthorpe Sta.
Museum
Hotel
ROWLAND ROAD
NEVILLE RD
HALLGARTH AV
CENTRAL WAY
NINE CHIMNEYS RD
APPLEBY MILL RD
BASIC SLAG ROAD
COKE OVEN AVE
REFINERY ROAD
NORTH LINCOLN ROAD
SERVICES ROAD
EASTSIDE ROAD
Rowland Recn Grnd.
BECK ROAD
COTTAGE BECK RD
ALBERT MARSON WK
EARL ST.
BEAUCHAMP WALK
TALBOT WALK
LYCON ST
CROMWELL AVE
North Lincs. Council (Cott. Beck Rd. Offices)
BANBURY RD
COLIN RD
KETTERING RD.
NORTHAMPTON RD.
AVON RD
PLUMTREE WAY
NEATH RD
REDBOURNE WAY
HAIG AVE
FAIRMONT CRES
Festival Gdns
Ch.
BRUMBY
MIDLAND ROAD
BILLET MILL ROAD
ROD MILL ROAD
FRODINGHAM SOUTH RD
QUEENS APP.
THE MIDWAY
SERAPHIM APPROACH ROAD
NOSTELL RD
LYDBROOK RD
KING EDWARD ST
MAPLE CL. W.
MAPLE CL. E.
ASHBY ROAD
BUSHFIELD ROAD
Brumby Cemy.
Chap.
CEMETERY ROAD
WARWICK ROAD
Jellicoe Court
KENILWORTH RD
WAVERLEY CRES
MIDLAND INDUSTRIAL ESTATE
ALBION PARK
LILAC AVENUE
LEAMINGTON CL
IVANHOE ROAD
WOODSTOCK RD
Redbourne Pitch & Putt
Sports Ground
Queens Gdns
Bushfield Inf. Sch
Occupational Centre
Sch.
101
C
E

A
98
B
5
6
7
8
1 WELLINGTON CT.
2 TAVISTOCK CT.
3 OKEHAMPTON CT.
4 COPPLESTONE CT.
5 DURSTONE CT.
6 WINSFORD CT.
7 WOOTON CT.
8 TORBAY CT.
9 TRURO CT.
10 TIVERTON CT.
11 FALMOUTH CT.
12 PORLOCK CT.
13 DAWLISH CT.
14 LULWORTH CT.
15 YEOVIL CT.
16 LYDFORD CT.
17 STRATTON CT.
18 NEWBURY CT.
19 BIDEFORD CT.
20 PENROSE CT.
21 HAYLE CT.
22 BRIXHAM CT.
23 RADSTOCK CT.
24 SALCOMBE CT.
25 HARTLAND CT.
26 LAMMERTON CT.
27 SHAFTESBURY CT.
28 WAREHAM CT.
29 CLOVELLY CT.
30 SWINDON CT.
31 KEYNSHAM CT.
32 BUDE CT.
33 LISCOMBE CT.
Central Park
A18
KINGSWAY BUSINESS PARK
North Lindsey College
West Common Sports Hall
BRUMBY COMMON LANE
WEST COMMON LANE
Brumby Common Nature Reserve
Parkland Caravan Site
LAGOON ROAD
LICHFIELD AVENUE
WESTCLIFF
Manor Park
RIDINGS
B1450
BURRINGHAM ROAD
Superstore
Ashfield Caravan Site
To M180 (Junction 3)
To Burringham
To M. 18 (Junction 5) & Doncaster
Scunthorpe Golf Club
Silica Country Park
SCOTTER ROAD SOUTH
ENDERBY ROAD
SOUTH PARK ROAD
SOUTH PARK INDUSTRIAL ESTATE
Green Acre Park
HIGH STREET
MOORWELL ROAD
Moorwell Business Park
M. 180
Grange Farm
Yaddlethorpe Grange
The Plantation
MOOR ROAD
YADDLETHORPE
Southfield Farm
Playing Field
Water Mill Fm.
Messingham Water Mill
Bottesford Beck
A
B

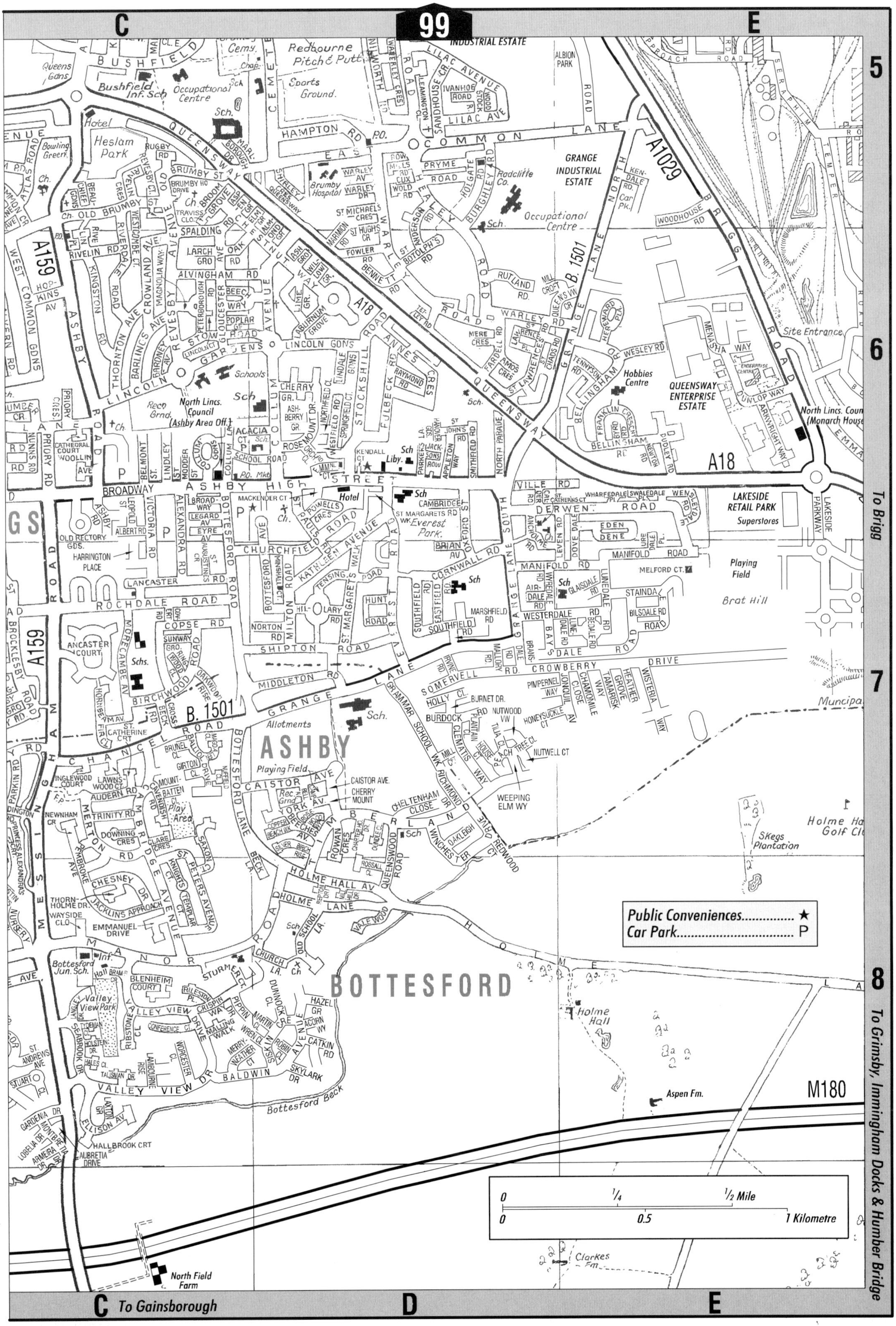
C
99
E
D
5
6
7
8
INDUSTRIAL ESTATE
Redbourne Pitch & Putt
Sports Ground
Cemy.
Chap.
Queens Gdns
BUSHFIELD
Bushfield Inf. Sch
Occupational Centre
Sch.
Hotel
Heslam Park
Bowling Green
QUEENSWAY
HAMPTON RD
LILAC AVENUE
LILAC AVE
IVANHOE ROAD
SANDHOUSE CR.
ALBION PARK
COMMON LANE
GRANGE INDUSTRIAL ESTATE
Radcliffe Co.
Occupational Centre
A1029
BRIGG ROAD
WOODHOUSE RD
KENDALE RD.
Car Pk.
Site Entrance
QUEENSWAY ENTERPRISE ESTATE
MENASHA WAY
DUNLOP WAY
ARKWRIGHT WAY
North Lincs. Council (Monarch House)
EMMA
Hobbies Centre
WESLEY RD
BELLINGHAM
FRANKLIN CRESCENT
TENNYSON RD
B. 1501
NORTH LANE
GRANGE LANE
A18
LAKESIDE RETAIL PARK
Superstores
LAKESIDE PARKWAY
To Brigg
PRYME ROAD
HOLGATE RD
BURGHLEY RD
WARLEY AV
WARLEY DR
WARLEY ROAD
Brumby Hospital
ST MICHAELS CRES
ST HUGHS CR
MARMION RD
FOWLER RD
BENNETT RD
ST. BOTOLPH'S RD
RUTLAND RD
MERE CRES
AMOS CRES
ST LAWRENCE'S
BRUMBY ST
OLD BRUMBY ST
BROOM GROVE
SPALDING RD
LARCH GRO
OAK RD
ALVINGHAM RD
BEECH WAY
POPLAR RD
STOW RD
LINCOLN GARDENS
LINCOLN GDNS
LABURNUM GROVE
STOCKSHILL ROAD
ANNES CRES
RAYMOND RD
FULBECK RD
Schools
Sch
North Lincs. Council (Ashby Area Off.)
Reco Grnd
CHERRY GR.
ASHBERRY GR.
ACACIA CT.
COLLUM AVENUE
SCHOOL ROAD
P.O. Mkt
Liby.
KENDALL CT
APPLETON WAY
SMITHFIELD RD
NORTH PARADE
ASHBY HIGH STREET
BROADWAY
MACKENDER CT
Hotel
CAMBRIDGE
ST MARGARETS RD
Everest Park
OXFORD ST
BRIAN AV
CORNWALL RD
CHURCHFIELD ROAD
KATHLEEN AVENUE
ST. MARGARETS WALK
TENSING ROAD
HILLARY
HUNT ROAD
EVEREST ROAD
NORTON RD
SHIPTON ROAD
MIDDLETON RD
SOUTHFIELD RD
MARSHFIELD RD
BOTTESFORD ROAD
VICTORIA RD
ALEXANDRA RD
LEGARD AV
EYRE AV
ALBERT RD
OLD RECTORY GDS.
HARRINGTON PLACE
LANCASTER RD
ROCHDALE ROAD
COPSE RD
SUNWAY GRO.
ANCASTER COURT
Schs.
MORECAMBE AV
BIRCHWOOD
B. 1501
GRANGE LANE
CHANCEL ROAD
ST. CATHERINE CRT
A159
ASHBY ROAD
WEST COMMON GDNS
HOPKINS AV
KINGSTON RD
RIVELIN RD
THORNTON AVE
BARLINGS AVE
CROWLAND AVE
REVESBY AVENUE
RUGBY RD
PRIORY RD
NUNNS RD
CATHEDRAL COURT
WOOLLIN AVE
BROCKLESBY
VILLE RD
DERWENT ROAD
WHARFEDALE PL
SWALEDALE
EDEN DENE
MANIFOLD ROAD
MELFORD CT.
Playing Field
Brat Hill
STAINDALE
BILSDALE RD
GLAISDALE
WESTERDALE RD
BAYSDALE ROAD
CROWBERRY DRIVE
SOMERVELL RD
HOLLY CL.
BURNET DR.
BURDOCK
NUTWOOD VW
PIMPERNEL WAY
JONQUIL AV
CHAMOMILE CLOSE
TAMARISK WAY
HEATHER GROVE
WISTERIA WAY
HONEYSUCKLE CT
NUTWELL CT
WEEPING ELM WY
PEACH TREE CL
CLEMATIS CL
Municipal
GRAMMAR SCHOOL RD
RICHMOND DR
Allotments
ASHBY
Playing Field
CAISTOR AVE
CAISTOR AVE.
CHERRY MOUNT
Rec. Grnd
YORK AV.
CHELTENHAM CLOSE
CUMBERLAND AVE
OAKLEIGH
WINCHESTER
REDWOOD
ROWAN CRES
QUEENSWOOD ROAD
HOLME HALL AV
HOLME LANE
BOTTESFORD LANE
BECK LA.
Holme Hall Golf Club
Skegs Plantation
Public Conveniences ★
Car Park P
HOLME LANE
Holme Hall
Aspen Fm.
M180
BOTTESFORD
CHURCH LA.
OLD SCHOOL LA.
DUNNOCK CL.
HAZEL GR
ACORN WY
CATKIN RD
ROBIN AVENUE
MARTIN CL.
WREN CL.
MERRYWEATHER CT
BALDWIN
SKYLARK DR
Bottesford Beck
STURMER CT.
PIPPIN DR
CRISPIN WAY
MALLING WALK
WORCESTER
VALLEY VIEW DR
LAMBOURNE RISE
Valley View Park
BLENHEIM COURT
Bottesford Jun. Sch.
MANOR ROAD
EMMANUEL DRIVE
WAYSIDE CLO
THORNHOLME DR.
CHESNEY DR
JACKLINS APPROACH
PEMBROKE AVE
MERTON RD
TRINITY RD
DOWNING CRES
CLARE CRES.
CAMBRIDGE AVENUE
ST PETERS AVENUE
SAXON
Play Area
AUDERN RD
LAWNS WOOD CT
INGLEWOOD COURT
NEWNHAM CR
MESSINGHAM ROAD
ST. ANDREWS AVE
STUART CL
GARDENIA DR
LOBELIA DR
MONTBRETIA DR
ARMERIA DR
AUBRETIA DRIVE
HALLBROOK CRT
ELLISON AV
To Grimsby, Immingham Docks & Humber Bridge
0
1/4
1/2 Mile
0.5
1 Kilometre
Clarkes Fm.
North Field Farm
To Gainsborough

Abbey Road B.6
Abbots Road C.6
Abercorn Street C.5
Abey Gardens C.3
Acacia Avenue A.3
Acacia Way D.6
Acer Close A.7
Acorn Way D.8
Agard venue B.4
Airdale Road D.7
Ajax Court C.3
Alan Crescent C.4
Alba Close B.7
Albert Road C.6
Alberta Crescent B.7
Albion Park E.5
Albourne Avenue C.4
Alexander Road D.4
Alexandra Road C.6
Alfreton Court A.4
Allanby Street C.4
Almond Grove D.5
Alveston Road B.5
Alvingham Road C.6
Amos Crescent D.6
Ancaster Court C.7
Ancholme Road D.6
Anchor Village F.7
Anderson Road D.6
Angerstein Road B.7
Annes Crescent D.6
Appleby Close C.7
Appelby Mill Road E.4
Appelton Way D.6
Argyle Court C.3
Arkwright Way E.6
Armeira Drive C.8
Armour Road E.4
Ash Grove D.6
Ashberry Grove D.6
Ashbourne Court A.4
ASHBY D.7
Asby High Street C.6
Ashby Road C.6
Ashdown Avenue B.4
Aspen Grove C.5
Asterby Road B.7
Atkinson's Way B.2
Atlas Road C.5
Aubretia Drive C.8
Auckland Road B.4
Audern Road C.7
Austin Crescent C.8
Avenswood Lane A.3
Avenue Cannes A.3
Avenue Clamart A.3
Avenue Fontenay A.3
Avenue Lourdes A.3
Avenue Rouen A.3
Avenue Vivian B.4
Avon Road D.5
Axholme Road B.4
Aylesby Road B.7

Bakewell Court A.4
Baldwin Avenue C.8
Balliol Drive C.7
Balmoral Court C.7
Banbury Road D.4
Bardney Avenue C.6
Barlings Avenue C.6
Barnes Crescent B.3
Barnetby Road C.7
Barnstaple Road A.5
Basic Slag Road E.4
Basildon Road B.3
Baslow Road A.5
Baysdale Road A.5
Beaford Court A.5
Beauchamp Walk A.5
Beck Lane D.8
Bedale Road E.7
Beech Avenue A.3
Beech Way C.6
Beeches Avenue D.7
Beesby Road B.7
Belgrave Square C.4
Bell Lane C.4
Bellingham Road E.6
Belmont Street C.6
Belper Court A.4
Belvedere Drive B.6
Bennett Road D.6
BERKELEY A.4
Berkeley Street C.4
Bessemer Way C.2
Betony Close A.2
Betula Way A.7
Beverley Court B.6
Bideford Court B.5
Bigby Grove C.7
Billet Lane B.1
Billet Mill Approach Road F.6
Bilet Mill Road E.7
Bilsedale Road E.7
Birchwood Road C.7
Birkdale Road A.8
Blackkthorn Close A.3
Blake Avenue B.6
Blenheim Court C.8
Bloom Lane B.1
Bluebell Close D.4
Bodmin Close B.5
Bolinbroke Road B.7
Bolsover Road A.4
Bonby Grove C.7
Bos Approach Road F.6
BOTTESFORD D.8
Bottesford Avenue D.7
Bottesford Lane D.7
Bottesford Road C.6
Boughton Avenue B.4
Bramley Crescent C.8
Brandon Road B.4
Brankwell Crescent B.8
Bransdale Road D.7
Brant Road B.4
Brian Avenue D.7
Briar Way A.3
Bridges Road B.6
Bridgewater Road B.5
Bridport Walk A.5
Brigg Road D.3
Brigg Road D.4
Bristol Road A.5
Brixham Court B.5
Broaway C.6
Brocklesby Road C.7
Brookdale Road B.4
Broom Grove C.6
Browning Close B.6
Bruce Street C.4
BRUMBY D.5
Brumby Common Lane A.6
Brumby Hall Gardens C.5
Brumby House Drive C.5
Brumby Wood Lane A.5
Brunel Close D.7
Buckfast Court
Buckingham Avenue C.3
Buckingham Street North C.3
Buckingham Street South C.3
Bude Court A.6
Burdock Road D.7
Burghley Road D.5
Burke Street C.3
Burke Street North C.3
Burn Road A.4
Burnet Drive D.7
Burnham Road B.4
Burringham Road B.7
Bushfield Road C.5
Buxton Court A.4
Byfield Road A.6
Byrd Road E.6
Byron Close B.6

Cadney House C.7
Caenby Road B.7
Caistor Avenue D.7
Calder Road D.6
Cambridge Avenue C.7
Cambridge Road D.6
Campbell Avenue D.7
Canterbury Close A.6
Carlton Street D.4
Castella Drive D.4
Castleton Court A.4
Cathedrral Court C.6
Catkin Road D.8
Cavendish Road C.7
Cecile Crescent B.4
Cedar Avenue A.3
Cemetary Road D.5
Centarl Way E.4
Chaffinch Close B.3
Chamomile Close E.7
Chancel Road C.7
Chandos Road B.6
Chapel Court C.3
Chapel Street C.4
Chapman Avenue B.6
Charles Lovell Way B.5
Charterhouse Drive D.7
Chatterton Crescent C.3
Chaucer Avenue B.6
Cheltenham Close D.7
Chelwood Road B.6
Cherry Grove D.6
Chesney Drive C.8
Chesterfield Road A.4
Chestnut Way C.5
Chiltern Crescent B.5
Church Court C.3
Church Lane B.4
Church Lane, Bottesford D.8
Church Square D.4
Church Street C.4
Churchfield Road C.7
Clare Avenue B.6
Clare Crescent C.7
Carendon Road B.6
Clarke Street C.4
Claxby House C.7
Claxby Road C.7
Clayfield Road B.2
Clematis Way D.7
Clevedon Road B.5
Cleveland Close B.5
Cliff Closes Road B.4
Cliff Gardens B.4
Cliff Street D.4
Cloister Close B.6
Clovelly Court A.6
Coke Oven Avenue E.4
Cole Street C.4
Coleridge Avenue B.6
Colin Road D.5
Collison Avenue A.4
Collum Avenue D.6
Collum Gardens C.6
Collum Lane C.6
Coltsfoot Close A.3
Comforts Avenue D.4
Commercial Road D.4
Concast Road F.6
Conference Court C.8
Conifer Close A.7
Coningsby Road B.7
Conway Square B.4
Cooper Beech Walk D.7
Coppestone Court A.5
Copse Road C.7
Cornwall Road D.7
Corporation Road C.4
Cottage Beck Road C.5
Cottingham Court C.3
Coventry Close A.6
Covery Road C.7
Cowper Avenue B.6
Cresta Drive B.7
Crispin Way C.8
Croft lane B.8
Cromwell Avenue D.5
CROSBY B.3
Crosby Avenue C.3
Crosby Flats C.3
Crosby House C.3
Crosby Road C.4
Cross Street D.4
Crossbeck Road C.7
Crowberry Drive D.7
Crowland Avenue C.6
Crowston Walk C.3
Cupola Way C.2
Cuxwold Road D.5

Dale Street C.3
Dale Street North C.3
Danum Road C.5
Dartmouth Road A.5
Davy Avenue B.4
Dawes Lane D.4
Dawlish Court A.5
De Aston Square B.4
Deacon Drive A.4
Dean Road B.6
Denby Close B.3
Derby Road A.4
Derwent Road D.6
Detuyll Street C.3
Detuyll Street West C.3
Devonshire Road C.6
Dewsbury Avenue A.4
Deyne Avenue C.4
Diana Street C.3
Digby Street C.3
Dolman Crescent C.7
Doncaster Road A.4
Donnington Gardens B.4
Dorchester Road A.6
Dove Dale E.7
Downing Crescent C.7
Dowse Avenue B.4
Dragonby Road B.7
Dronfield Court A.4
Dryden Road B.6
Dudley Road E.6
Dunlop Way E.6
Dunnock Close D.8
Dunstall Street C.4
Durstone Court A.5

Earl Street D.4
Earl Street D.5
Earls Walk D.5
East Boundary Road F.4
East Common Lane D.5
East Walk C.3
Eastfield Road D.7
Eastside Road E.4
Eastwood Court A.4
Eden Dene E.6
Edgbaston Avenue B.8
Edgemere Court A.4
Edward Jenner Court B.4
Edwards Road B.4
Elizabeth Street C.4
Ellison Avenue C.8
Elm Grove D.5
Emmanuel Court D.6
Emmanuel Drive C.8
Emmanuel Road E.5
Endcliffe Avenue C.8
Enderby Road B.7
Eryholme Crescent B.4
Ethel Court C.3
Eton Court C.7
Elton Drive B.8
Everest Road D.7
Exeter Road C.4
Exmoor Avenue B.2
Exmoor Road A.5
Eyre Avenue C.6

Fairmont Crescent D.5
Falmouth Court A.5
Fardell Road D.6
Farifield Road A.3
Farthing Avenue B.4
Fenton Street C.4
Fenton Street D.4
Ferriby Road B.7
Ferry Road B.3
Ferry Road West A.3
Fifth Avenue A.6
Fillingham Crescent A.4
Fletcher Close B.8
Flixborough Footpath C.3
Fotherby Road B.7
Fourth Avenue A.6
Fowler Road D.6
Fox Street D.4
Foxhills Industrial Park B.2
Foxhills Road B.3
Frances Street C.4
Franklin Crescent E.6
Frairs Road B.6
Frodingham Footpath D.4
Frodingham Road C.3
Frodingham South Road E.5
Fuchsia Croft A.3
Fulbeck Road D.6

Gardenia Drive C.8
George Street C.3
Gervase Street C.4
Gilliant Close C.4
Girton Close D.7
Gladstone Drive D.5
Glaisdale Road F.7
Glanford Lodge B.8
Glanford Road B.8
Glanford Way A.4
Glanville Avenue C.5
Glanville Crescent C.5
Glebe Road C.3
Gossop Road A.4
Gloucester Avenue C.6
Glover Road B.6
Goldcrest Close B.3
Goodwood B.7
Grammar School Walk D.7
Grange Avenue C.3
Grange Lane D.7
Grange Lane North E.6
Grange Lane South D.7
Grasby Road B.7
Grassmoor Court A.4
Gray Road B.6
Greengarth B.8
Greenhoe Road A.7
Grosvenor Street North C.3
Grosvenor Street South C.3
Gunby Road B.7
Gurnell Street C.4

Haig Avenue C.5
Hales Close C.8
Hallbrook Court C.8
Hallgarth Avenue D.4
Hamilton Road B.5
Hammerton Road B.7
Hampton Road D.5
Hanover Gardens D.5
Hardy Road B.6
Hargreaves Way D.3
Harrington Place C.7
Harrow Gardens C.7
Hartland Court B.5
Hartshead Avenue A.4
Hathersage Court A.4
Haworth Close A.3
Hawthorne Avenue C.5
Hawthorne Crescent C.5
Hayle Court A.5
Hazel Grove D.8
Headingley Avenue B.8
Healey Road D.5
Heanor Court A.4
Heather Grove E.7
Hebden Road A.3
Helston Walk A.5
Hemp Dyke Road B.4
Henderson Avenue C.4
Henderson Crescent B.3
Henry Street C.4
Hereward Place E.6
Heron Close A.3
Herrick Road B.6
High Leys Road B.7
High Street C.4
High Street East D.4
High Street Bottesford C.8
Highcliff Gardens B.4
Highfield Avenue B.4
Highgarth B.8
Hilary Road D.7
Hill Top Avenue B.3
Hillfoot Drive B.8
Hilton Avenue A.4
Hindon Walk A.5
Hinman Street C.4
Hinman Walk C.3
Holgate Road D.5
Holland Avenue B.4
Holly Close D.7
HOLME F.8
Holme Hall Avenue D.7
Holme Lane D.8
Holmfirth Road A.3
Holstein Close C.8
Holyrood Drive A.2
Home Street D.4
Honeysuckle Court D.7
Hood Road B.6
Hopkins Avenue C.6
Horbury Close B.3
Hornbeam Avenue C.7
Hornsby Crescent B.3
House Court D.7
Howdens Hill C.4
Hoylake Road A.7
Hudson Avenue B.3
Humber Crescent C.6
Hunt Road D.7
Hurst Lane B.8

Ilkeston Court A.4
Inglewood Court C.7
Irby Road B.7
Irvine Road D.7
Ivanhoe Road D.5

Jacklins Approach C.8
Jackson Road B.4
Jacksons Row D.6
Jellicoe Court D.5
Jesmond Avenue B.8
John Street C.4
Jonquil Avenue E.7
Jubilee Cottages C.5
Juniper Close A.2

Kathleen Avenue D.7
Keats Avenue B.6
Keddington Road C.7
Keelby Road B.7
Kelsey Avenue A.4
Kendal Court D.6
Kendale Road E.5
Kendall Court D.6
Kenilworth Road D.5
Kensington Road A.4
Kenya Drive B.8
Kestrel Road B.6
Kettering Road D.4
Keysham Court A.6
King Edward Street C.5
King Street D.3
Kingerby Road B.7
Kingfisher Close B.3
Kings Court C.3
Kingsdale B.8
Kingston Road C.6
Kingsway B.4
Kingsway Business Park B.5
Kingsley S.R. A.4
Kinsley Walk C.3
Kipling Avenue B.6
Kirkby Road B.7
Kirman Crescent B.8
Knights Court C.8

Laburnam Grove D.6
Laceby Road B.7
Lagoon Road A.6
Lakeside Drive A.7
Lakeside Parkway E.6
Lambourne Rise C.8
Lamberton Court B.5
Lancaster Road C.7
Landor Avenue B.6
Laneham Street C.4
Langley Drive C.8
Larch Grove C.6
Lavender Way D.4
Lawnswood Court C.7
Laxton Grove C.8
Leamington Close D.5
Lee Fair Gardens C.8
Legard Avenue C.6
Leonard Crescent B.4
Leopold Street C.6
Leslie Court C.3
Leven Road E.7
Lichfield Avenue A.6
Lilac Avenue D.5
Lime Avenue F.6
Lime Grove C.6
Lincoln Court C.6
Lincoln Gardens C.6
Lindale Gardens D.6
Lindley Street C.6
Lindsey Street D.4
Lindum Street C.4
Lindium Street D.4
Linnet Close A.3
Liscombe Court B.6
Lister Road A.4
Little John Street C.4
Lloyds Avenue B.5
Lobelia Drive C.8
Lockwood Court B.3
LODGE MOORS A.4
Lodge Road A.4
Long Road B.3
Lovell Road B.7
Low Leys Road B.7
Lowgarth B.8
Lulworth Court A.5
Lune Dale Road E.7
Luneburg Place A.3
Luneburg Way A.3
Lycon Street D.5
Lydbrook Road C.5
Lydford Court B.5
Lynmouth Drive A.5
Lynton Close A.3
Lysaghts Enterprise Park C.1
Lysaghts Way B.1

Machender Court D.6
Mackender Court D.6
Magdalen Close D.7
Magnolia Way C.6
Main Approach Road D.4
Main Road A.7
Maine Avenue A.3
Mallalieu Court B.3
Mallard Road B.6
Malling Walk C.8
Mallory Road D.7
Maltby Road B.7
Malvern Road C.6
Manby Road B.7
Manifold Road D.7
Manley Street D.4
Mannaberg Way C.2
Manor Farm Road B.6
Manor Road C.8
Mansfield Road A.4
Maple Avenue A.3
Maple Close East C.5
Maple Close West C.5
Mapletree Way C.5
Market Hill C.4
Market Square D.4
Marlborough Drive C.5
Marlowe Road B.6
Marmion Road A.6
Marsden Drive A.4
Marshfield Road D.8
Martin Close D.8
Mary Street C.4
Mary Summer Way B.3
Mason Drive B.8
Matlock Court A.4
Mavis Road B.6
Meadow Road A.8
Melbury Walk A.5
Melford Court E.7
Mendip Road B.5
Mercia Way B.2
Mere Crescent D.6
Meredith Avenue B.6
Merlin Road B.6
Merris Walk A.6
Merryweather Court C.8
Merton Road C.7
Messingham Road C.7
Middleton Road D.7
Midland Road D.5
Mill Croft D.7
Mill Field Road E.4
Mill Hill Drive D.8
Milton Road D.7
Minshall Court D.7
Minster Road A.4
Mirfield Road A.3
Moat Road B.1
Modder Street C.6
Monks Road C.6
Montbretia Drive C.8
Montrose Street C.5
Moor Road A.8
Moors Road A.8
Moorwell Road B.8
Morecambe Avenue C.7
Morley Road B.7
Mountbatten Close C.7
Mulgrave Street C.3

Neath Road C.5
Neville Road D.4
New Road A.6
Newbolt Avenue B.6
Newborn Avenue B.4
Newbury Court A.5
Newcomen Way D.2
Newdown Road B.8
Newland Avenue B.4
Newland Drive B.4
Newland Walk B.4
Newnham Crescent C.7
Newstead House C.7
Newton Road E.6
Nightingale Close B.3
Nine Chimneys Road E.4
Norman Crescent C.5
Normanby Road C.2
North Farm Road B.8
North Lincoln Road E.4
North Orbital Road A.3
North Parade D.6
North Street D.3
North West Orbital Road A.3
Northampton Road D.5
Northfield Close D.6
Northolme Crescent B.4
Norton Road D.7
Norwood Avenue C.4
Nostell Road E.5
Nuffield Close D.7
Nunns Road C.6
Nursery Close C.8
Nutwell Court D.7
Nutwood View D.7

Oak Road C.6
Oakford Close B.5
Oakliegh D.7
Oakwood Rise C.7
Ogilvy Drive B.8
Okehampton Court A.5
Old Brumby Street C.5
Old Crosby C.3
Old Rectory Gardens C.6
Old School Lane D.8
Ontario Road B.8
Orb Lane C.2
Orchid Close D.6
Orchid Rise C.4
Oriole Road B.6
Ormsby Road B.7
Oswald Road C.4
Ottawa Road B.7
Oundle Close D.7
Oxford Street D.7

Padstow Walk A.5
Park Avenue B.7
Park Court C.3
Park Farm Road B.1-C.2
Parkers Lane D.6
Parkin Road C.7
Parkinsons Avenue C.4
Partridge Close B.6
Pavillion Gardens B.5
Peach Tree Close D.7
Peacock Street C.7
Pembroke Avenue C.7
Penrose Court B.5
Percival Street B.4
Percy Street D.4
Permain Court C.8
Peterborough Road C.6
Peveril Avenue B.6
Pheasant Close B.6
Phillips Crescent B.4
Phoenix Parkway B.2
Pimpernel Way D.7
Pinchbeck Avenue D.4
Pippin Court A.3
Pippin Drive C.8
Plantain Close D.7
Plumtree Way C.5
Plymouth Road A.5
Poole Drive C.7
Poplar Gardens C.6
Poppy Close A.2
Porlock Court A.5
Porter Street C.4
Portman Road B.3
Powells Crescent D.6
Primrose Way A.2
Princess Alexandra Court C.7
Princess House C.3
Priory Crescent C.6
Priory lane B.6
Priory Road C.5
Pryme Road D.5
Purbeck Road A.5

Quantock Close B.5
Quebec Road B.7
Queen Street D.4
Queen Street D.6
Queens Approach E.5
Queens View Crescent D.6
Queensway C.5
Queenswood Road D.8

Radcliffe Court D.5
Radstock Court B.5
Ram Boulevard B.2
Ranby Road B.7
Ravensdale Street C.4
Ravensdale Street North C.4
Raymond Road D.6
Redbourne Close C.5
Redbourne Street D.4
Redbourne Way C.5
Refinery Road E.4
Reginald Road B.3
Repton Drive C.8
Revesby Avenue C.6
Revesby Court C.5
Ribstone Close C.8
Riby Road B.7
Richmond Drive D.7
Ridge Walk B.6
RIDINGS C.6
Rilestone Place C.8
Ringwood Close C.7
Ripley Court A.4
Ripon Close A.6
Rivelin Crescent C.5
Rivelin Place C.6
Rivelin Road C.6
Riverdale Road C.5
Robert Street C.4
Robin Close D.8
Robinson Close B.3
Robinson Road B.3
Rochdale Road C.7
Rochester Close A.6
Rod Mill Road E.5
Rose Walk D.4
Rosedale B.8
Rosemount Drive D.6
Rosewood Way D.7
Rossal Close D.8
Rothbury Road B.6
Rothwell Road A.3
Rowan Crescent D.7
Rowland Road C.4
Rowmills Road D.5
Rugby Road C.5
Russet Close A.3
Rutland Road D.6

Salcombe Court B.5
Salisbury Close A.6
Salmonby Road B.7
Sandfield Close C.4
Sandhouse Crescent D.5
Sandringham Crescent B.8
Sawcliffe Business Park C.3
Saxby Road B.7
Saxon Court C.7
Scawby Road B.7
School Road C.6
Scott Avenue A.6
Scotter Road A.3
Scotter Road South A.7
Seabrook Drive C.8
Seaton Road B.5
Second Avenue A.6
Sedgewood Way A.3
Selby Court B.6
Seraphim Approach Road E.5
Seraphim Road E.5
Services Road E.4
Shaftesbury Court A.6
Shakespeare Avenue A.6
Sheffield Park Avenue B.3
Sheffield Street C.3
Sheffield Street East C.3
Sheffield Street West C.3
Shelford Street C.4
Shelroy Close A.3
Sherburn Crescent B.3
Sherwood Vale B.4
Shipton Road D.7
Shirley Crescent D.5
Sidney Road A.6
Silica Crescent A.7
Silica Drive A.7
Silkstone Business Park D.2
Silver Birch Rise D.7
Siskin Crescent D.8
Sixth Avenue A.6
Skelton Road A.6
Skidby Court B.7
Skippingdale Road B.3
Skylark Drive D.8
Smith Street C.4
Smithfield Road D.6
Snowdonia Avenue A.2
Somerby Road B.7
Somervell Road D.7
Sorrel Way A.2
South Park Road A.7
South Ridge Crescent B.8
Southfield Road D.7
Southgate D.4
Spalding Road C.6
Speedwell Crescent A.3
Spencer Avenue C.3
Spilsby Road B.7
Springfield Close D.6
Springfield Court D.6
St. Albans Close A.6
St. Andrew's Avenue C.8
St. Augustine's Crescent C.7
St. Botolph's Road D.6
St. Catherine Crescent C.7
St. Catherines Court D.6
St. Chad's Road D.6
St. Davids Crescent B.8
St. Hugh's Crescent D.6
St. James Court C.4
St. John's Road D.6
St. Lawrence Place D.6
St. Lawrence's Road D.6
St. Margarets Walk D.6
St. Mary's Court A.3
St. Michael's Crescent D.5
St. Paul's Road D.6
St. Peter's Avenue C.7
St. Vincent's Avenue C.2
Staindale Road E.7
Stainton Drive B.7
Stainiwell Rise B.6
Stanley Road A.4
Station Road C.4
Stockshill Road D.6
Stow Road C.6
Strafford Drive D.5
Stratton Court B.5
Stuart Close C.8
Sturner Court C.8
Sunningdale Road B.7
Sunway Grove C.7
Sutton House C.3
Swaledale Place E.6
Swift Road A.6
Swinburne Road A.6
Swindon Court A.6
Swindon Court B.6

Talbot Walk D.5
Talisman Drive C.8
Tamar Walk A.5
Tamarisk Way E.7
Tanashi Dori Way B.5
Tansley Court A.4
Tattershall Court B.7
Tavistock Court A.5
Tealby Road B.7
Teale Street C.4
Teighmouth Court B.5
Temper Road E.5
Templar Court C.8
Tennyson Road E.6
Tensing Road D.7
Tetley Road D.6
The Vhequers B.4
The Circle B.3
The Cliff B.4
The Close C.5
The Crofts D.4
The Dales B.8
The Dell B.7
The Fairways A.4
The Midway E.5
The Oval B.8
The Rise B.8
Theodore Gardens B.3
Theodore Road B.3
Third Avenue A.6
Thomas Road C.5
Thompson Street C.4
Thoresby Road B.7
Thornhill Crescent B.8
Thorneholme Drive C.8
Thornton Avenue C.6
Tideswell Court A.4
Tilia Close D.7
Timberlands D.7
Tiverton Court A.5
Tomlinson Avenue B.4
Torbay Court A.5
Torrington Road A.5
Trafford Street D.3
Traviss Close C.5
Trent Street D.4
Trent View House B.6
Trinity Road C.7
Truro Court A.5
Tulip Road D.4
Tydeman Close C.8

Ulceby Road A.7
Uredale Place E.7

Valley View Drive C.8
Vancouver Crescent B.7
Vicarage Gardens C.4
Victoria Road C.6
Ville Road D.6

Waddingham Drive B.8
Walesby Road B.7
Wareham Court A.6
Wares Way A.4
Warley Avenue D.5
Warley Drive D.5
Warley Road D.5
Warping Way A.4
Warren Road C.3
Warwick Road D.5
Waverley Crescent D.5
Wayside Close C.8
Webster Avenue B.4
Weeping Elm Way D.7
Wellington Court A.5
Wells Street C.4
Wensleydale Road E.6
Wentworth Road A.8
Wesley Road E.6
West Common Crescent C.5
West Common Gardens C.6
West Common Lane B.6
West Street C.4
West View B.8
WESTCLIFF B.6
Westcliff Gardens B.6
Westcombe Court C.5
Westerdale Road D.7
Westfield Road A.6
Westfield Road D.6
Weymouth Crescent A.5
Wharfdale Place E.6
Whitestone Road A.7
Whitfield Road B.6
Whitman Road A.6
Wilkie Close A.4
William Street D.4
Willoughby Road B.6
Willow Grove D.6
Windsor Crescent C.8
Winn Street D.4
Winsford Court A.5
Winterton Road D.3
Wisteria Way E.7
Woodale Close A.3
Woodclose Road A.6
Woodhouse Road E.5
Woodland View A.4
Woodstock Road A.6
Woolin Avenue C.6
Wooton Court A.5
Worcester Close C.8
Wordsworth Road A.6
Wortley Street C.5
Wragby Road B.7
Wren Close D.8
Wybeck Road C.2
Wynmoor Road B.6
Wyredale Road D.7

YADDLETHORPE B.8
Yarborough Court A.4
Yeovil Court A.5
York Avenue D.7

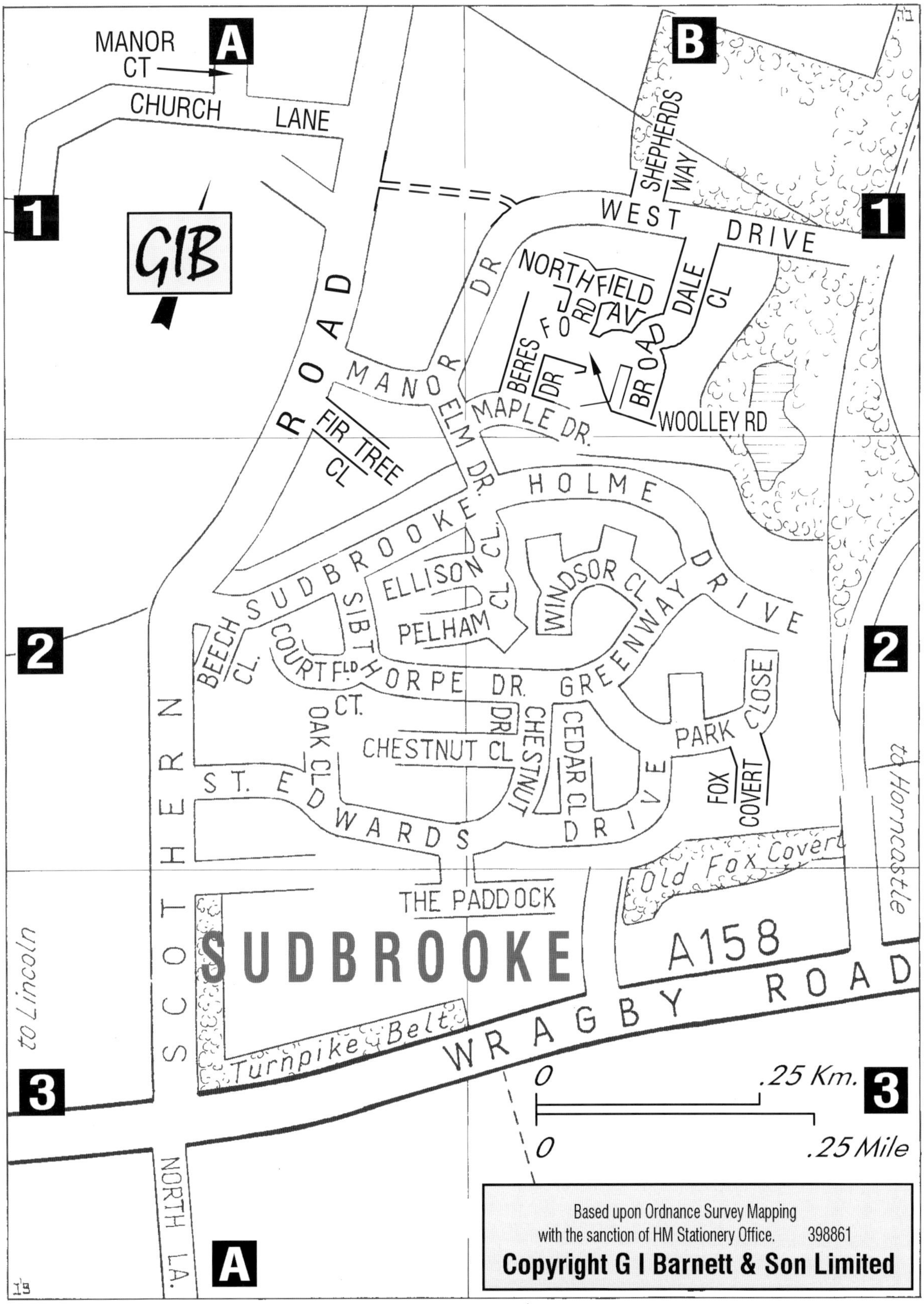

SUDBROOKE INDEX TO STREETS

Beech Close A.2
Beresford Drive B.1
Broad Dale Close B.1

Cedar Close B.2
Chestnut Close A.2
Chestnut Drive B.2
Church Lane A.1
Courtfield Court A.2

Ellison Close A.2

Elm Drive A.1

Fir Tree Close A.1
Fox Covert B.2

Greenway B.2

Manor Court A.1
Manor Drive A.1
Maple Drive B.1

North Lane A.3
Northfield Avenue B.1

Oak Close A.2
Old Fox Court B.3

Park Close B.2
Pelham Close A.2

St. Edward's Drive A.2
Scothern Lane A.3

Shepherds Way B.1
Sibthorpe Drive A.2
Sudbrooke Holme Drive A.2

The Paddock A.3
Turnpike Belt A.3

Windsor Close B.2
Woolley Road B.1
Wragby Road................B.3

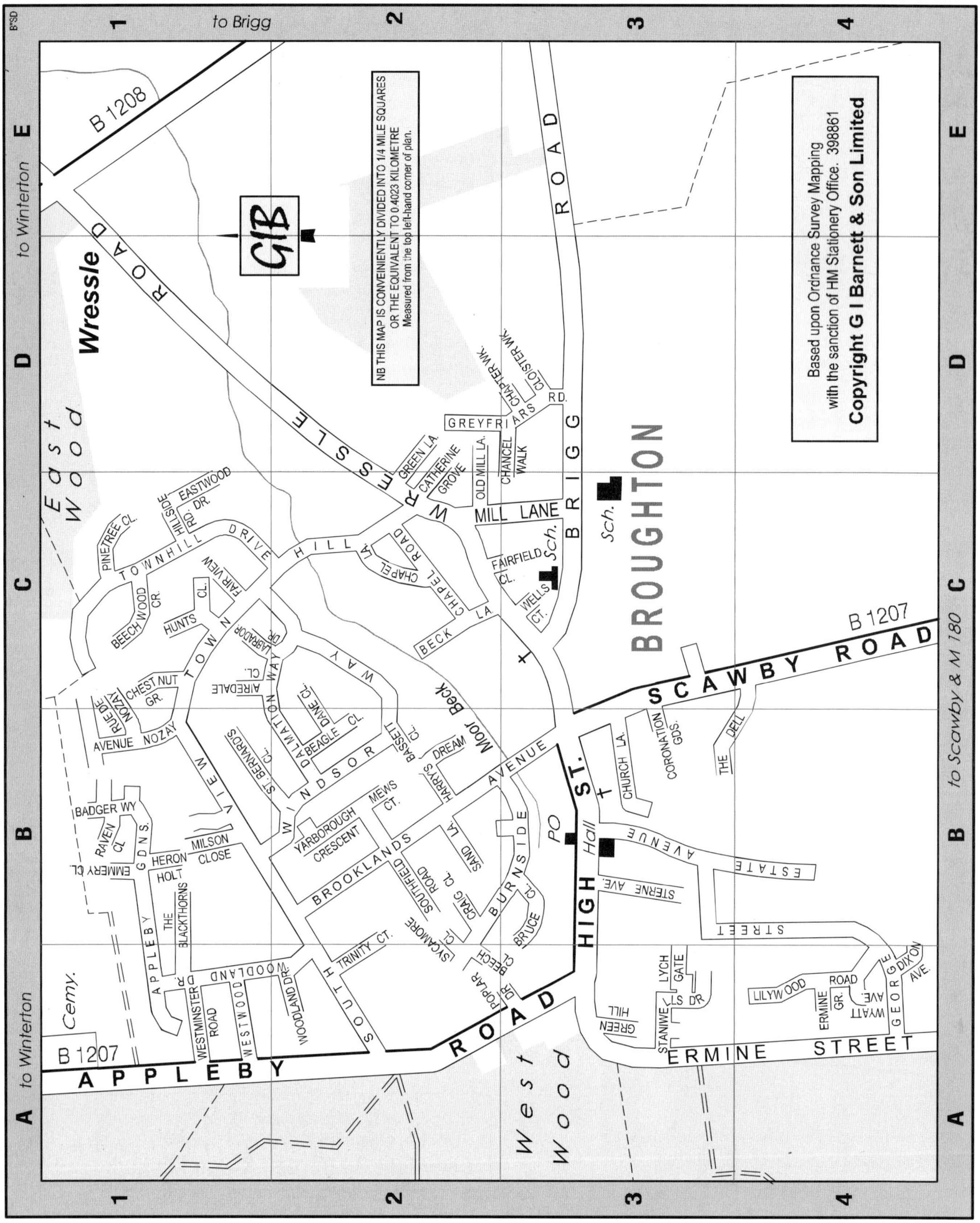

BROUGHTON INDEX TO STREETS

Airedale Close C.1
Appleby Gardens A.1
Appleby Road A.1
Avenue Nozay B.1

Badger Way B.1
Bassett Close B.2
Beagle Close B.2
Beck Lane C.2
Becchwood Crescent C.1
Brigg Road C.3
Brooklands Avenue B.2
Bruce Close B.3
Burnside B.3

Catherine Grove C.2
Chancel Walk D.3
Chapel lane C.2
Chapel Road C.2
Chapter Walk D.3
Chestnut Grove C.1
Church Lane B.3
Coronation Gardens B.3
Craig Close B.2

Dalmation Way B.2
Dane Close C.2
Dixon Avenue A.4

Eastwood Drive C.1
Emery Close B.1
Ermine Grove A.4
Ermine Street A.3
Estate Avenue E.4
Fair View C.1
Fairfield Close C.3

George Street A.4
Green Hill A.3
Greyfriars Road D.2

Harry's Dream B.2
Heron Halt B.1
High Street B.3
Hillside Road C.1
Hunts Close C.1

Labrador Drive C.1
Lilywood Road A.4

Mews Court B.2
Mill Lane C.2
Milson Close B.1

Old Mill Lane C.2

Pinetree Close C.1
Poplar Drive A.3

Raven Close B.1
Rue De Nozay B.1

Sand Lane B.2
Scawby Road C.3
South View A.2
Southfield Road B.2
Sterne Avenue B.3
Street Bernards Close B.1
The Dell B.3
Town Hill C.1
Townhill Drive C.1
Trinity Court A.2

Wells Court C.3
Westminster Road A.1
Westwood A.1
Windsor Way B.2
Woodland Drive A.2
WRESSLE D.1
Wressle Road C.2
Wyatt Avenue A.4

Yarborough Crescent B.2